The Professional
Story Writer
and His Art

The Professional Story Writer and His Art

by ROBERT C. MEREDITH

Associate Professor, Department of English

Chicago Teachers College

and JOHN D. FITZGERALD

THOMAS Y. CROWELL COMPANY

New York, Established 1834

PN
3373
.M14
1963

Designed by Laurel Wagner

Manufactured in the United States of America
by the Vail-Ballou Press, Inc., Binghamton, New York

Library of Congress Catalog Card No. 63-9201

Second Printing, March 1967

ACKNOWLEDGMENTS

The authors are grateful to the following authors, agents, and publishers for permission to include in this volume quotations from the
following stories:

The Citadel Press for quotations from "An Occurrence at Owl Creek
Bridge" from *Collected Writings of Ambrose Bierce.*

From *Points of View* by W. Somerset Maugham. Copyright © 1958
by W. Somerset Maugham. Reprinted by permission of Doubleday &
Company, Inc.

"The Colonel's Lady" from *Creatures of Circumstance* by W. Somerset Maugham. Copyright 1946 by W. Somerset Maugham. Reprinted
by permission of Doubleday & Company, Inc.

Farrar, Straus and Cudahy, Inc., for quotations from Alberto Moravia's
"Appetite," published in *Roman Tales,* copyright © 1956, 1957 by
Valentino Bompiani & Co., as a Signet Book by arrangement with
Farrar, Straus and Cudahy, Inc.

James Thurber, "The Catbird Seat," copyright 1942 by James Thurber, originally published in *The New Yorker*.

Ivan Turgenev, "Byézhin Meadow," from *The Novels and Stories of Ivan Turgenieff* (tr. by Isabel E. Hapgood), Charles Scribner's Sons.

Robert Louis Stevenson, "A Lodging for the Night," The Society of Authors.

Eudora Welty, "Petrified Man," from *A Curtain of Green and Other Stories,* copyright 1939 by Eudora Welty, Harcourt, Brace and Co., Inc.

Finally we wish to acknowledge a debt of gratitude to the following publications and authors:

Parts of Chapters One and Three were first printed in an article by John D. Fitzgerald, "So Wrong to Tell the Truth," *Writer's Digest* (February, 1960), pp. 37–9; 42–3.

For our critical approach to "Young Archimedes" in Chapter Four, and to "A Dill Pickle" in Chapter Five, R. W. Short and R. B. Sewall, "Manual of Suggestions," *Short Stories for Study,* Henry Holt and Company, 1952.

For some ideas concerning the nature of comedy in Chapter Two, Dorothy Van Ghent, *The English Novel: Form and Function,* Rinehart & Company, Inc., 1953.

The authors are grateful to agents, authors, and publishers for permission to include in the Appendix the following stories:

Vela DePeugh, "Maggie Mix-up," copyright 1961 by "21" Publishing Corporation, The Parents' Institute, Inc.; originally published in *Calling All Girls* magazine; used by permission of the publisher.

Anonymous, (author's name not for publication), "Winner at Bingo —Loser at Marriage," copyright 1961, Macfadden Publications, Inc.; originally published in *True Experience;* used by permission of the publisher.

James Gilmore, "Isn't It a Perfect Crime?" copyright 1961, by H. S. D. Publications, Inc.; originally published in *Alfred Hitchcock's Mystery Magazine;* used by permission of the author.

W. L. Heath, "No Margin for Error," copyright © 1960 by W. L.

TO ALL SINCERE NOVICE STORY WRITERS

Contents

the story. Definition of action. How to use action to bring character and complication to life. How to avoid the pitfalls of too much action. How to use action to bring description to life. Definition of narration. How to use narration to gain compression. Narration's importance in characterization and in cloaking the improbable. How to use narration to cloak improbable events. The uses of symbolism. Definition of symbolism. How to use symbols to capture the multiple issues of the story. The classes of symbols, conventional and private. Functional symbols defined, and their use. Structural symbols defined, and their use. Illustrations of the use of structural symbols. How to keep symbols within the literal events of the story. How the writer may test the effectiveness of his symbolism. Symbolism to be avoided until the writer has mastered the four tools. Exercises.

Characters result from artifice, and hence the need for the writer to understand traits of character. How to make a character a member of a group. How to distinguish him from other members of the same group. How to employ general, personal, emotional, and physical traits in characterization. Examples of the use of these traits in characterization. The relationship of the complication to the character of the protagonist. How professional writers test the character of their protagonists with the complication. Distinctions in the handling of character in pulp, slick, and quality stories. Definition of the resolution as a return on the protagonist's part to his group traits. Definition of the moment of truth, and its importance in characterization and structure. Relationship of the moment of truth to the protagonist's final decision. How quality writers use the moment of truth. Distinctions between commercial and literary conceptions of character. Illustrations of the way quality authors employ the moment of truth. The principle of unawareness in the artifice of character. How to characterize minor characters. The use of exposition, description, action, and narration in characterization. The methods of using exposition to characterize. The stream-of-consciousness technique and exposition. How to describe character. The use of indirect details in describing character. The use of action in characterization. How to make dialogue con-

vincing. *The use of dialect. The use of narration to characterize. The use of all four methods of characterization in fiction. The important distinctions between commercial and quality writers summarized. The value of learning commercial methods of characterization to acquire more subtle techniques. Exercises.*

Definition of situation, scene, and panorama. How authors use restatements of the central situation of the story. The relationship of situation to scene. How to know when to use scenes. The ingredients of the scene. The distinction between "big" and "small" scenes. Distinctions between commercial and quality writers in the handling of situations. Panorama used primarily in the quality writer's handling of situations. Definition of panorama. Illustrations of panorama. How commercial writers use panorama. The use of scene in fiction. Motivation defined. How professional writers reveal motivation. The use of adverbs in motivation. Distinctions between commercial and quality writers in their handling of motivation. How authors use objective facts and emotional facts to give the illusion of reality. The importance of the ability to feel. The relationship of emotions in the story to structure. How a narrative hook is used. How to discover the narrative hook in a story. Distinctions in the use of the narrative hook. Transitions and their use. How to make smooth transitions. The stream-of-consciousness technique and transitions. "Planting" defined. How professional writers use material as plants. How to plant details within character in order to give the illusion of consistency. Nomenclature defined. How authors use names that help characterization. The problem of repetition in naming characters. Style. Ten recommendations about the writer's character in order to acquire style. Ten ways in which to acquire a vivid style. Slanting. How authors may slant their stories. Why authors should avoid slanting. Revision. The development of critical ability in the writer. Revision and the development of an illusion. How professional writers go about revision. Techniques to aid in revision. The relationship between author and editor in revision. The problem of personality in revision. How professional writers use editing in order to acquire a critical sense. Exercises.

Preface

THE FUNDAMENTAL PURPOSE of this book is to present the techniques professional writers use in writing short stories so that the reader may become professional himself. Within such a purpose, we are aware of the possible uses to which our book may be put. It can be used for teaching creative writing at the college level. It can be used, as well, for teaching creative writing in adult-education programs. It can be studied in writers' workshops, writers' clubs, and other literary groups. But we have been primarily interested in making the language simple enough, in presenting such an abundance of clear illustrations, and in defining and examining techniques so thoroughly, that an inexperienced writer can learn by himself everything he needs to know in order to become successful.

We have intended to bridge the gap between commercial and noncommercial writing in order to enable the reader to discover his own level of abilities, to write stories in terms of his own unique talents. We have defined, explained, and illustrated every technique, method, principle, and term used by professional story writers.

The reason for including in this book a study of the techniques used by commercial writers is to provide the novice with the same opportunity to learn his craft as is given to students who attend a medical school, law school, art school, or conservatory of music. Upon the completion of his course, whatever it may be, such a student finds his own level in terms of individual talent. In the same way, it is our belief that a study of the basic techniques of story writing will aid the reader to find his own level in creative writing in terms of his own abilities. Only a very small percentage of the graduates of medical schools, law schools, art schools, and conservatories of music reach the top of their profession. But the techniques they are taught in school enable them to follow their profession and earn a livelihood after graduation. For every graduate of a medical school who becomes a famous doctor, there are hundreds who are competent but less able practitioners. For every graduate of a law school who becomes a highly distinguished judge, there are hundreds who become competent corporation lawyers, divorce lawyers, criminal lawyers, and insurance claim adjusters. For every art school graduate who lives to see his work hung in museums, there are hundreds who go into advertising. For every graduate of a conservatory of music who reaches the concert stage, there are hundreds who become teachers, or play with popular dance orchestras.

The separation of individuals into various levels of professional ability functions—let us repeat—in terms of the individual's own talent. And such a statement applies equally to the writing profession. We believe it possible to demonstrate how to tell a story successfully in any one of the major kinds of short fiction—granting only one condition, that the story teller himself be able to make the transition from one form to another. When a college course restricts itself to teaching only how to write purely literary work, it denies the would-be writer the instruction he needs to find his own level. Not more than one or two students in any given class in any college or university have the talent ever to create a short story on this level, for the same reason that not more than one or two students in the graduating class of a medical school have the ability to become outstanding in the field of medicine.

Yet there are thousands of would-be short-story writers who cannot afford to attend colleges, writers' workshops, or writers' conferences. They may live, indeed, in a place where they cannot meet in writers' clubs with other novices like themselves. In their search for knowledge they face a problem upon discovering that most textbooks on the subject confine themselves to the level of purely creative writing—and the several which do not, which speak about commercial fiction, do not go on to give the extension to the subject that it deserves.

Would-be writers are thus frequently denied access to information that would help them to sell their work. And as the reader will discover, the study of wholly creative techniques, as we have presented them, in terms of their being an artistic outgrowth from commercial forms, will lead naturally to the improvement of one's own writing.

We have sought, in other words, that kind of balance in the study of writing that will aid any apprentice writer to become commercially successful. Having once been apprentices ourselves, we know the joy of the young and aspiring writer when he makes his first sale, if only to a juvenile magazine.

The start, no matter how lowly, is exceedingly important. Many famous authors either got their start as hack writers or kept themselves alive to create later imperishable works by writing, for a wide audience, works that would sell. From the time of Daniel Defoe, story writers and novelists have written hack work and pulp fiction. The weight of actual practice is on the side of a course that follows a standard procedure in the development of artistic techniques. One may mention Henry Fielding, many of whose ephemeral stage plays were little more than dressed-up versions of newspaper accounts, but whose theatrical experience prepared him for the novel. George Meredith, in his early desperate years, wrote hack poetry and journalism, and according to one of his biographers, Lionel Stevenson, undoubtedly experimented with other forms of literature as well in abortive attempts to attract a public following. Arnold Bennett turned out a prodigious number of words yearly in the form of humor and mystery fiction, but the practice was undoubtedly valuable for the novel by which he is most remembered, *The Old Wives' Tale*. Thomas Hardy, H. G. Wells, Joseph Conrad, and D. H. Lawrence all wrote potboilers as a means of keeping themselves alive so that they could devote serious effort to literature. In France, Honoré de Balzac struggled for ten years as a pulp fiction writer before he made a name for himself. And the great and lucid French writer Colette acquired a mastery in the art of story-telling through her marriage to her first husband, a writer of slick fiction. In the United States, to mention only a few authors, Stephen Crane wrote his Whilomville stories, after an apprenticeship in newspaper work, to keep the wolf away from his door. Sinclair Lewis wrote apprentice material for nearly eight years after his graduation from college before his first novel, *Our Mr. Wrenn,* appeared. Sherwood Anderson wrote advertising copy in a Chicago agency for a number of years and experimented with his writing. F. Scott Fitzgerald, too, wrote slick fiction for *The Saturday Evening Post* and learned the secrets of technical virtuosity as a means of writing more enduring literature. Ernest Hemingway, as Charles A. Fenton makes abundantly clear in his book, *The Apprenticeship of Ernest Hemingway,* gained valuable insight into his craft by working on newspapers and imitating Ring Lardner. In sum,

xxi

the writer who starts at the top of his profession is that rarest of human beings. Most authors learn their craft by condescending to try whatever market exists.

On the other hand, the majority of pulp and slick short-story writers soon discover their own limitations and confine themselves to what they know they can sell. The successful pulp short-story writer may occasionally try his hand at a slick story, and the successful slick story writer may occasionally try his hand at a literary story—but only when the larder is full. Why should either of them waste their time writing stories that they know from experience they cannot sell?

We maintain it is a duty for any book on creative writing to guide its readers into exploiting their talents successfully. We consider it as rewarding to help young writers to sell pulp stories as it is to assist in the rare sale of a noncommercial story, for we have learned that it is not wise to scorn commercial forms, even for those who wish to write enduring literature.

We know it is impossible to teach anyone to become a successful writer unless that person has a desire to write. But we do sincerely believe that an individual who expresses such a desire and who attempts on his own to write shows thereby sufficient incentive to merit encouragement. Any expression of strong interest is a primary indication of inherent talent. This is true of all professions. Unless crushed by extraneous considerations, a person whose one consuming desire is to become a doctor and heal the sick invariably becomes a doctor.

The general principle by which we have organized this text is to proceed from the relatively simple fundamentals to the more advanced and relatively complex manipulation of those fundamentals. Such a method follows from a healthy regard for the values of good commercial fiction—values that one cannot get away from merely by using the word *commercial.* And it proceeds as well from the liberal view that there is no inevitable conflict between the various types of short story in terms of the techniques that every writer must learn to employ.

Before going further, it will be well to make clear what we mean by the terms *pulp, slick,* and *quality,* which we use in the text. In its original sense, a pulp story meant a short story published in a magazine that used a cheap grade of pulp paper. This was back in the days of the great pulp chains that published more than a hundred pulp magazines weekly. The term *slick story* in its original sense meant a short story published in a magazine printed on slick, or more expensive, paper. However, with the graduation of a number of confession magazines from pulp to slick paper, as well as with the development of men's magazines and others, the term *pulp story* in its original sense no longer applies. Some slick magazines publish condensed versions of novels on a cheaper grade of paper than that used for the rest of the magazine.

The terms, *pulp* and *slick,* are still in such general use that we decided to use them in this book, but we wish to define them in a more practicable fashion than in terms of the paper on which they are printed.

A pulp story is one that has a market value of from one to five cents per word. Pulp stories are published in confession, mystery, western, men's magazines, and so on, that advertise in their market requirements—as one may note in writers' guides to markets—that their editors use the foregoing rate of payment.

A slick story is one that has a market value of ten cents a word and up. The minimum word rate for practically all slick magazines is ten cents. The rate jumps, depending upon the names of author and magazine, with some slick magazines paying as high as one dollar a word for a short story. Slick stories appear in such magazines as the *Saturday Evening Post, McCall's, Ladies' Home Journal,* and so on.

Now what is meant by the term *quality stories?* We will now and again use as a synonym the word *literary.* Quality stories appear in such magazines as *Harper's, Atlantic, The New Yorker, Partisan Review,* in avant-garde magazines or the little magazines, in quarterly reviews and the like—in magazines, in short, that appeal to sophisticated literary tastes. It is significant that slick magazines are more and more in the market, too, for quality stories. Literary stories have no fixed rate of payment—that is, they may sell for as little as pulp stories, if in fact the author does not simply give his story to a small magazine for the privilege of seeing it published. On the other hand, some quality stories, written by famous authors, may earn several thousand dollars.

The distinction between these various types of story cannot be made hard and fast either in terms of rate of payment or, completely, in terms of what magazine the story appears in. A recent issue of a slick magazine aimed at a masculine audience contained an excellent quality story written by a famous Italian novelist and a pulp story written by a well-known American short-story writer. To use other criteria from those given will help in judging the classification of a particular story, but again, the distinctions given must be a trifle elastic. The pulp story deals with problems in a relatively superficial fashion, avoiding the deeper elements that lie in the subconscious, ignoring frequently the conflicting tangle of issues that may be involved within the plot, and coming to a solution that is, on the whole, facile rather than difficult. The slick story has a much more disciplined structure and makes the protagonist a dramatic figure by highlighting the struggle he must go through to bring about an effective solution. The quality story tends to do one of two things: either it dramatizes the struggle the protagonist makes, and more frequently turns the struggle and resolution into tragic rather than comic terms; or it follows a chronological form that tends to mute the struggle of the protagonist, showing him to be a creature who does not act but who is acted upon. And as one approaches the quality story, he finds more subtlety in technique since the issue becomes symbolic, ideational, a matter of deep-lying conscious or subconscious states of mind, and so on. So general in its effect does the development and theme of the quality story become, at times, that one must speak not of a protagonist, but of many: a group, a class, a culture.

This book is based upon our further belief that the apprentice writer needs to be given practical examples, and not merely precepts. The reader will find, throughout, illustrations of the various techniques employed by professional writers of pulp, slick, and quality stories. At the end of nearly every chapter, we have raised questions to alert the reader's attention to the various important matters we have dealt with in the chapter and to stimulate him to produce writing that he can measure objectively against the techniques we have described and illustrated. Mindful always of our commitment to proceed from the most simple to the most complex demands made upon the writer, we have so arranged the chapters as to journey from what the apprentice can most readily grasp to what will require more of him. The exercises help to pinpoint his trouble spots and assist him to overcome them.

Finally, at the very end of the book, the reader will discover an Appendix made up of representative examples of successful pulp, slick, and quality stories. For every story printed, there is an accompanying commentary that takes the story apart and demonstrates, from the writer's standpoint, how it is constructed.

We do not aim for a merely appreciative attitude on the part of the reader toward the short stories we have mentioned or used in this text. Instead, we wish to provoke him into discovering abilities in himself that he may recognize but that he very likely does not know how to utilize. We have been mindful throughout that the great art of story writing is itself an inventive, and not merely an analytic, process. What we have demonstrated, therefore, is a process that is ever flowing forward, one that captures the look and feel of the real world while at the same time selecting and exaggerating its characteristics into the forms of art. What we have written, we firmly believe, holds out the promise of that kind of creative excitement that constitutes the end and test of the human imagination. That we have considered the subject from the eminently practical standpoint of the apprentice writer's desire not only to write but to sell what he has written is to escape from mere dilettantism into one of the major conditions that all writers, minor ones as well as great, have always had to face.

1

How to Write
Salable Short Stories
by Using Exaggerated
Complications

BEFORE the beginning writer attempts to write a story, it might be well for him to ponder briefly the idea that short stories are contrived, together with all the implications of such an idea. In order to do so, he must first cease to read stories in his usual fashion, the fashion in which the mass of men do, which is to allow himself to slip into the illusion of reality that the short story presents. He must learn to see the way in which the illusion has been created or produced. Above all, he must make the distinction between fiction and "life." [1]

It is really easy to fail to differentiate between life and fiction, particularly when the fictional illusion is well maintained. Here, for example, is part of a scene that one may grant to have "reality":

> Once in the children's room he closed the door and felt secure for the first time that evening. Marianne fell down on the floor, picked herself up and calling: "Daddy, watch me," fell again, got up, and continued the falling-calling routine. Andy sat in the child's low chair, wobbling the tooth. Martin ran the water in the tub, washed his own hands in the lavatory, and called the boy into the bathroom.

[1] For some of the following ideas, we are indebted to Mark Schorer's "Introductory Comment," *The Story*, New York, Prentice-Hall, Inc., 1950.

"Let's have another look at that tooth." Martin sat on the toilet, holding Andy between his knees. The child's mouth gaped and Martin grasped the tooth. A wobble, a quick twist and the nacreous milk tooth was free. Andy's face was for the first moment split between terror, astonishment, and delight. He mouthed a swallow of water and spat into the lavatory.

"Look, Daddy! It's blood. Marianne!"

Martin loved to bathe his children, loved inexpressibly the tender, naked bodies as they stood in the water so exposed.

Carson McCullers, "A Domestic Dilemma"

Here certainly is a normal circumstance, a customary situation, a father taking care of his children, removing a loose tooth from his son's mouth, responding to the delighted animation of his daughter, and showing a quite common and valuable tender emotion for his children. We are, as in life, in normal and recognizable surroundings, listening to people talk who have names that are like ours, watching them act as we ourselves have acted. And we react to them as we react to people we meet, we judge them by what they do and say and the way they look. It is not strange that led by fiction we should think that writing merely reproduces reality. And it is easier to make such a mistake with fiction—and perhaps most of all with the short-story form—than it is with any other type of imaginative literature.

But very few actions in life ever work themselves out with the completeness, the unity, the well-focused point of view of the story. What we take as a representation of life as it may be said to occur is, in fact, upon close examination seen to be contrived, full of artifice, strained out of all the proportions of life, something quite exaggerated and changed into unity and harmony. There are many ways in which to observe such a principle.

Let us look at two of these ways, for they are more than any others critical in terms of artifice. These are, first of all, characterization and, secondly, the problem of complication. As a tentative definition, we can define the short story as consisting of a character who faces and resolves some complication in his existence.

So far as character is concerned, perhaps the dilemma of a story may appear farfetched, the setting strange, the speech uncouth or odd, and the style of the author stilted—but if there is good characterization, if the characters "come to life," we might yet maintain that the story is more "real" than "artificial." But it is noteworthy that a character never violates his nature in a story without a reason, which

2

has been fully given or suggested. If the character acts in a way beyond what we know of him, we feel cheated. In the excerpt from Carson McCullers' story, "A Domestic Dilemma," the father feels an excessive tenderness for his children, not only the normal human emotion of a father for his children, but because his wife has for the past year been drinking on the sly. Martin faces the dilemma that his wife's drunkenness poses: social disgrace, the gossip of his office co-workers, the humiliation of his own ego, the undermining of his will to achieve, and the possible psychological damage his wife's tippling may have for his children. The solution that Martin reaches is to treat his wife with the same love he has for the children. He realizes that she is immature. He sees her as young and filled with as much need for his guidance as his own children demand. It would be just as true to life for the family to split up, for Martin to get a divorce and to marry a woman of some sanity and balance. But this solution would violate what we know of Martin in the story. The character functions within the terms of a definition that the story establishes. The resolution of his difficulty depends entirely upon what has been given. What has been given has been exaggerated in order for us to see it. Hence any other solution becomes impossible. How then can the story be considered other than as contrived?

As a matter of fact, when a character within a story acts beyond what we know of him, we usually reproach the author with the statement that "we do not like him." What we very probably mean is that so flagrant has the author been about telling something true to life that he has not captured effectively the illusion of consistency of character. We are really reproaching the author because he has not been more guileful, inventive, and tricky. We reproach him because he has not told a big enough lie, so to speak.

The writer of a story is in a way a mere observer of what a person does of a certain particularized nature when, wanting something, that individual comes up against an obstacle or obstacles that deny his desires. People in real life are never so consistent. In actuality, people are tangles of conflicting desires, pulling one way and then another. They are consistent only in being relatively inconsistent. They lack the definiteness of the fictional character. Of course, some people appear to have a direction in them, but they are rare birds, and it would be possible to find wayward desires even in them if one could get under their surface. This is one reason that a short story must be artificial. The man of charity in real life is continually lapsing from its

3

rigorous demands. The visionary dreamer in real life deals with many practical decisions in quite a practical fashion during the course of a day. The thrifty soul, with scarcely a thought about the money, willingly buys cookies from the Girl Scout at the door, and he may do this through motives that are absolutely inconsistent with other attributes that mark his existence.

That a character is consistent is, in fact, only an illusion that we very readily grant when we pick up a short story to read. As a consequence, fiction proves to be a remarkable instrument for revealing what would happen if we were to be consistent. It phrases in the form of an hypothesis the way we could conceivably turn out if we did follow out one of our desires to the very limit, no matter what desire it was: ambition, hunger, righteousness, thrift, courage. Any one of these drives put into a plot becomes altered during the course of the story. Taken by themselves, they are never quite enough, and the story points this out by virtue of its form. It, like life, has movement, but unlike the action or movement of life, the action of a short story is never repetitious. It is impossible for a major character to retain his values throughout a story. There is an urgency, a compulsion, a pressure in the story that leads inevitably to change. Thrift alters and is widened by understanding; the coward finally sees the way around cowardice; the buffoon meets seriousness for the first time. Characters awaken to a new consciousness of themselves. There is no guarantee that life itself in its crude, raw, chaotic form ever provides this essential illumination. As Henry James remarked, "life has no direct sense whatever for the subject, and is capable, luckily for us, of nothing but splendid waste."

Not only are people inconsistent in real life, but also they are much too complicated to be valuable for fiction. Fiction has to simplify them in order to deal with them. It is when one strong emotion is dominant that one finds an interesting character. Byron will exemplify this. But the ordinary individual is filled with checks and balances for his wayward wishes, and he cancels himself out. He becomes dull in a way. He is always saying to himself, "By George, I'm going to break away from this situation which confronts me," but something, mainly himself, always gets in the way, and he doesn't do what he has sworn to do. That makes him safely dull and human.

The really bright and flashing birds in life, the peacocks in character, attempt to make life yield a full one-hundred-per-cent return for some extremely well-unified wish. Yet in life this is impossible. We

4

have to live in a situation in which we are punished for letting our wishes, whatever they may be, run away with us.

In characterization then may be seen the artifice of the short story, but we have also suggested in these remarks that the form of a short story has much to do with its being quite different from life. The form of most short stories is based upon a complication that must be resolved, upon some dilemma that cannot go on any longer without something drastic happening. Of course, complications occur in life. Life in fact consists of complications, trivial ones and serious ones. A door hinge becomes loose, or a tire blows out on the highway. A neighbor keeps borrowing things without returning them, or a child gets severely burned and hovers at the edge of death. But invariably, the short story deals with a complication that is inherently serious, never trivial—and unlike the complications that man faces in life and that very frequently he does not resolve, the complication in the story must arrive at some kind of resolution. It is in learning how to develop a serious complication and resolve it that the short-story writer learns to take the plastic material of life and bend and shape it to his purposes.

A recognizable character involved in some dilemma that he must resolve—these are the fundamentals of short-story writing. We shall learn later how to make our definition of a short story more subtle, and our technique in handling complications more refined. Let us investigate now, by specific example, how to deal with complication and character in the short story.

Perhaps one of the best ways will be for the reader to take some minor complication that has occurred to him and deal with that. Let us suggest several:

1. One misses a bus and is late for work.
2. Junior won't eat his spinach.
3. One hears some juicy gossip and tries to phone a friend to tell her, but she isn't home.
4. A neighbor throws a party and keeps one awake half the night.
5. A mother-in-law comes to visit and stays and stays.
6. A boy acquires a friend who is several years older than he is.

These complications are unequal in terms of seriousness, but they all share a similarity in that, as they stand, none of them will make a good short story by itself. The first thing a beginning writer must do with a minor complication is to make it more interesting than it appears in real life. Hence we derive our first principle:

5

I. To make a complication more interesting than it seems in real life, "lie" by exaggerating it.

One of the most frequent mistakes that new writers make in dealing with complications is to assume that an exaggerated complication will not make a good story because such an exaggeration could not possibly happen that way in real life. If it were written the way it happened in real life, however, it would never make a good short story. There is, therefore, a corollary principle to accompany the first:

IA. The more the writer lies and exaggerates, the deeper he makes his complication. The deeper the complication becomes, the better the story becomes.

Now keeping in mind that the method we are here following is fundamental to all short stories, let us take the last of the minor complications and develop a salable short story out of it. In order to accomplish this, we must make the minor complication inherently more artificial than it appears to us at first. We must make it a major complication. What could be serious about a boy acquiring a friend several years older than he is? This sort of thing happens all the time, and we know very well that such friendships may often be very good things. (Let us call the younger boy Benny, and have him just graduated from high school. He is seventeen years old. And let us call the older boy Duke, and make him about twenty.)

Step 1: Duke befriends Benny just after the latter has been graduated from high school.

Now let us try to make that situation worse:

Step 2: Duke is a bad boy; he has been breaking into houses and stealing things.

Now right away there has to be a reason why Duke befriends Benny, the younger boy. Why does he? (Once one has practiced plotting complications, he will find that each step begins to come readily since the challenge provides a stimulant to the imagination.) We know that Benny, the younger boy, is our protagonist and must be a sympathetic character. Therefore, we cannot say that Duke befriends Benny because Benny is more adept at breaking into houses than Duke is. Duke befriends Benny because of his fear—he wants an accomplice, someone to share his fears with. This is then our third invention.

6

Step 3: Duke befriends Benny because he is afraid, and moreover, he does not realize his own motives.

If we remember that our sole purpose is to make this complication as serious as possible, it means that the more miserable we can make Benny, the better our story will be. Obviously, Benny is a kid who wants friendship. Let us make him a youngster who is fat. All his life he has been kidded about being fat. He has felt particularly the way in which girls have treated him, and therefore he is shy and, at the same time, rebellious underneath it all. Duke is the first one who appears to have offered him any real friendship. But we know that at the back of this offer of friendship on Duke's part is fear. Benny does not realize this, however, and he accompanies Duke on a robbery for the first time in his life. This gives us the opportunity to make Benny really miserable.

Step 4: Duke savagely beats up the woman at the house they rob, and Benny discovers that Duke's proffered friendship is really a mask for cruelty and a desire for admiration. Benny wants to break off the relationship with Duke.

This is a pretty major complication, but yet it is not deep enough to make a really gripping short story out of it. And it is at this point in plotting complications that most beginners make one of the four fatal mistakes in plotting that result in a poor story. These four weaknesses are listed in the following principle:

II. Do not plot a complication
  1. *that is too unimportant.*
  2. *that is too easily solved.*
  3. *that is solved by some character other than the protagonist.*
  4. *that is solved by providence, accident, chance, or coincidence.*

Now if we stop with the fourth step of our outline, we will be committing one of these four mistakes. Let us assume that Benny, our protagonist, simply tells Duke that he will no longer chum around with him. Here we would certainly be committing the second weakness, plotting a complication that is too easily solved. Or let us suppose that some other character intervenes in our story, such as a priest who convinces Duke that he is a naughty boy, we would be using the third weakness. Or if we had some accident occur in which Duke was killed

7

and Benny was allowed to escape without blame, we would be committing the fourth weakness. The complication we have worked out so far escapes from the first weakness since it exaggerates upon a normal friendship between boys.

Fortunately there is a rule that tells one how to avoid committing any of the four weaknesses in plotting complications.

> *III. To avoid the four weaknesses in plotting complications one must demonstrate that something of importance will be at stake if the complication remains unsolved. And the solution of the complication must lie within the complication itself.*

A brief glance at popular stories will demonstrate that something of importance is always at stake in the complication presented. In one story, the reputation and career of a professor is at stake because a coed who had a crush on him told lies about him when he rebuffed her advances. In another story, an honest policeman stands to lose his job because some racketeers framed him. In a third story, a young woman's chances for marriage are at stake because she is the only one of the family who feels a sense of responsibility in caring for her neglected mother. In other words, the authors of these stories made certain that something of importance was at stake in the unsolved complication by employing the next method:

> *IV. To make certain that something of importance will be at stake if the complication is not solved, make the complication so serious that something vitally important becomes an issue.*

We will now employ this method in our story about the fat boy, Benny. Already in this particular complication, several important things are at stake. We know that Benny has been an accessory to several serious crimes: breaking and entering, larceny, and "mugging." And even though he is innocent of any real intention to do any of these things, he is subject to arrest and imprisonment, so that the boy's future is at stake. But we can make the complication even more chilling if we reflect about it for a moment.

Benny, as we picture him, is a boy who has been hurt many times because of his fatness, yet at heart he is a kind, sympathetic boy. His rebelliousness is easily explained. Everything in his experience seems to have been a matter for disillusionment. Girls have never taken him seriously. Even friendship turns out to be false. He is through school now and out in the world. Maybe he has not even tried to look for a job out of pure fear that a prospective employer would laugh at him. Now there is the danger in our plotted complication—inherent in Benny's character—that he might simply drift along, completely revolted at first by Duke's brutality and cruelty, but little by little becoming accustomed to it. In essence at stake in the story is the corruption of a character through his own weakness.

Yet we have overlooked what Duke's reaction would be to Benny's wish to get out. Obviously it strikes one that Duke beat up the woman in order to show off in front of Benny. He went out of his way to be cruel. He is not going very readily to let Benny get out now. And we are ready now for the fifth step.

Step 5: After the robbery, Duke shows Benny a gun that he has found. Benny then grows more frightened because he realizes that Duke will eventually kill someone. And Duke threatens to use the gun on Benny if Benny ever tries to inform on him or break off the relationship.

We have now made the complication so serious that something of even greater importance is at stake, and Benny must, at the same time, overcome his weakness and act. He rebels in his very soul at the thought of murder. If the complication is not solved, someone will be murdered, some innocent person, or perhaps Benny himself, a youngster who has gotten himself into a mess.

Now we must remember that to avoid any of the four fatal weaknesses in plotting, the solution to the complication must be found within the complication itself. If we go outside the complication by having an accident happen to Duke, or by the chance capture of Duke and Benny by the police, we will not have a complete and finished plot. Yet at this point in our outline, there just does not seem to be any way of avoiding the four weaknesses in plotting because no solution appears within the complication itself. Hence we must use one more principle in order to get our solution.

V. When the solution to the complication cannot be found within the complication itself, employ the principle of discovery and change. Discovery and change consist of letting a character discover something he did not know or did not realize before that leads him to a final decision.

We certainly cannot have Duke change his mind at this point. And we certainly cannot have Benny change his mind and accept the idea of

9

murder. But we can have Benny discover something about himself that he had not realized before. We are now ready for the sixth step.

Step 6: Benny discovers within himself his own weakness: his desire for friendship, based upon his own self-derision, has led him to make friends with a person like Duke. Benny realizes that all his life he has let his own fatness stand in the way of friendship based upon deeper than superficial values.

Now it is significant that this self-realization on Benny's part does make the complication deeper because it adds self-knowledge to the basic complication. It makes the situation worse by virtue of the fact that Benny now realizes completely and fully that he must break with Duke, even at the risk of getting himself shot. It might seem, then, that the only way to solve the situation is for the protagonist to walk out on Duke and then to await Duke's revenge. And if we visualize the psychology of Duke, we can be certain that Duke will do just what he says: he will shoot Benny in order to punish him and also to protect himself. If this happens, however, our story will come to a very unsatisfactory ending. Fortunately, there is one further principle which will save everything.

VI. The decision made in the ante-climax must point out the solution to the complication.

This is not as difficult as it sounds because if the decision made by the protagonist does not point to the solution, it simply means that the complication is still not deep enough and we have not sufficiently used our principle of discovery and change.

Now Benny is forced to make an agonizing decision. He must either continue going along with Duke, knowing now that he does it out of great weakness and fear of getting shot, or he must stop going with Duke and take his chances, exceedingly slim chances at that, that he will not get hurt.

Step 7: Benny makes the agonizing decision to stop going along with Duke.

Now this decision must point to the solution. But how? We have made the complication deeper by using the method of discovery and change. Let us project ourselves into Benny's thoughts. He has just made a very courageous decision. It is possibly the first time in his life that he has done anything truly courageous, that is, to put himself in such a situation that he might get killed in order to keep from doing anything to hurt anyone else. And this decision teaches him something about Duke. (Note that the principle of discovery and change occurs several times throughout the plotted complication.) He can now look at Duke not with the primary motive of fear but with understanding. Benny's realization of his own behavior through life teaches him that Duke is actually afraid underneath it all. Benny has made a line of mistaken interpretations about Duke from the very beginning. At first he thought that Duke was really a friend. Next he saw Duke as basically cruel and egocentric. Now he sees that Duke is a coward. Benny realizes that were he to continue going with Duke he would do so out of fear, and fear would lead him deeper and deeper, even to the extent of killing someone. Benny realizes, therefore, that the motive of fear in himself is the same motive behind Duke's actions. Now if Benny can show Duke up for what he really is, a coward, he will solve his complication. We are now ready for the next step of our outline.

Step 8: Benny's discovery about himself leads him to see that Duke is really a coward. In a last desperate attempt to prevent Duke from doing any more harm, Benny decides to expose Duke to himself.

The final step is easy.

Step 9: Benny's deductions prove correct. It is noteworthy that the story has at all times circled around the gun that Duke has found. If Benny can demonstrate that he is less afraid of being shot than Duke is, he will have shown Duke up. Therefore Benny asks Duke to play a game of Russian roulette. Duke does not want to, but at the same time he must, to save face. During the game, Duke cracks, Benny picks up the gun from Duke's hands, and then goes over to the telephone to call the police.

It is noteworthy that the complication is solved in using the principle of discovery and change once more, for it is Duke this time who discovers that he has less courage than Benny, and he changes his mind about himself. He recognizes that he is a coward.

Whatever the merits of the story will be in its final form, the complication outline just presented reveals the use of artifice in the construction of a story. For, first, there has been an exaggeration of a minor complication throughout. And, second, the character traits of the hero and antagonist have been implicitly exaggerated. In both

11

these ways, strangely enough, the story has acquired credibility even though it could not occur the way it has been presented in terms of real life. Thus in order to derive one further method in the construction of a story, one may state the following:

VII. *To make a complication and solution believable to the reader, the dominant character traits of the major participants should be exaggerated.*

It is quite unlikely that "Russian Roulette" would happen in real life in the way it has been presented. It is doubtful that Duke would pick out an inexperienced youngster of Benny's nature to chum around with. It is also doubtful that Benny, being basically kind and sympathetic, would accept the idea of robbing people to begin with. The story in its complication and resolution depends to a certain extent upon a mature insight into the hidden drives of people, and it is quite doubtful that a young person like Benny would be able to see into Duke's problem quite so deeply or so readily.

In order to make the story credible to a reader then, we have, among other things, to exaggerate the dominant traits of each character. It will be necessary to show Benny as a basically kind youngster who is sensitive about his fatness and somewhat rebellious against life, but who is also reflective. And to visualize Duke, we have to make him aggressive, egocentric, cruel, and at the same time cowardly. If we emphasize these character traits, the solution becomes that much more credible, since in real life it would be unlikely for Duke to accept the idea of playing the game of Russian roulette with Benny, a comparative nonentity.

The story "Russian Roulette" is, as it stands, not yet a finished story, for it can be told in any of three ways: as a pulp or confession story, as a slick story, or as a quality story, by which we mean a purely literary story, which uses techniques that are refinements of both the pulp and slick approaches. We have been concerned here only with plotting a complication and arriving at an outline. In order to complete the story, it will be necessary to change the steps of the outline in terms of their order, and it will be necessary to know in advance the implications behind the comic, the tragic, and the modern curves in the telling of the story. It will be the purpose of the next chapter to investigate the significance of these curves in the construction of a short story, and then we will turn our attention to the

12

methods whereby we can develop "Russian Roulette" into a finished tale.

There remain three more things to say about the artifice of the short story, and these things deal with the problem of theme, the nature of plotting, and the sources and nature of complications. It, first of all, should be noted that in outlining the story "Russian Roulette," nothing was said about the matter of theme, and yet the story has a theme. Such a statement should suggest to the reflective reader that the theme of a short story is not a prerequisite condition in plotting it. Now such a statement is both true and false. This is not to say that an author will necessarily be unaware of the theme of the particular story he is working on. The theme of a short story is what the author is trying to prove by pointing out a moral or teaching a lesson, as in juvenile, confession, and most pulp stories; or by pointing up some time-tested basic "truth," as in slick fiction; or by arriving at some intellectual codification of the conditions of life as they penetrate and interact with human character, as in quality fiction. For example the theme of most love stories is that "love will find a way." The theme of most westerns is that "the good guys always lick the bad guys." The theme of most mystery stories is that "crime does not pay." The theme of most confession stories is that "those who sin must suffer for it." And the themes of quality stories are endless in variety and significance.

But what is of primary importance for the novice writer who is just developing a technique in the construction of a short story is that to work on theme prior to developing the plot complication may lead, and very likely will lead, to his editorializing and moralizing so much about his story that the story will lose all entertainment value. In commercial fiction, except for juvenile and confession stories, the theme will take care of itself providing the complication is deep enough and the writer allows his characters to say and do what they must say and do. For the time being, with the exceptions noted, let it be taken as a matter of principle that the beginning writer concern himself not at all with the intellectual ramifications of his materials. He should concern himself wholly with the basic materials themselves. The novice writer should work, at the start, with visualization rather than conceptualization primarily.

The juvenile-story writer must concern himself with theme because writing for the juvenile market requires that the writer begin with theme. The confession-story writer must concern himself with theme or there will not be any confession "angle" to his story. To confess means to admit that one has been guilty of some wrongdoing and learned a lesson from it. The captions used in confession magazines beneath or above the titles of the stories express the theme. For example: I FAILED MY HUSBAND AND ALMOST ENDED UP IN THE DIVORCE COURTS. BY TRYING TO KEEP UP WITH THE JONESES I DROVE MY HUSBAND INTO A NERVOUS BREAKDOWN. And it is certain that the quality writer must understand consciously the theme of his story in order to select detail, to utilize symbolism, to underscore character traits, and so on.

Now so far as the nature of plotting is concerned, one of the first admissions to be made about a plot is that it is, in part at least, a mechanical rather than wholly creative act. How can this be otherwise when it can be demonstrated that short stories have certain basic forms? Let us face the issue squarely. It takes insight and imagination to create a bridge over the Straits of Mackinac, and the insight and imagination work in terms of technical knowledge. In the same fashion, it takes insight and imagination to utilize the techniques of plotting.

The final problem we wish to discuss here concerns the sources and the nature of complications. So far as the location of complications is concerned, the reader need not fear having an insufficiency of complications to use as basic story material. Minor complications abound in existence. No day's life is without one. And if an individual is fortunate enough to escape having some such problem present itself in the course of his daily existence, then he can turn to the agony columns of the newspapers, as well as to news stories themselves, to find a wealth of material ready at hand. The letters to Molly Mayfield, Ann Landers, and Jane Dare are full of more complications and unresolved situations than any one writer can handle in his lifetime.

Apart from the newspapers, other short stories themselves provide complications that are as yet unresolved. There are at least twenty good stories involved in Benny's growing up, if not more: Benny's attempts to get on the football team; Benny's first love; Benny's desire to overcome his weight problem; Benny's wish to have a friend. And if not other short stories, a family argument should provide enough material to fill out a number of short stories as well as a novel or two. Aunt Agatha, who never married and who has a passion for keeping pet alligators in her closet, should give a beginning writer pause.

14

It may be of help in exaggerating a complication to understand something of the nature of complications. Whatever the intellectual depth of a story, the story must communicate emotion to a reader. The only way a writer can communicate an emotion is first to produce it. Apart from questions of style, imagery, mood, and other means of arousing emotion in a story, the only structural fashion by which an author can produce an emotion is by complicating the lives of his characters. One simply cannot produce an emotion by writing about people who live contented and peaceful lives. One has to drop a monkey wrench into their peaceful scheme of things in order to arouse emotion in them, and this in turn—granting that the reader will be interested in the characters—arouses an emotional response in the reader. In its simplest terms, a complication is something unpleasant that happens to a person who, had he the freedom of choice of having it happen or not happen, would choose for it not to happen. The reason why a person would choose for a complication not to happen is that unpleasant things follow: heartache, sorrow, hate, anger, jealousy, sacrifice, frustration, disappointment, disillusionment, fear, etc. All stories, pulp, slick, and quality, are based upon complications. The struggle or conflict caused by a complication is the main structural device authors employ to produce emotion.

In order to demonstrate the emotions that struggle with complication arouses in a protagonist, let us view the emotions Benny goes through in the story "Russian Roulette." Benny's minor problem of fatness causes him to be left out of things. He feels humiliated and self-pitying, resentful, and at the same time, shy. With the appearance of Duke on the scene, Benny becomes joyful in discovering what he believes to be a true friend in the older boy. His feeling of joy leads him into the complication proper. Duke inveigles him into the robbery, and with this turn of events Benny feels apprehension, fear, and sorrow. The feeling of pity for the woman whom Duke has beaten up is replaced, however, by terror for himself when Duke threatens to shoot him. With the terror there is a mixture of compassion for other people whom Duke might hurt. The possibility that the woman (whom Duke has beaten) might die sends panic through Benny, and the panic is added to by a sick nervousness in his attempt to solve his dilemma. With the realization that all his life he has let his size stand in his own way, he feels a sense of his own stupidity, and he resolves to stop going with Duke. The resolution brings him a feeling of courage and self-reliance that is still partially fearful. And when

15

Benny does prove that Duke is a coward, he feels free of fear and emotionally strong.

EXERCISES FOR CHAPTER 1

1. Make a list of five or ten minor complications, and then by exaggeration, make each complication more significant, as in the following example:
Minor complication: A mother comes into the kitchen to discover her eight-year-old son stealing cookies from the cookie jar.
Exaggerated complication: A mother comes into her bedroom to discover her fifteen-year-old son stealing money from her purse.
2. Of the complications that you have listed, choose the one that appeals to you immediately as inherently interesting to you and develop an outline for it. (Keep two things in mind: it will be easier to develop such an outline if you are familiar with the characters and setting of the story—that is, do not choose a setting in an exotic place or characters whom you personally have never seen or observed; and be brief and to-the-point in developing each step of the outline.)
3. Make a list of the major characters involved in your complication, and after each character's name jot down three or four of his outstanding characteristics. Caution: use specific and concrete words rather than abstract and general ones. Do not use the word "good" when you actually mean "charitable," or "genial," or "incorruptible."
4. Check your outline against the principles listed in this chapter and make sure that you have used all of them.
5. An outline of a complication should reveal the essentials of action, and one of these essentials is motivation. Check your own outline to be certain that you have exposed the reasons why each character acts the way he does.

2
How Three Curves
Are Used in Fiction

WE HAVE SEEN in the last chapter how to construct the outline for a story by exaggerating a complication. Now before we proceed to discover how to turn such an outline into a finished story, it will be well to pause and consider what is really implied by the struggle of a hero and his eventual successful resolution of the complication facing him. For such a story yields the classic curve of comedy, and we have to realize that, in addition to a comic curve, there is a tragic curve, and there is a modern curve that differs from both of these.

The curve of comic fiction we can describe as concave. The hero begins in a difficulty that deepens and gets worse through his own mistaken efforts, and just when things seem blackest, just when the reader's ability to extricate the hero appears to be thoroughly nonplussed, the hero comes through with a resolution that neatly and surprisingly brings about an effective happy ending. It is obvious that the comic curve is optimistic in its very nature. We have begun the consideration of the short story, therefore, in terms of the widest popular appeal, the appeal to optimism, the appeal to the success that attends struggle. Virtually all of the pulp and slick fiction consumed in the United States is comic in nature. And one may well indicate as a corollary that in the predominance of such an optimistic view—involving, as it must have involved, the facing and resolution of countless complications—much is fictionally stated about the American character in the preponderance of slick stories, both written and televised, that flood the markets. And we say *fictionally* stated, using that qualifying adverb to show that such is not necessarily so in actuality.

Yet the comic curve does not tell the whole truth about existence, for it is equally obvious that a protagonist may find himself in such difficulties that no matter how he struggles he can never extricate himself. Such a story inevitably uses a tragic curve, and it is developed in just the opposite way from the comic curve, for the curve of tragedy is convex. The hero in the comic curve struggles to solve his problem and runs into difficulties, but eventually succeeds. The protagonist in the tragic curve struggles to solve his problem and appears to be virtually successful, save that an unanticipated difficulty robs him of success, and all is swept away in a crash about his head.

Both of these curves are illustrated metaphorically in the medieval picture of the Wheel of Fortune upon which people ride, dressed in various kinds of clothing to indicate their fortunate or unfortunate stations in life. The Wheel turns, indicating that they may begin doubtfully but end happily, or begin in promising station only to end miserably. In short, these curves use interchanges and reversals to impart either a sense of wonder and relief that life cannot always be niggardly or a sense of awe that life can humble even the greatest. Many of our common proverbs illustrate these basic curves: "A slow starter, an early finisher." "There's many a slip 'twixt cup and lip." "Pride goeth before a fall."

Disregarding for the moment other refinements in the art of short-story writing, one of the essential differences between the commercial and the quality story is that the former will not ordinarily tolerate failure or tragedy. This is not to say that all quality stories are tragic, for they are not. Many quality stories illustrate neither the comic nor tragic curves, but a relatively new type of basic conception that turns the hero into a passive, rather than active, figure, into one who is acted upon rather than one who acts.

It will be the purpose of this chapter to investigate the concepts of human nature that are implied by the comic, the tragic, and the modern curves in order to give the reader some perspective both about plotting and about the really essential distinctions in the various forms of short story.

What is stated about human nature in the comic and tragic curves? The essence of both of them lies in the struggle of a protagonist to extricate himself from his difficulties. The comic indicates that the will to struggle is an important attribute in any individual, that through the exercise of his own efforts—though he may land in difficulties—he nonetheless will succeed eventually. The tragic, no less significantly than the comic, relies upon the willed struggle of an in-

.dividual, a struggle that may indeed bring him near success only to have it snatched away from him by something in his own nature or in the nature of things, which he has not been aware of, toward which he is blind. The comic curve states over and over: "not to struggle against the odds is weakness, and success comes to him who fights." The tragic curve states over and over: "to struggle against the odds is futile, but there is something grand in the attempt, grand and moving and awe-inspiring." Even when one is brought to view the relative and terrifying puniness of a man, such as Oedipus, nevertheless the reader's tragic view of that individual lies in the idea that he has struggled against his destiny. There is, therefore, in tragedy a recognition of the same innate principle of human nature that is found in the comic curve: struggle in itself is valuable and necessary.

The comic and tragic curves represent very ancient conceptions of the human condition. These curves have dealt from early Greek times with a universe in which man's exercise of will led him either into freedom or into chaos and despair. A statement about human nature is in its own way a statement about the nature of the universe in which human nature must operate. The comic and tragic curves indicate fictionally that man has a will that is free; and that human nature has this capability in fiction must be granted. That human nature may not have such a capability in actual existence raises once more the problem of artifice in the short story. Quite apart from the fact that most individuals do not really struggle to overcome their problems—or if they face serious problems, frequently give up the fight altogether, there being few tragic heroes in real existence—quite apart from this fact, there is another conception of the universe that makes the older fictional view of human nature appear completely artificial: in actuality, human beings are not free agents.

According to a prevailing contemporary view, not only are the wills of men not free, the mere statement that the will is at least partly free, when made specific, invariably leads one back in an endless series of causes and effects to causes that lie eventually beyond the control of the individual: causes of heredity and environment—back, back, and yet further back to beginnings that are unknown over the generations. Such at least is a current view of human nature—a human nature tied by antecedents, restricted by formless outside causes, under the sway of accident and whirl and chaos.

Now what if the present-day writer, unconsciously or consciously, feels uncomfortable with the implications about human nature that the

19

classic comic and tragic curves give rise to? What if his view of human nature makes willed struggle impossible? What if, in short, a writer cannot take up the artifice of struggle on the part of his characters? Here, indeed, is a dilemma. For in effect, the modern writer denies himself that series of exaggerations about his characters that make it possible for them to assert themselves against the difficulties that harass them. He therefore denies himself the use of the comic and tragic curves. In an effort to come to grips with the actual truth of human nature, such an author must say:

Here is my character. To suppose him to be capable of struggling against the circumstances surrounding him is an impossibility. About the best that I can do is put him into a situation with which he cannot cope, and to show that he cannot cope with it, and why. I will not produce either a comedy or a tragedy, but at least I will be telling the truth. Or say that I put him into a situation with which he does cope. About the best I can say is that special circumstances are working in his favor, which enable him to succeed where others have failed. But the former is the more credible, the more true to life—that my character faces a complex of circumstances that are invariably too much for him. To pretend that he has the will to struggle against them is more than I can pretend. Half the time, what people call a struggle is merely something else—it is merely a strong expression on an individual's part of going along in a direction that has been given to him from outside himself, and therefore all I would be doing would be to make him a naïve character, blind to himself.

Some such series of reflections must animate the creation of many a quality story, particularly the stories of those writers for whom the expression of his own vision of the world, and not merely entertainment, is the chief motive in writing. Thus the desire for reality, for truth-telling, often prevents the use of the older classic forms in the short story; and instead of the comic or tragic curve, the curve of many a contemporary writer's story is, to be somewhat paradoxical, linear. Let us avoid the contradiction in terms, and call the modern story linear. And the method it uses is akin to that of biography or autobiography: a series of events added together linearly to produce the whole sum of a person's life. It is a form of addition, for its preoccupation is with the formation of a character as viewed *in toto*.

The linear story states certain things about human nature just as the comic and tragic curves do, but unlike them, the chief characteristic of the hero is his passivity. He does not struggle, and there

20

is no suggestion made that he can struggle against his dilemma. Yet the linear story borrows some of its emotional elements from the comic and tragic curves. From the comic comes the element of wryness, a kind of laughter that is without hope; from the tragic curve comes pathos. When we view a character inextricably enmeshed in circumstances beyond his control, we may be moved to wry laughter or to a sense of the pathetic. We will not feel the awe of tragedy, however, for such an emotion is reserved only for those who have the power to pit themselves against overwhelming odds. The passive character inextricably caught in a web may stir our sense of pathos, but not our awed sense of tragedy.

We will now analyze several representative examples of the linear story: Robert Louis Stevenson's "A Lodging for the Night"; Anton Chekhov's "The Kiss"; Gustave Flaubert's "A Simple Heart." Each of these represents an interesting variation of the linear story.

One form of the linear story is that in which the chief character is totally aware of himself and of the curtailments that his birth, fortunes in the world, abilities, personality, and so on, have erected around him. Such is the poet Francis Villon as Stevenson pictures him in "A Lodging for the Night." Villon is a man of tremendous self-understanding, who knows he must act in the way he does act. To struggle against the conditions of his existence is an impossibility, merely because he himself realizes that he is not free to struggle. Villon, forced to flee from a warm dwelling because of a murder that might implicate him, is reduced to facing a night of bitter cold weather, with only the prospect of being picked up by a patrol or the more immediate prospect of freezing to death as alternatives. In vain are his efforts to secure a lodging from relatives and erstwhile friends. He hovers in a doorway and steals a bit of money from a dead wretch, who has frozen. Quite by accident, he manages to obtain a lodging, warm food, wine, and safety from the elements at the home of a lord. He engages the lord in a conversation about the differences between their positions, remarking upon the fact that the lord's honor and position are fully as accidental as Villon's own poverty and necessity to steal from the dead. The lord maintains that a man can obtain honor and respect by desiring them, by repentance, by suing for God's grace. Villon, completely realistic, places the question of a man's morality upon the accident of his birth. Born rich, one can have honor, reputation, respect, and sue for God's grace. Born poor, one has to scrub, steal, lie, even murder merely to live on. The story

21

closes with Villon's leaving the house at daybreak, having insulted his host's intelligence at parting, and wondering whether or not the old man's goblets were worth stealing. The principal effect of the story is to convince one of the wryness of existence; there is a touch of pathos in our sense of the value of the poetry the real Villon wrote, but the chief mood is one of wryness. And Villon himself announces the doctrine of the linear tale: what is the purpose of struggling in a world where accident rules?

Like Stevenson's "A Lodging for the Night," Chekhov's "The Kiss" reveals a character who is aware of himself, of the limitations that his personality, physique, and abilities in life have placed around him, so that he cannot act. Before briefly analyzing Ryabovich, the protagonist—a characteristic Chekhovian hero in that he is in no way extraordinary—it seems worthwhile to cite two of Chekhov's statements about art: "The aim of fiction is absolute and honest truth"; and "It is . . . the duty of the artist not to solve the problem but to attempt to state it correctly." These statements reveal the preoccupation of the linear writer superbly. The emphasis shifts away from the imaginary to "reality," or "truth"; and away, also, from struggle and resolution to presenting a picture of the nature of the complication in which the passive hero is enmeshed.

"The Kiss" concerns one member of a group of soldiers who are invited to tea at the home of a local landowner. This particular soldier, Ryabovich, feels shut off from the others. He does not dance, he cannot make trivial and witty talk, he is not a swaggerer, he is shy, he is altogether aware of himself as a most uninteresting person: "There were times when he envied the boldness and swagger of his companions and was inwardly wretched; the knowledge that he was timid, round-shouldered, and uninteresting, that he had a long waist and lynx-like whiskers deeply mortified him, but with years he had grown used to this feeling, and now, looking at his comrades dancing or loudly talking, he no longer envied them, but only felt touched and mournful." During the course of the evening, an entirely accidental romantic interlude takes place. In moving back from the billiard room, Ryabovich loses his way, stumbles into a darkened room where a young lady, mistaking him for someone else, throws her arms around his neck and kisses him. She perceives her mistake instantly, and Ryabovich staggers from the room to spend the next months thinking about the incident, about the young lady, about romance, which has entered his life for the first time. He does nothing to discover her name, nothing to pursue the situation any longer; but yet his heart has been sorely torn. A new world opens up before him, yet the brigade of which he is a member moves away from the neighborhood. He is wholly preoccupied with that one chance encounter. For months he lives in a daydream. Then there is a chance to return to the neighborhood where the landowner lives. Ryabovich returns in a state of great excitement and uneasiness. He expects the local landowner to issue another invitation, but the invitation does not come. He does not even know the girl's name or her face. He takes a walk to the river near the landowner's home. He is impressed by the unintelligibility of the world. The river water symbolizes the ceaseless cycle of change without meaning. And the story raises the question, as Ryabovich ponders it: "What for? Why? And the whole world, the whole of life, seemed to Ryabovich an unintelligible, aimless jest . . . And turning his eyes from the water and looking at the sky, he remembered again how Fate in the person of an unknown woman had by chance caressed him, he recalled his summer dreams and fancies, and his life struck him as extraordinarily meager, poverty-stricken, and drab."

Ryabovich has a less virile intellect than Villon in Stevenson's story, and the story's dominant mood is one of pathos, rather than of the wryness of existence. But like Villon, he is a character too thoroughly conscious of his own limitations to wish to act, too much committed to a world of accident and disorder for any struggle to be meaningful. The universe has shrunk to unintelligibility in the linear story; the heroic act becomes impossible in it. Strangely enough, Villon, Ryabovich, Gabriel Conroy in James Joyce's short story "The Dead," and J. Alfred Prufrock, the protagonist of T. S. Eliot's poem, are all kin. Villon is the hardbitten realist who, in turn, bites the matter off with a wry grimace; Ryabovich, no less aware of his own limitations, has too little of the realist in himself to understand what characterizes his world from the very beginning; Gabriel Conroy comes to see himself as an ineffectual and bumbling fool who cannot arouse ardor in his wife; and J. Alfred Prufrock too self-consciously measures out his life in coffee spoons and visions that he cannot express without withering restatements that kill his own sense of action.

In both Villon and Ryabovich, one sees an inherent skepticism. Villon is openly skeptical. He makes the grace of God depend upon the economic circumstances of the individual. The story line brings highly dissident elements into confrontation with one another without

23

change occurring in the nature of the protagonist. Villon remains Villon at the end with no greater awareness of himself and his circumstances than at the beginning. The idealism of the lord's position is an impossibility for Villon, and Villon is shrewd enough to see it. In "The Kiss," change does occur in the protagonist, because although Ryabovich is aware of his limitations, he does get caught up in an idealistic vision. The romantic event that occurs becomes the source of a dream that invests the unknown woman with all the qualities of spiritual salvation for Ryabovich. We see him exaggerating the significance of the occurrence out of all proportion to its literal value. There is a blindness in the character, which we can put our finger on, and the collapse of his dream brings him back to the same awareness of himself that was there in the beginning. In terms of action, the movement of the story is linear. In terms of Ryabovich's mental experience, there is a curve resembling the tragic.

If one form of the linear story is that in which the chief character is aware of his own passivity, the other characteristic form is that in which the author, rather than the chief character, shows this awareness of curtailment, of hindrance to action. The author's knowledge, therefore, makes any attempt of the character to extricate himself from his situation impossible. Again there is no struggle. There is only a massive understanding of a character's life. There is no plot, in the conventional sense of the term, but there may be an attempt to present the life symbolically. Through symbols the author may reveal a character's subconscious desire to struggle, a desire that he lacks in his conscious life. Thus, the principal mood is again one of either wryness or pathos. What the character says and does, we more or less totally understand. The hero, here, is somewhat like a bug skewered on a pin, raised up still squirming to our gaze. Struggle implies a consciousness that the character lacks and a will that he cannot have, so that life touches and maims him with almost utter disregard for the character's own wishes or interests. Here is the source of both pathos and wryness. It is wryness without hearty laughter; it is pathos without tragedy. It is a picture of the helpless human being. And such is Félicité, as Gustave Flaubert views her, in "A Simple Heart."

Again, as with Chekhov, it is interesting to observe that Flaubert hoped to write with such objectivity and realism that, as he remarked in his *Correspondence*, posterity would not be occasioned to wonder whether he himself had lived: he believed in the complete subjection of the artist to his materials, the complete abandonment of the artist's own personality. This is only another way of stating that the writer should write in terms of objective fidelity to his subject, not in terms of his own subjective exaggeration. Thus, in "A Simple Heart," we get a faithful portrait of a faithful servant, a picture of a character eminently naïve, almost totally without desire to struggle, for there is no conscious knowledge of the need for struggle.

The story is very much like a biography. It covers the life of Félicité from her eighteenth year, when she came to work for Mme. Aubain, until her death fifty years later, at a time when she "spoke to shadows of her own from time to time," and was incapable of seeing the stuffed effigy of her precious parrot Lulu, because she was "blind now." The use of the plural, or the suggestion of habitual action, throughout the story is an interesting way of creating a regularly unfolding or linear progression: "She rose at daybreak to be in time for Mass, and worked till evening without stopping. . . ." "At all times of year she wore a print handkerchief fastened with a pin behind. . . ." "Every Thursday regular visitors came in for a game of 'Boston,' and Félicité got the cards and foot-warmers ready beforehand. . . ." "On Monday mornings the dealer who lodged in the covered passage spread out all his old iron on the ground." "This adventure was talked of at Pont-l'Évêque for many a year." "On days when it was too hot they did not leave their room." Félicité learns her catechism "by dint of hearing it" over and over; and the few particularized scenes give way once more to the general plural: "From sheer habit Félicité went into Virginie's room in the mornings and gazed at the walls." Or, "He arrived on Sundays after Mass, rosy-cheeked, bare-chested, with the scent of the country he had walked through still about him." Characters enter the story and leave it; they appear for a time, are particularized, and then they disappear, and life goes on in terms of a set series of actions. Mme. Aubain's children grow and leave home, and the daughter dies, and they mourn, and then "years slipped away, one like another, and their only episodes were the great festivals as they recurred. . . ." Félicité gets the parrot, and we have particular times and places and descriptions, which turn into the episode of the attack of quinsy, of earache, and then "Three years later she was deaf; and she spoke very loud, even in church. . . ." The parrot dies and Félicité has it stuffed, Mme. Aubain dies, and we are told of Félicité that "her eyes grew feeble. The shutters ceased to be thrown open. Years and years passed, and the house was neither let nor sold."

The alternation of particular scene and generalized plural—the particular and timely giving way to the habitual and routine—this is the technique used to present Félicité's whole life story. One gets the impression of knowing the character fully and completely, much more fully and completely than the character can be said to know herself. What is more significant, Félicité shows no struggle. There is never a moment in her life in which she attempts to fight against the constrictions around her. She accepts what befalls her with complete passivity. Any attempt on Félicité's part to struggle would be absurd, in fact, for the author has dammed up the very sources of the will to struggle by making Félicité totally unaware that life could be different for her. She is so entirely faithful and good that the narrowness of Mme. Aubain's family, the callousness of Félicité's previous lover, the cruel withering away of her own faculties by time, none of these things offer challenge, but acceptance. The story is thus linear; it is marked by a tremendous sensitivity to the linear and often unrelated episodes of life as they occur and act upon a passive protagonist.

Thus, as we said before, there is no plot in conventional terms, but there is an attempt to present the life of the chief character in symbolic fashion in order to make her appear to have a knowledge or will in her unconscious existence that she lacks, through no fault of her own, in her conscious life. And this knowledge is presented to us in the story through the use of religious imagery. Félicité is a religious figure: she renounces struggle, accepts the demands of life, feels the blows of events, and in the end is rewarded by a vision of her existence and her salvation, which has only symbolically been suggested. Is the story tragic or comic? Neither of these words will do to describe the net effect, which is one of pathos. The suggestion of Félicité's great joy and happiness, which she experiences in her dying gasp—the mystic vision that will unite her finally with the parrot, now a symbol of union with Christ—may come to the devout as a hope extended from heaven to man. But the real terms in which Félicité's life has been stated must convince us of the pathos without either the tragedy or the joys of existence.

Flaubert's "A Simple Heart" shows the linear story in its pathetic, nontragic aspects with almost complete fidelity to the abstract description given it. Human nature in the story is nearly the same as human nature outside the story. Félicité does not struggle, for there is no pretense made that a will to struggle is possible. She cannot succeed as comic protagonist, nor fail as tragic protagonist because she makes no attempt. What is left is life treating human nature as life does, with many things demanded and given and changed. What is left is understanding. We understand Félicité perfectly. We know what makes her "tick." She is very much like a living person. We feel the pathos of that life—as surely as we feel the pathos of any human life if we know it entirely—for all real human lives are in their own way pathetic.

There are many other illustrations of the linear story, but there seems little need to examine them here, once the main characteristics have been made sufficiently clear. In any case, so widespread is the occurrence of the linear tale and so important is the effect upon modern literature of the passive hero that we will return to this form again and again. The reader is not to make the mistake of believing, however, that all quality stories are linear tales. The literary artist uses, as well, the other curves in fiction. We have been describing only one particular form of quality story.

One matter that may now puzzle the reader concerns our statement that all short stories deal with a complication that has been made inherently more interesting than it would be in real life through the process of exaggeration. For the modern writer as artist has professed a desire to abandon such an artifice, to deal with life "in the way that life really is," in short, to tell the truth. We do not propose, at the moment, to comment fully on these aims, since we wish to raise the question of artifice in examining the plot structure of the quality story in Chapters Four and Five. Yet we may remark that there are two ways of exaggerating a complication. One of them is to blow it up out of all proportion to its actual size in life, and thus to call forth from the protagonist an exaggeration of his own attributes in dealing with it. The other way is to present a complication and so minimize the character's willingness to face it, or his blindness toward it, as to suggest, in effect, that the complication is too large for him. In the linear story the complication gains its exaggerated quality by virtue of the hero's passivity.

We have shown in the first chapter how to exaggerate and develop a complication in order to produce an outline for a story. What we have done essentially is to form a true comic plot: the hero struggles; he meets a difficulty; he succeeds. In this chapter we have indicated that certain other considerations—almost extraneous ones, at first sight, to plotting a short story—must be taken into account of the nature of the complication and the protagonist if the writer is to plumb the full resources of his art. We have not intended to imply any denigration of the use of comedy by indicating that much modern fiction has moved away from the comic resolution of difficulties, which the protagonists of commercial fiction still effect. Comedy remains a great and permanent achievement of mankind, and cannot be harmed by any commercial exploitation of its methods or literary reluctance to consider human beings as capable of will and success. In fact, when it comes time to examine quality stories in greater detail with a view to showing how the comic formula may be adapted to their structures, let the reader remember that story writing is artifice—all of it—and not the less so for deserting the market place.

Before demonstrating how the reader may turn the outline of his complication into a quality story, however, let us consider the methods a writer uses in adapting such an outline to the demands of pulp and slick stories. Later, after much experience, the reader can dream up a plot that will call upon the hidden reservoirs of his mind and spirit and represent his own vision of reality. Right at the moment, let us begin with a thorough awareness of the choices available to the apprentice writer and with his conscious manipulation of his materials. Exercise comes before perfection.

3

How to Plot Formula
and Chronological Stories

ESSENTIALLY, as we have stated, the outline for a story produced according to the methods presented in Chapter One will be comic in nature. Now there are two ways in which to develop such a story, either in terms of a formula plot or in terms of a chronological one. Let us first consider the formula story.

In telling a formula story, we begin with a much tighter, more sophisticated, and much more dramatic structure than is possible in a chronological story. For it is in this form of story that we get what we call, strictly speaking, a developed plot. A plot may be described as the objective chain of events in a story that has a beginning, a middle, and an end. Or we can say of the plot that it is the device that holds together the beginning, middle, and ending of a story, giving it continuity and enabling the writer to exploit its dramatic elements in such a way as to elicit the greatest interest and excitement in the reader. The formula story is the conventional method of writing a short story, and as we speak of it here, it not only forms the structure of the great bulk of commercial fiction, but it also serves as the most elementary approach to the structure of the quality story. It is the most popular of story forms, comprising approximately seventy-five per cent of all published stories. Let us, therefore, consider the divisions of the formula story, the beginning, the middle, and the end, and the elements that compose them.

THE BEGINNING

The beginning of the formula story has seven separate requirements, or we can speak of the beginning as accomplishing seven different aims.

I. The beginning must be placed in time as close to the ending as possible.

Like the beginning *in medias res* of the epic, the formula story commences either with a full-blown complication or with a minor problem that swiftly leads to a major complication, so that the reader may grasp immediately that something exciting is at issue. This method exploits the dramatic interest of the story in order to pique the reader's curiosity and to present simply and cogently to him the nature of the dilemma.

II. If the complication itself is not immediately presented, a minor problem leading to the complication must be given.

The structure of the short story is very much like a funnel. At the opening of the funnel, there is a relatively large space for the volume of liquid to move about in. But very quickly, the walls of the funnel narrow, and the liquid, if it is not to spill over, must rush through the constriction. So with the beginning of the short story. Very rapidly must the reader's interest be brought to flow in a narrow and tightly directed channel, so that it will have an aim and a focus.

III. The scene must be set.

The poet's eye may roll from earth to heaven in a fine frenzy, but the net result of his effort must be to give to his airy fancies a local habitation and a name. In the same fashion, the short-story writer may have airy fancies at the back of his mind, but he will cheat the reader by not placing him in some time-conditioned, concrete reality. The reader, in short, must know where he is when the story commences.

IV. The principal characters must be introduced with an indication of the approximate ages, and the point of view must be established.

The psychology of a reader is a curious thing. Once he has begun reading a story, he will invariably tend to attach the greatest importance to those characters who first appear, for he will think that the story is about them. It will bewilder the average reader to delay the introduction of major characters until well after the story has begun, for he will already have made the foregoing assumption. And it is obvious that the point of view must be established immediately. Through whose eyes do we see this story. The author's? One of the character's? With which one, of all the characters, are we to identify ourselves? We begin by taking sides, by asserting sympathy, by placing ourselves in the dilemma. The short story must appeal immediately to this basic desire of the reader, who wants to know where he stands in relation to what is going on.

V. The tone of the prose must let the reader know what type of story he is reading.

This requirement of the beginning simply makes specific in one more way what has already been stated: the reader must know where he stands. A romance, a mystery, a western, a story of intrigue, and all other types of stories have their own moods, styles, and peculiar atmosphere.

VI. The beginning must imply what ending is desired.

Here again, whether comic, romantic, or any other type, the story must suggest to the reader at the very beginning what he wants the ending to be. The plotted short story has a very tight structure, and a large part of the sense of inevitability that one feels in reading certain short stories comes from the recognition that all the concrete details of the story point to a definite choice of direction. It is, in fact, by means of the unstated assumptions that the reader is led to make that the author whets curiosity and bestows eventual satisfaction. This is the technique that adds to illusion.

VII. The reader must be trapped into reading the story through the use of a narrative hook.

The short story should begin with some action which, through swift characterization, movement, dialogue, will hook the reader into reading the remainder of the story. The most elementary form of hook consists of anything that will cause a person's attention to fix itself. A policeman flags down a motorist as one passes by; one cranes his neck and slows down, trying to hear the first words. A little grade-school girl on a crowded bus giggles and thoughtlessly keeps poking

31

her umbrella into an elderly woman by whom she is sitting. If one happens to be a passenger, where will his eyes be glued? Ordinarily, the narrative hook should contain the leading character or characters, and the action should in some direct fashion indicate what the dilemma or complication of the story is to be.

So much for the elements that the beginning of the story should contain. Let us turn now to the middle of the formula story; the middle has four requirements.

THE MIDDLE

1. The middle must give the background of circumstances that produced the complication.

If the reader considers even momentarily what has been said, this prescription will make immediate sense. One of the most obvious questions to occur after the presentation of the minor or major complication is what produced the situation in the first place. Again a reference to the ordinary psychology of the human being is in order. Our minds customarily demand satisfaction in terms of the historical or causative elements of an event. That is, whenever a circumstance occurs that cries for some kind of solution, our normal question concerns how it happened.

It is worthwhile digressing here to point out two of the most common mistakes beginning writers make in handling this portion of the formula story. One is the relatively simple one of the verb tenses employed in telling the story. It is a fairly common convention that most short stories are told in the past tense. Thus, the past tense— "mouthed," "sat," "said," "awakened"—is, in effect the present time of the story. To represent any action in the background leading to this "present" time, therefore, requires the writer to use the past perfect tense: "had mouthed," "had sat," "had said," "had awakened." For some reason, many beginning writers fail to make clear this distinction in time when writing their stories, and as a consequence there is a vast confusion in the mind of the reader as to just when any specific action takes place.

An even more fatal mistake, however, in handling this first element of the middle is to present the background action *en masse,* as it were. Thus, in one fourteen-page story handed in by a student, the first two pages set the scene, the complication, and in general followed the requirements of the beginning. The subsequent ten pages were devoted entirely to giving the background of causes that produced the complication, and the final two pages were devoted to the resolution of the complication. Even so mechanical a method of analysis as counting the number of pages devoted to the beginning, middle, and end reveals that this writer has started his story at the wrong point and has sacrificed dramatic interest for the sake of nondramatic background information.

A cardinal principle, therefore, in presenting background material is to let it trickle through into the present action, keeping the reader's eye mainly on the development of present events within the story, and citing the past only as events in the past clarify, illuminate, and put into relief what is of present significance. A story that is told mainly in the past perfect tense can hardly be said to have movement.

II. The middle must present a series of efforts (usually three) in which the protagonist attempts to solve the complication only to meet with failure.

We shall see later that in outlining a complication, this step required by the formula story is always omitted. The writer will have to create these attempts when he fuses his own outline to the steps of the formula plot. It is enough to remark here that this step is an essential one in the formula story since each successive attempt of the protagonist to solve his complication—if the writer handles it with skill and originality—will more and more move the reader into an impasse. When the reader gives up and imagines that no means exist by which the protagonist can extricate himself from his difficulty, then the successful solution, which the reader will come to see as truly "right," will surprise and delight him. And he will say to himself: "Of course, that is the only way it could have ended."

The prescription that the protagonist must make three attempts at a solution, rather than two or four, is merely conventional and need not be followed slavishly. Yet here again, one may refer to the nature of the human mind as in its own way prescribing three attempts. Only one try, ordinarily, will strike the reader as but a feeble gesture toward solution. A second attempt is better, and by its very nature should be the antithesis of the first, for our minds, in the face of a dilemma, tend to go from one extreme to another; and thus by inference—having canvassed all the intermediate stages that could be starting points for an attempt—a third effort, based upon reasoning not employed in the first two tries, will produce or suggest an impasse. Three attempts, therefore, tend to operate in terms of the reader's psychology, but once again, such a technique is not to be followed with slavish rigidity.

III. *The middle must present, therefore, a situation of ante-climax in which it appears that the protagonist will finally solve the complication, only to meet with such disastrous failure that it leaves the reader convinced that there is no hope of a satisfactory solution.*

The reasoning here has just been presented above, in discussing the second element required in the middle of the story.

IV. *The middle must force the protagonist to make an agonizing decision that will point to the solution of the complication.*

How definitely will the decision point to the solution? It must be remembered that in short-story writing, suggestion is everything. Curiosity feeds on suggestion, rather than upon overwhelming amplification of facts. And our sense of the surprising, too, requires the writer to skirt the obvious and to produce what at first appears startling, even though after the initial wonder wears away, the solution will appear so inevitable that the reader will come away from the story saying to himself: "Well, I wouldn't have thought of that, but just so . . . I could think of no other solution that would be better." All too frequently poor short stories result when the solutions presented are pat and stereotyped, or when the reader can anticipate without difficulty what will occur.

THE END

The end of the story has just one requirement:

I. *The solution to the complication must be satisfactory and believable to the reader.*

To return once more to our analogy of the funnel, as being a concrete representation of the short-story structure: a visual object that represents the converging lines of possibility for flow. If we let the reader's interest and attention be represented by the liquid that is to flow through the funnel, we can see that very rapidly in the story we establish the line and direction of the flow, bring it into a tighter and tighter direction, at the same time as we persuade the reader that the story may turn out disastrously, and then direct the flow through the narrow orifice of the ending before the reader will quite have spotted the direction we, the writers, are forcing it to take. After the experience, the reader will see that he has been tricked into following a development that he could, perhaps, have put his finger on from the very beginning, had he been as clever as the writer.

So far, the plot of the formula story has been presented abstractly. Let us try to make the foregoing comments and requirements concrete by considering how we would plot the story "Russian Roulette" as a formula story. It is obvious that the outline we produced in Chapter One will have to be changed about in order to make a formula story of it, using the type of plot most commonly seen in all magazines.

The beginning of the formula story is the most difficult to write because the middle and ending are a result of it. Most new writers know that the beginning must be placed in time as close to the ending as possible, but unfortunately make the wrong choice for the opening scene. To avoid making a wrong choice, let us look once more at our complication outline and with the basic steps before us, work backward from the last to the first step, attempting to discover the best place to begin.

Step 1: Duke, a cruel twenty-year-old, befriends Benny, a fat and sensitive kid, just after the latter has been graduated from high school.

Step 2: Duke is a bad boy; he has been breaking into houses and stealing things.

Step 3: Duke befriends Benny because he is afraid, and moreover, he does not realize his own motives. Benny accepts Duke's offered friendship because Duke is, so he thinks, really sincere.

Step 4: Duke savagely beats up the woman at the house they rob, and Benny discovers that Duke's proffered friendship is really a mask for cruelty and a desire for admiration. Benny wants to break off the relationship with Duke.

Step 5: After the robbery, Duke shows Benny a gun that he has found. Benny then grows more frightened because he knows that Duke will eventually kill someone. And Duke threatens to use the gun on Benny if Benny ever tries to inform on him or break off their relationship.

Step 6: Benny discovers within himself his own weakness: his desire for friendship, based upon his own self-derision, has led him

35

to make friends with a person like Duke. Benny realizes that all his life, he has let his own fatness stand in the way of friendship based upon deeper than superficial values.

Step 7: Benny makes the agonizing decision to break away from Duke.

Step 8: Benny's decision leads him to see that Duke is really a coward. In a last desperate attempt to prevent Duke from doing any more harm, Benny decides to expose Duke to himself.

Step 9: Benny's deductions prove correct. It is noteworthy that the story has at all times circled around the gun that Duke has found. If Benny can demonstrate that he is less afraid of being shot than Duke is, he will have shown Duke up. Therefore Benny asks Duke to play a game of Russian roulette. Duke does not want to, but at the same time, he must save face. During the game, Duke cracks, Benny picks up the gun from Duke's hands, and then goes over to the telephone to call the police.

Now we obviously cannot begin our formula story with the last step, for that is the ending of the story. Steps 7 and 8 clearly fit the fourth requirement of the middle of the formula story: that the protagonist is forced to make an agonizing decision and that this decision will point to the solution. Step 6 of the complication outline is really in the mind of the protagonist—it is a moment of discovery and change, when Benny sees how he himself has failed to make friends, and that his own girth has led him, indirectly, to make friends with a person like Duke—and hence, if we used this step, it would be difficult to present the protagonist in any dramatic fashion. Step 5 would, however, fit all the requirements of the beginning. Duke points the gun at Benny and threatens to shoot him if Benny tries to back out now; and Benny realizes that Duke will murder someone. We have here a dramatic scene, a fully developed complication: the hero is enmeshed in what appears to be an insurmountable difficulty. We can present the principal characters, establish the point of view, let the reader know what kind of a story he is reading, and so on.

It just happens that nine steps were required to outline "Russian Roulette." The number of steps used in the reader's own complication outline may differ from this so that one cannot automatically say which step will be used to begin a formula story; but the principles discussed remain the same. Bearing these things in mind then, let us line up the complication outline in terms of the requirements made by the plot of the formula story:

36

Complication Outline	Formula Story
	Beginning

	⌈ 1
	| 2
	| 3
Step 5	⟨ 4
	| 5
	| 6
	⌊ 7

Now let us turn to the middle of the formula story and see which steps of the complication outline satisfy those requirements.

Complication Outline	Formula Story
	Middle
Steps 1, 2, 3, 4 (background leading to complication)	1
Step 6 (ante-climax, failure to reach solution)	3
Steps 7 and 8 (agonizing decision)	4

And of course, the ending of the formula story will coincide with the last step in the complication outline.

	Ending
Step 9	1

Now as we pointed out, the second step in the middle of the formula plot is always omitted in outlining the complication. This occurs every time since, in such an outline, we are interested only in developing and solving the complication and not in the minor attempts of the protagonist to solve it. We know that when we get to this portion in the middle of the formula plot that we must create some situations showing the protagonist's attempts to solve his complication. As the writer develops skill and finesse, he will find that his subconscious mind has been working for him to create these minor efforts of the protagonist, and that they will flow forth upon demand.

As a matter of fact, with greater experience the writer will not need to develop first of all a complication outline and then fuse it consciously to the plot of the formula story; he will think in terms of the formula plot right from the very beginning. But until such time as a writer becomes capable of doing this subconsciously, it will be best to take time to develop a complication outline and then rearrange it to meet the demands of the plot of the formula story.

Of course, the process of plotting and of ordering the plot, particularly when set forth in a step-by-step progression, seems mechanical. We have attempted throughout this chapter to show, in terms of the various requirements of the formula story, that plotting, although it follows a mechanical pattern, nevertheless also satisfies the demands that the human mind makes when confronted by the dramatic situation a protagonist is involved in. Undoubtedly, any reader's first stories will seem to him to be mere manipulations. He may feel somewhat uncomfortable at first with the discipline that the formula story imposes upon his efforts, and despite our advice to treat the "rules" with finesse and subtlety, he will not know without experience how to be skillful.

The formula plot is the oldest method of telling a story, and hence it has the qualities that belong to any classic structure: discipline, form, and unity. Chronological stories are, by contrast, much looser in construction and generally lack the finesse in craftsmanship used in the formula story. Why then consider them at all? Not long ago, a short story told in chronological order could not be sold because most short stories were formula stories in which, as we have seen, the beginning must be placed in time as close to the end as possible. But since the confession magazines have great popular appeal, the chronological story has found a ready market. The main reason, however, for describing the plot of the commercial chronological story is that its structure is largely the same as that of most linear stories, and hence can provide a ready and elementary way to gain practice in this form. Particularly interesting in this respect are the confession stories. Since the confession story is told in the first person, there is an important element of introspective awareness amounting to self-pity that tends to move the story away from dramatic action into subjective self-analysis. Such, as we have pointed out, is one of the main characteristics of the linear story.

In the chronological story, then, there are no flashbacks: the action always takes place in the present. The reader lives the story in the order in which it unfolds. One writes what the characters say and do as things happen, as events occur. Thus the plot of the chronological story makes use of the following conventions:

THE BEGINNING

I. *The beginning must set the scene.*

II. *The principal character or characters must be introduced with an indication of approximate age, and the point of view must be established.*

III. *The tone of the prose must let the reader know what type of story he is reading.*

IV. *The beginning must give the background of circumstances that eventually lead to the complication.*

V. *The reader must be trapped into reading the rest of the story by presenting a minor problem that later results in the complication, or by arousing interest in the protagonist's welfare.*

THE MIDDLE

I. *The middle must present the complication.*

II. *The middle must present a series of efforts (usually three) in which the protagonist attempts to solve the complication only to meet with failure.*

III. *The middle must present, therefore, a situation of ante-climax in which it appears that the protagonist will finally solve the complication, only to meet with such disastrous failure that the reader is left convinced that there is no hope of a satisfactory solution.*

IV. *The middle must force the protagonist to make an agonizing decision that will point to the solution of the complication.*

THE END

I. *The solution to the complication must be satisfactory and believable to the reader.*

Note that there are only five steps in the beginning of the plot structure of the chronological story. In this form of story the writer cannot imply what the desired ending will be because the complication is not made known to the reader until later, and the beginning cannot be placed as close in time to the end as possible because the story must be told in the chronological sequence of events in which it happened. But starting with II of the middle section, the plot structure is identical with that of the formula story.

In what ways must the complication outline be changed in order to develop a chronological story? As we have seen, for the formula story we had to juggle the steps of the complication outline around in order to squeeze out as much dramatic excitement as possible. For the chronological story, it will not be necessary to alter the complication outline at all. We might, perhaps, begin the chronological story a little earlier than the start of the outline. If a situation exists earlier that will satisfy the chief requirement of the beginning of the chronological story—that we have our interest aroused in the protagonist's welfare—we can show him involved in some minor problem, which will lead to the complication. In the story "Russian Roulette," for example, we could commence the chronological version by showing the humiliation Benny experiences in high school because of his size. From then on, the story will simply follow the steps of the complication outline.

We have delayed until now discussing two deviations from the plot structures of the chronological and formula story, which professional authors use occasionally. The first of these, which we call the "reversal of struggle," occurs most frequently in steps II and III of the middle. The reader learned that steps II, III, and IV of the middle, and the single requirement of the end are identical in both the formula and the chronological story. The technique of reversal of struggle is used when the complication is based on the antagonist's wanting to take something away from the protagonist that the protagonist wants to keep. For example, in several stories in current magazines, the authors used the principle of the reversal of struggle in the following ways:

1. A western story: the antagonist attempts to take the protagonist's ranch away from him.
2. A career story: the antagonist attempts to take the protagonist's job away from her.
3. A love story: the antagonist attempts to take the protagonist's good reputation away from her.
4. A mystery story: the antagonist attempts to take the life of the protagonist.

Hences comes the term "reversal of struggle" since it is the antagonist who struggles to take something away from the protagonist. The deviation occurs most frequently in steps II and III of the middle of the plot structure as follows:

THE MIDDLE

II. *The middle presents a series of attempts by the antagonist (usually three) to take away something from the protagonist that the protagonist wants to keep. The attempts meet with failure.*

III. *The middle, therefore, presents a situation of ante-climax in which it appears that the antagonist is certain to get what he wants from the protagonist, which leaves the reader convinced that there is no way for the protagonist to prevent it.*

IV. *As a consequence, the protagonist is forced to make an agonizing decision that will point to the solution of the complication.*

THE END

I. *The solution to the complication must be satisfactory and believable to the reader.*

The use of reversal of struggle in steps II and III of the middle does not change either step IV of the middle or the single step in the end of the formula and chronological story.

As we have indicated, the attempts by the antagonist to wrest something from the protagonist occur most frequently in the middle of the story, but this is not always so. The antagonist may attempt to take away something from the protagonist in the beginning of the story as well as in the middle. A good example for the study of this technique occurs in the slick story "I Will Not Talk," which is contained in the Appendix on page 382.

The other deviation in the plot structures of the formula and chronological story, which we call the "minor decision," is employed in step IV of the middle. The reader will recall that in both forms of story the protagonist is forced to make a major decision, and this major decision points to the solution. The deviation is employed when the agonizing decision made by the protagonist might otherwise be unbelievable to the reader. Thus, in the middle when the minor decision is used, step IV will read as follows:

IV. The protagonist makes a minor decision that will force him to make an agonizing decision. The major decision then points to the solution of the complication.

A good example of this deviation occurs in the slick story "Precious Moment," which is found on page 382 of the Appendix. Although the minor decision is not often so obvious as it appears there, it is used in many stories. In step 6 of the complication outline of "Russian Roulette," Benny actually makes a minor decision about himself when he discovers his own weakness and realizes that he has let his size prevent his making real friends. He is thus led to make the agonizing decision to break off with Duke, a decision that the reader otherwise would find unbelievable.

Besides these deviations within the plots of the formula and chronological story, some commercial stories deviate in terms of the entire plot structure. Such a story is called most frequently an "off-beat" story. There was a time not too many years ago when the off-beat story was shunned by most magazines. Times have changed so far as the reading public is concerned. A cursory glance at the "100 Best Markets for Short Stories" in the *Writer's Yearbook* reveals that quite a few magazines now list off-beat stories in their market requirements.

The mere fact that a story is called off-beat indicates that it is difficult to define in precise terms. About as close as one can come to describing an off-beat commercial story is to state that it differs from the normal commercial story in terms of the nature of the protagonist, in terms of theme, and in terms of structure. Originally, the off-beat story was one that violated some editorial taboo, such as stories with unsympathetic protagonists, or stories about drug addiction, prostitution, or crooked law-enforcement officers, stories with too much sex, or those that were irreligious, stories containing racial bias, stories that offended good taste, or stories in which virtue was not rewarded. But as the off-beat story became more and more acceptable to the editors of magazines, it tended to imitate the quality story by violating the formula plot of commercial fiction. Here is perhaps the most significant element of the off-beat story.

The reader learned in a previous chapter that all pulp and slick stories are essentially optimistic because the complication is always solved so that the ending is happy or satisfactory to the reader. Such is not true of some off-beat commercial stories. For example, in a current copy of a slick man's magazine, there is an off-beat story about an unsympathetic protagonist who is a heel insofar as women are concerned. His dominant character trait is that he is a woman chaser who loses all interest in a woman once he has seduced her. In the story, he meets the heroine. The complication he faces is his desire to seduce her. After several attempts, only to meet with failure, he lies and says that he loves her. He promises to marry her later if she will allow him to seduce her. After the seduction, he brutally tells the girl that he lied to her, that he has no intention of marrying her, and that he loses all interest in a woman once he has caused her to surrender. The story ends with his leaving the girl as he plots his next conquest.

Admittedly, the complication was solved in terms of the protagonist's interests; the ending was certainly satisfactory so far as the protagonist was concerned; but the reader who sympathizes with the heroine would have preferred that she not let the man have his way. The ending is neither a happy nor satisfactory one to the reader. The story violates the basic commercial plot of CONFLICT TO OVERCOME AN OBSTACLE TO SOLVE THE PROTAGONIST'S COMPLICATION AND REACH A WORTHWHILE GOAL. While it is true that the goal of seducing the girl may be worthwhile to the protagonist, it certainly is not a worthwhile goal to the reader. The reader finds himself hating the protagonist as the story ends, which is probably the reason why the editor of the magazine bought the story. He knew that the characterization of the protagonist would stick in the reader's mind long after the reader had forgotten the other stories in that issue of the magazine.

Now, why did not the author make this a formula story? He could have easily enough. The formula would have required the protagonist, after failing to seduce the heroine, to make the agonizing decision that he had fallen in love at last, so much in love that he was willing to give up his philandering ways and marry the girl. But the author knew if he did that that he would be walking right into a trite situation that has been done over and over so often in stories, in movies, and on T.V. that it has become a cliché. By violating the plot of the formula story, the author avoided the cliché and came up with a provocative story that the reader will long remember. Moreover, to have made it into a formula story would have resulted in its being unbelievable to the reader. The characterization of the protagonist was such that it would have been completely unrealistic for him to change his character drastically and fall in love with the heroine.

Every writer will occasionally get an idea for a short story that cannot be told as a formula or chronological story. He may end up by writing an off-beat story. But the mere fact that the protagonist is unsympathetic is no guarantee that the story will classify as an off-beat story. Many mystery stories present an unsympathetic protagonist who violates the basic plot in that the goal to be reached—whether murder, robbery, rape, or what have you—is certainly not a worthwhile goal so far as the reader is concerned. Such mystery stories, however, do not violate the single step in the end of the formula or chronological plot, because the unsympathetic protagonist is always punished for his crime. The ending is, therefore, satisfactory to the reader.

We repeat, we cannot define the off-beat story in concrete terms. We can only generalize about it. The current off-beat commercial story is not so much a violation of editorial taboos as it is a violation of the plot of the commercial story. The violation is necessary to make the story convincing to the reader and the characterization of the protagonist believable. In this respect, many slick off-beat stories could become quality stories were they written with greater depth and artistry.

The inexperienced writer is cautioned against trying to write off-beat stories until he has become truly professional. The market for off-beat stories is still so limited that editors rarely buy them except from established authors. The unestablished writer's chances of selling a formula or chronological story are perhaps a thousand times better than his chances of selling an off-beat story.

There are several other matters to stress about plotting. A plot depends essentially upon conflict. Conflict in a short story is created by the complication and the protagonist's struggle to solve it. Therefore, conflict occurs when the complication is deep enough. If the writer does not produce conflict between the protagonist and somebody or something in his attempts to solve the complication, it simply means that what is at issue is not major enough to warrant a struggle.

When one considers the possible conflicts that can confront an individual, it will readily and somewhat surprisingly be seen that there are only three generic plots possible in commercial fiction. Man can conflict with man; man can come into conflict with obstacles; man can confront and conflict with nature. To restate these three basic plots in more formal language, there can only be:

I. Conflict to eliminate an opponent to solve the protagonist's complication and reach a worthwhile goal.
II. Conflict to overcome an obstacle to solve the protagonist's complication and reach a worthwhile goal.
III. Conflict to avert a disaster.

It is interesting to compare these with the dictionary definition of the word *conflict*. *Webster's New Collegiate Dictionary* defines conflict in the following way:

1. A strife for mastery; hostile encounter; a fight; battle; esp., a prolonged struggle. 2. Clash or divergence of opinions, interests, etc.; esp., a mental or moral struggle occasioned by incompatible desires, aims, etc. 3. A dashing together, as of waves.

Once more, let us caution the reader to learn whatever rules we mention, for the reader will discover as he proceeds throughout the book that we will mention more and more of them. It may, indeed, be well for him to pause at this point and read the selections in the Appendix in order to fix more permanently in his mind the operation of these rules within the short stories printed there. In this way he can avoid becoming confused. And in any event, when the reader begins to write his own short stories, he will need to be thoroughly conversant with the various steps of the story form he is using in order to make his structure successful.

We will turn in the next two chapters to the structure of the quality story and consider there the more complex deviations in plot that quality writers have developed from the formula and chronological story.

EXERCISES FOR CHAPTER 3

1. The exercises of Chapter One asked the reader to develop a complication outline from a minor complication that the reader exaggerated. Take this outline and arrange it in terms of a chronological story.
2. Take the same outline and rearrange it as a formula story. Plot step two of the middle part of the formula story after you have rearranged your whole outline in terms of the plot structure of the formula story.

45

3. Read several formula stories in current magazines, dividing each story into the three parts of beginning, middle, and end, and then check each part to see how the various requirements for each part of the story have been carried out.
4. Make a special study of the narrative hooks of each of the stories you have read. Determine their average length, decide what elements make the hook interesting or exciting, and then write a narrative hook for your own formula story, imitating the techniques that seem to you the most valuable.
5. Study and memorize the various steps required by the plot of the formula story until you are able to write or recite them at will.

4   *How Structure Is Used*

in the Quality Story

IN THE SAME WAY that all commercial stories can be said to be based on one of three basic plots, there appear likewise to be three basic plots available to quality stories. Let us consider the following examples:

> *1. Stories that present a complication that the protagonist attempts to solve only to meet with failure which forces him to accept the complication as a part of life*

In this sort of story, the movement of the plot is toward tragedy, though it may not reach the scale of tragedy. For though the protagonist attempts to solve his complication and fails, if the attempt he makes is primarily a mental or intellectual one, and represents a failure in understanding, then the story cannot properly be labeled tragic. Tragedy involves a struggle that is dramatic, one that brings doom to the individual, and belongs to the world of action rather than thought. The tragic protagonist is not really tragic if his failure has not been made final in the realm of concrete actuality. He is only tragic if his attempt meets some rebuff from the very substance of his universe. An intellectual failure requires only a different point of view, a different effort at understanding. A true tragedy uses harsh reality, and while we are in the grip of the tragic nemesis, we are made to feel the very rocklike substance of events by which the tragic figure is overwhelmed. Some quality stories are true tragedies; some tend toward the tragic.

2. *Stories that present a complication about which the protagonist does nothing, either blindly or passively accepting
the complication as a part of life*

We have previously covered this type of story, labeling it as linear in
its structure. It must be remembered that within the basic linear tale
the protagonist may either not be aware that he faces a complication,
in which event he is blind and naïve and hence passive; or being aware
of the complication that faces him, he may protest, but doing nothing,
he is yet passive.

3. *Stories that present a complication that the protagonist solves
through his own efforts or has solved for him by accident,
providence, chance, coincidence, or by another character*

In this kind of story there is again a certain noticeable ambivalence.
On the one hand, if the protagonist solves his own complication, the
plot is truly comic. On the other hand, if the protagonist's complication reaches a resolution through the operation of forces outside himself, the plot may be labeled comic, but the comedy will be of a rather
different order. That is, the protagonist may be regarded as bumbling,
ineffectual, or circumscribed by other limitations, but the universe
around him may be viewed as ironically and comically capable of
satisfying the protagonist's desires. Thus, some quality stories are true
comedies; others tend toward the comic.

The reader may notice a certain reluctance to classify quality stories
too rigorously. As one turns from pulp and slick story writing, one
moves away from the set plot toward a freer and looser handling of
complications. About the most that one can do is to make an attempt
to differentiate among the various kinds of quality story in the hope
that they will be described sufficiently well so that a perceptive reader
will be able to grasp with some intelligence any new type that he may
stumble across. Within the three groups of stories described above
may be found a number of distinctive forms, and about the most one
can do is to describe these by means of examples. It therefore becomes obvious that there will be more kinds of structural devices used
in the quality story than in commercial stories.

Nevertheless, it would be impossible to understand the structure of
quality stories at all without some basic knowledge of the plot of the
formula story, for implicit in the quality writer's work will be his
awareness—perhaps even subconscious awareness—of its structure

and he will make use of its various elements to suit his own ends. This is merely another way of stating that all stories have as their basis the use of a complication—and there are just so many ways of dealing with a complication. Pulp and slick stories, as we have seen, deal with the complication in a comic fashion. Quality stories ring the changes on the way any complication may be dramatized.

Before discussing the various types of structure used in quality stories, it is worth noting that the three plots of commercial fiction, mentioned at the end of Chapter Three, and the three used in quality fiction touch only at one point; and for the most part cannot be brought into any congruency. This will be obvious if we place both sets of plots side by side.

Pulp and Slick Stories	Quality Stories
1. Comic: conflict to eliminate an opponent, solve the complication, and reach a worthwhile goal.	1. Tragic: protagonist struggles and fails to solve the complication, or simply yields to it as a part of life.
2. Comic: conflict to overcome an obstacle, solve the complication, and reach a worthwhile goal.	2. Linear: protagonist either is unaware of the complication, or passively accepts it as a part of life.
3. Comic: conflict to avert a disaster, solve the complication, and reach a worthwhile goal.	3. Comic: protagonist may solve the complication himself, but more frequently solution comes through the operation of chance, providence, accident, or another character.

In a tragic quality story, the conflict either ends tragically, or it is so muted that it hardly has dramatic existence because of the nature of the protagonist's attempts to solve the complication. In the linear story, the protagonist makes no attempt at all to solve his complication. In the comic quality story, if the protagonist struggles and successfully solves his complication, then we have the one point of harmony in terms of structure with pulp and slick writing. But for the most part, comic quality stories violate the formula plot, either by making the protagonist's success ironic or bitter, or by showing the world outside of the protagonist to be comic and thereby muting his struggle. It is interesting to observe the quality writer's tendency to assume—in contradistinction to the assumptions of pulp and slick writers—that human beings find it exceedingly difficult, if not impossible most of the time, to solve complications truly satisfactorily.

Not alone in the techniques of craftsmanship does the quality story differ from the commercial story, but also, and perhaps more im- portantly, in terms of approach. The quality writer utilizes as an operating principle the principle of subtlety. He tends to work less directly with overt statement, more implicitly by means of suggestion, implication, symbolism. We shall disregard for the purposes of this chapter the principle of subtlety in the questions of characterization, description, dialogue, narration, exposition, action, and point of view. We are here concerned mainly with the application of the principle of subtlety to structure. For though some quality stories do follow the formula handling of a complication, in the main the great distinction between quality and commercial stories lies as much, if not more, in the structural manipulation of the complication.

The quality writer constructs the complication in his story in terms of one of two basic time distinctions: he makes the time of the story the same as that of the complication—the form of structure this chap- ter will discuss; or he makes the time of the story follow the actual time of the complication—with which form of structure the following chapter will deal.

Incidentally, in discussing the stories we have chosen as examples, we will avoid oversubtle analysis of the story—that kind of analysis based on an appreciative, almost word-by-word rereading—for the sake of presenting the story's structure in its boldest pattern.

I. The complication is stated; the resolution is merely implied.

A great many quality stories use the device of foreshortening the resolution in order to gain the principal effect this foreshortening gives, namely that the protagonist's conflict will be solved by a change in attitude without his necessarily having to act out for us its actual result. If the reader cares to refer to the various steps of the complica- tion outline, the quality writer is here simply halting his story at step 5, at that moment, in other words, when the protagonist discovers some- thing he did not know or did not realize before which leads him to change his mind.

We have already referred to Carson McCullers' "A Domestic Dilemma" in Chapter One. This story is an excellent example of how a resolution may simply be implied, and we will therefore give the main outlines of the story in greater detail, in order to see how the author implies a resolution. The protagonist, Martin Meadows, is a sensitive, responsible person who faces the problems brought about by his wife's emotional disintegration during the past year. The author has established Martin's values: he is one of those people in life who carry out the major tasks of taking care of what he owns, rearing his children with love and yet with firmness, keeping his home neat and orderly, establishing a sense of security for his family. And his wife for the past year has begun to drink, to reveal a latent coarseness in her nature, to let her household chores go slack to such an extent that at one time she even carelessly dropped her daughter and hurt her. Martin is worried over his future, the problems at the office which his wife's drinking entails, but more than anything, over the destructive effect her drinking has upon his marriage, the possible mental harm that is being done to his children. His wife comes downstairs in a drunken state; there is a scene; Martin tries to comfort the children. His wife goes to bed, and Martin puts the children to sleep. He hates his wife because she has been unable to adjust to the move the family has made from Alabama to New York. Then he goes to his bedroom. In his wife's slumbering form he sees the way in which his children's faces have been passed down from their mother. His anger and his hatred vanish in the desire he feels for her, in the recognition of her immaturity, in the terrible complexity of a love that mixes desire and sorrow together. By implication, the protagonist discovers that he must play a changed role toward his wife, not as husband primarily, but also as father.

Of course, any reader's interpretation of the story may differ from the one given; but the very circumstance that differing interpretations are possible demonstrates precisely the point that the story's resolution is not stated but implied. The complication is presented fully and concretely. The resolution, however, moves by implication and suggestion, by indirect statement. In terms of the basic formula plot, the resolution of "A Domestic Dilemma" appears to come abruptly, with surprising speed, and to rest primarily in the mind of the protagonist rather than in any overt action. If what we know of the protagonist has been made concrete enough, we may imagine that the changed attitude of the protagonist will solve, over the course of a period of time, the dilemma that faced him. Such a suggestion, therefore, has a tendency to make the new attitude appealing to us as a recommended course of behavior for any other individual caught in a similar dilemma, granting only that he have the sensitivity of Martin. The great danger in such a resolution lies in the tendency toward sentimentality, if one can consider the sentimental to consist of the idea that ideas themselves may be supposed to have an intrinsic value quite apart from the practical acts that ensue from them. But, of course, an author may be objectively aware of this.

Another story that illustrates the way in which a definite complication is stated and the resolution only implied is Irwin Shaw's "The Girls in Their Summer Dresses." The story is simple, the complication resulting from the fact that a supposedly happily married young couple finds itself emotionally bankrupt through the husband's penchant for staring at pretty girls and his admission that he may wish someday to have an affair. The husband, Michael, and his wife, Frances, are out for a Sunday stroll. They appear to be happily married, to have few cares in the world, to be young and gay. The author allows us to see Michael appraise a girl passing by. The second time this occurs, Frances reproaches her husband. She has noticed, prior to this, his habit of looking desiringly at other women. She decides to give up part of the day she had gaily planned, a tour of the Art Museum, and they walk to a bar to have a drink. There Michael speaks of his interest in other women. It is for him an exciting thing to look at them. For Frances, his wife, his talk becomes an admission of his latent desire to be free sometime, to follow out his impulses, to deny her.

They had been invited out to the country by friends, the Stevensons, but Frances had not wanted to go. She would rather have spent the day with her husband. She asks Michael to keep his talk about women to himself, and then coolly reminds him of the invitation. She changes all her plans for the day. Despite Michael's real faithfulness toward her, she is just another woman to him, attractive, perhaps even beautiful. He regards her in precisely the same fashion as he regards all other women as she walks away from the table to telephone. The day, which had begun with happiness, has ended in a truce. She has nothing more to say to him, and he really has little to say to her. They will go to the Stevensons'; the afternoon will be bright and giddy with meaningless cocktail chatter; they will be immersed in people who actually don't matter to them. For the moment, there is a truce—but the resolution that is implied is somewhere in the future. We are aware of what will happen inevitably. Michael is too selfish to consider women as other than mere objects to acquire. Frances, though wounded, is too fearful to force the issue to a crisis. In both "A Domestic Dilemma" and "The Girls in Their Summer Dresses," the protagonist faces a situation that cannot be resolved ideally. There is a movement

52

toward the pathetic, and in both stories the resolution is not acted out but rests only in the mind by implication.

II. *The complication is implied, and the stated resolution is used to make the meaning of the complication clear.*

This variation in structure is often used when an author is exploring a character who may not be aware initially that he faces a complication at all; and it is also used when the complication, if explicitly stated, would appear to be too brash, too blunt, perhaps even too vulgar.

Both the stories chosen as examples, Katherine Mansfield's "Bliss" and Alberto Moravia's "The Fanatic," deal with the problem of sex. In both, the protagonists have arrived at a moment in which their sexual natures have become aroused. Bertha, in "Bliss," is only in the most obscure way aware of this. The taxi driver in "The Fanatic," though aware of it, is not aware of its depth, of its true nature as it strongly marks his own character.

In "The Fanatic," a taxi driver finds himself approached by three fares, two men and a woman, who wish to go to a beach outside Rome. The taxi driver looks at his passengers-to-be, dismissing the men first, and then concentrating on the woman, who had "a narrow body in a tight green dress that made her look like a snake." He also notices her "full, red mouth, like a fruit, and beautiful eyes, black and shining like wet coal." Because of the way she looks at him, he agrees to the first price they offer. The taxi driver drives them outside Rome, and then at the woman's laughing suggestion, he takes a narrow winding track that wanders through a pine woods beyond which is a deserted beach. In this desolate area, one of the men, who is riding in the back seat, shoots at the taxi driver, but misses because the other man, in the front seat, lunges against the driver. The trio had purposely enticed the taxi driver to this lonely place in order to murder him and steal his taxicab. But now neither of the two men has the courage to make a second try. The driver, in fact, displays a good deal of courage in telling the trio off. They argue over what is to be done. Eventually the taxi driver drives the woman back to Rome; she has indicated a possible intimacy. But the driver refuses to take the two men, and of course they are just as contented to be left where they are. On the way toward the city, the taxi driver tries to seduce the woman, but she refuses him. When they arrive at Rome, angry at the waste of his time, the use of his gasoline, and the resistance of the

53

woman, he shouts at her that she should be glad that he doesn't take her to the police. She replies, "How fanatical you are!" and leaves him "with an insolent and haughty walk, wriggling all over in that tight, snake-like dress. . . ."

The complication in the story does not consist of the attempted violence against the taxi driver, but of the unspoken yet well-realized complication that faces, one may suppose, the Latin man of hot blood and impulsive temperament, the desires of the flesh. It is because of this desire that he agrees to take his passengers at their own price where they wish to go, that he is stirred by hopefulness when they turn toward a deserted beach, that he transcends the attempt on his life by displaying courage before the woman, that he is so pliable in allowing the men to escape scot-free after their attempt at murdering him, and that he becomes so enraged at the woman on reaching Rome after having spent his time for nothing. All these things are summed up in the one words she hurls at him, the word "fanatical"; and we thus see at the close of the story the state of the man's mind at the very beginning of it. For the complication produced by sexual frustration and sexual interest is there, unspoken, unstated, implied, and it becomes fully accounted for in the girl's remark.

In the story "Bliss," we are introduced to a young married woman, Bertha, who returns home from a walk with elation burning unaccountably in her breast. She tries to put into words its cause and, although she partially divines it, shrinks away from the meaning she has stated. There is to be a party at her home that night. She arranges some fruit, feeling again the unaccountable elation, a rising hysteria over its beauty, and driven by the feeling, disturbs the nurse in order to clutch her three-year-old daughter to her breast and show her love for the child. The party that Bertha gives is a study, in many ways, of the frustrated, the repressed, the eccentric in personal character—exemplifications of the general state of a society that moves people into superficial and meaningless talk and inhibits the flowering of their masculine and feminine natures. In the midst of this, through an amazing symbol, the pear tree at the end of Bertha's garden, we get an insight into her past sexual frigidity, her purity and chastity, into a feminine nature whose passions, through some quirk of society, have been repressed, but are nevertheless now in flower. And we learn that the relationship between Bertha and her husband Harry has been that of "really good pals." Life seems to Bertha to have an exquisite fullness. At the party is a woman whom Bertha has invited, a Miss Pearl

Fulton, toward whom Bertha feels some obscure yet extremely intimate fellowship, bordering even, so extremely suggestive is the symbolism in this story, on the area of perverse sexual interest—though this, too, is merely implied. It is not until the guests begin to leave the party that Bertha finally becomes aware that she will be alone with her husband, in a darkened room, in a warm bed. And for the first time in her married life, she desires him. Here, at last, nearly at the story's end, does the complication, marked by her ecstatic feeling of bliss, her unaccountable yearning for something that has produced the radiant glow in Bertha, become stated. And hard on the heels of the statement comes the resolution. As Bertha bids the guests good-bye, she accidentally sees her husband and Miss Fulton kissing in the hallway and arranging for an assignation on the morrow. She sees Harry, her husband, a man of sardonic character, showing a violence of animalistic passion, and Miss Fulton's heavy-lidded response. And Bertha is left wondering what will happen now. The conclusion becomes a means of stating the way a woman such as Bertha, the victim of repressive times and repressive training in sexual matters, ironically arrives at an understanding of the life-urge—surely a Lawrencean phrase is not inappropriate in analyzing the story—only to find herself cheated of its fulfillment. She becomes, therefore, in her unaccountable yearning at the beginning of the story, suggestive of the repressed sexuality that society has been responsible for, and of the marital complications that ensue in a world that allows men greater liberty of action than it allows women. It is the resolution of the story that makes one understand the nature of the complication at the beginning.

Again, it is noteworthy that in both "The Fanatic" and "Bliss" the complication facing the protagonist leads eventually only to disappointment. The writer's handling of the complication and resolution, by moving away from explicit statement, either of complication or of resolution, tends naturally to suggest the painful, the pathetic, the tragic, the ironic, the sardonic, as qualities of the action.

III. *The complication is delayed—though eventually it is stated and resolved—in favor of descriptive detail, characterization, thematic statement, or incidents that imply what the complication will be.*

At first sight, this device may not seem substantially different from that just described in II. And in truth there are broad similarities. To

55

a certain extent, indeed, such a structure prevails in many quality stories, otherwise distinctive in pattern. The slow beginning, the often implicit presentation of theme through the use of carefully selected descriptive detail, the generation of interest in character prior to our knowledge of what situation the character may be involved in, the approach to theme through explicit statement—these are the marks of many quality stories. But III differs from II primarily in the fact that the resolution in III is not used to make the meaning of the complication clear. And another distinction is that the device of delaying the statement of a complication gives the writer the ability to generalize upon the complication, to universalize it, so that when the complication proper follows it may be seen to be one illustration of some large and universal problem. As we have noted earlier, the quality story tends in certain ways to move away from the dramatic toward the nondramatic presentation of material—and this motion is pretty well marked in the above device, for whatever the concrete language used in descriptive details, characterization, or thematic statement, at issue is a fairly large abstraction that the complication proper is to exemplify.

Again two examples will suffice to show the use of this sort of structure in the quality story. Many readers will be familiar with Somerset Maugham's long short story "Rain," and they will already have remarked on the carefully casual manner in which Maugham introduces the principal characters of the story: first, Dr. Macphail, "precise and rather pedantic," "shy but no fool"; Mrs. Macphail, fussily proud over their shipboard acquaintance with the Davidsons; Mrs. Davidson, dressed in black, a small woman with "brown, dull hair" and a face "like a sheep's"; Mr. Davidson, his face cadaverous but with surprisingly "full and sensual" lips; Miss Sadie Thompson, plump, coarse, pretty, ingratiating. In a leisurely way these personages are introduced, and along with them, the suggestion of those problems that sweep with trade into the remote Pacific islands: the mixing of occidental cultures with island cultures; the rubbing together of the mercantile and the primitive; of native disease compounded by imported illness; of native customs that are explicitly sensual and, to Mrs. Davidson's eyes, disgusting; and the introduction of a religion that is rigid and puritanical in cast and brooks few human emotions.

We see the events of the story from the viewpoint, primarily, of Doctor Macphail, a man of science, more objective by far than Davidson, the clergyman, willing enough at first to be stirred by Davidson's apparent sincerity, yet at the same time brought eventually to anger through his irritation at the tropical rain, through his irritation with the unceasing efforts of Davidson to entwine Sadie in a mesh of guilty repentance, aware within the depths of his being of the missionary's language as essentially deceitful. The themes of the story intertwine and fuse in the principal action, which involves the unhealthiness of suppressing human emotions and desires, and the final resolution in Davidson's suicide and Doctor Macphail's understanding of Sadie Thompson's final words. But it is the beginning of the story, the characterization, the description of setting, the thematic statements, which occur from time to time, that give to the efforts of Davidson to force Sadie to repent and the clinical view of Macphail their extended significance.

Another story using the same device of delaying the complication is Aldous Huxley's "Young Archimedes." This, too, is a long short story, brilliantly realized. It is a story about the humanizing effects of genius upon the land, upon the inhabitants of the land, and upon the generations of mankind. And the story begins appropriately enough with many descriptive paragraphs that serve to prepare us in terms of theme and mood for the appearance of genius and for the sad death of the boy genius of the story. Not too strangely, Huxley has chosen to use the region around Florence for the story's setting, for this is the area of great art, of great geniuses of the past, of their works in cathedrals, of buildings that rise from the land, shine in the light, and disappear in the shadows that fall when the sun hides behind a cloud. The landscape perpetually shifts and varies before the narrator's eyes. A scene from the valley, brilliant and distinctive emerges, shines fitfully in the splendor of the sun, then is clouded by mist or darkness—"the hills and the white houses shone as it were precariously, in a dying splendour, on the brink of some fearful calamity." It is this landscape that has been humanized, civilized for man's occupation by countless generations, but above all, by the men of genius, those relatively few men in the world's population who have used ideas creatively. "Sometimes," the narrator remarks, "upon those who live in the midst of it there comes a longing for some place that is solitary, inhuman, lifeless, or peopled only with alien life. But the longing is soon satisfied, and one is glad to return to the civilized and submissive scene." Also, within this "civilized and submissive scene" are those moments of darkness, of shadow, and we are thus prepared to see, both indirectly and directly in the later statement,

57

that "fiendish influences as well as divine haunt these total solitudes"; we are thus prepared for Signora Bondi's assault on the boy genius, Guido, and for his tragic death. The rest of the story follows the thematic description at the beginning. We are aware of the tremendous significance that the narrator is later to attach to the boy and of his remorse at not having foreseen what would happen when he left the villa for a time so that his charge, Guido, is left prey to the designing Signora.

We shall now, however, postpone discussion of the remainder of the story until later, for although illustrating perfectly how a complication may be delayed in favor of a descriptive thematic statement at the beginning, in its over-all structure it is also an example of a complication whose time occurs prior to that of the story proper.

IV. The complication is delayed until the very end of the story: the function of the story is to state the complication.

This is an interesting variation in the handling of a complication, and particularly upon the structural device explored in III above. Here the complication is again delayed in favor of a build-up accomplished through characterization, description, suggestions of the theme, but unlike III, when the complication is finally stated, the story ends. The principal effect that such a structure has is to suggest that for the protagonist the complication cannot be resolved satisfactorily.

Sherwood Anderson's story "I Want to Know Why" illustrates very well this sort of structural form, where the statement of the complication forms the conclusion. The story concerns a fifteen-year-old Kentucky boy who, with three companions, takes off on a lark away from home to see the horse races at Saratoga. The boy is a lover of horses, and he admires, by extension, people who have anything to do with the training of horses or with horse racing. For the boy, "horse racing is in every breath of air you breathe." It is in terms of this environment that the boy's idealism is stated. He is incapable himself of saying precisely what his values in life are, but he is tremendously aware of their importance to himself: "I'm getting to be a man and want to think straight and be O.K. . . . ." And thus the environment of horse racing is fascinating to him, for here, within the concrete realm of the race track, he can visualize his ideals: "There isn't anything so lovely and clean and full of spunk and honest and everything as some race horses." At Saratoga the event happens that forms the complication that the story's ending states. For at Saratoga, two great horses are to race, Middlestride and Sunstreak; and the boy, in visiting the stalls of the two horses, knows deep inside himself that Sunstreak is going to win. It is a moment in which there coalesces all his admiration for the values which, the story has stated, are most significant in his life. And the boy shares this moment with Jerry Tillford, the horse's trainer. It is a moment of deep feeling, in which the boy recognizes that his values are embodied in another human being. He feels he loves Jerry Tillford even more than he does his own father. Sunstreak does, indeed, win the race the next day; he breaks the record. That night after the race, the boy wants to be near Jerry and searches him out. He discovers him at what he terms a "rummy farm house," and he peers in through the window to see with horror that his admired Jerry Tillford is consorting with low, hard-faced women and indulging in "rotten talk" and bragging about the race, just as though he, and not the horse, had won it. The boy is bewildered about the things he sees and hears. How in one and the same day can a person like Jerry Tillford, who has come to embody all the boy's ideals of clean living, honesty, and courage turn around like that and brag like that and kiss a woman like that and deny in his actions everything that the boy has felt? The story ends with the statement, "I want to know why"; and thus with the story's ending we have the complication stated.

Another story that uses the same structural patterning is Ray Bradbury's "I See You Never." Mrs. O'Brian, a landlady, opens her kitchen door at a knock, to find her favorite tenant, Mr. Ramirez, standing there between two policemen. He has been picked up because he has overstayed his visa for six months and now must be deported to Mexico. Mr. Ramirez is heartbroken, for he has clearly loved the life he has led in Los Angeles, the big city's sights and sounds, the restaurants, the money he has earned which has enabled him to buy a radio, a watch, jewelry for an occasional lady friend. He has appreciated the clean room in Mrs. O'Brian's home, her cooking, her strict kindliness. And now he must go back to the scorched landscape of a small village in Mexico, its dust, its isolation, its loneliness. Suddenly, Mr. Ramirez weeps and clutches Mrs. O'Brian's hand and says, "Mrs. O'Brian, I see you never, I see you never." After he has gone, Mrs. O'Brian sits down to supper with her children, and then she pauses in her eating, with her hand to her face, under the realization that she will never see Mr. Ramirez again, either.

The story seems only to be an incident or an episode, without any complete plot. And it does not have a complete plot, for like Anderson's story, it is told merely to state the complication, which neither of the principal characters realized until it was too late: that they were strongly attached to one another. Mrs. O'Brian's realization of this points up the complication, the separation of two people through legal machinery at just the moment before they discover a mutual attachment.

V. *The complication is solved by violating the plot and using one of the four fatal weaknesses in plotting.*

The formula story, as we have seen, insists upon the protagonist's solving a complication through his own effort. The assumptions, which the formula-story writer makes, are that the protagonist will be ingenious and intelligent enough to solve the dilemma he faces. Obviously, however, the formula-story writer must thereby leave out of consideration the operations of chance, coincidence, and accident. The quality writer, as we have suggested, through a more skeptical attitude about the free will of human beings, and through a less optimistic viewpoint about the nature of the universe, will at times allow accident to rule over the events of his story.

An excellent illustration of the use of accident or chance event which solves the complication without the protagonist's effort is another story by Alberto Moravia, "The Perfect Crime." A slender and self-effacing waiter in a restaurant learns to hate a fellow waiter who is much bigger, much more virile looking, for this waiter, Rigamonti by name, steals away the girl friends of the smaller man at every opportunity. The small waiter begins to brood about Rigamonti's presumptuousness, and he learns to hate him passionately for his aggressiveness, his physical superiority. One night when they are both at an American movie, the small waiter discovers from the movie the perfect plan for killing his enemy, Rigamonti. He fills Rigamonti's head with the notion that a young girl has fallen in love with him. Rigamonti in his masculine vanity and sense of superiority believes, of course, that the girl is pining away for him. It is the small man's plan to lure Rigamonti to a meeting with the fictional girl on a railroad embankment at just the moment when an express train will roar by, to murder Rigamonti, to return to a café and pick up a parcel, which he has earlier left there purposely, and to be in bed in sufficient time so that he will have an alibi. In fact, he does convince Rigamonti to accompany him; they reach the railroad embankment, a lonely spot, and at that moment, Rigamonti sees a woman approaching them and thinks her to be the one the small waiter has spoken of. But the woman cannot, of course, be the fictional girl, and in fact turns out to be an aged prostitute, perhaps sixty years old, a true physical horror. Rigamonti excuses himself and leaps away down the embankment, obviously thinking that the waiter has played a monstrous joke on him. The waiter realizes that his perfect crime is evaporating, but with it also goes his hatred for Rigamonti. In fact, he feels sorry for the aged harlot, for himself, even for the man he has hated. The next day, Rigamonti bears him no grudge, and the small waiter invites Rigamonti to go out with him and a new girl, Amelia, but Rigamonti refuses, and the waiter is to a certain extent disappointed that Rigamonti is not going to steal Amelia away from him.

The accidental encounter has completely blocked and thwarted the plans of the small man to avenge himself upon Rigamonti, but at the same time, through sheer accident, the waiter gains a sense of the physical sadness of desire, and this frees him from his plot and his envy of Rigamonti.

It is not surprising that in a story by one of the modern French existentialists the plot is violated by accident. For the existentialists, there is a great split between the yearnings within man for some kind of wholeness in his view of things, and the discord and irrationality of the world outside the individual himself. Jean-Paul Sartre's story "The Wall" reveals the doctrine of absurdity as an element of the function of plot. In fact, an accidental revelation made by the protagonist in this story, a revelation that is a mere shot in the dark, an attempt to pull the leg of a Falangist officer, is the means whereby the protagonist is allowed to continue living. There can be no more significant way of indicating that causality in the events of life can have little explanation.

In the story, Pablo and Tom, both members of the International Brigade, and Juan, the younger brother of an active soldier fighting against the Falangists, are condemned to death for their support of the enemy cause. After the interview with the Falangist officers, the three are taken down into a dank, cold cellar where they are to wait all night before facing the firing squad in the morning. In this dilemma, what can they do? Each one reacts in a different fashion. Juan, the youngest, is the least able to face the fact of his death. Tom, also horror-stricken, must talk, must act, while his imagination provides him with pictures of the horror that he faces. Pablo, the narrator, wishes to die a decent death, but feels himself becoming more and more disassociated from all the loyalties, the friendships, the trusts, the ideals for which he has given himself. The mere fact of death takes "the charm" out of everything—even the memory of his former life, even the desire for Concha, his mistress. He discovers that he has lost "the illusion of being eternal," which it is absolutely necessary to feel in order to enjoy the things of life. Now that that illusion is gone, he seems to be remote from everything, even from his own body which sweats and turns gray beyond his will, beyond his control. In such a state, Pablo becomes aware of the ludicrousness of existence. Tom and Juan are taken out to be shot. An hour later, Pablo is taken out to be questioned about the whereabouts of his comrade, Ramon Gris. He is offered the opportunity to inform on Gris and save his own life. Yet Pablo finds, absurdly enough, that he cannot inform on Gris, even though his friendship for Gris has evaporated along with his love for Concha. Nothing has importance, yet he stubbornly refuses to divulge the information. Finally, aware of the absurdness of the Falangists, who too will die sometime, but who are now occupied in rustling through papers, carrying on a kind of unimportant busy work in the face of their own mortality, Pablo discloses that Gris is hiding in the cemetery. Of course, this is a joke, for Gris is hiding, so Pablo thinks, in his cousin's house a couple of miles outside the city. The Falangists bustle off, and then after some time, they return, and Pablo is sent to wait down in the big courtyard while the tribunal decides his case. He is perplexed. His life has been spared. And then he learns that Ramon Gris, through folly, had gone and hidden in the cemetery and was caught and executed there. Pablo is stunned by the information, and when he finally realizes it he "laughed so hard the tears came to [his] eyes."

In Sartre's story, we have a resolution to a complication brought about by sheer accident. The accidental has been raised even to the status of an element within a philosophical system, for the absurdity has had nothing to do with the significant stubbornness with which Pablo continues to conceal Ramon's whereabouts even when he no longer has any personal interest in Ramon. It is, perhaps, at this point that the reader may be inclined to argue that Pablo's mistaken revelation of Gris' whereabouts is not strictly speaking an accident, for in the absence of any rational explanation of causes among events, all things become accidental. But as readers of a story, examining the way the complication is resolved, quite apart from any philosophical system erected about the story, we must find the complication resolved through mere accident, certainly not through the agency of the protagonist.

VI. The complication is handled as it is in the formula story.

It would be a mistake to assume that all quality stories alter the structure of the formula plot. It is true that the quality writer generally tends to impart a different structure, but there are some stories that faithfully follow the structure of the formula story. Such a statement will, of course, raise the question in the reader's mind: what, then, is the distinction between the quality story and the slick story? The distinction may be a perfectly extraneous one, having nothing to do with the "quality" of the writing at all, but with the name and reputation of the author. That is, a writer of some reputation will be able to sell to a quality magazine a story that an unknown writer could not sell. But this is certainly not the case with those quality stories that manage, in using the formula plot, to become a part of our literature; and the distinction therefore lies in the degree of subtlety that a writer gives to the formula story—this time, not in terms of structure, but in terms of characterization, description and exposition, dialogue, and so on.

James Thurber's story "The Catbird Seat" is such a formula story. The protagonist faces a definitely stated complication; there is exposition of background to indicate how the complication was produced; there are attempts of the protagonist to solve his dilemma; and there is eventual success. In this story, in other words, we have the true comic curve. The story illustrates, as well, what variety there is in the emotional tone of comedy.

In "The Catbird Seat," Mr. Martin, the shy, punctual office worker, head of the filing department of the firm of F & S, has determined to "rub out" Mrs. Ulgine Barrows, an appalling woman whose braying laugh, whose baseball slang, and whose whole effect on the office staff at F & S are terribly disconcerting. The story begins with the decision to "erase" Mrs. Barrows, the preparations Mr. Martin has made, the project perfected. We have the flashback then: the first meeting of Martin and Mrs. Barrows, the "blatant and persistent attempts" of Mrs. Barrows to introduce efficiency into the firm, and the minor crisis when Mrs. Barrows pops into Martin's office to cast a goggly orb at his filing cabinets with a view to introducing efficiency there, too. It is Mr. Martin's plan to introduce himself into Mrs. Barrows' apart-

63

ment, drink a drink, an unusual thing for him, smoke a cigarette, one more red herring to cast across his trail, and then with gloves on, murder Mrs. Barrows with some weapon which he will discover there. Of course, the plot goes awry. He cannot find a suitable weapon, and then a vague idea stirs in his mind. He confides to Mrs. Barrows that he has a scheme to bomb old Fitweiler, the head of the firm. Martin smokes, he drinks, he confesses to taking heroin. He uses Mrs. Barrows' own slang. He cautions her to secrecy, and then he leaves, aware that Mrs. Barrows will report him to Fitweiler. She does, and of course Mr. Fitweiler, weighing the evidence of Martin's years of studious devotion to the company in the light of Mrs. Barrows' preposterous story, refuses to believe her charges. Mrs. Barrows is dismissed as an incurable case of psychological breakdown, and Martin returns to his beloved office files, light of step, discreetly happy.

VII. The complication is not faced, either through passivity or blindness on the part of the protagonist, and the resolution is based on this refusal.

We have saved this method of approaching the complication for the last in this group of quality stories, where the time of the story is the same as that of the complication. The reason may occur immediately to the reader, for the statement in VII is simply another way of describing the linear story. If some quality stories follow the formula structure, either in essence or in terms of variations upon the handling of the complication, a great many others utilize the peculiarly modern viewpoint toward human nature which we have described in Chapter Two: the idea that action or the will to action on the part of the protagonist is impossible, and hence that the story can only depart completely from the comic or tragic curves and become linear.

The reader may wonder—if the linear story is described here as one of seven forms of structure—why so much point was made to discuss its nature at length in the aforementioned chapter. The reasons are the following. First, the contemporary viewpoint toward human nature is so all pervasive that, even in those quality stories described in I–VI above, the protagonist will be seen to partake somewhat of the nature of the blind or the passive individual that we find in the linear tale. Martin, in "A Domestic Dilemma," merely mentally finds a resolution. Michael, in "The Girls in Their Summer Dresses," merely looks at women without acting, and his wife retreats without a struggle. Bertha, in "Bliss," is blind to the causes of her ecstasy. The cabdriver, in "The Fanatic," is unaware of how deeply he is a fanatic. The boy, in "I Want to Know Why," has too little experience with life to be able to see why Jerry Tillford acts as he does. Mrs. O'Brian and Mr. Ramirez, in "I See You Never," are both unconscious until too late of a mutual attraction. The small waiter, in "The Perfect Crime," is unaware of the sadness of desire. Second, as an effect of the apparent blindness or passivity of the protagonist, the authors of these stories give to the protagonist a quality of "life-likeness," under the assumption that most people do not readily view, visualize, or understand the complications which they face; and discussion of the linear story aids one in understanding the artifice of character that most quality writers use. Finally, the linear tale adds a new dimension to the classic short story in departing from the curve of comedy or tragedy altogether. For these reasons, it has seemed important to consider the linear story, first of all, as a separate phenomenon.

As we have described the linear form prior to this, it is not necessary to repeat the major points here. Nevertheless, it might be wise to regard two examples of the type in order to reinforce our understanding of its nature.

James Joyce's short story "A Painful Case" illustrates superbly the way in which a hero, through sheer passivity, refuses to face a complication, and hence, as a natural result, faces a resolution that is not of his own choosing. Like some of the other stories in *Dubliners,* the volume in which this story is found, the complication reaches its critical point in terms of the question of death. Mr. James Duffy, an obscure and retiring bank clerk, methodical in his personality, grubbily attached to a routine existence, meets and is attracted to a married woman. He pursues a platonic affair with her until he realizes that she wishes to become physically intimate. Then he drops her brusquely. She becomes morose, begins drinking, and is the victim of an accident; she is crushed to death by a train. The protagonist has been aware of the complication she presents and he refuses to face it, writing to himself: "Love between man and man is impossible because there must not be sexual intercourse and friendship between man and woman is impossible because there must be sexual intercourse." After the woman's death, which Duffy reads about in a newspaper account, he first of all thinks of her reproachfully as a degraded woman, hardly worthy of the attentions he had given to her; and then little by little, he begins to realize that she is now a memory. He has no one to share his confidences with; he begins to feel "an outcast from life's feast." His habits deteriorate rapidly. He goes to a bar and drinks, and then in wandering alone through a park afterwards, aware of the lovers lying there, of their desire for him to be gone, of the failure of his memory to evoke her presence, he realizes to the full that he is really alone.

The story is told chronologically. As usual in the linear tale, we have the passive character, a complication that the character either does not see or refuses to face—in this case, the latter—and a dominant mood of pathos rather than of true tragedy. These are the marks, also, of the other linear story we shall discuss: "Mr. Penfold" by H. E. Bates.

The initial description of Mr. Penfold should alert us immediately to the kind of story this is: "Mr. Penfold . . . a painfully shy, retreating man with almost invisible eyelashes, who looked as if he would have been much happier walking backward. . . ." Mr. Penfold is a traveling draper and haberdasher, who calls on a widow, Mrs. Armitage, and her young daughter every other Thursday. He has been so regular in his visits that the Armitages have taken to calling the day "Mr. Penfold's day." Naturally, Mrs. Armitage begins to discover a liking for Mr. Penfold, and she hopes that the casual acquaintance will ripen into more than mere friendship, so that she will no longer be lonely. But it is the daughter, Katie, who attracts Mr. Penfold far more than he is aware; the years pass, and then he begins to notice the changes in the girl. He is totally unaware of the attitude of Mrs. Armitage to him, totally blind to her indirect statements about her loneliness, totally perverse in his failure to see what secret her heart holds. But when the girl grows up and returns for a summer vacation, then Mr. Penfold is smitten by astonishment and shyness: "But he could not say anything and gradually his great sense of astonishment was repressed and folded away, to become in turn part of his shyness, to become as time went on something that he could not speak about or reveal." The girl gets a job, and continues to grow ever more beautiful to Mr. Penfold, but he evades the issue: "He knew that he could not sit there at the table with the girl any longer without something happening; something momentous or foolish or even, to his way of thinking, something terrible." Three years pass, and he finds himself one evening alone with the girl and talking on much more intimate subjects than he ever has before. The girl reveals a rebellious attitude toward her mother—everything she earns, the mother saves and then doles the girl out a small allowance. Here is a moment in which, if he can overcome his reserve, Mr. Penfold might perhaps win

66

the girl, but he is painfully shy. He manages only to rest his arms on her shoulders as she, sitting on the floor beside him, sobs out her troubles. When Mrs. Armitage comes unexpectedly into the room, he beats a hasty retreat. On his next visit, he learns that Katie has gone away from home to live and work, and Mrs. Armitage shows a strange hostility toward him, almost as though she blames him for the girl's leaving home. He does not call on his next time to visit, but instead dreams of buying a small shop where he and Katie can live. Finally he can bear the dream no longer. He returns to the home of Mrs. Armitage, determined to overcome his shyness and to speak of his longing for the girl. He discovers that Katie is back, and after the girl leaves the room, Mrs. Armitage bitterly tells him that Katie is going to be married because she has become pregnant. Mr. Penfold "knew that there was nothing he could do or say," and he departs, aware that all the hope of his life has been dashed out.

In "Mr. Penfold," we find that our protagonist is both passive and blind. He faces really two complications: the one produced by the mother's longing for him prior to her daughter's growing up, where he does not really understand the situation; and the other that his shy longing raises when Katie does grow up. The story proceeds completely in the present without flashbacks; and because the protagonist is at first unaware of the complication, we get a peculiar tension, set up within the linear tale, where both comedy and tragedy are possible; but since the protagonist remains virtually the prisoner of his own nature and appears incapable of the will to act, the comic and tragic elements fade away into the emotional moods of wryness and pathos.

The seven forms of plot structure presented so far do not exhaust those used in the quality story based on the formula or chronological plot. The next chapter will consider the ways that a writer gives structure to his story when he makes the actual story time follow the time of the complication.

But before turning to these additional forms, it will be of interest to see how the seven structures just discussed are contained within the three basic forms of plot for the quality story, suggested at the beginning of the chapter:

I. The complication is stated; the resolution is merely implied.

This clearly uses the first plot with a possible shading into the second. The reason this is so, is that an implied resolution indicates either a failure on the part of the protagonist to resolve his complication by action, or an acceptance of the complication as an element of existence.

II. The complication is implied, and the stated resolution is used to make the meaning of the complication clear.

Again, this sort of structure is based on the first or on the second form of plot: the tragic or the linear. Since the protagonist may be blindly unaware that he faces a complication, or since the resolution is used to make the meaning of the complication clear—which implies that the protagonist himself actually fails to resolve what he did not, at first, see—we have a situation in which either the protagonist yields to the complication as an element of existence, or shows blind passivity toward it.

III. The complication is delayed—though eventually it is stated and resolved—in favor of descriptive detail, characterization, thematic statement, or incidents that imply what the complication will be.

If the complication is stated and resolved through the protagonist's own efforts, even though there is a delay, then we have either a tragic story developed from the first form of plot, or a comic story based on the third one. But as we have already pointed out, the device used above is more or less representative of all quality stories.

IV. The complication is delayed until the very end of the story: the function of the story is to state the complication.

Now if it is true that we do not actually get the complication until the very end of the story, then the story itself will present a protagonist who is unwittingly involved in a situation that he, as soon as he becomes aware of it, cannot solve. Thus such a story fits the description of the second or linear plot.

V. The complication is solved by violating the plot and using one of the four fatal weaknesses in plotting.

It seems quite obvious that this would come under the third of the plots, that in which a solution is produced though not through the agency of the protagonist.

VI. The complication is handled as it is in the formula story.

Here again, we find the third form of plot, this time in terms of a true comedy: success is achieved through the protagonist's own efforts.

68

VII. The complication is not faced, either through passivity or blindness on the part of the protagonist, and the resolution is based on this refusal.

In every instance, this would be the second or linear form of plot.

Some readers will invariably object to any attempt to fit short stories into a given scheme, to classify them, to set up artificial terms and categories for their structure, their themes, their techniques. And they will do this from the best of motives, from the assumption that such an analysis inherently prevents enjoyment. It inhibits the delight that is to be gained from the mere act of reading. But as we pointed out at the very beginning, the best of motives for the reader is the worst for the writer. Anyone who wishes not merely to read short stories, however discriminating he may be in his reading, but who wishes more to write them, must invariably concern himself with technical elements—and the more he immerses himself in the study of form and structure, the more will he find it rewarding in terms of the attempt to improve the form of his own stories. To demonstrate that a formula story, such as we have plotted in "Russian Roulette," may be turned into a quality story requires a knowledge of the structures available in quality writing; and after we have finished our present discussion of the structure of quality fiction, we will demonstrate how "Russian Roulette" may be transmuted into that form of story. Now let us turn to those kinds of quality story where the time of the story follows the actual time of the complication.

5

How Structure Is Used

in the Quality Story

(Continued)

IT IS NOT merely an arbitrary exercise to consider those quality stories where the time of the story is later than the time of the complication as distinct and separate in structure. The distinction exists in actuality, and it provides an author with some very interesting and suggestive tools. There are not many forms of these stories, but those that exist can give the beginning writer a chance to view the complication with a new perspective. He will be free to envision the complication from a perspective that he would not normally think of using in telling a story; and this new perspective may, and probably will, suggest imaginative directions his own work can take.

VIII. The time of the story occurs late in the complication sequence, the early steps having been dropped or suppressed in order to avoid sensational elements and to bring peripheral elements of the complication to the foreground.

Many a reader may question this description. Do not such stories begin in a moment of drama as most formula stories do? The answer is that they may, but that a stronger tendency is for them to start *following* such a dramatic moment. And in any event, the interest deliberately shifts away from what created the drama, the antecedent circumstances, to deal with the effect the complication and its resolution have on bystanders. Two examples will clear up what may seem baffling and will illustrate very well what other authors have done.

They are Hemingway's famous short story "The Killers" and Erskine Caldwell's story "Daughter."

Hemingway's story is sufficiently well known so that it hardly needs a massive retelling. But what is frequently omitted in the usual critical appraisal of the story is that Hemingway has begun with the last act, so to speak, and has deliberately shifted the perspective toward tangential characters, who have had nothing to do with the original complication.

The formula version of the story would have to go somewhat like this. A heavyweight boxer by the name of Ole Andreson becomes involved with gangsters who seek to control him. Perhaps he is a man of pride, perhaps of stubbornness, perhaps of stupidity. He is unaware at first just what is demanded of him, but when he is told to throw a fight, he fails to do so. The gamblers lose a lot of money on him, and he realizes that they will kill him. He starts running, but he is aware that behind him are his pursuers, cold, efficient, inexorable. He has no one to whom he can turn. At length he simply gives up. The killers close in on him. Burdened by his oppressive sense that ordinary humanity will not listen to him, Ole nevertheless appeals to his landlady for help. She is sympathetic, and she knows the local police very well. As a consequence, Ole solves his immediate complication and learns that people are not so callous and hardhearted as he had thought. The killers are caught, and humanity is served.

Now in the first place, Hemingway's vision of the world would not allow him in this story to write a comic ending. The story had to end with the protagonist's failure, but if Ole failed to secure help, the reason was that there was no one actually to appeal to. And in order to demonstrate the truth of this, Hemingway shifted to a scene and characters who are actually tangential to the plot. Thus the critical idea that no one can help Ole required, for dramatic purposes, that the story begin with our viewing the effect upon others of Ole's dilemma. It required a deliberate juggling of the usual time values of the formula story.

The tangential characters lie outside of the actual complication, and in exaggerating their significance Hemingway is using George, Sam, and Nick Adams as symbolic personages. They symbolize the humanity that Ole has been unable to appeal to in his previous flight from the killers: Sam, the cook, doesn't want to get mixed up in what is of no concern to him; George has seen enough of the world to know that this is not his business; and Nick, young and impressionable, is in-

71

effectual in preventing the monstrosity from happening and too little the hero to be able to do anything but get out of town and forget. Thus the tangential personages acquire symbolic stature, and the story gains an allegorical cast. Henry's lunchroom, with its ordinary menu, its standard service, its commonplaces of setting, becomes Anyplace, USA, and the killers themselves, typed in appearance, dress, and speech, become the relatively commonplace antithesis of the "good" people; that is, those people who "stay in line," "follow orders," "keep their troubles to themselves." It is interesting to notice the allegorical and moral quality in this story—very much as in the morality plays of the Middle Ages—for such a quality indicates how far away from the merely sensational elements of Ole's story the writer is enabled to move by means of the altered time perspective.

Hemingway accomplishes one other thing by deliberately shifting the time of his story to the last stages of the complication, and it seems so normal a result of the technique that it deserves comment here, though certainly such a question belongs, strictly speaking, to the problems that will be discussed in our later chapter on point of view. In accepting the complication as a fact that has already virtually happened, and in bringing peripheral characters to the foreground, the author is aided in making his story seem taut, condensed, highly packed. Little by little we learn of antecedent events, but what little we learn serves mainly to answer our most immediate questions. What we are chiefly concerned with is the reaction of the tangential characters to the climactic part of the complication. Thus the tangential characters acquire a dramatic interest that they would not have at all in the formula version of such a story. They would be nameless, well-nigh featureless, and certainly unimportant to us in the formula story except in the aggregate effect their refusal to aid Ole would have.

The second story that illustrates the use of time displacement in the complication is Erskine Caldwell's "Daughter." The formula-story version of "Daughter" would have to consider the poverty-ridden Carlisle family sharecropping on Colonel Henry Maxwell's acres. Jim Carlisle's child is hungry, the times are poor, there is little to eat, and yet the harvest appears to be shaping up into a good one. Then through no fault of Jim's, one of Colonel Maxwell's mules dies. Jim, oppressed by the moaning for food of his child, is blamed for the mule's death, and Colonel Maxwell highhandedly takes Jim's shares away from him as recompense for the mule. Now it is at this point that the formula story would very probably begin, for the event is one that produces all

72

the essentials of the complication and would provide a satisfactory moment from which to underscore the injustice of Colonel Maxwell. As another way of stating the matter, the event arouses the reader's interest in and concern for Jim's plight, as well as a good deal of curiosity as to the way in which he will solve the complication. The formula writer, mindful of the need of reproving Colonel Maxwell for his lack of heart and of giving Jim something to live for, would search for a solution for Jim, which is possible, though perhaps farfetched. Jim has been accused of having killed one of Colonel Maxwell's animals. Either he can prove that the animal's death resulted from causes which could kill off other animals Colonel Maxwell owns—Jim here becomes more than the ordinary animal husbandman—or he can attribute the death of the animal to an enemy of Colonel Maxwell, or he can discover ways in which to recompense the loss of the mule. Whatever solution the formula-story writer hits upon, he *has to avoid* the solution that Caldwell arrives at; i.e., the killing by the father of his own flesh and blood. Crazed by his troubles, Jim kills his daughter, and by killing his daughter, Jim actually solves his complication; that is, if the complication is that there is not enough food to eat, then to lessen the number of mouths that eat the food is one way to increase the relative abundance of nourishment—Swift's suggestion in "A Modest Proposal."

Curiously enough, those who would scorn the slick writer's solution of Jim's dilemma are brought to sympathize with the murderer of a child—no matter what the justifications are. Had the story played out the complication in a regular time sequence, Jim Carlisle would become a demented monster, and the absence of Swift's satiric tone would raise moral questions that no reader could sidestep. By shifting the time perspective of the story, Caldwell has accomplished three things: he has made the question of child murder less important than the question of social injustice; he has focused attention upon anonymous humanity and its appeals for humane economics; and he has provided a rationale that upsets normally conceived opinions about legal systems; he takes the side of the coolie against the sahib.

However, as we are all aware, very frequently, if not always, the solution to a complication is merely another way of posing another and different complication. The resolution of one story provides the source for another. In both "The Killers" and "Daughter," the immediate complications that the protagonists face have, in actuality, been resolved: Ole Andreson gives up running and passively accepts the fact that the gunmen will kill him; Jim Carlisle, in a half-demented fashion kills his daughter. The acceptance of the resolution on the part of both Hemingway and Caldwell as substantial fact about which nothing can now be done allows them to concentrate their attention upon the peripheral characters. The peripheral characters can either fail to do something about it, or they can act. Hemingway in "The Killers" poses the problem of humanity's reaction to an instance of cold, unemotional brutality, and comes up with a pessimistic conclusion. Caldwell raises the same problem and comes up with an optimistic conclusion.

As in "The Killers," "Daughter" has a highly dramatic, compact and taut style. There is hardly an excess word. Descriptive detail is kept to a minimum; there are no dialogue tags to indicate the tone of a speaker's voice, or the way in which he makes his statement. It is not simply the situation of the story that arouses our emotions: the situation of the poor sharecropper who having killed his daughter stands in a jail surrounded by his curious fellows. The ballad-like quality and the use of refrain in the sharecropper's speeches—"Daughter said she was hungry," a variation of which Carlisle repeats some nine times, the one elemental answer to all the questions put to Jim by his acquaintance—establishes the resolution of the story in the most direct fashion. It is the source of the crowd's feeling that a gross injustice has been done Jim and that the only way to serve justice is to "spring" him from the jail. Unlike Hemingway, however, who gives his peripheral characters significant character traits so that they lose their anonymity, Caldwell purposely conceals the distinctive attributes of the members of the crowd who aid Jim. They are "several men"; "six or seven men"; "other men"; "somebody"; "the crowd"; "a man"; "men." The avoidance of personal attributes in the peripheral characters adds to the allegorical quality of the story—Everyman has a love of justice. This form of story structure allows the author to deal with great abstractions in the most concrete and dramatic way.

IX. *The time of the story occurs much later than the time of the original complication so that the complication can be renewed and resolved through nostalgic reminiscence.*

Now as the reader will recall, in the first two of the basic plots described at the beginning of the last chapter, either the protagonist attempts and fails to solve the complication that he faces or he blindly and passively accepts the complication as a part of life. The resolution

74

thereby achieved may be a good one for the character at that time, but what if we allow a fair length of time to go by? What if we allow the protagonist to grow older, to gain more experience, to undergo a change that deepens or strengthens his character, and then renew the original complication by having him face it once more? Such a device tends to impart a lifelike quality to the story, violating as it does in a way the very nature of the short story. The original structure of the short story implies by its very nature that a final conclusion to the complication of the story has been reached. But the device discussed here asserts structurally that no one complication in life is ever really and truly solved immediately, and that life consists of our facing and refacing over a matter of years the same old complications, solving them and re-solving them unsatisfactorily, until at length we change sufficiently to solve them finally. Such a statement need not imply that the complications of existence ultimately face a happy conclusion, that the protagonist, if he has failed in the past to resolve his dilemma, must eventually reach a satisfactory solution, after changing and maturing—though of course such a possibility exists. Yet it may be that the resolution that the matured character now reaches will depend upon his having changed so much that there can be little comedy and much ironic bitterness in renewing a complication after a much earlier failure. It is possible to win in such a way as to lose more than one gains; and it is possible for the protagonist to fail again, but this time for good.

But whether or not the final solution has satisfactory or merely wry or completely tragic overtones, the emotional mood established by such a structure tends in the main toward melancholy, which often predominates in any thought about the past. "If I knew then what I know now" is a statement in which is recorded the fact that human history is a catalogue of blunders, wry hindsight, and, often, vexed longing for another chance to rectify what is past changing.

Two stories will illustrate the way a complication is renewed through reminiscence. They are Katherine Mansfield's "A Dill Pickle" and Chekhov's "Old Age." Katherine Mansfield's story begins with this revealing sentence: "And then, after six years, she saw him again." One knows immediately that the complication is between a man and a woman, that the woman has in the intervening period of time been thinking about "him," that whatever produced the split between them has now been altered by the change of time, and that finally there is to be a renewal of the complication and a new resolution, this time

75

founded upon the changes that have taken place within the characters.

Vera and the man meet in a tea shop. She recognizes him first, and then after a moment, the man remembers her. He invites her to sit down. They talk of their past. They have been two people who shared certain similar qualities of imagination, taste, and sensitivity; these qualities were responsible in the beginning for their having been drawn together. And the changes that have occurred? She is conscious of having grown older, of being still single, and there is a suggestion or two of that fussily neurotic quality that is the mark, at times, of the unmarried woman. She is poorer than she was—at least, she has sold her piano—and she has not been able to travel to those places that she and he used to talk about going to. On the other hand, he has "lost all that dreamy vagueness and indecision" that once characterized him. He has become more self-assured, certainly more wealthy and worldly, and he has traveled widely. At the same time, certain irritating habits still cling to him: his trick of interrupting her, his habit of not really listening to what she says, his petty stinginess, the faint yet perceptible callousness, cruelty, and egotism that mar his character. These qualities in him caused her to reject him in the past, but now conscious of her loneliness, of his successful life, and once more responsive to his other qualities, she feels that she committed a terrible mistake in rejecting him that first time. The longing for him stirs within her. She feels that she could be the glove that he is now drawing caressingly through his fingers. But there is the sudden thrust, the sudden cruelty, the pricking of her dream with his laughing statement that in the old days they were such foolish egoists they had no real concern for anyone but themselves. The sudden revelation of his complete selfishness forces her to leave his table, and the story comes to an end, the complication having been renewed once again and solved in the same way as before, by the woman's again rejecting the man for his hidden qualities of hardness and callousness, but this time, her utter rejection of him resolves the complication for good.

Chekhov's story "Old Age" suggests by its title, of course, that the story will characterize a time of life—but in order to characterize old age, it is necessary to contrast it with an earlier time of life. Hence, there is in the subject matter of this story a compulsion to return to the past, contrasting it with the present, by way of reminiscence.

Uzelkov, the protagonist, returns to his home town after an absence of eighteen years to find that "everything had changed." Trying to find some contact with that former life and failing, he searches out

Shapkin, the shyster lawyer who had managed the once-notorious divorce between Uzelkov and his wife, an affair of twenty years ago. Uzelkov, an architect by profession, has come back on a commission to examine the church where his former wife lies buried. Shapkin, now turned into "a modest, grey-haired, shrunken old man," suggests that he accompany Uzelkov to the church, which of course makes their return to the grave of Uzelkov's former wife in a mood of reminiscence seem perfectly plausible. And through Shapkin we learn the sordid story that had taken place those many years ago: of Uzelkov's marriage that was undertaken in a spirit of "caprice"; of the details of the divorce; of Uzelkov's bribing Shapkin to bribe Uzelkov's wife to "take the guilt on herself"; of Shapkin's expropriation of part of the bribe money, a third of it in fact, as a sharp way in which to mulct Uzelkov; of the woman's degradation of character through her becoming no more than a prostitute in accepting the bribe; of her feeble gesture to retain command over her personality by flinging the money in Shapkin's face, and of her then buying back a minor amount of it with her body; and of her eventual death. It was a terrible thing that Uzelkov callously perpetrated those many years before, and for the first time in his life he is aware of this. When the two former acquaintances are standing before the grave in the church he suddenly discovers that he wants to sob, to weep bitter tears, tears that will relieve him of his sense of cruelty and guilt. Moisture actually comes to his eyes, but he is too aware of the presence of Shapkin. When he finally has a chance to return to the grave alone, he discovers that before the "little white monument," which marked the grave of his former wife and which "stared at him absently, so sadly and innocently, as though a girl and not a wanton divorcée were beneath," he cannot weep, try as hard as he might. The longing for atonement, for some relief from the guilt of his former years, this longing is his old age.

It is significant that, although Uzelkov originally managed to solve his complication by ridding himself of his wife in a, to him, satisfactory yet exceedingly brutal fashion, the story now ends in pathetic terms. Uzelkov, now grown old, now mature and lonely, must inevitably be a judge of his former self, must inevitably fail to solve that previous complication as he had so callously done when he was young.

X. A weak or abstract complication may be made strong through retelling or reminiscence.

The words "weak," "abstract," and "strong" require attention if the statement is to make sense to the reader, particularly since the way these words are used differs, to a certain extent, from their normal meaning.

It may help in understanding these terms to make the general observation that very few people—if any at all—who go through an absorbing experience are able immediately to state the ultimate meaning of that experience. Art recollects and interprets experience. It ordinarily requires time, reflection, and further acquaintance with the world for anyone to be able to realize the true significance of an isolated experience. Particularly is this true when the experience or event is of any complexity, strangeness, or deep emotional impact. Therefore, if we were to confront a stated complication that is vast in its import, unless we have had previous personal experience of a similar situation, we are very likely to find that such a complication is "weak," and that its real significance is not apparent. Yet at the same time, in certain stories, the author wishes to deal directly with this very fact, as directly as a fictional statement will allow. The device described above allows one to deal more or less seriously with the tangle of issues involved in the rubbing together of two cultures or civilizations. It is interesting to observe that a story that presents an Englishman in France, or an American in Japan, in such a way that the story time and complication time are the same often tends to be comic in nature and to deal with the superficial distinctions in culture, which are evident in language, dress, local customs, looks, family arrangements, and so on. It may take many years before the deep-seated conflicts between cultures become visible to any participant in a foreign world; and hence the form of structure under discussion is very useful for getting at the serious, indeed often tragic, distinctions that separate mankind into cultural islands.

Here, for example, is a complication of a wide scope and complexity: the world owes its civilization and progress to a mere handful of geniuses in history, and yet the world consistently brutalizes, misunderstands or destroys the live geniuses in its midst. Readers may recognize this statement as being the thematic complication of Aldous Huxley's story "Young Archimedes," an aspect of which was discussed in the last chapter. Let us now return to that story briefly to illustrate its structure in a different fashion. It is significant that the protagonist, who tells the story, classifies himself along with the rest of humanity, excluding the geniuses, of course, as one of the "teachable animals." He is a man of a certain intellectual culture, of sensitivity and taste: a man who can recognize genius and provide an environment for genius to sprout and flourish; but also, a man who can fail to understand immediately, without further reflection and experience, how absolutely necessary genius is as a base for his own culture. The ego gets in the way; it takes reflection to see that one's intellectual attainments, particularly if they are not slight, are insignificant in comparison with the mental gifts of a young stripling, a mere boy. It is upon this failure and several others of the narrator that the story turns. Not alone is the designing and worldly Signora Bondi responsible for the boy's death. The narrator is, also, in his failure to understand completely what civilization owes to such a boy as he has in his charge—how much do the opening descriptive passages depend upon his appreciation of the civilized valley; but this appreciation follows his experiences with Guido. The descriptive scene is a reconstruction in the narrator's mind; it is an extension into humanistic and historical terms of the qualities of genius. The narrator fails properly to appreciate, also, how much of a threat to the boy-genius is Signora Bondi, how much significance his leaving the villa for a number of weeks will have on the boy. The story is told at a time later than the complication in order to convey the attitude of self-reproach on the part of the narrator—and, of course, no such attitude would be possible were the time of the story and the time of complication to be one and the same.

Now the superstructure of ideas in this story is based on the relationship between the boy and the narrator. We have already remarked upon the fact that in certain forms of quality story the complication is delayed until after descriptive passages occur that set forth the theme indirectly. And we have already pointed out that "Young Archimedes" follows this procedure. If the reader will also recall, in the first chapter we cautioned him not to concern himself with theme in developing a complication outline, for a concern with theme might lead a writer into direct sermonizing about his story. In the quality story, however, the author must be aware of the thematic implications of his complication so that he may select detail, present character, utilize symbolism, and otherwise structure his story. Such a statement is preeminently

79

true of the types of story structure discussed in this chapter, for the device of using a perspective of time requires an author to be aware of the net result of his complication, prior to his writing the story.

"Young Archimedes" has a weak complication made strong in the sense that an abstract idea appears to have been thought of first and then made specific and relevant to us in the literal events of the story. It is noteworthy, therefore, that such a story inverts the usual short-story order; the complications of stories such as in Hemingway's "The Killers" and Caldwell's "Daughter" may have far-reaching meanings; but these meanings do not depend upon the author's more or less direct statement as much as they do upon the imaginative insight of the reader. Hence the stories of form X are virtually the antithesis of the stories of form VIII, being much looser in structure, less dramatic, more directly thoughtful and philosophical. The stories described under VIII have an allegorical quality; the characters symbolically represent abstractions. The stories of type X—by explicitly pointing up the intellectual significance of the characters—tend to move away from allegory into a form of prose-essay statement. Nothing bursts the illusion of allegory so much as having an author intrude himself into the story by making a direct statement on the allegory's meaning. In the stories of type X, however, a narrator deals directly with the theme and the extended significance of his complication.

Now let us see how a different meaning may be attached to the word "weak" in our descriptive statement of type X. A weak or abstract complication may be made strong through retelling or reminiscence if the complication's weakness consists of its incapacity to stand alone as a credible and moving story. Here the word "weak" has very much its normal meaning. An example of such a tale is Ring Lardner's "Haircut." In the story, one must distinguish immediately between the events, the characters, and the narrated complication—the attempts by Jim Kendall against Julie Gregg, Julie's love of Doc Stair, the boy's defense of Julie—and the use the author makes of them. The author uses those events to solve a complication of his own, the desire of a stranger to take up residence in a small town. If it were not for the barber's attempt to convince the stranger in his chair of the values of small-town life, if the story omitted the barber and actually related only to the events dealing with Julie Gregg, one would have to doubt the story's credibility.

"Haircut" consists of a story that is framed by a story: the hair-cutting operation with its suggestions of congeniality on the barber's

80

part, the stranger's initial interest, and his unstated but growing disgust with the small town surrounds and is fed by an internal story. Lardner uses as a principle throughout that whatever the barber says will appear to us as overstatement, as exaggeration: "We have pretty good times"; "They used to be plenty fun in here Saturdays"; "He was certainly a card." The speech of the barber is that of an illiterate person, and because he is uncultivated, his language reveals how little capable he is of making those moral judgments of others with which the story deals; of Jim Kendall and his noxious practical jokes, for example. The judgment of the barber, already suggested by his language, is further shown to be distorted by the conflict between his business practicality and the latent recognition—which the barber suppresses— that Jim Kendall is actually crude, unprincipled, criminal in tendency, vulgar and essentially base. It made for good business to have Jim Kendall in the shop, and the story concludes, "It probably served Jim right, what he got. But still we miss him round here. He certainly was a card!"

The internal story in itself provides a good illustration of a weak complication being made strong through retelling. As told to us by the barber, it is in the nature of melodrama and could hardly stand by itself. A would-be rapist, the town loafer and drunk attempts to get revenge upon a small-town heroine who is too good for the town. His motives lie in the fact that the girl has snubbed his attempts to force her to yield to him, and in the fact that Doc Stair has apparently won the girl's affections. Jim Kendall parades his desire for Julie in front of his companions at the barber shop. He attempts one night to rape her. He voices publicly a desire for revenge.

The actual revenge that Jim Kendall exacts, to expose Julie Gregg's admiration for Doc Stair, both to herself and to the town rowdies—a humiliation of an unspoken love, which puts it in carnal and odious terms—cannot provide a satisfactory solution to the complication, for the complication itself is monstrous. Jim Kendall is a married man with two children, and Julie Gregg has already indicated a detestation of him, which the reader heartily shares. In addition the attempt at revenge is so puerile that the only way in which we can swallow it as the action of a man is through the testimony of the barber. The barber actually applauds the ingenuity of Jim Kendall in mimicking voices; and in fact, were it not for the barber, the news that Julie Gregg was attracted to Doc Stair would not likely have reached Jim Kendall's ear.

Following Kendall's attempt, the complication is left dangling. Jim

Kendall has humiliated Julie Gregg, but he is afraid to let the affair leak out to Doc Stair. There is an inherent weakness in the internal story as a result. The love or admiration for Doc Stair that Julie Gregg feels is unknown to the doctor, so that he does not become Jim Kendall's antagonist because of it. The only way in which the internal story can move to a solution is through, once again, the agency of the barbershop. It is there that the retarded boy, Paul, learns of Jim Kendall's action.

It is noteworthy that if we were to tell the story without its framework we would now be forced to leave out a very significant aspect of the internal story. The barber has all along expressed a sneaking kind of admiration for Jim Kendall in his desire for Julie, at the same time as he has also felt a latent sympathy for Julie: "Poor Julie! She didn't show up here on Main Street for a long, long time afterward"; and, "It probably served Jim right, what he got." Without such an ambivalent point of view being expressed by the barber, we would be led to conclude that the braggart Jim Kendall was a monstrosity, a freak in any environment, and certainly not in any way typical of any aspect of life in a small town. As it is, however, he does represent in his actions toward Julie part of that curious distortion of values that finds expression in the barber's speech. And if we regard, as the barber does, Jim Kendall's desire for Julie Gregg in any way sympathetically and realize the impossibility of his ever resolving such a desire in human terms, then we must grant that the only solution left to Kendall will be criminal in nature. As a result, the only way to solve such a complication is to become advocates ourselves for criminal action against Kendall. Thus, curiously enough, as readers we are brought to sympathize with the boy's murder of Jim Kendall, our sympathy somewhat influenced by the fact that the boy cannot, being a retarded child, be considered legally a free moral intelligence. But not completely. The final exaggeration still stands that we wished to stop Kendall by criminal means.

Doc Stair's finding that it was an accidental shooting is merely a way of granting, in the face of a chain of accidental events, that Jim did have what was coming to him: the events were the boy's overhearing accidentally what Jim Kendall had done to Julie; the doctor's involuntary and angry remark that anybody who would do something like Kendall did "ought not to be let live"; and the again coincidental desire of Kendall to go duck-hunting, and his accepting Paul in place of Hod Meyers as a companion. Once again, if the internal story had been left to stand by itself, these accidental events would seem nothing but wishful inventions on the part of the author so that such a monstrous person as Jim Kendall could be punished.

But as the events are narrated to us by an actual participant, we accept them as credible because our real interest is fixed on something else. It is fixed on the fact that we—as the stranger sitting in the barber's chair—are actually having recommended to us as one of the elements of charm in small-town life, and with the idea that we will endorse them, such statements as that Jim Kendall was a "card," even though "he had it coming to him"; that Julie should have been made fun of for her love for Doc Stair, and yet that she was a "poor girl." And finally, we who are civilized beings and do not go about taking the lives of people have wished with all our might to see Jim Kendall "get it." Thus, the statements of the barber finally reveal just the opposite of what he intended. They reveal that the "fun" of the small town consists of a return to the emotions of the jungle; and the final, solicitous remark of the barber, "Comb it wet or dry?"—the conventional indication that one must soon pay for his services is accompanied by a distinct desire to pay up, to leave, to return to civilization away from the small town, and never to return.

In short, the internal story of "Haircut," without a frame of reference to direct it, to give it point, to make its accidents acceptable and credible and its malevolence understandable, would be too weak to stand by itself. It requires the use of reminiscence to make it strong and effective.

So much for our analysis of quality stories where the time of the story follows that of the time of the complication. There are only three ways to construct such stories, but within them, great variety is possible, and they suggest an opening-up of imaginative possibilities in the recasting of any formula story.

Now, let us see if the types of story structure investigated in VIII through X are based on the same three plots we mentioned at the beginning of Chapter Four. The first was tragic in its implications; the second was linear; and the third was comic.

It seems fairly obvious that stories of type VIII can be told in terms of any one of the three plots. In Hemingway's "The Killers," the protagonist Ole is a linear character, passively accepting the complication as a way of life, and this same passivity is characteristic of two of the peripheral characters, Sam, the cook, and George; Nick Adams appears to make a movement toward a solution of the complication, only to give up and accept it as a part of life. In Caldwell's "Daughter," Jim Carlisle attempts to solve his complication by killing his daughter, and he must be rescued from the terrible injustice that has been done to him by the actions of others. Stories of type VIII, therefore, may be tragic, linear, or comic. Had Hemingway shown Ole to be the focus of interest—which as protagonist in the formula version of the story, he would be—the story would certainly be linear. But since our interest in Ole is less significant than our interest in the way the other characters react to Ole's plight, there are obvious possibilities for tragedy or comedy, also. The fact that the story suggests these possibilities and moves to the linear is a great indictment of ordinary humanity. The potential emotional range in stories of this kind undoubtedly contributes to their dramatic excitement.

Stories that fall under our heading IX, in which a complication is renewed much later than its original occurrence and resolved through reminiscence, can never be linear: they must either be tragic or comic since it is part of the structure of such a story that the complication to be renewed will be faced by the protagonist for the very last time. In Katherine Mansfield's "A Dill Pickle," the heroine solves the complication that the meeting with her previous admirer has raised, and in solving it, repeats her earlier resolution of the complication. It is a victory over his charm and his meanness, and like the victories of a good many quality stories, carries with it a sense of the ironic loss one sustains even in the very moment of success. Chekhov's story "Old Age" demonstrates a complication renewed in ironic fashion. Uzelkov had successfully resolved the earlier complication, the capricious marriage, but again such a satisfactory solution carried with it its load of bitterness which, when the complication is renewed after the character has aged, shows up the complication for what it was, a cheap, shoddy, and brutal victory. The story, therefore, ends with the tragic implications of our first form of plot, that in which the protagonist, attempting some way out of his difficulty, ends by accepting the complication.

Stories of type X, those in which a weak or abstract complication is made strong through retelling, lean most heavily toward either the tragic or linear plot. It must be noticed that in the form of story where the main complication is what faces the narrator the internal story which he tells is merely an example, an illustration of the complication on a concrete basis. The story thus asks structurally: will the narrator

84

be able to resolve the complication through a retelling? Will he simply retell it, driving toward an acceptance and understanding of the complex issue that faces him? Or will he be able, after reflection and experience, to deal with it successfully, or partially so? As we have seen, the great point of the story "Young Archimedes" is that the narrator lives in an aura of self-reproach for his failure to appreciate in its total significance the appearance of such a genius as Guido, and for his failure to protect him. The story generally indicts the more talented and sensitive members of humanity for their neglect in the face of the threat imposed by the Signora Bondis of the world. Hence "Young Archimedes" is included under the first of our quality plots.

Yet the fact remains that stories of type X may have a linear structure. James Buechler's short story, "The Proud Suitor," a story of type X, consists of the narrator's recounting the actions which took place "about thirty years ago," really, in fact, prior to the marriage of his parents, in which his own moral values were determined by the irreverent and superficial values of the society in which his parents lived and which led them, particularly the mother, to fail to understand the dignity and solid virtues of an Italian immigrant. The complication of the narrator is past solution. All the protagonist of "The Proud Suitor" can do is to state the clash, which occurred in the past between two ways of life, in order to find some way of illustrating and understanding the poverty of his own spiritual heritage. About his own heritage, he can, of course, do nothing; he is forced to accept it passively.

There remains in stories of type X the possibility of a comic conclusion, but it is only a very slight one. The weak complication, as we have observed, is in one sense a very large complication; indeed, so large as to require such experience and ability on the part of the individual to understand his immediate experience as to make it nearly impossible for him at the time to react in any other than a groping and blind fashion. It is even possible, in such a story, for the narrator to present the concrete issue of a complication that he has not himself personally experienced as a means of stating the significance of that spiritual condition that he feels is a part of his life. Since he does not participate in the complication itself but is merely attempting to understand it, the story cannot be other than linear. By and large, the stories of type X will be those that lean most heavily toward tragic or linear plots.

Now it seems time to summarize briefly what the preceding chapters, including this one, have had to say about the subject of complications and the structures that appear to be characteristic of the various types of short story.

The structures of all pulp, slick, and quality stories are based upon the handling of a complication, and short stories vary structurally and derive their most significant qualities from the way the complication is handled.

Contemporary short stories may be divided into three categories: pulp, slick, and quality. Pulp fiction is divided into the adult and juvenile fields.

Adult pulp stories present a complication and solution to it in the lives of one or more characters, which must seem more interesting than the complications discovered in real life, and yet at the same time believable to the reader. Pulp stories of the adult variety are found in confession, adventure, mystery, and western magazines.

Juvenile pulp stories present a complication and solution to it in the lives of one or more juvenile characters; they strongly stress theme by pointing out a moral, teaching a lesson, or pointing up some time-tested truth. Juvenile stories are found in magazines aimed primarily at the juvenile market.

Slick stories present a complication and the solution to it in the lives of one or more characters, which must be more interesting than it would seem in real life, and at the same time believable to the reader. Slick stories employ a much more literary, sophisticated, and subtle style than pulp stories. Slick stories may be found in such magazines as *Cosmopolitan, Saturday Evening Post, Ladies' Home Journal,* and so on.

Pulp and slick stories are always optimistic because the complication is always solved in terms of the best interests of the protagonist. The story must have a happy or satisfactory ending.

Quality stories are divided into three sorts: the tragic, the linear, and the comic:

Tragic stories present a complication that the protagonist attempts to solve only to meet with failure, which forces him to accept the complication as a part of life.

Linear stories present a complication about which the protagonist either mentally protests but does nothing, or that he passively or blindly accepts as a part of life.

Comic quality stories present a complication that the protagonist either solves through his own efforts or has solved for him by accidental, providential, or chance events outside of himself, or through the actions of another character.

Quality stories tend to escape from direct action and make subtle appeals to style, symbol, idea, states of consciousness, and mental attitudes. Such stories may be found in the *Atlantic, Harper's, Partisan Review, The New Yorker,* and the quarterly magazines. With increasing frequency, one finds quality stories appearing in such magazines as *Playboy, Esquire,* and others devoted to a feminine market, both adult and juvenile, such as *Vogue, Mademoiselle,* and *Seventeen.*

Linear stories and those with a tragic curve are always pessimistic because the complication remains unsolved. Quality stories can be either optimistic or pessimistic, depending on whether the solution to the complication results in a satisfactory or unsatisfactory ending so far as the protagonist is concerned.

As one moves from commercial to quality stories, one finds that the nature of the complications presented differ widely. Let us now attempt to define the differences in complication. As we pointed out in the first chapter, a complication in pulp and slick writing consists of something unpleasant happening to an individual that, had he the power of choice, he would choose not to have happen. The story is always aimed at arousing an emotional response in the reader. It offers him a vicarious existence in which he can experience dramatically the emotions he is made to feel in terms of a protagonist's reaction to and solution of the complication. All stories of all types communicate emotion, as we have seen, but in the quality story the emotions tend to become more complex, more subtle, darker and more ironic, though retaining a greater range than merely the pathetic or potentially tragic. In addition, the emotion of the quality story is made to carry a heavier intellectual freight.

One may liken the use of emotion in fiction to the amount of force or energy required to move a given mass. The emotions in pulp and slick stories, by being limited to the range of feelings that a protagonist experiences who has the ability to solve the complication, therefore cannot, or at any rate do not, suggest complexity but a relative simplicity and directness of response. This relative simplicity is geared to the complication which, though universal in terms of its probability, does not have the same kind of universality of application that is used in the quality story. The complication in a quality story is more intellectualized, more extended in meaning and consequently greater in range. The writer of quality stories must be aware of the intellectual or thematic significance of his complications, therefore, in a way that pulp and slick writers are not, for the author is attempting to make a statement of philosophic depth in his story. Thus, on the level of structure, as well as on that of craftsmanship, he has developed many more ways of dealing with a complication: we have seen that the quality writer can arrange his complication in terms of a time perspective, so as to gain an extra vantage point from which to view it; and he can use any of a number of other ways in dealing with the complication, implying or stating it, implying or stating a resolution, exaggerating the protagonist's inability in the face of the complication, and so on. And in addition, through all the media of language, the quality writer can use subtle rhythms of style, imagery, symbolism, detail, rhetorical devices, allusion, connotation—all the techniques, indeed, of the poet —to give emotional impact and depth to the situation and to the protagonist's response.

To define then, at least in part, the complications of quality stories, a complication consists of an event whose intellectual significance disturbs the universe of the protagonist. Had he free choice, he might or might not wish for the complication to occur—if indeed, he understands that he faces a complication at all. But granting that he is not a blind, linear protagonist, it frequently requires a change in attitude, in the conditions of his culture, in the qualities of his personality, or in the mere nature of things, for the protagonist to face and resolve his complication. Even so, the complication must always arouse emotion in the reader for the protagonist; it must be exaggerated and made more interesting than it would seem in real life; it must, inherently, be contrived. As we pointed out at the conclusion of Chapter Two, the complication in the quality story can be exaggerated in one of two ways: either directly, by means of the same kind of inflation that the commercial writer uses; or indirectly, by so minimizing the ability of the protagonist to deal with the complication that the complication appears far larger than it would in real life. That the literary artist tends to favor the latter method seems obvious when one recalls the complications facing the protagonist in the various quality stories we have summarized.

One can, in other words, take almost any quality story and prove that it would not happen in actual life the way the story asserts that it does. Insofar as complications are concerned, the writers of quality stories, also, use just as much direct exaggeration as do pulp or slick writers. And in terms of the extended significance of these complications, the exaggeration is further heightened. Hemingway's "The Killers" is a classic example of this. In order for Ole to give up running away from the killers and to accept in complete passivity his death at their hands, all humanity must have turned a deaf ear to his plea for aid and sympathy. Is there no exaggeration in this? Is it entirely realistic that Nick Adams, horrified by the callousness of the whole event, should not make some further attempt to save Ole rather than merely to warn him? Hemingway exaggerates the passivity of ordinary humanity to the coldly callous and the brutally mechanical in order for us to see it. Nothing more. The exaggerations of fiction are an aid to our insight.

In effect, what gives lifelike character to the quality story is the subtle structure built from a normal complication. A cab driver waits for fares, and fares do come along, one of them a woman. A woman feels a sense of bliss before really understanding why she does. A man does think, after having been pursued by gangster killers from town to town, that ordinary humanity may not aid him. Again, certain forms of the quality story acquire quite a lifelike character by implying that complications must be faced again and again before they can be resolved through the growth and maturing of the protagonist.

However, an even more important contribution to the apparent realism of the quality story lies, for us as modern readers, in the reaction of the protagonist to the complication. If commercial stories exaggerate the ability of the protagonist to win out over his difficulties, given perseverance, shrewdness, determination, adequate intelligence, and so on, quality stories, in effect, exaggerate the inability of human beings to solve them. If one has, at times, in the slick story the feeling that the complication is a tempest in a teapot, his reaction to the quality story, at other times, is that the protagonist is a mere teapot in a tempest. In effect, the resolution achieved in most quality stories muddies the streams of pure comedy and pure tragedy—and hence those stories appear to have, for us, a lifelike quality.

The modern passive hero is a creature of our times, formed out of a world in which the intelligence is staggered by the adjustment it must make to the complexities, the pressures, the organizational patterns of existence. The twentieth century has seen the development of a technological and scientific civilization far in advance of the ability of human beings to adjust to it; it is a civilization pretty largely forecast by Matthew Arnold's phrase, "with its sick hurries and divided aims." It is no wonder that the modern writer should so often deem it essential to exaggerate the passivity of his protagonist to the manifold and complex demands made of him. But to call such a hero true to life, or real, is to overlook the essential artifice of the story writer who, as artists have always done, is merely demonstrating by exaggeration and selection the qualities of the age he lives in.

Not only is the structure of modern life so complex as to make complications inherently difficult, but there is at the root of the complications in much of modern literature a presumption in favor of the abstract: the protagonist is "real"; the situation that confronts him is not; it tends toward the nebulous. We are more preoccupied with the protagonist's reactions to the situation he faces than with the situation itself. The modern protagonist in the linear story is a creature of a profound spiritual malaise. He is a critic of his world without a message, without a belief, without a concrete commitment. His commitments come as a result of his disaffection rather than through conviction; and therefore, the protagonist can only exhibit the consciousness of a loss of innocence. The very sources of his disillusionment and passivity form the blind alleys of his emotions. The modern protagonist is very much like Amory Blaine in F. Scott Fitzgerald's novel *This Side of Paradise,* whose self-knowledge forms at once the great criticism of his existence and the source of his defeat:

He was in an eddy again, a deep, lethargic gulf, without desire to work or write, love or dissipate. For the first time in his life he rather longed for death to roll over his generation, obliterating their petty fevers and struggles and exultations. His youth seemed never so vanished as now in the contrast between the utter loneliness of his visit and that riotous, joyful party of four years before. Things that had been the merest commonplaces of his life then, deep sleep, the sense of beauty around him, all desire, had flown away and the gaps they left were filled only with the great listlessness of his disillusion.

He can end only with the cry, " 'I know myself, but that is all.' "

In effect, what makes the quality protagonist and the quality story appear lifelike to us is this *cri du coeur* of the quality hero. The complication turns frequently into something so large that he cannot even define its limits. What he can do is to communicate his helplessness, or his paradoxical sense of his insignificant significance, or the depth of his critical awareness of himself with the fear of turning into something else if he acts, or the strange convolutions of personality and emotion without the possibility of dramatic projection, or the configurations of his self-pity coupled with a snobbish condescension toward those who

90

discover a value in any dedication—and because the protagonist communicates these things to us, he is, therefore, to us "real." For we are, as human beings, in his boat. Each one of us, as intelligent and sensitive beings, is aware at some point or other in his life of the iron necessities of change, of time, of the directions his life has taken and the reasons for them, of the way in which he has been formed or maimed, and of the fundamental irony of death, which always robs what experience has enriched.

The modern hero very often speaks to us in the accents of the human condition, no matter what complication he actually faces in the story: the complication serves only as a leaping-off place for what is essentially the lyric impulse of the writer to sing about the sad perplexities of human life. And hence many quality stories establish a mood that has truth for us, an atmosphere that has interpenetrated our beings, a set of emotions with which we are conversant. But the artist of other times has also defined the truth that his hero is enabled to act with a consciousness of what he faces and somewhat greater faith in his powers to grapple with a concrete dilemma. Once we admit two truths which are radically divergent, we must come to the conclusion that all is artifice.

The complication, furthermore, in the modern quality story, unlike that in slick or pulp stories, may consist of something potentially pleasant, which happens to the protagonist. Bertha in "Bliss" discovers her feeling of ecstasy to be the deep stirrings within her of a woman's desire for her husband, free from the silly artificialities of a guilt-ridden, quasi-theological horror of the body. Ryabovich in "The Kiss" meets, in the midst of a humdrum, routine, and boring life, the possibility of self-fulfillment through romance. In "Young Archimedes," a sensitive, talented, and civilized person faces one of those rare opportunities in human life to foster a boy-genius. Mr. Penfold in H. E. Bates' story faces not only the prospect of a satisfactory marriage with a widow who is anxious for his attentions—and we may suppose capable of satisfying the loneliness of his heart—but he later faces the prospect of an alliance with the woman's daughter. It is obvious that in order to arrive at the ironic or the pathetic, one of the devices of structure that a writer may use is to involve an inept protagonist in a potentially pleasurable, rather than unpleasant, situation, and this will heighten, by contrast, the ironic reversal: the inability of the protagonist to come to grips with the complication, even when it seems most possible and, chiefly, most tangible.

In short, to define the quality complication, we may phrase it in the following terms:

> *A quality complication consists of an event, situation, or idea of pleasant or unpleasant nature that disturbs the universe of the protagonist, causing him to try to fit such an event, situation, or idea into his scheme of things. The complication will as usual be exaggerated, either in terms of its abstract quality —it will be so large or complex or universal in scope that the protagonist cannot possibly deal with it satisfactorily short of outside help—or if it is concrete and capable of being dealt with, the protagonist may, and often will, be blind or passive or inert in the face of it. In some forms of quality story, the complication calls for a change in attitude on the part of the protagonist; in others, it calls for an attempt at action; but in most it calls for understanding on the protagonist's part.*

Now as the reader will recall, we have already demonstrated how to take the outline of a complication and develop it as a pulp or a slick formula story. We have postponed until now any discussion of how to take the same outline and tell it as a quality story—at least in terms of the structure of the quality story. Whether or not the reader will be capable of going far enough in matters of structure to produce quality craftsmanship in the telling of a story will be the only thing to inhibit his using any of the structures we have mentioned. Let us, therefore, take up once more our story "Russian Roulette" as an example, and attempt to see further things in the story than the structure of the formula story allows.

The rationale of "Russian Roulette" was based, for the pulp and slick versions, on the supposed—and necessarily highly exaggerated—ability of the protagonist to see exactly why he had accepted Duke as a friend, and to move from that discovery into an act that finally releases him. The story admits that a boy who has developed a sense of self-effacement and self-ridicule through no fault of his own, through the mere accident of his glandular system, can easily involve himself in a situation where his desire to rebel and break away from his lot will lead him into physical and moral danger. Now there was one point in our outline where Benny could easily have become passive in the face of his complication. Granted a sense of horror at Duke's beating up the woman, if that feeling cannot overcome an undercurrent of satisfaction in Benny at the mere act of rebellion, then Benny will continue to go with Duke until he has passed a point of no return—until he has, in fact, lost all his compunction and sensitivity and has become as cruel and compulsive as Duke is.

Now such a realization on the writer's part is the first step in creating a passive rather than an active protagonist. This will cause us to regard Benny as the net product of certain forces in society, which kill, little by little, the kindliness of a person like Benny, and which emphasize in his character a rebelliousness that is actually criminal passivity. What are these forces? Here the experience of the writer in modern life must be called into play. It is here that we become conscious about the thematic implications of the dilemma. These forces may, and possibly will, be the failure of people to be sympathetic toward an unfortunate person; to overemphasize the romantic achievements of the young as the criterion of value; to stress the importance of outward appearance at the expense of internal character; to wage the polite warfare that adults so often wage against the young in this society by making the young person feel impotent in the face of the world's complexity. Whatever the forces, and the necessary exaggeration made of them, the important thing is that Benny has here moved from the formula plot in which the protagonist overcomes an opponent to reach a worthwhile goal to the linear plot in which the protagonist may protest about the complication he faces but about which he does nothing, either blindly or passively accepting the complication as a part of life.

Similarly, the story can be told—at least this particular slick story can be—in terms of either the tragic or the comic plot of the quality story. As tragedy of the traditional kind, it will be sufficient to emphasize the protagonist's awareness of those very same forces that have made him a partially passive character and to have him consciously attempt to struggle against them only to fail. He is trapped by the things he struggles against, but he acquires heroic stature in the struggle. As tragedy of a more modern sort, where the effort of the protagonist is directed at understanding the nature of his plight rather than at striving to overcome it, it will be necessary to emphasize the perplexity that Benny faces in acting a part that has no place in his emotional life. What he does and the way he feels are two different things. The attempt to understand why he cannot carry out the demands of his own rebelliousness in the face of a conscience that attacks him and tortures him with guilt would make the story tragic in a modern sense.

93

His tragedy here would be to emphasize the illumination of his own motives without suggesting in him the power to act successfully in terms of such an understanding. As a comic quality story, the general outlook could perhaps stand as it is, granted sufficient literary ability on the part of the writer—and for this, one must in effect wait upon the judgment of critics. But it would be of another order of comedy; indeed, if the resolution of Benny's complication were taken from his hands and were given to mere accident, the emotions of terror and the will for righteousness could be shown as absurd.

In thinking of the formula story as a possible quality story, in other words, what one does is in actuality to emphasize or de-emphasize the characteristics of the protagonist. If the reader will recall, for his formula story he was urged to choose several, perhaps as many as four, attributes that marked the character of his protagonist. In Benny's case, these attributes were rebelliousness, reflectiveness, shyness, and sensitivity. Emphasizing more rebelliousness than sensitivity, we move to the linear protagonist. Given more qualities of understanding than of action (as implied by the attribute of rebelliousness) would yield the modern tragic character. Emphasizing sensitivity, minimizing rebelliousness, and having the story resolved through accident would yield the modern comic approach.

Hence, the ways to turn the outline of a formula or a chronological story into a quality story may be stated as follows:

1. *Determine at which steps in the complication outline the protagonist might travel along the paths indicated by the generic quality plots.*
2. *Determine which emotional attributes within the protagonist would become predominant in terms of the generic plots of the quality story.*
3. *Determine the thematic implications of the story in terms of each of these plots.*

It will be at this point that the reader can make use of the varying types of structure that have been presented in this and the previous chapter. For it will be up to him, in terms of his own imaginative realization of the possibilities presented by the story he is mulling over, to choose that form that will most effectively represent the best way to tell his story. Here, a frank admission of the necessity for models and for imitation is in order. And it might be well to close a fairly long chapter with the sprightly comments of a professional

94

writer of the eighteenth century that may put into focus both the demand for formal knowledge and the need for experience on the part of the writer if he is to be successful. In one of the introductory chapters that form a brief set of esthetic rules for each book of *Tom Jones,* Henry Fielding remarked that "the nimbleness of a dancing-master is not at all prejudiced by being taught to move; nor doth any mechanic . . . exercise his tools the worse by having learnt to use them. . . ." Yet "a man should have some little knowledge of the subject on which he treats," and to give a picture of the manners of men, it is requisite for a writer to live among mankind, for here book-learning "will not do the business."

EXERCISES FOR CHAPTER 5

1. Reread Katherine Mansfield's short story "A Dill Pickle" or Chekhov's story "Old Age." Using the characters from either story, construct a plot outline which depends upon the time the complication in either story originally took place. Now work up your outline as a chronological or formula story. Apart from matters of style and technique, what particular gains or losses are there in your telling the story at the time the complication first occurred?
2. Take the story you have just written and begin it late in the complication sequence in order to show the effect the complication has upon a peripheral person. Are stories of violent action better suited to such a device? That is, would it be easier to use Chekhov's story "Old Age" in this way than it would be to use Katherine Mansfield's "A Dill Pickle"?
3. Read Joseph Conrad's short story "The Lagoon." What reasons can you discover for Conrad's using a narrator in the telling of this story? Do you consider the complication which Arsat faces either weak or abstract? Why, or why not?
4. Determine which of the following complications seem more suited to commercial stories than to quality stories:
   a. A lonely bachelor faces the prospect of falling in love with a married woman.
   b. A boy jeopardizes his father's election chances by "throwing" a tournament game in basketball.
   c. An idealistic young couple go to Europe in order to collect expensive curios and then return to live in dissatisfaction in the United States.
   d. A young boy discovers that his father is having an affair with "another woman."

e. A man discovers that recent business successes have made him unable to tolerate his wife.

5. Memorize and recite the ten sorts of plot structures mentioned in Chapters Four and Five, as well as the three generic plots available to quality stories.

6

How to Select
Point of View
in the Story

OF ALL THE ELEMENTS in a short story, the question of choosing the point of view from which the story is told can be the most troublesome to an inexperienced writer, and it is also the one element in structure that can destroy an otherwise salable story. It may seem strange to the beginning writer to read that point of view in the story is a structural device. Such a statement must wait upon the contents of this chapter for proof and illustration. Nevertheless, the way a story is told depends upon the decision a writer makes—and the story sometimes makes for the writer—as to what point of view is eminently right and just for all the elements of the story, for otherwise the whole becomes a barren manipulation without central intelligence, confusing at best, at worst unintelligible.

Of the many distinctions that can be drawn between commercial and quality stories, the differences in the handling of point of view are undoubtedly one of the most significant. For here a literary crafts-man's greater subtlety and suggestiveness show up in critical fashion. One can indicate the differences between the three major categories of short story in the following way: pulp stories invariably use the point of view of the protagonist; slick stories generally, though not always, use the protagonist's point of view; and quality stories, like slick stories, use either the point of view of the protagonist or a minor character, or they may establish the point of view even more subtly by placing it outside the story proper. Since these distinctions exist, and since we have arranged our material in order of difficulty, proceeding from the simplest to the more complex, let us first of all investigate the points of view a writer may use in writing pulp and slick stories. Now a rule exists that governs point of view:

1. *Only those things that the character who has been given the point of view personally knows, experiences, observes, or deduces can be included in the story.*

The writer, therefore, must first investigate the difficulties that he might encounter in choosing one character over another to tell the story. For the reader will identify himself with the point of view of this character, interpreting the story through the character's personal frame of reference, and living the role of the character vicariously.

To illustrate the difficulties and solutions that professional writers have met and dealt with effectively, here are several examples of interest in the question of point of view. In the first, a slick story, the story is told by the ten-year-old daughter of a couple headed for divorce. The story could not be told impartially from the point of view of either the father or mother, and had the author tried to use one or the other, it would have been unsalable. The complication seen through the eyes of the ten-year-old girl, however, becomes the substance of a successful story. The second story concerns the difficulties of a couple who married very young, and who lack the experience and maturity to see just how to face their problems. The author, therefore, tells the story from the point of view of a maiden aunt with whom the young couple make their home. The third example provides a classic illustration of the way in which an author has given credibility to his stories by using the right point of view. These stories are the Sherlock Holmes stories. Seen through the eyes of Doctor Watson, the things Sherlock Holmes does are wholly convincing. Were we to see the same performances from the point of view of Holmes himself, he would appear to us an insufferable creation. We have included in the Appendix on page 397, a slick off-beat story by C. Y. Lee, author of *The Flower Drum Song,* as another illustration of the right choice in point of view. The story "The Casanova of Kearny Street," because it is seen through the eyes of a minor character, is wholly credible; if it had been told from the point of view of the main character, it would seem unbelievable.

Nearly all pulp and slick stories use the point of view of a single character, and the preponderance of them are told in the third person.

(An interesting exception to the customary practice of slick stories to maintain the viewpoint of only one character occurs in the story "I Will Not Talk," which can be found on page 382 of the Appendix. The author skillfully shifts the viewpoint back and forth between two of the characters throughout the story in order to characterize, to arouse suspense, and to bring in information that one character alone would not possess.) Telling a story in the third person, unfortunately, is apt to give the new writer a good deal of difficulty. For one thing, the novice at writing seems to have an invariable tendency to violate the rule governing point of view, which states that only that portion of the action can be conveyed that the character whose viewpoint is being used personally knows or witnesses. As a result, a second difficulty arises: in order to make it appear that a character obtains knowledge of things really outside his ken, the writer includes faulty exposition, wild improbabilities, and coincidences, overheard conversations, chance meetings, and so on, to keep his character informed; all such flaws can only weaken a story.

The best way to avoid these difficulties is to use the following method:

II. In order to avoid violating the rule governing point of view, as well as subsidiary and related errors, write the original draft of a story in the first person and then, on revision, change the first to the third person.

Here is a specific example of how to use this method. The original draft of a story reads in this fashion: "*I* kept *my* hand over the gun in *my* coat pocket so that the elevator operator would not notice the bulge as *I* entered the fashionable apartment house where *my* friend, Stanley Randolph, lived." After writing the first draft, the novice simply underscores all the first-person pronouns, gives his character a name, and transposes the narrative to the third person: "John Steele kept his hand over the gun in his coat pocket so that the elevator operator would not notice the bulge as he entered the fashionable apartment house where his friend, Stanley Randolph, lived."

There are both virtues and limitations in using this technique, and one must be aware of them. It is obvious, so far as the virtues are concerned, that it helps to avoid violating the rule governing point of view and all the errors that come from such a violation. In addition, it tends to ensure good continuity in a story; and finally, the use of the first person often helps to involve the writer in his character more closely. One can imagine one's own emotions in a given situation much more intimately than those of a third person.

However, as we indicated, there are also certain limitations. The writer, in the first place, may tend to use his story merely as a sounding board for his own convictions. He may sidestep the actual involvement of his characters in order to leap to the expression of his own personal, political, religious, social, and moral beliefs and persuasions. Nothing will destroy a story more quickly than the intrusion of foreign matter. In the second place, the writer must be able to identify himself so thoroughly with the character's point of view that he will have conviction and sincerity when he speaks through the character. The use of the first person may actually create a gap between writer and character if the writer is psychologically unable to project himself into his character. For example, if the central character is a ravishing and untrustworthy *femme fatale* and the writer happens to be a rather dowdy but respectable middle-aged housewife, it would be better for her to avoid identifying herself in the first person with her creation, unless she is able to surmount the barriers of her own psyche, physique, and environment. If the protagonist is a hard-boiled policeman, the writer must, if he is to use the first person, be sufficiently an actor to transcend his own personality. If the writer cannot project himself into his character, the character will be a mere puppet and the story will be unsalable.

Although most pulp and slick stories are told in the third person, some are told in the first person, and one particular group of pulp stories, confession stories, are always told in the first person. It will obviously be to the beginning writer's advantage to practice using the first person until he becomes thoroughly familiar with the rule governing point of view and is able to keep it consistent throughout the story.

The use of more than one point of view can weaken a reader's grip on the story, burdening him with the confusion of readjusting to a new angle from which to view the action. The beginning writer, therefore, should limit the point of view to a single character, using either the hero or the heroine, whichever will be the more sympathetic to the reader, until he becomes adept enough to tell his story through the eyes of a minor character. And it will take a very great amount of practice and skill, indeed, to produce the shifts in point of view that are often used in quality stories.

Obviously in outlining and developing his plot, the writer will tend to use the viewpoint of his protagonist, seeing the action, looking at the setting, and regarding the other characters with his eyes. The initial statements of the story, in which the point of view becomes established, follow from the development of the complication—unless the writer, in studying what he has produced, can discover a more effective vantage point from which to tell the story.

Now when a story is told in the third person, it is obvious that the person who is actually telling the tale exists outside of the story proper. The third-person element refers, of course, not to the person of the narrator—if the person who is telling the story were to speak he would have to use the pronoun "I"—but to the characters within the story, all of whom are written of in the third person. Certain distinctions exist in stories told from the third-person point of view in terms of the relative entrance or exclusion of the author from the story. That is to say, the author as narrator may give himself the privilege of entering the story at any point he chooses, interrupting it, and making a comment upon it from the outside, as it were. In doing so, he willfully breaks the thread of the action to point out something that he wishes the reader to know or think about. Again, the author as narrator, although he realizes that he has the privilege of entering his story, may wish to conceal himself and not exercise that privilege quite so obviously. Yet he may retain something of that power, intentionally and consciously shifting the reader's focus of interest. A third and final type of third-person story is that where the author suppresses himself completely as narrator, feeling that what he has to say about the characters can best be shown by their actions and that for him to intrude would only destroy the story's dramatic value.

These three methods of narrating a story exhibit the wide range of techniques available to the writer, all the way from the presentation of a broad panoramic sweep of events under some overriding view or philosophy the author has of life, to the exploitation of character and the use of environment as extension of character, to the exhibition of sheer dramatic action without interpolated comment.

Let us look more closely at each of these methods, analyzing them in terms of their advantages and disadvantages, as a way of exploring the choices available to the writer. In order to aid the reader, it will be helpful to give names to each distinctive kind of third-person story; substituting the word narrator for author, we will according call them:

1. The omnipresent narrator
2. The concealed narrator
3. The suppressed narrator

The omnipresent narrator

The point of view used here is the oldest in the craft and art of fiction, and in certain respects it is one of the most difficult, though its basic supposition that the author himself is telling the story is perfectly apparent and appears to give freedom. When this point of view is used, the story, we are fully aware, is seen through the mind of the person who is most acquainted with all its sweep as well as with all its minutiae. The author can set the scene, describe the characters, and then drop them momentarily to make a series of remarks about the significance of what he is doing before he turns back to the scene. The reader is thus conscious of the narrator at all times. He is aware that the author is telling the story, is manipulating it—if that is not too strong a word—though the manipulation does not appear to be a grievous fault if skillfully handled. The author, as omnipresent narrator, has the right to regard the whole panorama of his tale as he would were he in the theatre to step up front on the stage and simply remark upon the whole of what he intends to present; or he can step within the tale and move about freely, as he would were he to enter the scene on the stage and make his own comments upon the actors or their speeches. Although in using this point of view the author does not always penetrate into the deeper consciousness of his characters, he may if he wishes, for the assumption is, of course, that the author knows everything. As Fielding remarks in *Tom Jones:* "Reader, I think proper, before we proceed any farther together, to acquaint thee that I intend to digress, through this whole history, as often as I see occasion, of which I am myself a better judge than any pitiful critic whatever. . . ."

The use of an omnipresent narrator seems more appropriate to the sweep and play of large forces or events upon the stage of life than it does to the more intimate aspects of personality. The device is, therefore, most useful for an author who views life from some philosophical perspective, some large and all-enveloping thought structure that serves to give reason and significance to even the tiniest details of his observation.

The obvious disadvantages of its use lie in the difficulties of commenting on the story without losing the reader's interest; of intruding on the action without forcing the reader to feel cheated of his sense of identification with the story and its characters; of presenting a sweeping view of life without falling into vague generalities that find no concrete existence within the story proper—or in other words, of presenting the story so that it remains an unfolding action with its own *raison d'être,* and is not smothered by explanations.

An illustration of a very subtle use of the omnipresent narrator is found in a short story by Ambrose Bierce, "An Occurrence at Owl Creek Bridge." The story concerns a Southern planter who, caught in an act of sabotage against a bridge now occupied by Union forces, is to be hanged by them from the bridge. The bulk of the story occurs within the planter's mind as he is forced to drop from the bridge with the rope round his neck. In those seconds the man reviews the events that have led to his hanging, imagines that the rope has miraculously parted, that he is swimming in the river, that he escapes from the efforts of his captors to kill him, and that he works his way back home to his wife. At just the instant she opens the door to welcome him, he reaches the end of his plummeting drop; the rope does its work, and his body sways lifeless beneath the timbers of the bridge.

In order to give us an understanding of the essential irony of warfare, the author enters the story to address the reader directly in such statements as the following:

Death is a dignitary who when he comes announced is to be received with formal manifestations of respect, even by those most familiar with him. In the code of military etiquette silence and fixity are forms of deference.

Evidently this was no vulgar assassin. The liberal military code makes provision for hanging many kinds of persons, and gentlemen are not excluded.

In order to let us know what the doomed man thinks as he falls from the bridge, the author tells us, "As these thoughts, which have here to be set down in words, were flashed into the doomed man's brain rather than evolved from it the captain nodded to the sergeant." The author of the story is thus outside the story proper, but by intruding in it, to look at it and comment on it, he is also able to tell us what goes through a man's mind in the last moments of life.

Now a question occurs in looking at the device of using an omnipresent narrator. If the author appears in the story putting himself between the reader and the story, who precisely is the character whose point of view is being used? The answer is that it is the author as omnipresent narrator who is the point-of-view character. But what then do we call the central character in the story? To get around this difficulty, we can use the term *focus of interest*. The focus of interest in a commercial story is almost invariably the protagonist. That is, our interest is always centered on the hero since he is the one involved in the complication, he is the one who attempts to extricate himself, and he is the one who eventually succeeds. Ordinarily in commercial stories using the third person, the author conceals himself and does not force his reflections upon the reader's notice. As a consequence, the point of view and the focus of interest are both placed in one and the same character. But it is obvious that if the device of omnipresent narration is used, the point of view will be that of the narrator himself simply because he calls himself to the reader's gaze and fulfills the function of having us see the story through his eyes. The focus of interest within the story will center, therefore, on whatever person or idea, scene, or action within the story the author wishes to make predominant. The focus of interest may remain absolutely constant within the story, as it almost always does in commercial fiction, or it may shift from one character to another or to anything else the author wishes to stress.

The concealed narrator

This method of telling a story can be divided into two main branches, A and B. In both forms of this sort of story, the author is concealed and does not choose to obtrude himself on the reader at all in any direct way. Yet it is possible for the concealed narrator to back away from the story, as it were, and view it from the outside, just as the omnipresent narrator does when he steps out to the front of the stage and speaks directly to the audience. When the concealed narrator, however, finds occasion to direct his audience's gaze to certain things within the story, he does it as briefly and as subtly as possible.

To clarify the way the concealed narrator operates in a story, let us look again at the analogy between the story writer and the dramatist by imagining that the dramatist wishes to emphasize certain things for his audience, but that he does not want to be overt in telling the audience what he feels. What can he do to let them know without at the same time intruding his presence? Dramatists have solved the problem by using a character to present a prologue or epilogue, acting the part of an allegorical figure who comes on and tells the audience what the dramatist feels yet did not want to say personally. The story writer does not have such freedom, for his characters must be a part of the action; at the same time, he wants this subtlety. Therefore, he uses one or many of the characters in his story to serve, each in his own turn, as the character who has the point of view. It is essential to remember that whatever the point of view established by a concealed narrator the story is still seen from a third person's viewpoint by the reader, for such a character is always spoken of in the third person.

To represent the distinction between a concealed narrator's using the point of view of one or many of the characters in his story, we have divided the subject, as we stated, into two branches: A and B. In form A, the concealed narrator uses either a minor character or the protagonist to establish the point of view. Only what such a character himself knows, sees, and experiences can enter the story; and hence with hidden narrator A the rule governing point of view that we gave at the beginning of this chapter operates very strictly. Almost all pulp and slick stories told in the third person belong to the category of concealed narrator A. An excellent and far more complex use of the form is shown in Stephen Crane's "The Open Boat," which we will discuss in a moment.

If the writer wishes, however, to give the point of view of more than one character in the story, he will use the device of concealed narrator B; that is, many characters, each in turn, are used to give their points of view. The narrator himself being concealed within the personality and perspective of the different characters, the rule governing point of view is, therefore, not nearly so rigid as with concealed narrator A. It is true that the viewpoint will be limited in terms of each character's own knowledge, so that the rule governing point of view applies to each specifically. But for the story as a whole, the rule is far less confining because of the fact that each character is able to bring his own bit of insight, knowledge, or ideas into the story, which would have had to be omitted if a single character's point of view were used.

The subtlety that narrator B can give to a story is very great. Let us, for example, take a number of characters, such as John, Mary, Bill, and Ed. Now if each of their viewpoints can be presented, it is obvious that we can get four different points of view of the protagonist. Once again, we must use the term "focus of interest." If John is the focus of interest, we can look at John from varying points of view, from the points of view of Mary, Bill, Ed, and of John himself. The one thing that keeps the use of so many views from turning the story into a hodgepodge is that the focus of interest must remain fixed. If the writer adopts John as the focus of interest, he is committed, and he must retain this same focus throughout the story.

The advantages of using diverse points of view are many, for the varying viewpoints of all the other characters in relation to John will allow us to know John even more thoroughly than we would know him if the author were present as omnipresent narrator. At first sight, such a statement may seem hard to believe, for surely the omnipresent narrator knows everything about the story and characters, nothing being too minute for his all-seeing, all-discerning eye. Yet however brilliant an observer of character, however profound a vision he may have, the author when he is present in the story can give only one point of view, his own. We may see John through the author's eyes and know him; but to see John through the eyes of Mary, Bill, and Ed, in addition, will be to know John even more thoroughly. The character who acts as the focus of interest, when concealed narrator B is used, can therefore be studied in depth, in terms of his actions and interactions with other persons. Another great advantage of using concealed narrator B is that nothing in the story becomes really irrelevant, so long as the focus of interest remains fixed. Exposition of past events, descriptive passages, summaries of action are all conveyed in terms of the feelings and behavior of many characters. In essence, the author who acts as concealed narrator B can take the reader within the consciousness of his characters and then expose external events in their interaction to that consciousness without creating a gap. When the author is omnipresent, the reader is always aware that the author is hovering about the character, explaining him, pointing out his thought processes, bringing up relevant facts to our gaze. With the device of concealed narrator B, the reader perceives only dimly, if at all, that the author has for the time being penetrated the character, assumed his biases, his failures, and his virtues; and thus, while cloaked, actively established his character's nature.

In concealing the narrator in a story we get away from the ponderous and the pompous—the dangers implicit when the author is omnipresent. The author does not appear to have any bias, for he allows his characters to view life on their own terms rather than his. Yet for all the obvious advantages of subtlety, depth, and objectivity, there are also disadvantages. The writer may tend to subordinate dramatic action to the analysis of conditions operating upon the characters, primarily upon the character who is the focus of interest. In the hands of the inexperienced writer, it is all too possible for the action to be halted and the dissection of focal character made so minute that the whole fabric becomes hopelessly dense and impacted. The very virtues of the use of concealed narrator B tend to be faults if the writer has not learned or is unable to subordinate minute details to whole observation.

Now to return to Stephen Crane's "The Open Boat" as an illustration of the method of concealed narrator A. What makes this story interesting to the student of writing is that Crane has also used both the devices of the omnipresent narrator and of concealed narrator B to forward the purposes of his story, and then quite clearly has established the story toward the end as one actually told by concealed narrator A.

The story in terms of plotted action is quite simple. Four men, the captain, the cook, an oiler, and a newspaper correspondent, have escaped from a sinking steamer by means of the dinghy, an open boat. The sea is tremendously rough. The boat is small and easily capsized. Yet they are not far enough away from shore to be drowned for a certainty, nor is survival a certainty either, since no landsman understands their plight. Finally, after struggling to beach the boat, one of the men, the oiler, is drowned, and the others reach the safety of land. The story ends with the words, "and they felt that they could then be interpreters."

Of what are they to be interpreters? In essence, they are to interpret the nature of the universe as neither malevolent nor beneficent but as flatly indifferent to those who inhabit it. Man tends too easily to impose his own ego on the outer world, to conclude that if he is to die unjustly, it is some force in nature that caused the injustice. Man can either sue for grace before this force or "throw bricks at the temple." But in reality, before the vast indifference of the scheme of things, neither action is meaningful. As a consequence, when man is forced to view his own situation correctly, he can then only understand and value the doctrine of brotherhood.

The theme of the story imposes the technical problem of point of view. Crane is talking not of a particular man's understanding, but of any man's understanding. And to show that it is not the private point of view of only one person in the situation, Crane makes use of the minds of the four men. Notice such a statement as "The men in the dinghy had not discussed these matters, but each had, no doubt, reflected upon them in silence and according to his mind." Such a statement would seem as if it must come only from the author, for it is obvious that if the men had not discussed their common sense of brotherhood, they could share it only as an intuitive feeling. Thus in this statement, and in a number of others throughout the story, the author appears to be the omnipresent narrator, looking at the situation from the outside and talking about it. Here is another example:

A singular disadvantage of the sea lies in the fact that after successfully surmounting one wave you discover that there is another behind it just as important and just as nervously anxious to do something effective in the way of swamping boats. In a ten-foot dinghy one can get an idea of the resources of the sea in the line of waves that is not probable to the average experience which is never at sea in a dinghy.

And again:

Viewed from a balcony, the whole thing would doubtless have been weirdly picturesque. But the men in the boat had no time to see it, and if they had had leisure there were other things to occupy their minds.

The trouble with stating that Crane uses the device of omnipresent narrator, however, is this: he refuses to climb up on the balcony to view and explain what is occurring. At the very beginning of the story, he lets us know we are in the boat, rather than in his mind:

None of them knew the color of the sky. Their eyes glanced level, and were fastened upon the waves that swept toward them. These waves were of the hue of slate, save for the tops, which were of foaming white, and all of the men knew the colors of the sea. The horizon narrowed and widened, and dipped and rose, and at all times its edge was jagged with waves that seemed thrust up in points like rocks.

For the sake of illustration, let us rewrite the opening lines of the story as the true omnipresent narrator would have viewed the circumstances:

To a perceptive mind, a vast expanse of sea is a lesson in viewing properly the station that man occupies in the universe. There is nothing quite so suggestive of the illimitable as a rolling sea forever rushing in multitude of sight and sound. The blue sky is an impersonal thing, for we can not touch it. But man is very close to the sea. His primal consciousness is of the waters from which all life has come, and if he would learn a lesson from his experience, he might learn to cling to brotherhood, for only in this way can he feel secure. The sea itself does not care. . . . There were four men in a boat struggling against their mother and destroyer, the sea. . . .

108

In Crane's passage, the waves "swept toward them." The horizon narrows and widens, dips and rises. Only from the boat can we see these things.

Crane purposively moves into the boat and looks at the situation from the eyes of the men in the boat, who are bobbing about on the waves. Yet once in the boat, he does not speak in his own person, nor does he speak explicitly in the person of one of the boat's occupants. Why is this so? Again we must return to the technical problems that his theme raises, as well as to the editorial rule governing point of view. Since only that part of the story can be covered that the character whose point of view is being used can personally observe or deduce, it is obvious that no one person in the boat can speak of the common sensation (or intuition) of brotherhood without usurping the theme to himself, so to speak, and becoming a sentimental observer:

It would be difficult to describe the subtle brotherhood of men that was here established on the seas. No one said that it was so. No one mentioned it. But it dwelt in the boat, and each man felt it warm him.

Crane was undoubtedly aware, in writing the story, that he had to be able to penetrate sufficiently within each man so as to make clear to the reader the idea that each man felt their "subtle brotherhood." Now as we have observed, the author as concealed narrator B has this power. He can explore each of his characters in turn, using the viewpoint of each character to establish an idea, the idea of brotherhood.

We find Crane doing this throughout the story. Note how frequently he shifts the focus of interest from one man to another until he has successively described each one:

The cook squatted in the bottom and looked with both eyes at the six inches of gunwale which separated him from the ocean. . . . The oiler, steering with one of the two oars in the boat, sometimes raised himself suddenly to keep clear of water that swirled in over the stern. . . . The correspondent, pulling at the other oar, watched the waves and wondered why he was there. The injured captain, lying in the bow, was at this time buried in that profound dejection and indifference which comes, temporarily at least, to even the bravest and most enduring when, willy nilly, the firm fails, the army loses, the ship goes down.

Now though Crane shifts the viewpoint from one man to another, in order to establish a commonality of feeling and response to the

109

situation, there is one other aspect of his theme that prevents him from adopting completely the device of concealed narrator B. It is not sufficient for Crane's purposes for each man simply to feel a "subtle brotherhood." He wants the reader to think about the doctrine of brotherhood as a final and inescapable conclusion to the view that the universe is quite indifferent to man. The doctrine, in other words, has to be an articulated doctrine. No one man in the boat speaks of the idea of brotherhood. Each thinks "in silence and according to his mind." But there is one man of the four who is capable of stating his theme, and that is the correspondent. He, alone, is the one whom Crane establishes, at the very beginning of the story, as being most preoccupied, not with the mere question of physical survival, but with "why he was there." As a consequence, although Crane shifts from one to another of these silent men he, nonetheless, keeps coming to rest principally in the thoughts and reflections of the correspondent. As the story continues, we move more and more into the mind and point of view of the correspondent. In the last few pages, the story is certainly there.

We have dwelt at some length upon "The Open Boat" to point up several things about the use of point of view. The mere fact that one can classify distinctions among points of view does not commit a creative writer to a rigorous and undeviating use of one point of view to the exclusion of all others. A writer of quality stories must develop a certain elasticity in his techniques, and the way he becomes elastic is to consider the intimate relationship that exists between his meaning, the point of view he uses, and the ultimate structure of his story.

As the reader has already seen in the chapter on the structure of quality stories, within every quality story there is concealed and altered, but nonetheless present, the formula story. So, too, is this true of "The Open Boat." The formula story that is concealed there *is* the correspondent's story. The complication that faces all the men in the boat appears to him as a problem belonging not alone to the physical realm, but to the intellectual, even the spiritual. Why are they in this predicament? It is he who sees most clearly the irony of their situation. They are saved from their initial destruction by drowning only to struggle most viciously for their lives, and this only to face once more, and most unjustly, the prospect of drowning all over again. It is he of all the four who has been most cynical about men and comradeship. And finally, it is he who understands most clearly "the serenity of nature amid the struggles of the individual—nature in the wind, and nature in the vision of men." Through a new recognition of the nature of the universe, the correspondent learns the answer to his initial question. The complication of the formula story is imbedded in "The Open Boat," but it has been raised from mere dramatic action alone to a level of universal significance.

The suppressed narrator (or the story of dramatic objective)

There is now only one further type of third-person narrator to consider. To give some appreciation of this method, let us once more return to the analogy we have been using between the stage and the short story. With a suppressed narrator, the action takes place upon the stage without its being at all apparent that the author is present, either in his own person or concealed to use the point of view of a character or number of characters. In effect, with a suppressed narrator it is very difficult to determine the character with the point of view, for the simple reason that the action unfolds before our gaze as though we, and not the author, established the significance and values of the events and characters. In both the preceding forms, the audience is aware, either overtly or covertly, of some point of view at work that clarifies theme, plot, and character. In the method of suppressed narrator, nothing seems to stand between portrayal of the events and the reader.

Actually, of course, these events have been selected by the author, who then removes himself completely from the scene. Thus, in this particular method, the only way in which to determine the views of the author is to regard what other words he might have chosen, what other scene he might have rendered for us. The attempt to get at the suppressed narrator's point of view, however, is mainly an academic one. The fact of our interest in the intelligence that has presented the action dramatically has little to do with our appreciation of the story. The story exists on its own feet, as it were, and it seems to state, "Well, here is what happens—make the most of it." It is, therefore at the opposite pole from the one using an omnipresent narrator where the author tells us his story while we loll about in easy chairs and listen to his voice.

With a suppressed narrator, there is no character who speaks a soliloquy, none who comes down to the footlights and lets us know what he thinks of the action. Each character is involved in the plot directly and immediately, and we must determine from the action both what he and the story are all about. Thus, all the reader or viewer can do is to appreciate what the characters are like from their outward appearance—whether cowardly, brutal, passive, frightened, or what have you—but this is not the same as to penetrate into the depths of character. The suppressed narrator, having effectively walked away from the vision he has conjured up, leaves it up to his reader to have the taste, the values, and the judgment to determine the significance of what is going on. The reader can know the characters only from what they reveal in speech and action. And the characters within the story are aware of one another, perhaps may even penetrate momentarily within the hidden recesses of another person's character, but only momentarily. What relationship exists between characters is found on the stage where the dramatist purposefully avoids a definite viewpoint.

An excellent illustration of the use of suppressed narrator is seen in Hemingway's "The Killers." In discussing the story in Chapter Five, we remarked that the shift in time perspective allowed Hemingway to emphasize dramatically the effect that the complication has upon peripheral characters. The tautness of the action, the avoidance of description, the use of a great deal of dialogue, and the focusing of the reader's gaze upon the setting in which the characters move, all these things belong to the more modern forms of drama. Like drama, too, our interest is never exclusively concentrated upon the speech and actions of any one character, for each in turn claims our concern. Nevertheless—and this pretty clearly separates the short story as a medium from the drama—no matter what point of view the author uses, the author must at one time or another use the viewpoint of one or more of his characters. On the stage, in movies, and in television plays, the authors can appeal only to sight and sound; the person watching interprets the drama by what the actors do and say. The audience knows, for example, that an actor is terrified by the look of terror on the actor's face; they interpret how an actor feels by the inflection in his voice. "The Killers" gives us an indication that no author is ever really capable of transforming the written word directly into dramatic action. He must, at some point or another, enter into a character's thoughts, even if only for a moment. It is here, in other words, that our analogy breaks down. Hemingway shows in "The Killers" a subtle, yet nonetheless explicit, use of the point of view of the concealed narrator from time to time. When Al orders George and Max to group themselves along the counter, we get a sentence that belongs to George's consciousness: "He [Al] was like a photographer arranging for a group picture." Or again, "George watched them, through the window, pass under the arc-light and across the street. In their tight overcoats and derby hats they looked like a vaudeville team."

It would seem fairly difficult to determine the main character in "The Killers" because, as we have previously indicated, the story functions to make a comment upon the mechanically organized existence that prohibits the effective functioning of individual human sympathies. The point of view of Nick Adams, like that of George, enters into the story; he is allowed to move away from events and view them on his own. Even so, the penetration into consciousness is on only a superficial level. The author appears to be less interested in character *per se* than he is in social forces meeting and colliding; and profound studies of character tend to subvert the revelation of externally imposed social pressures.

There are certain obvious advantages in using a suppressed narrator. The story gains whatever the drama offers in immediacy, raciness, action, and conflict. It is a subtle device; it is indirect. The reader must spot the tiny clues, the meaningful details with a minimum of help. There is a quality of lifelikeness. Finally, the story with a dramatic objective (our other term for a story that uses a suppressed narrator) is an effective way to deal with external events that act upon characters without involving us deeply in their psychology or the whole range of their personalities. Thus, it is most useful for exploring with cool objectivity the brutal facts of existence, or for dealing with patterns of existence that do not allow room for any liberation of the individual's desires.

There are disadvantages also in its use. The device of suppressed narrator has little to offer a story that must cover a sweep of events or of time; it is too immediate and too dramatic for that. Again, it obviously limits the author tremendously in building up or creating character. Character in such a story is not subtle, but exceedingly open; whatever exists below the surface remains hidden. The very objectivity in such a story rules out the subjective elements in life. As a result, its photographic quality may tend to place a serious curtailment on the rhythms of style that suggest the richness or amplitude of life.

The three ways of telling a story that have been discussed so far do not by any means exhaust the range of possibilities in point of view. For convenience, they have been listed in terms of the way an author can enter a story at will and speak in his own person, can conceal his own person and give the points of view of the characters, or eliminate himself entirely so that he disappears, leaving behind him an objective picture or vision of his theme. And as we have indicated, though these devices may be considered separately, the author of a quality story may fuse one with another. Stephen Crane accomplishes such a feat in "The Open Boat." Another master in the use of alternating points of view is F. Scott Fitzgerald. His story "The Jelly Bean" for example, begins with the comments of an omnipresent narrator, uses next the concealed narrator, turns then to use the suppressed narrator, and concludes by returning to the omnipresent narrator. Whatever appears to serve his purposes best in the story he makes use of; and as a consequence, the story gains from the tremendous range of values that alternating points of view can suggest. Once more, it seems worthwhile to point out that the great distinction to be made in handling point of view in pulp, slick, and quality stories depends on understanding the curtailment in viewpoint that is placed on its use in the first two types. The commercial writer must ordinarily confine the point of view to one character in the story, whichever is initially used. He does not have the liberty that the purely creative writer has to carry out his intentions.

Now let us turn to the discussion of the sorts of point of view represented by stories told in the first person. When we speak of a first-person story, what we indicate is that the author has himself moved within the frame of reference of the story; or he has concealed himself and he does not speak in his own person—he may conceal himself by speaking in the person of a minor character; or he may suppress his own point of view and adopt that of the protagonist. The analogies are obvious with the devices we have already discussed where we have seen distinctions based upon how thoroughly, or how little, the author reveals himself. In order to conceal or even to cloak his role, we have seen him manipulating various points of view as a concealed narrator, or using the techniques of modern drama as a suppressed narrator. So here, in first-person stories, the author speaks openly as himself, conceals himself as a minor character, or completely suppresses his character by adopting that of the major character. To distinguish among these forms, we will use the following terms:

1. Author as narrator
2. Minor-character narrator
3. Chief-character narrator

Author as narrator

Certain first-person stories exist in which the author speaks as himself in the story. It is true that relatively few authors wish to speak in their own persons, but sufficient numbers of such stories exist to merit more than passing attention.

Now immediately the reader may wonder how a story with an author-narrator differs from the one having a chief character narrator. After all, it would appear that in this case the author *is* the chief character. The significant point is that, even though he may be the chief character, he does not immerse himself in another character and use that character's point of view; he never loses his own personal identity.

One may mention, as examples, the stories of Colette in which she writes of Sido, her mother, and of herself as a young girl. And there are other stories in which Colette writes of herself as a music-hall performer, such as in the story "Gribiche," or of herself as a writer, such as in "Bella-Vista." Maxim Gorki's "One Autumn Night" and Dostoevsky's "The Peasant Marey" are also excellent illustrations of the first-person author-as-narrator type of construction. Another recent group of stories by Christopher Isherwood, *Down There on a Visit,* illustrates the fascination that autobiographical materials have for fiction. In these four stories, told by a narrator who is Isherwood himself, we get a revelation of Isherwood's own emotions from the 1920's up to the 1940's.

Authors who write as themselves in the first person show an awareness, frequently, of themselves as writers or as distinctive personalities. If they speak of the stress of circumstance in the formation of their lives, they are not self-conscious about revealing the strain. Dostoevsky in "The Peasant Marey" casually remarks at one point in the story: "Perhaps it will be noticed that even to this day I have scarcely once spoken in print of my life in prison. The *House of the Dead* I wrote fifteen years ago in the character of an imaginary person. . . ."

Of what value are such confessions? Is their interest purely biographical? Admittedly, such stories do not form a large group. Nonetheless, they are of great technical interest, just as they may be of great biographical interest. For here the fusion of fiction and fact appears to go on under our very eyes.

To see how in any story an author establishes his point of view is to expose the endlessly fascinating ways in which an author submerges himself within the materials of his story. The identification of the author with the characters in his story follows the very essentials of the artistic process since it is impossible for him otherwise to exploit the peculiar talent that is his: an ability to give himself up, as it were, to externals. Keats remarked of the talent as the "Negative Capability" of the poet; T. S. Eliot referred to the process as "the continuous extinction of personality." If Shakespeare found it necessary to be Othello, he certainly also found it necessary to be Iago. Yet in the type of story under discussion, it seems that the author as narrator manages to avoid this necessity.

For here we see an author making use, not alone of what we know of him as a character within the story, but also of what we know of his character outside the story as a means of enlarging the reader's interest. Within the story proper he functions as if he were as omniscient as the author who is concealed or outside the third-person story, with this distinction, that he is omniscient solely toward himself, not toward the other characters. He can, also, go outside the story proper, as Dostoevsky does—"I have scarcely once spoken in print of my life in prison"—to give impact to the dilemma that he wishes to write about in his prison existence. And what greater authority for the story can there be, we are led to think, than that of the author who tells a story about himself? His authority is, indeed, unlimited, for we are inclined to take what he says of himself as the willing self-revelation of a known person under crisis.

How are we to judge such stories? As stories? Or as mere autobiographical anecdotes? The first-person point of view does not always form the story's whole structure, though it contributes to its formation. If as Dostoevsky does in "The Peasant Marey," the author pictures himself in a dilemma and solves it, we have the structure of the short story underscored by a sense of the factually true, the biographically ascertainable. A writer who uses the technique skillfully has thus a golden opportunity to convert what appears to be fiction into what appears to be solid fact. At the same time we can be on our guard immediately. No man ever speaks the complete truth about himself, and those who are notorious inventors of fabled deeds about others may be no less inventive when they rewrite history in their own behalf. Whether their inventions are successful in such a form, it seems to us, is frequently disputable, if for no other reason than that fiction and fact mix together well only when fiction takes the precedence. Colette in "Bella-Vista" states: "I shall not finish my task as a writer without attempting, as I want to do here, to draw them [former acquaintances] out of the shadows to which the shameless necessity of speaking of love in my own name has consigned them." Some of her stories told in this fashion are her least successful.

Minor-character narrator

We have already pointed out the fact that certain slick stories use the point of view of a minor character within the story and that it is used in quality stories as well. There is little difference between this device and that of the first-person author narrator with this exception, that the author has now managed to conceal himself within a character who speaks in the first person and who exists at the periphery of the story's action.

One of the immediate advantages of such a device is that, given a sufficiently credible reason for participating in the action as an observer, the minor character can be used to give something of the Olympian view of the author himself without making it appear that the author is himself moralizing. Using such a narrator is very useful, therefore, when the chief characters are inexperienced or unaware of their problems. It has another advantage, too. Since the minor character is at the periphery of the action, he can back off from it, as it were, and view it as a whole, meditate upon its meaning, and treat the events elastically, summarizing the unimportant, or developing the important ones scenically. Difficulties in the method arise when we cannot accept as credible the appearance of the minor character in particular scenes, or when the minor character's involvement is weak. It sometimes occurs that the story told by a minor character is a good story, but that the reader can find little reason for the character's having known about it. The minor character's authority, therefore, is quite limited since he must be shown to be enough entangled in the complication so that his presence as a witness is solidly credible. Nevertheless, his is the authority of an eye witness, and looking through his eyes at an event can heighten or enhance the reality of the story. If a minor character's qualities are, to us, sympathetic—and in most cases they must be for him to be used at all—we not only get a report on the action, but a sense of the immediate and justifiable response to it through the eyes of someone whose opinion we value.

It may happen, however, that the minor character who is used as narrator is not either sympathetic or objective in his point of view; and the author must therefore use his biased and unfair report of the story for some positive effect. Technically this is difficult to do, for it is then more difficult to explain his presence as an observer, and not as a participant in the action. The very nature of the device seems to demand, as a rule, that the first-person observer be objective and sympathetic, though emotionally involved in the action. It is for this reason that we have spoken of the author's point of view being concealed within the minor character. He can, thus, enter his own story as a witness and gain whatever elements of credibility an eye-witness account can give without using the more cumbersome device of speaking in his own person. We mentioned previously the use of this device in C. Y. Lee's "The Casanova of Kearny Street." That the author's point of view is concealed in the minor character does not mean, of course, that such a character has no personality in his own right. It seems generally essential, however, that he have one aspect of the author's personality, an objective yet sympathetic interest in the characters of the story; and it is for this reason, alone, that it seems justifiable to consider the minor-character narrator to be, in fact, a mask for the author.

Chief-character narrator

The final means of establishing the point of view is for the author to suppress his own personality completely in that of the chief character of the story. Here, there is no problem about explaining the involvement of the character in the story, for the action of the story is his action. First-person stories of all kinds are told by and from the viewpoint of the chief character.

William Saroyan's "The Circus" begins in this fashion:

Any time a circus used to come to town, that was all me and my old pal Joey Renna needed to make us run hog-wild, as the saying is. All we needed to do was see the signs on the fences and in the empty store windows to start going to the dogs and neglecting our educations. All we needed to know was that a circus was on its way to town for me and Joey to start wanting to know what good a little education ever did anybody anyway.

It is obvious that such a story depends upon the thoughts and feelings of the hero—what passes in his mind and how events act upon him form the story.

In both the points of view represented by the author as narrator and minor-character narrator, the author seems to have more freedom to allow his first-person spokesman to form conclusions about what goes on in the minds of other characters and in his own mind than he does when the central character is the narrator. The reason for this is apparent when one reflects upon the fact that the author in both the first two types has not had to disguise his omniscience so completely as he does when he uses the chief character's point of view. As a consequence, one very frequently finds in stories where the viewpoint of the protagonist is used an interesting technical problem; the protagonist will tell the story without truly understanding what he tells although the reader will. The protagonist, whose point of view is given in the story, may be absolutely blind to the nature of the complication, and the reader, therefore, finds a dramatic interplay between what he sees and understands as the story develops and what the protagonist fails to grasp. A good many stories of this sort deal with the eventual recognition by the chief character of his blindness.

In all stories told in the first person, the editorial rule governing point of view applies, though as we have seen where an author himself is telling the story he is privileged to range into the materials of his own life and to bring them into the story proper. Otherwise, stories told in the first person absolutely require that the first-person narrator cover only that portion of the action that he can personally observe or deduce.

It is not to be expected that the inexperienced writer will be able to profit immediately from all the material set forth in this chapter. First, in order for him to do so would require him to attempt to use devices for which he is still not fully prepared in terms of his own experience. In the second place, he must also make a special study on his own of every story he reads in order to investigate the problems that are solved by the use of particular viewpoints. We have only pointed out the general ways point of view can be used, for otherwise what we have written would have become prohibitive in length. To repeat, the inexperienced writer should discipline himself by telling his story in the first person if he has any trouble at all with faulty point of view. And he should confine himself to the single third-person viewpoint of his protagonist until he has become successful and believes himself qualified to experiment, either by telling a story through the eyes of a minor character, or by using more than a single point of view.

EXERCISES FOR CHAPTER 6

1. You will have already written a formula story by this time. Now you should take this story and invent a credible minor character who views the story's events. What losses and what gains might occur in retelling the story in such a fashion? In telling the story from the point of view of an omnipresent narrator? Or in using any of the other points of view mentioned?

2. Read the following stories and determine what points of view their authors used: Jean Giono's "The Corn Dies"; Katherine Mansfield's "A Dill Pickle"; Joseph Conrad's "Heart of Darkness"; Ernest Hemingway's "In Another Country."

3. Define the difference between point of view and focus of interest. In what types of point of view must these two things be identical? Why?

4. How do the following things indicate a fault in the point of view adopted: frequently overheard conversations; chance meetings; coincidences; lengthy explanations accounting for a character's presence?

7 How Professional Writers Employ Exposition, Description, Action, and Narration— and the Use of Symbolism

THE PREVIOUS CHAPTERS have dealt with plot and structure in the story. Plotting, as we have pointed out, depends upon recognizing a complication, realizing through an understanding of the protagonist's character how he will deal with it, and understanding the implications of such a confrontation between character and complication in order to choose the right fictional curve and point of view for the story. The ability to plot is not necessarily an inherent ability. Practically anyone, with practice and experience, can learn to plot.

But now we come to the art and craft of composition, the aspect of short-story writing that does demand inherent ability. It seems safe to state that not everyone has an equal facility with everyone else in the use of the basic tools of composition, for they demand an innate talent in the imaginative handling of words to convey pictures, sights, sounds, information, and so on. The basic elements of prose composition are exposition, description, action, and narration. Despite the fact that the skillful use of these elements demands individual talent, certain techniques within each one can be explained as a way of helping the inexperienced writer to expose and explore his own ability. And there is an important subsidiary tool for the beginning writer to consider, for with it, a writer can transform the literal elements in exposition, description, action, and narration to a wider and more inclusive sphere. This tool is the use of symbolism.

EXPOSITION

We turn, then, to the first of the four elements we have mentioned. What is exposition?

> *Exposition is the way the reader is given the knowledge of past circumstances that he must have to understand and believe in the story and characters.*

Faulty exposition—one of the most common causes of failure in the work of beginning writers—destroys a story in two ways: one, faulty exposition burdens a story with needless detail and explanation that smother the action; two, the characters, laboring under faulty exposition, become unrealistic and the story becomes unbelievable. Both failures arise because the words used to convey information lie outside the story proper: they are the writer's words, not the words of the characters; and especially if the structure of the story allows him to speak in his own person, the writer may overlook what is really essential in the complication and succumb to telling everything.

The detection of faulty exposition is easy. For example, when two characters for no visible reason give facts about the past to each other of which both characters are aware, then the words are the writer's and not the characters'. In order to correct such flaws, the writer should use one of the following devices:

> *I. To impart needed information to the reader, bring in a character who also needs the information.*

An effective example of this technique occurs in Chekhov's story "Old Age." Uzelkov, the architect, in returning to his home town after an absence of eighteen years, questions a hall-porter as to whether or not the hall-porter remembered the famous divorce case between Uzelkov and his wife. Does the hall-porter know Shapkin, the notorious shyster lawyer? Yes, Shapkin is still alive; he is prospering. Had Chekhov had Uzelkov go immediately to Shapkin's house, it would have seemed a much less credible way to convey this essential information.

To clarify the use of the technique further, here is an example from a slick story. The information the author wanted to convey to the reader, because it is important later in the story, is that Helen Sutton jilted Tony Marco several years before the opening scene takes place. The story is told from the point of view of Bill Wegher, who already possesses the information. Present in the scene is his wife, Dorothy, who also possesses the information. The author brings in a third person, Jerry Pearson, who has not seen Bill or Tony since their college days:

"The years have been kind to you, Bill," Jerry said, as Dorothy served them coffee. "A prosperous business, a nice home, a wife who is not only beautiful but a wonderful cook, and two fine boys. I suppose Tony and Helen have a houseful of kids by now. Tony always said when they were married he was going to raise a baseball team."

Bill felt uneasy as he looked at his wife who nodded her head sadly. He took a deep breath. Jerry had idolized Tony during their college days.

"Helen jilted Tony and married a man you don't know, named Steve Braddock, several years ago."

Jerry just sat there staring at the creases on the table cloth he was making with his spoon.

"And Tony?" he finally asked without looking up.

"He never married," Bill said. "He's a lonely man, hurting inside all the time."

II. Let two characters in possession of the information bring it out during an argument.

Arguments disturb old memories. An excellent illustration occurs in Ernest Hemingway's "The Snows of Kilimanjaro" in which the protagonist's situation—his gangrenous leg and approaching death— as well as the relationship with his wife and the sense of class distinction between the man and woman are related for us bit by bit in terms of dialogue.

Here is another example, taken from a slick magazine. The information the author must convey to the reader is that before George Manners married Alice Carver, he used faithfully to take her out to parties or to a dance every Saturday night. The story is told from Alice's point of view:

Alice knew exactly what she'd see when she entered the living room. Good old George would be sprawled out in the easy chair with a can of beer and a bowl of pretzels on the end table. There he would sit staring at the television until bed time, leaving the room only to get another

123

can of beer or go to the bathroom. It had been the same every Saturday night since their honeymoon. Well, good old George was due for a surprise tonight. She wiped the last of the dishes, took off her apron, and walked into the living room.

What a pleasure it was to march over to the T.V. set and turn it off. Good old George couldn't have looked more surprised if she'd said she wanted a divorce.

"What's the idea, hon?" he asked.

"We are going out tonight, George," she said, making her voice as firm as possible.

"Out where?" he asked with a shrug.

"I want to go where there are people, laughter, music, and fun," Alice said, feeling better just by saying it.

"But there's a good fight on T.V. tonight," he protested.

"There's been a good fight on T.V. every Saturday night since we moved into this apartment," she said. "I've been cooped up here day and night since we got back from our honeymoon."

"You know we are trying to save enough money to buy a new car," he said getting up and walking over to the T.V. set.

Alice felt as if he'd struck her as she heard the click of the dial.

"You used to take me out dancing and to parties every Saturday night before we were married," Alice said, as she felt a tear. . . .

III. Other forms of emotion raised by a particular situation may cause a character to review the past and thus convey needed information.

When two people suddenly meet one another, it frequently happens that an element of their past relationship emerges in terms of the self-pity of one of the characters. Other emotions will do as well as self-pity, such as reminiscent nostalgia for the past on the part of the characters, for example. Nostalgia, however, may be said to be only another form of self-pity, for it implies that a change has occurred for the worse in the lives of characters: the past beckons and gleams as a golden age of unconscious happiness. Of the two stories chosen as illustrations, one we have previously remarked upon, Katherine Mansfield's "A Dill Pickle"; the other is F. Scott Fitzgerald's "Babylon Revisited." In "A Dill Pickle," as we have observed, Vera meets a man she loved in the past and recaptures that past through nostalgic reminiscence, which conveys to the reader what he once meant to her.

In "Babylon Revisited," the protagonist, a leading irresponsible spirit among a group of expatriate Americans living in Paris, returns to a bar, one of his former haunts, after an absence of eighteen months. There he talks to the barman and we have the mood of that collapse of excitement and frenzy that accompanied the stock market crash of 1929. The story is a very effective example of past events being retold in dialogue between the protagonist and a former acquaintance.

IV. The central character may review the past and through his own unspoken thoughts give the needed information.

An effective example of this method is found in Herbert Gold's "Love and Like." The protagonist calls his wife from whom he has been separated for a month, and after the conversation on the telephone, we get a recapitulation in his own unspoken thoughts of their ten-year-old marriage and the suggestion of what has caused the split between them.

Here is another example taken from a pulp story. The information the author wants to convey is about Stella Marshal, the central character, her husband Roger, whom she caught on the rebound, and Vangie Harrison, the woman who first attracted Roger. Some time has passed since the marriage took place:

Stella could almost hear Edna Farley purring as she hung up the receiver. Trust Edna to be the first to let her know that Vangie was back in town and divorced from Tom Singleton. Anger gave way to uneasiness as Stella looked around the living room of the home she loved. But it would not be a home to love without a husband to love. She had loved Roger since childhood but believed it to be a hopeless love. She had never had a chance against Vangie, who even as a small girl had small boys fighting for her favors. Like everyone else in town she had believed marriage between Roger and Vangie was inevitable.

Then a miracle had happened. Tom Singleton had come to town and after a whirlwind courtship, he and Vangie had eloped. Stella was more than willing to catch Roger on the rebound. She would never forget that day just a couple of months after Vangie's elopement when he'd asked her for their first date.

The reader then remains transported in the past while Stella relives in her memory that date, the courtship, and her marriage to Roger.

The inexperienced writer should always test his stories in terms of the effectiveness of their exposition, making certain that all needed information is conveyed not in his own words but in the words of his characters. Such a prescription holds good for all kinds of stories except those that use an omnipresent narrator. Here it is obvious that the author purposively enters the story, very frequently with a message of his own; and here there is great danger that the combination of message, explanation, and background of past circumstances may prove to be over-great temptations leading to wordiness and inflation. About the only way in which to avoid all the pitfalls in exposition is to treasure the following precept:

> *The writer must keep constantly before his mind and the mind of his readers the complication in which the protagonist is involved.*

In such a way only is it possible for the author to avoid bringing in what can only be extraneous.

DESCRIPTION

Description is the way the writer appeals to the reader's five senses in order to make the story's characters and setting real and believable.

In order to make his story believable, the writer must be able to arouse an emotional response in the reader by letting him look, feel, taste, smell, and hear through the words written on the printed page. (This is not to mention other aspects of the use of language, such as rhythm, rhyme, alliteration, assonance, and other devices whereby a writer may appeal to the reader's senses.)

An older fashion in story writing, based no doubt upon a less time-conscious generation's reading habits, allowed the writer to indulge himself in using description. Today, however, readers will not tolerate lengthy descriptive passages except in quality stories, and even in those, the descriptions must serve to advance the complication, the characterization, the action of the story.

I. Description is very important in making the characters real to the reader.

As an illustration, let us take the following:

Johnny was of medium height with sandy hair and gray eyes. He was twenty-three years old and a veteran with four years service in the South Pacific.

Here we have, instead of a person, a photograph. Now let us appeal to the reader's senses of sight and feeling, and see if we cannot breathe some life into Johnny:

The war had robbed his face of its youth. He was only twenty-three, but there were wrinkles around his mouth from compressing his lips during battle. Countless nights of squinting into the black nothingness from a foxhole had etched crows feet under his eyes. His sandy hair was bleached with spots of white from the tropical sun. Deep shadows under his high cheek bones gave him a gaunt, almost hungry look. Watching men die during four years of dirty infantry fighting in the South Pacific had sucked the life from his gray eyes. He was a young man with an old man's face.

II. Description must never be extraneous to the complication.

Such a rule, phrased with all the exactitude of scientific law, nevertheless allows a good deal of latitude, for it is obvious that the broader the complication, the more extensive survey an author can give of the external setting of his story. For example, the very beginning of Aldous Huxley's "Young Archimedes," as we have previously noted, covers the view of landscape surrounding the protagonist's villa. Yet, as we also noted, certain dominant features of the description are carried over to convey to the reader the nature of the complication. A reader will do well to state the complication of any story he reads and then study the descriptive material in order to see how the author has managed to keep the senses of the reader alerted to the story's dramatic content.

One of the great paradoxes of the imaginative work of art is that it evokes real experience. Perhaps this will not be paradoxical for those who take their imaginations as both literal and evocative. But it is truly one of the difficult feats of the human mind to imagine reality. Who can imagine the scent of mimosa mingling with a dull political speech on a rainy Sunday afternoon? What is so paradoxical is that the imagined experience communicates on the concrete level at the same time as it may be modified by, and modifies, the structure of the short story. In the same way the imagination of the artist is controlled by, and at the same time controls, his structure.

One must consider that there is far more to description, therefore, than simply those passages which, *en bloc,* as it were, set a scene or an atmosphere; description also consists of those bits or pieces of depiction that interweave with the action, the narration, and the exposition to give a story body—and the word *body* can be taken quite literally as meaning the flesh, the blood, the nervous system, the entire living aspect of what is contrived. Certainly, the only stories that live for the reader—whether or not the reader is aware of the exaggerations contained within the story—are those in which the experiences of the story function in terms of sense impressions. It is good advice that states that the writer must cultivate the sharpness and firmness of his own sensations. He must be aware of the direct and immediate cause, rather than the effects, of his impressions, for only by communicating through the senses will the writer be able to produce an effect on the reader. Make the coins "chink," remarks Chekhov, rather than emit a merely pleasant sound.

Yet although the writer must strive constantly to evoke sense impressions, he also faces the danger that such descriptions will escape control and begin to substitute themselves as claimants on the reader's attention, rather than advance the action, the characterization, the multiplicity of structural interests that lie within the story. One of the striking things, for example, about the initial stories of students who possess sensitivity is that while the range of their impressions may be great, and at times sharp and clear, the whole of what they write lacks order, unity, and narrative excitement. The sensory detail swamps the interest, and everything becomes evocative without direction. Sense impressions must be so structured in the story that they do not serve as actors in their own right, apart from their ultimate effects on the whole structure.

In other words, the description of sense impressions forms another way in which the writer can exaggerate life and bring artifice to his story. How vital these same impressions may be in real life is debatable, yet the minute they form part of the structure, they cause added reality and interest.

If this is true, description should not occur only as one writes the story, but should be a part of the planned effect, the whole conception held by the writer. Not alone will it suffice to determine to write with sensitivity to external impressions; one must order that sensitivity from the start. Certain stories will exclude certain sensory images; they have no right to be in a particular story, though they may be right in another story. They are right for one character and wrong for another. They are right for one point of view and wrong for another. The right sensory experience, in essence, forms the most intimate approach possible to an appreciation of the whole story, and it destroys that appreciation the more it ceases to work for it.

Two short stories will illustrate how authors gifted with an ability to render the "feel" of things manage to state the complication in terms of sensory impressions. One is a story by Ivan Turgenev entitled "Byézhin Meadow." The other story, which appeared in *Esquire* (July, 1958), was written by Anthony C. West, and is entitled "Song of the Barrow."

In the simplest terms, "Byézhin Meadow" deals with the adventures of a hunter during one day, one night, and the following morning. He has hunted during the day. Toward dusk he turns homeward only to lose his way, spends the night near the encampment of four boys who are out pasturing horses, and with the sunrise he returns to his home. The action would seem hardly sufficient to hang much of a story on, but a story is indeed implicit in the complication and emerges through the sensory images the author uses. The daylight at the very beginning is slowly diminishing—but it had been a time primarily of light, light which dispells vain fancies and is ideal for daily tasks. It "is the sort of weather which the farmer craves for harvesting his grain." The conclusion of the story, with the dawn, returns to the conception of the dark-dispersing light, and "everything began to stir, awoke, began to sing, to make a noise, to chatter." Within these two poles of light, connecting them and contrasting with them, we learn of the hunter's getting lost in the growing darkness, of his many sensations of foreboding and perplexity, of desperation and fright, and finally of the hunter's stumbling across the welcome encampment of the boys, where he presently lies down to sleep. But instead of sleeping, he overhears the boys telling one another fearful and superstitious tales about demons in nature, inexplicable events, drownings, and reappearances of the dead. The night evokes and incarnates the primitive consciousness of man. It frightens him with vague and shadowy fears. It forces him to invent a spirit world to account for, as well as to substantiate, his fears. It comes as an extreme irony, therefore, when the hunter reveals at the very end—once more safely back in daylight, once more in the midst of a beautiful, and hardly fear-inspiring, universe—that one of the boys, the one he most admired, later died. The boy's death occurred through no more supernatural an event than a fall from his horse; and the narrator concludes with a statement that belongs to the world of daylight reality: " 'Tis a pity, for he was a splendid young fellow!"

In "Song of the Barrow," the protagonist faces at the age of fourteen the perplexing ambiguities of life, and these ambiguities are not only concerned with springtime and youth, but also with death and the identity of men who must face, not changeless institutions, but their own common mortality. The central experience concerns the

129

boy's going on a hoped-for Saturday during May down to the peat bogs to watch the men at work, to tumble with other lads, to feel the dazing contentment of the warm spring day. While there, near the lake, he observes a school of spawning bream, and shouts out the cry. Immediately the men desert their work to tumble in the water, almost insensate in their excitement; and a lad whom the protagonist had admired for having arrived at strong-backed manhood is drowned. The father laments, the men work over the lifeless body after bringing it back to the shore, and the protagonist takes his unnoticed leave, walking slowly away, having met for the first time the mortality of man, the fact of change itself. Though sensory impressions abound in the story, the chief one is that of sound: the sound of the barrow's wooden wheel whining on the axle-tree, the sound of wind-swept branches, the humming of a flight of bees, and the lugubrious slow toll of the church bell. The first elements of the story deepen and intensify. They increase during the story, so that the sounds coalesce to form an experience of life; we define life itself in terms of youth's thoughtlessness, awakening perplexity, and finally that loss which is at the same time a gain, the melancholy knowledge of the whole cycle of mortal man. This is the story, then: sense impressions exaggerated to form a whole, turning the disparate and separate experiences of life into a unity.

III. In order to make description function to state a complication, use indirect rather than direct statement.

A story submitted by a student will serve as an illustration. The story was by no means original in plot, but for the most part it was well told and convincing. A cowboy of some thirty-odd years of experience saw one day a wild stallion out on the range. He was so smitten by the looks of the horse that he just had to capture it. He tried and failed. The stallion was too intelligent to be trapped. The summer faded away into winter, and one wintry day, while rounding up strays, the cowboy saw the horse again. It had stolen some of the hay left out on the range to keep the cattle from starving. The cowboy once again tried to capture it, but his mare was not fleet enough in the drifts, and the stallion got away. The cowboy returned to the ranch and took care of his horse:

Now I knew I had to own that horse. The game had become one whose stakes were his freedom or my peace of mind. We could not exist together in the same country. Never in my thirty-one years of ranching

130

had one animal so outwitted and humiliated me. As I rubbed down my weary mare, I vowed I would catch that horse; for I knew there would be no rest for me until this free spirit had been chained by my own power.

Here we have a direct statement of the complication, and there is a flatness to it, a repetitive lifeless quality, that tends to detract from our appreciation of the situation.

In order to bring the story to life again, we must resort to sensory impressions; and it is necessary, then, to capture them at the moment when the cowboy's unspoken thoughts are being given to the reader. What is the cowboy doing during that moment? By describing what he does in terms of sense impressions, it is possible to state the complication indirectly:

The mare's flanks trembled as he rubbed her down. From her back in the dusky light of the barn rose a slight steam. The heavy, sweet-sour smell of hay and sweat and animals that thirty years of cowpunching had taught him were in the man's nostrils as he worked. He rubbed down the mare's slight legs remembering the flashing gait of the stallion as it seemed to fly headlong and careless through the drifts. He heard once again the snort as the great animal reared its proud head and turned. The man stopped in his work to look at the face of the mare. Her nostrils were not curved and proud, nor was her head high. She seemed to droop with the cold ride, and her dark eyes were mournful, yet trusting. The proud eyes of the stallion had flashed across the wintry waste, and the man wondered at that free spirit out there in the snow. He rubbed the mare's neck affectionately. Yet his mind was with that other animal, too proud to be curbed, disdainful in the ripple of his muscles, even in the winter preferring cold to his need and hunger.

Of course, the descriptive passage tends to be longer. The writer must judge for himself whether or not the direct or indirect statement is preferable at any given moment of the story. Yet if a story is to live, the writer must be careful to weigh the gains against the losses, and he may often serve his purpose and keep his story alive by means of descriptive details, which stimulate the reader's senses.

ACTION

Action allows the reader to participate vicariously in a scene through identifying himself with the character.

Some texts consider the use of dialogue and action separately. We shall consider them as being, for all practical purposes, one and the same, as they are in their effect on the reader. Action is used for the following purposes.

I. Only the most dramatic and exciting scenes in a short story are to be put into action.

We will study later how to select such scenes. For the time being it is essential to understand the differences between action and narration. Narration is a discourse in which events are related chronologically so that they become compressed and swift in the telling. Action, like narration, also renders events chronologically, but with the intention of exploring these events in terms of scene, giving their minutiae, their look, their feel.

Here, for example, is narration:

Tena left the Forester house in tears, ran home, and confronted Earnest, distraught by her failure to help him.

The same events retold as action might read like this:

As Tena left the Forester house, she pressed a handkerchief to her eyes to check the sudden flow of tears. She was still crying when she arrived home.

Earnest walked across the room and took her in his arms.

"Oh, Earnest," she cried pitifully, "they wouldn't listen to me, and I was so sure I could make them understand."

"Please don't cry."

"I can't help it," she wailed. "From the time you were a little boy, I've always been able to help you . . . to nurse you when you were sick . . . to help you solve your problems. And now, now when you're faced with the greatest crisis of your life, I can't do a thing. I feel so helpless, so useless. . . ."

By allowing the reader to participate in the action, we have helped to make Tena's plight more realistic, and we have aroused an emotional response in the reader by letting him know how Tena feels about her failure.

II. The writer must avoid using too much action in his stories. To do so is to write under the mistaken belief that action is always more exciting, dramatic, and interesting than exposition, description, and narration.

The beginning writer fails frequently to realize that only a very few scenes in the chronological and formula story merit being portrayed in action. He will do well, for example, to draw a red line in the margin of the stories he is reading to indicate scenes of action and to study how relatively little space they occupy in the short story.

Interestingly enough, however, the experienced creative writer may develop his story so that it is told primarily in action or dialogue. Such a statement is true of Irwin Shaw's "The Girls in Their Summer Dresses," Ernest Hemingway's "The Killers," and Chekhov's "Old Age." And quality stories exist in which action, as we have defined it, is kept to a minimum and much of the story is narrated or lies in description, as for example in James Joyce's "A Painful Case."

III. A cardinal rule to remember about action is that it slows down the pace of a story and tends to work against the effect of compression.

A scene that takes five hundred words to portray in action can be told in fifty words of narration. Those writers who take any form of dramatic entertainment, such as television plays, motion pictures, and stage plays as their models, may gain a mistaken notion about the importance of action in the short story. In all the dramatic media, there must be action: characters must do something, say something, or both. The story works its way out by means of dialogue and movement; but the writer who employs action exclusively—unless he has studied how to compress his complication—will find he loses pace and speed and writes overlong works in place of the brisk narratives he hoped for.

IV. Action is also a useful way to make description more animated, interesting, and believable.

One of the chief flaws of description, no matter how good and effective it may be, is that it tends toward the static; or perhaps one can say that the only thing that moves is the observer's eye (and hence the reader's eye) as it looks at a person, or a place, or an object. For example, the static quality of description emerges here:

The small hotel room had cracked and peeling wall paper. The furniture was battered and needed painting. The carpet was worn so threadbare the floor boards showed through in several places. It was about as shabby a hotel room as Dan Hogan had ever seen.

Note how the use of action can bring the description more to life:

Dan Hogan got up from the creaking bed and after stretching, looked around the small hotel room with its cracked and peeling wall paper.

133

He walked in his bare feet across a carpet so threadbare the soles of his feet touched the floor boards in several places. He put his hands on the battered dresser. It needed painting. He stared at his face in the cracked mirror. He shook his head slowly. This was the crummiest hotel room he'd ever seen.

NARRATION

Narration is a discourse in which events are related chronologically so that they become compressed and swift in the telling; narration does not allow the reader to participate in the action.

Although in our discussion of action we have already defined narration, we have repeated the definition here and clarified it by adding one important ingredient.

I. Narration is employed to keep a story moving.

Narration allows one to write with extreme compression. It is the only way a writer can give rapidly the movements and actions of the story's characters. Hence, a story that is too long or appears to drag in spots can be speeded up by using narration. In the example cited above, the narrative account of Tena's actions was given in nineteen words; the same actions rendered dramatically employed one hundred and twenty.

II. Narration, as the workhorse of fiction, not only allows one to write with compression, but it also has an important function in characterization.

Description, particularly of facial features, is a common enough way of characterizing people—quite apart from the other means of developing character. Managed skillfully, description need not have a static quality, although it tends toward such an attribute. To render character by narration, however, voids the rigid pose and helps to capture essentials. One might compare the following passages, for example: the first, descriptive; the second, narrative.

Sam Smith had a long, lean, melancholy, and sullen visage. Eyes of a dirty yellowish hue glared from under bushy eyebrows that drooped down in sagging arcs to give him the look of a beaten dog that will nevertheless bite the hand that feeds it.

Sam Smith came home drunk, kicked the dog, put his kids to bed without supper, and then beat up his wife.

III. Narration can make a reader believe something that if put into action would be totally unbelievable. The use of narration disguises the improbable that would glare out in action.

If one put into action Sam Smith's coming home drunk, kicking his dog, sending his children to bed without supper, and then beating up his wife, the reader would find it difficult, if not impossible, to believe that any man could be so contemptible. Narration, because of its rapidity, allows the reader to swallow what would otherwise be rejected as improbable.

An interesting illustration of how narration persuades the reader to accept the incredible occurs in Robert Louis Stevenson's "The Sire de Malétroit's Door." The story is interesting, also, in terms of several other aspects of short-story writing, for in it we have the very essence of the use of exaggeration to give an effect of verisimilitude. A young man of honor is persuaded by circumstance and a girl's character to fall in love, with a love so sincere that it prevents the almost certain death that would have been the lot of the young man had he failed to love. Probably no man in the history of the short story has had the alternatives of love and death so forcibly thrust upon him as young Denis de Boileau in this story—and it is not entirely certain that Stevenson was not teasing about the improbability of romantic love by turning the story into a satirical farce with still some rudiments clinging to it of realistic psychology. However that may be, the story turns upon the fact that Denis de Boileau must somehow be conveyed into the house of the girl's uncle, who represents the enemy, without a possibility of escape. Stevenson has him stay at a friend's house until late at which time it is dangerous to go about the streets, has him meet a roistering crew of soldiers who would as lief kill him as ask questions, and has him seek escape through a door that opens to him and then closes fast upon him without any apparent means of reopening. Narration is here combined with action to make the events believable to the reader. The minute the door has closed upon Denis de Boileau, Stevenson resorts to action to show Denis's attempts to reopen the door. Such is the technique of a skilled writer who realizes that he is forcing his reader to believe the improbable and who first uses narration and then turns swiftly to action to make the whole account believable. That is to say, we accept the narration to begin with, and then to dispel any lingering doubts in our minds, the writer turns to action as a way of supporting our belief. If we are given the unbelievable in narration, it seems that we move rapidly into simple faith when we are given the opportunity to inspect the way a person will act directly afterwards under the established circumstances.

IV. Another important function of narration is that it establishes the past for the reader. In the middle of the plot of the formula story, the reader must have conveyed to him the circumstances that produced the complication and the best way to do this is by narration.

In Katherine Mansfield's story "The Fly" the author uses narration to transport the reader into the past:

It had been a terrible shock to him when old Woodifield sprang that remark upon him about the boy's grave. It was exactly as though the earth had opened and he had seen the boy lying there with Woodifield's girls staring down at him. For it was strange. Although over six years had passed away, the boss never thought of the boy except as lying unchanged, unblemished in his uniform, asleep forever.

Now if a writer knew nothing about exposition, description, action, and narration, nevertheless, in writing a short story he would use all four of these elements. His exposition might be faulty, his description weak, and he might use action when he should have used narration, or narration when he should have used action, but he would use these four elements because there just is no other way to write a short story.

SYMBOLISM

It may seem, in view of what we have said above, that symbolism is an extraneous consideration. And in terms of the use of symbols to characterize, to stand for ideas, to represent values, to give a visual "handle" to an abstraction, symbolism might more profitably be considered elsewhere. But there is one function of symbolism that is not extraneous to the materials in this chapter and makes it necessary to consider it here. That function is to present in a brief, vividly graphic fashion what would otherwise have to be given in much lengthier, and perhaps less satisfactory, exposition, description, narration, or action. When a symbol is used to compress the structure of a short story, it becomes a means of bypassing one or the other of these four elements.

Since we must touch upon the general subject then, let us deal with it in its entirety, and consider the special ways that symbolism may be used as a structural device to avoid using one of the four basic tools of composition.

It has become fashionable among writers of quality stories to make use of symbolism rather extensively, to show a preference for indirect means of presentation rather than for the explicitly direct. The advantages gained by using symbolism are many and varied, and the disadvantages, especially for the inexperienced writer, numerous, also. Let us first define symbolism, and then look at the way writers use symbols, as well as at the dangers that exist when the unskilled use them.

> *A symbol is a visible sign that stands for or suggests something else, a person, place, idea, attitude, value, feeling, or action. A symbol is, therefore, a concrete object used to suggest the nature or attributes of something that is usually, though not always, abstract.*

Certain symbols have a simple and uncomplicated relationship with the things they symbolize. For example, an arrow indicating a curve on a road sign suggests no more than a curve in the direction the arrow points. The conventional marks of punctuation symbolize a pause, a break, a question, an exclamation, a list of things to follow, and so on. A double yellow line on the highway symbolizes danger, a no-passing zone, or a direction in the line of traffic. In none of these instances are symbols multiple in significance. We have been trained from our earliest years to recognize many symbols of this nature.

Although the writer may use such symbols, he generally does so in terms of their usual significance. He does not try to obscure their meaning or to reinterpret their significance. After all, he is bound, as the reader is bound, to give conventional meanings to conventional symbols. On the other hand, the writer may wish to use a concrete object as a symbol to represent things, or ideas, or values that he would otherwise find difficult to state directly. And since his whole effort in writing is to bring the reader to feel a sense of the multiplicity of issues and emotions that inhere in and arise from any given moment of his story, he frequently has to resort to symbolism. Thus, for instance, the riding whip of Cipolla in Thomas Mann's story "Mario and the Magician" is not only a mark of the hypnotist who needs something that will make a noise to bring people out of a trance; it also suggests the brutality of the man, the coercive drive of the

137

Fascist to control the masses, the sense of superiority of Cipolla himself, as well as the overweening nationalistic sense of superiority of an entire nation momentarily gone demented. It would take a great deal of exposition, description, narration, and action to bring these as forcibly to the reader's attention as Thomas Mann has done by giving Cipolla a whip.

Since the writer is bound to give conventional meanings to conventional symbols, we must therefore divide symbols into two main classes. First, there are conventional symbols whose meanings have been established by long practice and long use. The skull is the emblem of death; the fern and the flower symbolize life, youth, and hope; winter is the season of decadence, death, or sterility; spring is the season of rejuvenation and regeneration; the fallen leaf is the fallen hope, or the blasted or the wasted; the new buds mean renewed vitality; the rose is love; and water is spiritually cleansing; the song of the nightingale is the sad song of ravished love; and the song of the turtledove, happy love and fulfillment. But there are other symbols whose meaning lies not so much in the conventional terms of their usage as in the private world of the author's imagination and their use in a particular story. Such, for example, is the meaning of rain in Somerset Maugham's story "Rain"; the meaning of the pickle in Katherine Mansfield's story "A Dill Pickle"; and the meaning of gooseberries in Chekhov's story "Gooseberries." And an author may frequently trade upon the conventional meanings implicit within a concrete object— the way Thomas Mann does in "Mario and the Magician"—to expand the conventional meaning within the world imagined for us. Perhaps in this way, certain authors demonstrate their imaginative power: to make a conventional symbol yield new meanings, in addition to the old, indicates an author's awareness of both past and present.

There are two different ways to use symbolism in a story:

I. Symbols have a functional use in the story to represent character, place, idea, attitude, value, or emotion.

The word *functional* is here opposed to the word *structural*. It means simply that the use of the symbol is dependent on the explicit or direct statement of the complication. If one removes the symbol, the story, though maimed, will still be a story.

To multiply examples is not really necessary, for some examples have already been given, and the reader will be able to discover—in fact, is often too prone to discover—symbolic meanings within the literal facts of any given story. Nevertheless, very satisfactory uses of the symbolic occur, as we have hinted, in Hemingway's use of the characters within "The Killers." And a really imposing use of symbol occurs in D. H. Lawrence's story "The Rocking-Horse Winner." Those who have read the story will recognize that the complication consists of a family's, particularly a mother's, desire for money that crushes and thwarts the natural maternal love she feels for her children. In order to secure his mother's love, her little son Paul determines to become "lucky"; that is, to earn or somehow acquire money so that she will be unable not to love him. The story thus deals with a curiously ironic perversion of values: the mother's withholding her love because of her materialism and practicality, the boy's using intuition to acquire money for the sake of his nonmaterial yet vital need for maternal love. The irony carries over into the rocking-horse, which he rides to "pick a winner," and which being used as a symbol has many implications. It is a child's toy used for an "office," a business, a way of earning money. It is itself a material bit of luxury for the child who uses it to gain another "luxury," maternal love. The boy's riding on it duplicates in a graphic fashion a real horse race; but, of course, the rocking-horse never arrives at a finish line: it can move up and down but never go forward. It, therefore, symbolizes the boy's distortion of his own nature and his inevitable failure to win love from his mother. And the mother, in acquiring money, wants more and more. The gambler's psychology, which the boy, a mere child, takes upon himself, is a complete obstruction in terms of any emotional winning. The terribly withdrawn and violent way the boy rides the horse expresses an alienation from the world as a means of winning the world for his mother. The rocking-horse is not a real horse, but a make-believe horse, like the make-believe world in which the mother indulges herself and which the boy attempts to ride into. The story, in short, exists independently of the symbol; but certainly the symbol does much to compress the meaning of the story.

II. Symbols may be used structurally to state the complication or the resolution of a story.

As the reader will recall, there are two sorts of short-story structure that require implication instead of direct statement: the first is where the complication is implied and the resolution is used to make the complication clear; the second, where the complication is stated directly and the resolution implied. One of the best ways of implying

139

rather than explicitly stating is to use a symbol, or a symbolic action. Here, certainly, symbolism is not merely functional, within the limited definition given above, but a structural device: without the symbol the story would collapse, and there would be no story.

Interestingly enough, if a symbol or symbolic action is to function as a way of stating the complication, it can be successful only if the protagonist is blind toward his real complication and is consciously aware only of a minor complication. Here, once more, our understanding of the use of artifice in characterization is important, for it happens frequently enough, though not always, that in quality stories if the character cannot realize the complication he faces, he will assume something else, less significant, to be his dilemma. Thus the character will face and act out his real complication within the terms of a symbolic action, remaining unaware frequently of what he does, or only becoming aware of what he does afterwards. Again, if the resolution is implied, while the complication is explicitly stated, the best way to imply it is through a symbol—for a symbol is vivid in its implications. In both these forms of story, the writer thus avoids what he would otherwise have to state directly, using lengthier description, exposition, narration, or action.

The reader will find in the commentary on Katherine Mansfield's "The Fly," contained in the Appendix on page 406, a discussion as to the way the author, involving the protagonist in a minor complication, implies the real complication symbolically, and arrives at a resolution without ever allowing her protagonist to know what he has done consciously. On the other hand, in Alberto Moravia's story "Rain in May" we have the complication directly stated and the resolution implied symbolically. A young waiter, happening to acquire a position in a restaurant, falls under the spell of Dirce, the restaurant proprietor's daughter. The father, Antonio Tocchi, is a hopeless sort of man, unfeeling, coarse, and small minded. His daughter has a dream of refurbishing the restaurant, which is located on a hill overlooking Rome, in order to increase its clientele and to earn more money. But the unimaginative father argues constantly with the girl and frequently slaps her. The girl, in hatred of her father, uses her sexual attractiveness upon the young waiter, attempting to persuade him to become an accomplice in the murder of the father. At last, through frustration, the young waiter agrees. They are to kill the father down in the wine cellar; and thus one evening at a signal, when the father calls to summon the daughter, the young waiter picks up a poker from the fireplace to carry out his purpose. But at just that moment, a man ap-

140

pears at the door and asks for help. His cart, loaded with stones, is stuck in the mud outside, and his horse cannot free it. The carter is brutish in looks, and he is in a rage. The waiter, not really thinking, follows the carter out, where he sees the man, now growing more and more enraged at his plight, seize the poker, which the waiter had set down, and rain blows upon his hapless animal. After the infuriated carter kills the horse, the young waiter leaves the restaurant and takes a tram to Rome.

At one or two points, Moravia underscores the significance for the waiter of this seemingly extraneous event, but for the most part, the symbolic action alone is used to resolve the complication: the rage of the brutish carter toward the dumb animal symbolizes effectively the planned assault of the young waiter against the father, allowing him to recognize his own bestiality. The violence done saps away the waiter's motive for violence. The use by the daughter of the young waiter's sexual drive is in essence a violence committed against his own ethical feelings, a killing of the moral code within himself. Many things coalesce within the symbol as a means of resolving the waiter's predicament. And it is certain that had Moravia resolved the story primarily in terms of literal significance, he would have had to say a great deal more in order to arrive at a satisfactory resolution.

Now there are certain things about the use of symbols that a writer should understand:

> *III. A symbol acquires its power of compression from the actual events of the story: a symbol is* basically, *by being a concrete object or action, the same thing that it is literally.*

All too frequently, the beginning writer, persuaded that he can only become a deep or profound author by using symbolism, sets himself the task of confounding the reader with obscurity. Now although it is true that some symbols within literature rise beyond the heights of comprehension, they can only do so by virtue of their initial literalness within the action. One might mention, as illustrations of profound symbols, Joseph Conrad's Grove of Death in "Heart of Darkness," or Herman Melville's Moby Dick, the whale that is that and so much more.

> *IV. As a consequence, symbols must never attract undue attention to themselves.*

The real aim of the author is to convey, by exaggeration and selection, the illusion of reality. What after all is a short story? As a result of the search for obscurity on the part of many a modern author, the notion has arisen that because a story is not obscure it, therefore, has no value. One can only applaud and echo Somerset Maugham's attack on obscurity in writers. In *The Summing Up,* he makes these statements: that obscurity arises from "negligence" or from "wilfulness"; that the author is "unsure" of what he wants to say; that his "pen originates the thought"; that the obscure writer has no power of "precise reflection"; that he is masquerading any talent he may have under a pose of "aristocratic exclusiveness"; and that very frequently what passes for the profound is a mere "contortion" in language that hides "very commonplace notions." And to Maugham's statements may be added yet one more reflection: when a writer wishes to call attention to his symbols, he is making his story function for its parts, and not the parts for the story. He is deliberately cultivating a serious breakdown of unity for a few paltry effects.

> *V. The writer must be able to state the complication and the resolution in direct rather than implied terms before he can deal effectively with symbols. If he cannot state directly what his complication or resolution consists of, he will only be an obscurantist.*

A student's short story will serve as an excellent example of what is meant. Quite by accident, the student turned in a good story and was terribly disappointed to discover that it was not "profound." His story consisted of the following complication: a young farmer went to town, a drive of some three hours on back country roads, in order to get supplies and a few incidental toys for his children. When he arrived, he discovered that a terrible storm had been forecast for the area. His friends attempted to dissuade him from returning home, but the man was adamant. He had built his home not far from a creek and he was frantic that the storm would unleash a flood that would sweep away not only his possessions but his family. Escaping from his friends, he borrowed a fresh horse, and struggled off through the breaking storm. His efforts were monumental ones, but he became injured. His friends instituted a search party, which failed to find him lying unconscious in a forest. Finally the farmer, regaining consciousness, struggled to his feet and resumed his journey. He reached home to find his house destroyed, but not far away on a bluff, he found his family safe from harm.

Quite literally, the story was extremely well done. The style was very effective: one realized with the shock of actuality the raging of the storm and the physical efforts of the man, his perfectly natural anxiety about his family, and the warmhearted concern of his friends for him. All in all, a very creditable performance so why was the student disappointed? Well, he wanted the storm to be a symbolic storm: he wanted it to be a storm of doubt and insecurity within the man's mind as to whether or not he really loved his family enough to venture his life for them! Symbolically, the story would have been a hodgepodge. On its literal level, and certainly by accident rather than by intention, it turned out very well. And one was left questioning whether or not, in fact, it was not just as "profound" for a man willingly to risk his life for his wife, his children, and possessions as it would be for him to doubt the attempt's value.

In summary, the inexperienced writer does well to learn what values there are in the four basic tools of the writing craft before he goes on to explore the use of symbolism. That these four tools have a directness and simplicity in them means simply that the writer has something of value to use in clearly stating what he wants to state. The skills that they impose upon the writer of the pulp story are the same as they impose upon the writer of the quality story—and if the writer of the latter really does write in terms of "quality," it will be by virtue of his being well versed in those techniques he will have learned as an apprentice, perhaps even as a pulp writer. To scorn clear statement in writing seems as foolhardy as a surgeon's preference for a penknife rather than a scalpel, a mere private notion that may satisfy the wayward eccentricities of the surgeon but is not particularly appreciated by the patient.

EXERCISES FOR CHAPTER 7

1. Selecting a few short stories of all three types, label those parts of the story that use exposition, narration, description, and action. Then test what the author accomplishes in the story by his use of exposition, description, narration, and action.
2. Outline the plot of a complication and then try to state either the complication or the resolution in terms of a symbolic action on the part of the protagonist.
3. Read the following stories and determine what symbols occur in them, whether they are conventional or not, and whether they are functional or structural: Somerset Maugham's "Rain"; Katherine Mansfield's

"Bliss"; Ernest Hemingway's "A Clean Well-Lighted Place"; Guy de Maupassant's "The Necklace."

4. Practice converting scenes of action into narration. Determine for each one what is gained and what is lost, not only in terms of the scene, but also in terms of the story in which the scene occurs.

5. Practice using action to enliven descriptive passages. Can the protagonist be made to move through a described scene?

6. In scenes of description, underline all words of a concrete nature. Concrete words name or describe things perceived by one or more of the five senses. They may be either general or specific. For example, *chair* is concrete and general; *Morris chair* is concrete and specific. Determine in descriptions you consider effective whether or not the author has preferred to use more concrete, specific words than concrete, general ones.

8

The Techniques of Characterization and How Professional Writers Employ Them

THE IMPORTANCE of vivid characterization in a short story should be self-evident. We do not, therefore, propose to urge the beginning writer to try to develop his characters sufficiently so that a reader responds to them. The result of his failure to do so, and hence of his failure to interest his audience, should be reason enough for him to vow to make his characters come alive. Since the very substance of a short story concerns the involvement of a recognizable character in a complication more exaggerated than in real existence, it follows automatically that the story will be credible only if the characters who face it seem real to the reader.

Now there are a number of ways of making a character credible and vivid, but let us begin at the start by recognizing that the fictional character, whether based on a real person or not, can live only in terms of the artifice of the short story, and not in terms of actual existence. And the short story demands, first, that we know not only the surface of the character, but also the character's thoughts, feelings, and motives; second, that there be a simplification of character (as opposed to the relative complexity of a human being) so that the complication will gain sharpness and dramatic impact from its effect on specific and recognizable traits within the character; and third, that there be a consistency in character so that the outcome of the story will follow the laws of logical probability. In all three of these ways, the character in the story comes alive, but the lifelikeness is only an illusion in contrast with the real life of a person.

The methods a writer uses to create believable characters are the same in every form of short story. The differences between characters in quality stories and those in commercial ones are, for the most part, a matter of the greater suggested depths in their intellectual, moral, and spiritual qualities. We will point out how this depth is achieved in the quality story as we examine the methods used in common by all short-story writers.

If the whole of society were to call a man a rascal, there would be little, short of a miracle, to prevent that individual from living up to the name that society had given him. This is only another method of stating the melancholy truth that names serve to imprison people, forcing them into the general patterns of behavior expected of the name, at least so far as those persons expose their public, not their private, faces. What is true of life becomes an exaggerated truth in the story. In life, a bus driver may know and quote Shakespeare. In the short story, the writer is constrained to describe such a man as an eccentric character, a mutation in terms of type, unless the writer substantiates with skill such a departure from the norm. In a story Caesar's wife must always perform those homely little chores, such as banquets and state dinners for roving ambassadors and high-flying dignitaries, that befit her position; it will do her little good to keen about the good old days when she was married to no more than an aspirant to the title. The first two principles, therefore, to be observed in characterization are the following:

> I. *The writer reveals to the reader the sort of person a character is by characterizing him as a member of some general group and then by distinguishing him from the group's other members.*
>
> II. *Any variation from the pattern of general traits given a character must be fully substantiated.*

Now a writer must know the characteristics that form the usual patterns of behavior for any individual in terms of profession or occupation, or in terms of nationality or culture, or finally in terms of a person's general social identity. It will benefit the reader in considering such matters to ponder over George Orwell's essay "Shooting an Elephant" in which the author investigates the dilemma facing him in being simultaneously a human being, full of certain sympathies and aversions, and a police official, representative of British imperialism in Burma. As a human being, Orwell finds himself quite lonely and isolated because he hates British imperialism, and he hates as well being taken by the Burmese as a representative of it, and certainly not as an individual. In order to save face, therefore, he must act against his own humanity by shooting an elephant before a mob of attentive Burmese, so that he will have fulfilled their expectations of how the white man should behave. And there is no one to turn to at the very end, for in obeying the will of the mob, he is merely, and quite ironically, demonstrating the authority entailed in his official position.

GENERAL TRAITS

Let us, for illustration, list general traits that we associate with certain groups of people. The British are known for their reticence, the Orientals for saving face, the Irish for a sense of humor, the Scotch for their thrift. In addition, all criminals are *ipso facto* against society, farmers love the land, policemen are honest and brave, teachers are dedicated to children. And finally, a libertine should not be trusted alone with an unmarried (or married!) and pretty young lady, a thief should not be hired to guard the family treasure, and a liar is no person to employ as a bank examiner.

There will be found no inconsistency with the two principles already stated when we add that being conversant with such general traits and using the normal ones will not save a writer from making his characters dull. As society progresses in levels of tolerance and understanding, these traits change; as social upheavals take place, as political and economic crises develop, they also change. It is instructive, for example, to see the way the wealthy were pictured in the films of the thirties and how they are pictured today. What was yesterday's stereotyped view appears today very much like a savage and almost unmerited satire. And there is nothing to prevent a writer from choosing different traits to characterize a group from the ones held current today. The only danger is that he may court rejection slips by attempting to open the eyes of society to their errors, their static evaluations, and their lethargy. Some authors, such as Oscar Wilde and Bernard Shaw at the very end of the nineteenth century, were tremendously

147

successful in characterizing people, not with old customary names, but with more proper new ones.

Personal traits establish, in effect, another series of general attributes except that they give us a more specific way to characterize human beings. Perhaps the term *general attributes* will seem strange, but personal traits involve great abstractions. Nonetheless, these are the traits that allow us to distinguish individuals, one from another, within a certain large, general, professional or cultural group:

> Some of us are brave, and some are cowardly.
> Some selfish—some unselfish.
> Some bold—some meek.
> Some argumentative—some passive.
> Some loyal—some two-faced.
> Some ambitious—some lazy.
> Some faithful—some fickle.

The list is almost endless. Now there is a median position for every extreme, as Aristotle pointed out in his *Ethics*. Such characteristics can be arranged in triads with a middle or median quality between the two extremes. For example:

> Humility—modesty—pride.

But the purpose of fiction is to arouse an emotional response in the reader, which is generally done best by using extremes.

EMOTIONAL TRAITS

The tendency is for emotional traits to depend upon general and personal traits. That is, a scientist tends, so far as he is typically a scientist to be studious (personal trait) rather than intellectually inert, and hence to be emotionally disciplined—even cold, if not dispassionate—in terms of his temperament. It is logical and valid that general traits will exercise some control over personal traits, and that as a consequence the individual will have certain emotional tendencies. This does not mean, however, that ironclad necessity operates in the determination of character, and it is certainly as wise to consider that character follows the inscrutables and imponderables of heredity, environment, and accident, as that it be consistent and explicable.

Another way of describing a person is in terms of physical characteristics. And right at the start, we must assert that what we associate as characteristic between a person's outer appearance and inner nature is not necessarily true in terms of scientific observation. The fictional truth is that we associate—as did Shakespeare—lean and hungry men with the suspicious in character, and the fat with the jolly. Thus, throughout literature we have been made to feel that certain physical types have certain mental, moral, and emotional characteristics. A student can find much in literature—classical, medieval, renaissance, and even up to and including the nineteenth century—to reinforce his belief that there is a coupling between the physical and the moral character in individuals. And today, driven by an increasing scientific interest in the relationship between physical and mental-moral characteristics, such an investigator as W. H. Sheldon has attempted to make such an accurate classification possible.[1] Yet whatever may be the value of such scientific observation for the writer, he seems committed, to a certain extent at least, to follow the general preconceptions of humanity about character and physical appearance. This much may be said, therefore, as a guide to the beginning writer: the association between physical traits and the other aspects of character must always seem to be logical and valid. And the way to do this is to make the physical traits a way of explaining or demonstrating the other traits. In essence, physical traits, by virtue of being visible, are actually symbols of the other characteristics.

Before proceeding further, let us look at several illustrations of the way authors establish a character, using general, personal, emotional and physical traits.

1. Cousin Eva in Katherine Anne Porter's story "Old Mortality":

A very thin old lady [physical and general traits] raised choleric black eyes [personal and physical traits] and fixed upon her a regard of unmixed disapproval. She had two immense front teeth and a receding chin [physical traits], but she did not lack character [personal trait] . . . Aunt Amy had threatened to be an old maid [general trait] like Eva. Oh, Eva, the trouble with her is she has no chin [physical trait] . . . Eva has given up, and is teaching Latin in a Female Seminary [general trait]. Eva's gone out for votes for women [general trait]. . . She sighed with a humorous bitterness. The humor seemed momentary, but the bitterness was a constant state of mind [emotional trait].

[1] In *The Varieties of Human Physique* and *The Varieties of Temperament*.

149

There are several other aspects given of Eva's character, her "brisk rustling energy," her portentousness, her hatred of romantic love, her "small voice of axiomatic morality," which have not been represented in the description quoted—and particularly there is her habit of dwelling in the past, which is fundamental to the story. Nevertheless, it is obvious that Katherine Anne Porter has used all the traits so far mentioned to make Eva's character vivid to the reader.

2. Eagle in Herbert Gold's story "Home Is Where a Man Dwells":

Everyone knew that Eagle had no home [general trait]: he never received mail, he spoke of no place but the circuit, he married himself to the carousel rented each spring from a retired carnie [general trait]. A gypsy had named him Eagle because his baldness and the great shiny nose hooking out from his face and the piercing rasp of his voice [physical traits] . . . had reminded the gypsy of an eagle . . . That was all right: the name stuck. Eagle liked it, or at least never complained, for a short memory can become a professional habit [general and personal traits] . . . The others, too, were homeless. What carnie expects a home [general trait]? The others, however, generated itches which they periodically felt as love, making it a substitute for a home . . . Eagle could not be fooled; he never pretended, earned neither love nor a home, refused to be consoled by an itch [general, personal, and emotional traits]. He understood that feelings happened in men, but love, like a home, is something a man dwells in [general trait] . . . He constantly rehearsed the habit of expecting nothing further [general trait], and as middle-age embraced him with an insulating fat, he shed his hair and his mournful face retreated from his nose, so that the beak alone pointed out [physical traits], toward those others, the paying customers, the suckers for whom the carousel lights winked and the calliope music flirted [general traits].

3. Peyton Farquhar in Ambrose Bierce's story "An Occurrence at Owl Creek Bridge":

The man who was engaged in being hanged was apparently about thirty-five years of age [general trait]. He was a civilian [general trait], if one might judge from his habit, which was that of a planter [general and physical traits]. His features were good—a straight nose, firm mouth, broad forehead, from which his long, dark hair was combed straight back, falling behind his ears to the collar of his well-fitting frock coat [physical traits]. He wore a mustache and pointed beard, but no whiskers; his eyes were large and dark gray [physical traits], and had a kindly expression [personal trait] which one would hardly have expected in one whose neck was in the hemp. Evidently this was no vulgar assassin [general trait]. The liberal military code makes provision for hanging many kinds of persons, and gentlemen [general trait] are not excluded.

The reader can discover for himself further examples of the way that established writers select and use the various traits to establish their characters.

It is now time to discuss more fully the relationship between character and complication, for one can deduce it as a rule that:

III. A complication brings out character because it threatens the status quo *of the protagonist's personality.*

A complication always involves a demonstration of character. Given such-and-such a personality, an event that threatens the personality in any fashion will always cry out for some kind of resolution. Let us once more look at several examples.

In the story "No Margin for Error," printed in the Appendix on page 331, the *status quo* of the protagonist is endangered. Jack, the protagonist, belongs to the group of young, $12,000-per-year executives with a bright future. As a result of the error (the complication), Jack becomes distinctive from his group because he is now a young, $12,000-per-year executive who may not have any future. In terms of his personal traits, Jack is self-respecting, honest, and decent. As a result of the complication, the *status quo* of his personal traits is threatened. He considers becoming dishonest and deceitful, and he even starts to lose his wife's respect. In terms of his emotional traits, Jack is happy and satisfied in his marriage and general position. As a result of the complication, a rift develops; he becomes unhappy and dissatisfied. He is forced to experience, as a result of the complication, emotions that he might never have experienced otherwise: anguish, dismay, fear, apprehension, disillusionment, hopelessness, and so on.

In the slick story "Precious Moment" found in the Appendix on page 372, Dave Lomax has general characteristics that belong to a few million other young men. He is a happily married young adult with a couple of children, another on the way, and a mother-in-law. As a result of the complication, the *status quo* of his general traits changes, and he is made distinctive from his group. He is still a happily married young adult with a couple of children, another on the way, but he has a mother-in-law for whom he has no name. Of the millions in his group, Dave is probably the only one who has no way to address his mother-in-law. In terms of his personal traits, he is considerate, kind, friendly, and very sensitive about hurting others' feel-

151

ings. As a result of the complication, the *status quo* of his personal traits is threatened. He wants to be kind and friendly to his mother-in-law; he does not want to hurt her feelings; but because of his inability to find a suitable name to call her, he is in danger of doing this. In terms of his emotional traits, he is happy and contented. As a result of the complication, the *status quo* of his emotional traits changes. He becomes miserable, ashamed, even a little desperate.

In the short story "Russian Roulette," which we developed earlier in the book, we find a young high school graduate, who has never made any friends. The complication is a threat to Benny's nature, for in acquiring Duke as a friend, he discovers that he cannot accept the role Duke requires of him. In James Thurber's story "The Catbird Seat," Mr. Martin, retiring, discreet, methodical, discovers his whole character is endangered by Mrs. Ulgine Barrows. In D. H. Lawrence's story "The Rocking-Horse Winner," in attempting to win his mother's love, Paul's nature as a young boy is not only threatened but violated. In Herbert Gold's story "Home Is Where a Man Dwells," Eagle, a representative of the "carnie" world, who fleeces "suckers" and has crushed within himself the desire for love, because of a true "carnie's" appreciation of the profits of his meretricious trade, meets a girl who, by attracting him outside his group, threatens to cause a change in his previous character.

The rule holds good for all forms of stories. Here for example are the plots of two slick stories, which illustrate how their authors have developed their complications on the basis of a recognition of the traits of their particular characters. In the first, we have a college girl who is made distinctive from her group by being shown to be wholly uninterested in an education. She is going to college only to have a good time and find a husband. In her personal traits, which are closely coupled with her emotional traits, she is headstrong and selfish. During the story, she is seen as confident when she finds the man she wants to marry, disappointed when he says that he does not want to marry until he is more firmly established, desperate as she tries to seduce him so that he will have to marry her, frustrated when he refuses to be seduced; and finally joyous she eventually solves her complication. In the second story, we have as protagonist a criminal lawyer who is made distinctive from his group by his weakness for fancy neckties. In terms of his personal traits, he is honest and dedicated; he will not take a case unless he believes his client to be innocent. The story shows him as doubtful that his present client is innocent, disappointed when he cannot shake off his doubt, apprehensive as he realizes that should his client be innocent he will be letting an innocent man go to the chair undefended, frustrated when, after he takes the case, the prosecutor produces a surprise witness that makes conviction almost inevitable, and elated as he solves his complication and establishes the innocence of the defendant.

Now although in all stories the complication will consist of a threat to the character of the protagonist, it is only the purely creative writer who will demonstrate the tragic or pathetic implications of a protagonist's moving outside of his group. In pulp and slick stories, the emotional traits of the protagonist move almost invariably from a point of doubt or disappointment in the beginning, to despair and frustration in the middle, and eventually to joy at the ending of the story. The use of the comic curve in pulp and slick stories appears to make such a range of emotional change inevitable. For the most part in quality stories, with the exception of very few examples, the complication that threatens the general traits of the protagonist and carries him to a point outside of his group almost always culminates in some kind of disaster. Thus, we can establish another rule:

> *IV. The resolution may, though it does not need to, return the protagonist through the principle of discovery and change to his original traits of character.*

In the story "Russian Roulette," therefore, we arrive at a moment when the protagonist discovers the truth about himself and sees himself for what he really is; and because of this insight, he returns to himself, as it were. It is exactly as though he had been led away from himself by the complication and had gone so far out of himself as to recognize that his own being is threatened.

In the story "No Margin for Error," when Jack discovers that he is not the sort of person who can let another man lose his job and shoulder all the blame for his error, he confesses and returns to his original characteristics in the group of young, $12,000-per-year executives, whose implied general trait is self-responsibility. Thus, Jack returns to his personal traits of being self-respecting, honest, and decent. He returns, as well, to his emotional traits of being happy and contented.

The principle involved in rule IV, describing that moment in the story in which self-discovery occurs, is so important in every form of story that we wish to suspend briefly any further discussion of methods of characterization in order to deal with it further. Rule IV we can, therefore, restate in the following fashion:

> *IV. A moment of truth occurs in the story when the protagonist must face up to the truth about himself and see himself for what he really is. The moment of truth always results from the complication the protagonist faces, for the complication tests the character of the protagonist and in so doing exposes his weaknesses.*

Now, keeping in mind that to every rule there is an exception and that this rule does not hold true for certain quality stories, for reasons that we will advance later and that the reader may already surmise, let us look at the way this principle is actually used in certain stories.

As we have already seen, Benny in "Russian Roulette" faces a moment of truth. If the reader will recall, step 6 of the story's outlined complication reads as follows:

Step 6: Benny discovers within himself his own weakness: his desire for friendship, based upon his own self-derision, has led him to make friends with a person like Duke. Benny realizes that all his life he has let his own fatness stand in the way of friendship based upon deeper than superficial values.

In a commercial story, the moment of truth usually occurs just before the agonizing decision, which the protagonist makes in step IV of the middle of the chronological and formula story. Why is this so? As one can see, the insight on the protagonist's part into his own inherent weakness is what determines him to make the agonizing decision that follows. Thus, Benny sees himself for what he really is and determines through a new-found courage to make the decision to break away from Duke.

In a pulp story, the heroine is a married woman whose devotion to her married children and grandchildren is so great that she completely neglects her husband. Her moment of truth occurs when her husband is locked up in jail for being a drunkard. She realizes that her neglect is making him an alcoholic; this insight forces her to make the agonizing decision to alter completely her relationship with her children so that she can devote all her time to her husband.

In the slick story previously alluded to about the college girl, the girl's purpose in going to college, simply to have a good time and snag a husband, leads to a moment of truth. After she has tried to seduce the hero and he has rebuffed her advances, she sees herself for what she really is. The moment of truth forces her to recognize that she is unworthy of the hero's love.

In both of the above stories, the moment of truth occurs as a prelude to the decision that the protagonists make to return to their essential natures. The complication has been a test of their characters. We pointed out the ways "Russian Roulette" could be changed in order to make it a quality story. If the protagonist were to accept or yield to his weakness rather than overcome it, the moment of truth in the story would depend upon forces greater than the protagonist's nature to resist them. In other words, what we are suggesting is that the moment of truth in quality stories may involve a corruption of the protagonist's character. The protagonist in most quality stories may, by moving outside of his group, actually so upset the *status quo* of his original character as to undergo an alteration that is frequently a violation.

While the moment of truth in commercial stories also occurs after the agonizing decision has been made, it invariably points to the solution. Thus, in one pulp story, the heroine makes the agonizing decision to divorce her husband because he spends too much money on doctor's bills and too much time with his mother, who is ill. Her moment of truth occurs after the divorce is granted when she realizes how selfish she was, how lonely she now is, how much she misses and really loves her husband.

In another slick story, the heroine is an ambitious understudy to a Broadway star. The heroine is positive that she is a much better actress than the star if she can only get the chance to prove it. The show, after a successful run, is due to close in a few days. In desperation, the heroine makes the agonizing decision to put knock-out drops in the coffee the star always drinks, just fifteen minutes before curtain time. The heroine then gets her chance to take the star's place for one performance. Her moment of truth comes when, after the critics call her performance mediocre compared to that of the star, she realizes she does not have the talent she thought she had.

In quality stories, the operation of rule IV is not nearly so uniform as it is in commercial fiction. The central reason lies in this: the purely creative writer appears to place much more serious emphasis on the possibility that a threat to the general traits of the protagonist cannot occur without doing some damage, perhaps even permanent damage, so that if the protagonist does return to his accustomed traits, he does so often at the risk of disaster.

It will be well, here, to suggest some of the variations that quality writers make in the moment of truth. And since there are certain quality stories that follow the plot of the formula story, let us look at one, James Thurber's "The Catbird Seat," in which the moment of truth operates in nearly the same precise terms as it does in its prototype. The moment of truth occurs when discreet, mild Mr. Martin realizes that it is beyond him to murder Mrs. Barrows:

> When Mrs. Barrows reappeared, carrying two highballs, Mr. Martin, standing there with his gloves on, became acutely conscious of the fantasy he had wrought. Cigarettes in his pocket, a drink prepared for him—it was all too grossly improbable. It was more than that; it was impossible. Somewhere in the back of his mind, a vague idea stirred, sprouted . . . The idea began to bloom, strange and wonderful.

Thurber does not, however, reveal what this idea is. To do so he would have had to make Mr. Martin as self-explanatory as a commercial story's protagonist. We can perhaps show the distinction by rephrasing the idea latent in Thurber's characterization:

> When Mrs. Barrows reappeared, carrying two highballs, Mr. Martin, standing there with his gloves on, became acutely conscious of the fantasy he had wrought. Cigarettes in his pocket, a drink prepared for him—it was all too grossly improbable. It was more than that; it was impossible. Never would he be able to murder Mrs. Barrows—that was obvious. Filing clerks never murdered anyone. They just padded around filing things away in discreet, but nonviolent order. Yet somewhere in the back of his mind, a vague idea stirred, sprouted. If he could convince Mrs. Barrows that he really *was* violent, that, say, he had a plan for doing in even old Fitweiler—Yes, but wouldn't he run a terrible risk in convincing her of this? He eyed her, with the whiskey in his hand. It was a risk he had to take. There was no other way.

Of course, to rephrase Thurber's story in this fashion does much to destroy its humor and originality, but it is equally obvious that his protagonist faces, in a moment of truth, his own characteristic qualities and from this confrontation arrives at a decision.

In the quality story, the moment of truth may *be* the resolution of the story. That is to say, the writer may so manipulate the moment when the protagonist arrives at a consciousness of his true character as to minimize the importance of any decision he might make, in favor simply of that recognition. If this occurs, the protagonist will return to his general traits, but almost invariably with a sense of change that is melancholy. He finds that he is the same, yet somehow different, and frequently saddened.

In Carson McCullers' story "A Domestic Dilemma," as we previously cited, the resolution is only implied. It comes when the protagonist finally gazes at the slumbering form of his wife, "delicate . . . full-bosomed, slender and undulant." He is aware that his wife has the same characteristics as his children; and he goes to sleep with his "sorrow paralleling desire in the immense complexity of love." The protagonist in a sense returns to himself from his anger and fear, but the change in his character as suggested in this moment of truth is in a growth of "sorrow."

Again, in Herbert Gold's story, "Home Is Where a Man Dwells," we have a suggestion that the protagonist comes back to his true self, but with a depressing self-recognition. After having asked the girl to live with him, after having expressed words of love, Eagle denies the girl's son; and he is conscious of his deceitfulness: "He hated his easy sleek sucker-words. . . ." And a little later, when on the point of giving in to her plea, "the words stuck a moment when, like a true carnie, he calculated the risks." The moment of truth lies in Eagle's reawakened awareness—now with a sense of self-hatred—that he belongs to his group, to those who "fleece" the "suckers." He reaffirms his general traits and returns to the carnival where "the lights of the Ferris Wheel, revolving amorously against the night sky, gave him the way back to his only home." Eagle has been brought to see himself as incapable of love, and hence the moment of truth that he faces suggests a disastrous weakening.

Though we stressed the idea in both versions of rule IV that the moment of truth is universal in all short stories, in certain quality stories it is not the protagonist who consciously faces a moment of truth as much as the reader. Given the artifice that the protagonist may be unaware of the complication he faces, he may be equally unaware of what the moment of truth reveals. In the last chapter, we pointed out that a writer could involve the protagonist either in a symbolically stated complication with a directly stated resolution or in a directly stated complication with a symbolically stated resolution. Stories that employ symbolism in either the complication or the resolution frequently involve their protagonists in situations to which they are blind, call forth traits in them of which they are unaware, and reach moments of truth whose meanings are far more apparent to the reader than they are to the characters. Once more we refer the reader to Katherine Mansfield's "The Fly" and to our extended commentary upon that story, both contained in the Appendix on page 406. Two other examples, however, we will discuss briefly here, in order to clarify our meaning for the reader.

The first story is by Chekhov and is called "The New Villa." Although Chekhov protested that it was not the business of the writer to deal as a specialist with social conditions, political ideas, or problems of a practical nature, but only to tell the plain truth and let others decide what should be done, nevertheless his stories often do, in fact, give rise to an instinctive zeal to remedy social conditions. His celebrated objectivity enables him to present not only individual characters but whole groups of people who have lost their way; they continue to act their parts as ineffectual gentlemen, sentimental landholders, idlers, self-deceivers, drunkards, lowly peasants, although the spirit of their times has moved away from them and seems to cry for new insights.

In "The New Villa," an engineer named Kutcherov comes to build a huge bridge two miles away from a village. His wife, charmed by the lowly village, persuades her husband to purchase land, and they build a "pretty house" there. They, thus, become an aristocracy or, at least, a gentry class to the peasant folk of the village, who are frequently impoverished, some of them having very large families, many of them being indigent and thriftless. Incidents occur. Cattle from the landowner's estate get into the meadows of the villagers; the engineer cheerfully pays damages of five rubles, and the peasants promptly spend the money on drink. At the same time, the peasants invade the property of Kutcherov to steal wood, trample in his garden, and destroy his copses. When Kutcherov attempts to reason with the peasants in a friendly fashion, the peasants are surly and truculent. The engineer's wife visits the village, and doing a few small charities, attempts to win the sympathy of the peasants. She, too, came from the laboring class, she tells them, and married above her station. She now seems to lead a lonely, unrewarding life despite her wealth and possessions, but the peasants remain sullen. The rift grows between the gentry and the peasants: there is anger; and when there comes a time for Kutcherov to interpose in a quarrel between a father and son, he remains silent. Kutcherov and his family move away from the village. A long while afterward, after people have grown older and some have died, we see certain of the peasants trudging homeward. They are tired out from sawing wood, as well as from the ceaseless and unre-

deeming poverty of their lives. A new owner has come to take charge
of the engineer's former home; but he is seldom there, and he is cold
and aloof. The villagers think of the engineer and his wife and wonder
why none of them got along together:

Why had they parted like enemies? How was it that some mist had
shrouded from their eyes what mattered most, and had let them see
nothing but damage done by cattle, bridles, pincers, and all those trivial
things which now, as they remembered them, seemed so nonsensical?
How was it that with the new owner they lived in peace, and yet had
been on bad terms with the engineer? And not knowing what answer
to make to these questions they were all silent. . . .

A brief summary of "The New Villa" cannot do the story justice,
yet it does give us insight into the way its moment of truth reveals
more to the reader than it ever can to the villagers who are protagonists. For although the bridge in the story is in one sense quite literal,
it is also the bridge of human sympathy and concern that Kutcherov
and his wife tried to extend to the peasants. The only one of the peasants who is aware of such an effort, as is characteristic of Chekhov,
is Rodion, an old man in the story, who feels the sympathy but mistakes its nature. He understands everything "in some peculiar way of
his own." In other words, he goes back to the past for his answers,
wishing to be treated as a serf again and to bow and scrape before his
betters, so that even he cannot understand the symbolic significance
of the bridge. Thus in this story, the moment of truth reaches the
reader with a quite different impact from the way it reaches the characters, who "not knowing what answer to make to these questions
. . . were all silent. . . ."

Our second example is "Bliss" by Katherine Mansfield. As we have
already noted, in that story the protagonist is a repressed woman
who, aware only at the story's end of an awakened and now normal
sexual interest in her husband, discovers that he is having an affair
with another woman. But throughout the story, Katherine Mansfield
has carefully hidden from Bertha, by means of symbolism, the true
nature of her situation. Bertha errs in understanding the repressed
quality of her guests at the party. She mistakes Miss Fulton's apparent
sensitivity to herself as a latent, nameless, yet exciting emotion. Her
moment of truth comes when she realizes that, after the guests have
gone, she will be alone with her husband in a darkened room and a
warm bed. But Bertha is never so fully aware as the reader, even when
she faces the moment of truth about herself, that she as well as her
guests are all victims and results of outmoded social conventions and

mores. The story has far more meaning to the reader than it does to the characters, and particularly to Bertha in the moment of truth.

Before departing from the subject of general, personal, emotional, and physical traits to look at the ways writers make these traits apparent to a reader, there remains a word or two about the handling of minor characters. So far, our discussion has concentrated wholly on the central characters in the story. As we see from the following rule, there is no need to invest minor characters with all the attributes we have mentioned:

> *V. In a short story it is usually sufficient to identify a minor character by his general traits.*

For example, if a minor character is a policeman, it is enough, usually, to do no more than say so. The reader will deduce from this description that the minor character is honest, law-abiding, brave, etc. Of course, just how much weight a character will carry in the story depends upon how significant a part the character plays in the story. It is possible, therefore, that what might seem a minor character will nevertheless need sufficient personal, emotional, and physical characterization in the story to become vivid in his own right. Such a character, for example, is Cousin Eva in Katherine Anne Porter's "Old Mortality"; for it is through an accidental meeting with Cousin Eva that the protagonist reaches a moment of truth and resolves, as the author points out, "in her hopefulness, her ignorance," to cut all her ties with the past. Cousin Eva has to be, therefore, fully enough delineated to bring the protagonist to this decision.

Now how do writers actually create major characters? What methods do they use to convince readers that the people who move upon the printed page have reality? Characterization employs the same basic aspects of prose we investigated in the last chapter, singly and in combination.

> *Exposition. To characterize by exposition, convey information to the reader about a character through the observations, thoughts, or feelings of another character; through the character's own observations, thoughts, or feelings toward himself; or through the observations, thoughts, and feelings of the author as omnipresent narrator.*

In pulp and slick stories, it is more common for characters to establish their identity by exposing the identities of other characters, than it is for the author to step directly before the reader and indicate what his characters are like. One example of characterization by using the observations, thoughts, and feelings of another character is the following:

Mama was sitting in her maple rocker with her hands clasped tightly in her lap. This, I thought to myself, is the first time I've ever seen Mama's hands idle. They were always busy hands, sewing, mending, cooking, and washing. It was as if she had to hold them to make them rest.

And here is how Henry James characterizes his protagonist in his story "The Beast in the Jungle":

He was satisfied, without in the least being able to say why, that this young lady might roughly have ranked in the house as a poor relation; satisfied also that she was not there on a brief visit, but was more or less a part of the establishment—almost a working, a remunerated part. Didn't she enjoy at periods a protection that she paid for by helping, among other services, to show the place and explain it, deal with the tiresome people, answer questions about the dates of the buildings, the styles of the furniture, the authorship of the pictures, the favourite haunts of the ghost?

In both the above examples, the characterization of one individual is accomplished through the thoughts of another.

Here are a couple of illustrations of a character's thinking, observing, or feeling about himself in a way that characterizes:

There was no joy in knowing she was in love with Matthew. It was a love that should never have been born. She could not pretend the precepts by which she had been reared did not exist. It was abhorrent even to think of breaking her engagement to Wade. She must marry him.

He knew that about a pretty face he could not be trusted. About money, yes. He could carry on his shoulders the whole daily deposit of the Chase National Bank, and it would be safe with him, not a check wasted in the mud, not a bill squandered. He returned library books on time, never borrowed a rake from a neighbor without bringing it back, and he walked by saloons without a hesitant quiver in his knee. But a pretty face. Well, he had to stop and talk, to stare and admire, to while away the time and smile while feeling that time was passing, that he had other things to do; but glory be, wasn't a pretty face a marvelous thing?

The use of the omnipresent narrator's point of view in the quality story tends to give a greater possible range to characterization by

161

exposition than do the points of view where one character thinks of another or a character thinks about himself. (It is worthwhile to recall that the device of omnipresent narrator has not the general favor and currency it once had in fiction, but that it is, nevertheless, often employed is indisputable, and it is frequently merged with some other type or types of point of view.) Here, for instance, are two examples of the omnipresent narrator using exposition, as well as other means, to characterize; and it is noteworthy that in these characterizations may be found a sense of time, of time past and time present; of area or locale; of group rather fully elaborated upon; and lastly of an attitude toward the character that we can take to be valid, it being possible that when one character remarks about another, or when he thinks about himself, there may be deception.

F. Scott Fitzgerald begins his story "The Jelly Bean" by directly establishing his protagonist:

Jim Powell was a Jelly-bean. Much as I desire to make him an appealing character, I feel that it would be unscrupulous to deceive you on that point. He was a bred-in-the-bone, dyed-in-the-wool, ninety-nine three-quarters per cent Jelly-bean and he grew lazily all during Jelly-bean season, which is every season, down in the land of the Jelly-beans well below the Mason-Dixon line . . . Jim was a Jelly-bean. I write that again because it has such a pleasant sound—rather like the beginning of a fairy story—as if Jim were nice. It somehow gives me a picture of him with a round, appetizing face and all sorts of leaves and vegetables growing out of his cap. But Jim was long and thin and bent at the waist from stooping over pool-tables, and he was what might have been known in the indiscriminating North as a corner loafer. 'Jelly-bean' is the name throughout the undissolved Confederacy for one who spends his life conjugating the verb to idle in the first person singular—I am idling, I have idled, I will idle.

The other example of the technique is taken from several paragraphs in "The Patented Gate and the Mean Hamburger" by Robert Penn Warren:

For Jeff York had a place. That was what made him different from the other men who looked like him and with whom he stood on the street corner on Saturday afternoon. They were croppers, but he, Jeff York, had a place. But he stood with them because his father had stood with their fathers and his grandfathers with their grandfathers, or with men like their fathers and grandfathers, in other towns in settlements in the mountains, in towns beyond the mountains. They were the great-great-grandsons of men who, half woodsmen and half farmers, had been shoved into the sand hills, into the limestone hills, into the barrens, two hundred, two hundred and fifty years before and had learned there the way to grabble a life out of the sand and the stone. And when the soil had leached away into the sand or burnt off the stone, they went on west, walking with the bent-kneed stride over the mountains, their eyes squinching warily in the gaunt faces, the rifle over the crooked arm, hunting a new place. But there was a curse on them. They only knew the life they knew, and that life did not belong to the fat bottom lands, where the cane was head-tall. . . .

The opening paragraphs, prior to what is quoted above, of Robert Penn Warren's story are excellent examples of characterization by means of descriptive details.

It might be worthwhile, here, to remark that writers who are followers of James Joyce and Virginia Woolf have gotten rid of one conventional form of characterization, the revelation of a character through his own thoughts, by plunging us, not into the thoughts of the character, but into his mental experiences so that these things appear not so much in terms of grammatically expressed statements as in terms of a patterning of sensory impressions and awakening consciousness. We are on the very threshold of thought before it has been given shape by the character, made consecutive and logical in his own consciousness. The character reveals himself through his interior impressions, to be sure; but many a reader may feel that he has been plunged into such a welter of details that he can make little of the character whose consciousness he is experiencing. Before the new writer practices such a technique as stream of consciousness for the revelation of character, it would appear good advice to insist on his using methods that are more readily intelligible. This is hardly to scorn the attempts of the experienced creative writer, for as we have hoped time and again to make clear, our intent is not to place rigid restrictions upon methods and exclude the untried or unconventional. It would be equally unfair, however, to insist that the stream-of-consciousness technique must be, because it is different, a wholly satisfactory method for those who have not yet learned to make characters credible by other, more intelligible, means.

> *Description. To characterize by description, describe a character's appearance, mannerisms, habits, and favorite expressions of speech in order to make the character distinct and individual.*

We can, of course, tell the reader about a character by using exposition, and granted that we tell the essentials, we can make that character interesting and credible. But it is conventional in most stories for the writer to give factually descriptive details to aid in the presentation. Thus, for example, when we say that Silas Pickering was the meanest man in town, such a statement tells the reader what kind of a man Silas Pickering is, but it fails to differentiate him from others of his kind, so that he remains virtually a puppet. He does not really come alive because every town has at least one meanest man, and we must make him distinct in terms of other characteristics. Let us therefore try to fill out the portrait:

Silas 'God's Truth' Pickering was the meanest man in town. He was a tall, gaunt man with hollow cheeks that sucked inward to reveal narrowly defined, sharp cheekbones. He looked perpetually hungry. He had lost all but the lobe of his right ear in a hunting accident and had a habit of pulling at the lobe with his thumb and finger, when talking to anyone. He made a living lending money at exorbitant interest rates to people the bank had turned down for a loan. He was called 'God's Truth' Pickering because any time anyone asked him for an extension on a loan, he would look pious and say sadly, 'God's truth, I'd like to help you, but business is business.'

Silas has, in terms of descriptive details, now become individual and distinct from others in his group. There are many tall, gaunt men with hollow cheeks, but in describing his face as hungry, we have used a physical detail to symbolize his character, which tends to make Silas distinctive. Every town has mean men, but now many of these men have nothing but the lobe of their right ear, and how many have a habit of pulling on that lobe when talking to people? And how many mean individuals have a habit of using the expression, "God's truth"? Incidentally, as we observed before, to link physical traits with the other traits of character, we must use those physical traits as symbols. To prevent a reader of commercial fiction from mistaking the clues that are given, the writer usually couples the physical traits with the other traits very firmly. In the pulp story "Why I Killed My Father," for example, the author did not wish his readers to mistake the character of the prosecutor:

As the prosecutor moved back and forth in front of the jury, turning now and again to indicate me, I watched him with something of the same fascination. He was a tall, heavy-set, broad-shouldered man with

164

a deep voice that rang with conviction; a hard, brutally handsome and florid face which flashed with indignation; iron-gray wavy hair which lay like a mane on his head, giving him an appearance of solidity, respectability.

As we move toward quality fiction, however, it becomes more and more conventional for the writer to work through indirection, rather than by overt statement, when describing a character. Note the greater reliance upon physical description, the lesser reliance upon direct statement in Stevenson's description of Francis Villon in "A Lodging for the Night":

The poet was a rag of a man, dark, little, and lean, with hollow cheeks and thick black locks. He carried his four-and-twenty years with feverish animation. Greed had made folds about his eyes, evil smiles had puckered his mouth. The wolf and the pig struggled together in his face. It was an eloquent, sharp, ugly, earthly countenance. His hands were small and prehensile, with fingers knotted like a cord; and they were continually flickering in front of him in violent and expressive pantomime.

And yet, the passage directs the reader very firmly at times in the use of such words as "greed," "evil," "wolf," "pig."

Is it necessary, when characterizing by descriptive detail, to give all four outward aspects of character: appearance, mannerisms, habits, expressions of speech? No, it is not, for appearance alone reveals a great deal. In certain types of stories, it is quite necessary to make much of appearance—in love stories, for example, in which the reader wishes to know what the hero and the heroine literally see in each other. But though appearance can do much by itself, it is usually better for the inexperienced writer to give other aspects as well. For example let us consider the statement: "Floyd Thompson was a small man with a hairline mustache." Though the appearance suggests something of his individual personality, Floyd Thompson does not really live for the reader; and the writer, therefore, reinforces the suggestion behind the appearance by adding a distinctive habit:

Floyd Thompson was a small man with a hairline mustache. He owned twelve pairs of patent leather shoes which he took better care of than some men do of their children. He always carried a big silk handkerchief, and at the first sign of a speck of dust on his precious shoes, he'd whip out the handkerchief and wipe it off.

The example just given suggests another fashion by which we can describe a character, and this is indirectly, by the things he owns, the possessions that surround him, the taste or lack of taste revealed in his furniture, his house, his books: the myriad of things, orderly or disorderly, that make up the objective environment surrounding the character, forming it, perhaps, or simply reflecting it. Therefore, under description, we can state a subsidiary principle:

> *Description. To characterize by description, examine the immediate and personal environment of the character in order to capture his attributes indirectly.*

People either belong in a place, or they wish to escape from it—in either situation, the writer can add substantially to his characterization by examining the character's environment. In pulp stories writers sometimes put great stress on an individual's desire to escape from his objective situation, and hence the details of environment that come into the story serve indirectly, as well as directly, to indicate the dreams and the illusions that the character wishes to follow. In general, however, commercial stories tend to avoid anything that seems to be static, and hence the details of environment used for characterization are usually worked into the thread of narrative or action. The purely creative writer, who is not so self-consciously devoted to action, will frequently pause to look at environment with an eye to extracting from it as much as possible that will contribute dimension to his characters. Here, for example, is the technique practiced by James Joyce in "A Painful Case":

Mr. James Duffy lived in Chapelizod because he wished to live as far as possible from the city of which he was a citizen and because he found all the other suburbs of Dublin mean, modern and pretentious. He lived in an old sombre house and from his window he could look into the disused distillery or upwards along the shallow river on which Dublin is built. The lofty walls of his uncarpeted room were free from pictures. He had himself bought every article of furniture in the room, a black iron bedstead, an iron washstand, four cane chairs, a clothes-rack, a coal-scuttle, a fender and irons and a square table on which lay a double desk. A bookcase had been made in an alcove by means of shelves of white wood. The bed was clothed with white bedclothes and a black and scarlet rug covered the foot. A little hand-mirror hung above the washstand and during the day a white-shaded lamp stood as the sole ornament of the mantel-piece. The books on the white wooden shelves were arranged from below upwards according to bulk. A complete Wordsworth stood at one end of the lowest shelf and a copy of the *Maynooth Catechism*, sewn into the cloth cover of a notebook, stood

166

at one end of the top shelf. Writing materials were always on the desk. In the desk lay a manuscript translation of Hauptmann's *Michael Kramer,* the stage directions of which were written in purple ink, and a little sheaf of papers held together by a brass pin. In these sheets a sentence was inscribed from time to time, and, in an ironical moment, the headline of an advertisement for *Bile Beans* had been pasted on to the first sheet. On lifting the lid of the desks a faint fragrance escaped —the fragrance of new cedar-wood pencils or of a bottle of gum or of an overripe apple which might have been left there and forgotten. Mr. Duffy abhorred anything which betokened physical or mental disorder.

These lines form the opening of the story. Joyce then goes on to describe the physical, personal, and emotional traits of James Duffy, and finally to discuss his general traits. The story, in other words, seems to give a straightforward description of environment by an author who has not yet learned to experiment and to omit, to suggest rather than to present directly. But what is noteworthy is that by the time we are told that Mr. James Duffy "abhorred anything which betokened physical or mental disorder," we have already been made very much aware of his character.

A word of warning is appropriate, and Virginia Woolf has given it to us in her essay, "Mr. Bennett and Mrs. Brown," on the art of characterization in the novel—and in terms of the above convention that short-story writers and novelists alike use in the creation of character. All too frequently writers have described the situation and habitation of the Mrs. Browns of the world, thinking that by giving a picture of the house, they have automatically given us the character of the person who lives there, whereas this may, in fact, lead us away from our concern with the human being to things that are just not the proper concern of the novelist or story writer at all: taxes, rentals, upkeep, economic conditions and upheavals, social institutions, and so on.

Action. To characterize by action, demonstrate a person's character by what he says and does.

This statement will, of course, remind the reader that in this book dialogue is considered as a form of action; and we must now indicate how dialogue is made convincing to the reader. First of all, dialogue is an index to the character of the speakers—i.e., it is revelatory. The talk may be about something else, but for the writer, one of its principal points lies in its power to reveal character, although, of course, through dialogue he may also give any information he wishes to the reader. Even so, dialogue does double duty, and perhaps even triple or quadruple duty. Here is a bit of dialogue that reveals character:

'Personally,' Whitey Connors said, 'I am very grateful for the pattern of human nature that supplies me with suckers to fleece, because I have a very strong aversion to carrying a dinner pail.'

Or again, from Eudora Welty's "Petrified Man":

'Reach in my purse and git me a cigarette without no powder in it if you kin, Mrs. Fletcher, honey,' said Leota to her ten o'clock shampoo-and-set customer. 'I don't like no perfumed cigarettes.'

The vulgarity of both characters is manifest, but in the first, there is the attempt to mask it by the studied use of orotund language, and in the second, Leota is openly brash, breezy, and vulgar.

Written dialogue, in the second place, though imitative of real speech, is never a literal transcript of it. The writer may find it amusing and at the same time instructive to attempt to take conversation down as it occurs. He will be fascinated by the fact that his literal transcript seems but the sorriest and flimsiest imitation. Dialogue requires selection, arrangement, artful tricks of repetition, of indications of intonation of voice.

In the third place, in order to be convincing, dialogue follows the forms of colloquial language, rather than of standard formal English. In colloquial speech, there is a good deal of slurring, combining of words, looseness of grammar. It is "I don't," rather than "I do not"; and "you'll," instead of "you will." People speak, furthermore, not always in full sentences but in terms of sentence fragments, or mere phrases. One of the things that makes Henry James so difficult for many people to read is that his conversations are frequently so formal and convoluted that the reader is constantly in danger of losing the thread of the illusion of life in mere exasperation with the speech of the characters. The attempt to get characters to speak as they normally speak requires not only an accurate ear for recognizable mannerisms of colloquial speech, but also for distinctive traits that mark the characters' intonations, and not those of the author.

Again, many stories require the use of dialect or regional language. Certain conventions exist in the form of special words for distinctive areas of the country: "You all" or "y'awl"; "kin" (for *can*); "hain't" or "ain't"—and literally tens of dozens more for the South. And then others for the North, for New England, for the West, for the big city, for the country village—the distinctions are many. Along with dialectal forms, one can place the shoptalk of specific occupations and professions, the language of the underworld, of the con man, of the literate, of the uneducated. So many distinctions exist and are so important, not alone to characterize but to establish the illusion of a story, that indeed a whole volume could be written on the subject. About the most profitable way, however, a writer can become adept in extracting for his dialogue the flesh and blood of character is to cultivate a sensitive pair of ears and to practice diligently—reading aloud his own dialogue and polishing it to capture the rhythms of ordinary speech, while artfully bending it to his fictional purposes.

Incidentally, there is a distinction to be drawn between commercial and quality stories in the amount of dialect permissible: by and large, commercial editors do not like writers to use too much dialect, if any at all. A writer can insert a few words or turns of speech, which will indicate a region, a character, a nationality, a type; but an editor of a national magazine aims at an audience that transcends strictly regional barriers, and he does not wish to offer —except in the case of a truly unusual story—what might offend either in terms of reading difficulty or of individual feelings. Quality stories, on the other hand, are not bound by these restrictions, and many stories exist in which the writer has made a much more thorough-going attempt than the pulp or slick writer to capture the sounds and forms of dialectal language.

Finally, although the principal point of dialogue is to reveal character, this is only another way of stating that dialogue serves to advance the complication: character revealed makes the complication significant. Returning, then, to the use of dialogue to represent character, it is obvious that the writer must think in terms of the general, personal, emotional, and physical traits of the character when he has him speak. What does a high school girl say about the elaborate ball gown she has seen in the shop window? What does the genial and kindly old gentleman say to the pretty miss who has inadvertently caused him to stumble? What are the intonations of voice of the young lover who has just fancied a slight on the part of his loved one? Dialogue is appropriately the dress of the character and the very heart, at times, of the complication.

Not only does a character's speech reveal him, but also so do his actions. Of the two, speech and action, action is by far the more solid way of creating character. In the great days of comic literature, in the plays of Molière and the novels of Henry Fielding, the conflict that existed between the speech of the character and his actions, between his verbal view of himself and the actual traits of his character, were made to yield a particularly delightful species of comedy. Today, however, the much more usual view of the way to treat character exists in the statement that what a character says and what he does must be made more or less consistent. The possibility always exists, however, that a writer can exploit the distinction between a person's speech and his actions in order to bring about an ironic revelation of real character. In many ways this is precisely what Henry James does in his story "A Beast in the Jungle."

At any rate, here is an illustration, from a commerical story, of characterization by action:

Phyllis stopped to see why the group of miners on the wooden sidewalk were laughing. She saw Herb Sanger in the middle of the street, so drunk he couldn't get to his feet. Every time Herb tried to get up, his feet flew out from under him. She walked toward him, unmindful of the ankle-deep mud. She placed her hands under his arms and helped him to his feet. The mud on his clothing was ruining her new riding habit, but she didn't care as she helped the drunken man to the wooden sidewalk.

In John Steinbeck's story "Flight," the actions of the protagonist, Pepé, serve constantly, with the exception of his final action, to contrast incongruously with what Pepé thinks of himself and what his mother thinks of him. The story concerns a boy of nineteen who, true to his Spanish-Mexican-Indian heritage, wishes to be thought of as a man. He is given the task of riding into Monterey from his poor, struggling little farm to buy salt and medicine. In town, he visits the home of a friend of his mother's, drinks a little wine, is insulted by another man, kills him with his knife, and flies away— first, home to store up provisions, and then to the mountains to escape revenge. Pepé consistently thinks of himself as a man. His mother is inclined not to think that he has yet reached man's estate, although he is close to it. But his actions reveal him most of all: the practice-throwing of a knife to gain the admiration of his younger brother and sister; the impulsive killing of the man because of a few insulting words; the loss of his coat, his rifle, his horse during his flight, all the result of inexperience; the flight itself instead of a watchful ambush in a relatively secure place. Only at the very end, when weakened by his wound, by thirst, and by flight, he stands up in full gaze of his pursuer to accept what is inevitable, his death, does Pepé truly become a man. Throughout the story, Steinbeck has continually pointed out, by Pepé's actions, the ambiguity of his estate, his boyishness close to manhood, his manhood yet leavened with immaturity and inexperience. It is only in this way that Steinbeck can arrive at his final equation, which is so much a part of the heritage of the people whose lives he deals with in this story, that manhood involves great danger, even the calm acceptance of death.

By and large, it can be taken as a rule that the actions of the character must be consistent with his nature. If there is any disparity between the way a character is described and the way he acts, then the reader must not be left to puzzle out the writer's intention. The writer must either consciously utilize such a disparity, or he must make his character act consistently in terms of his description. Too often to ignore, novices at writing receive such penciled notes as the following from their teachers or, worse still, from editors: "The story has possibilities, but you do not give your characters any life —what happens in the story is contrived—the characters are made to do things or say things that they could not possibly do or say. . . ."

Narration. To characterize by narration, present the actions of a character over a wider time span than can be given in action.

Narration, as we observed before, avoids the minutiae of action in order to arrive at a compressed and rapid presentation. Action tends toward the microscopic: it is an analysis and gives a scene, in terms of particulars, details, motions, gestures, speech, in order to approximate, psychologically, the same amount of time it would take in real life. Narration avoids real time and gives us an effect of character engaging in numerous actions. Obviously, narration can therefore give an impression of character. For example, let us take the sentence which we previously used:

Sam Smith came home drunk, kicked the dog, sent his kids to bed without supper, and then beat up his wife.

Such a rapid narration of events gives us a fair idea of the type of person Sam Smith is.

Another example of narration used to characterize—though combined with exposition—is this passage from Somerset Maugham's story "The Colonel's Lady":

For before his marriage he had been in the Welsh Guards. At the end of the war he retired and settled down to the life of a country gentleman in the spacious house, some twenty miles from Sheffield, which one of his forebears had built in the reign of George II. George Peregrine had an estate of some fifteen hundred acres which he managed with ability; he was a justice of the peace and performed his duties conscientiously. During the season he rode to hounds two days a week. He was a good shot, a golfer, and though now a little over fifty could still play a hard game of tennis. He could describe himself with propriety as an all-round sportsman.

In discussing the various methods of characterizing people, we have been forced to analyze them separately. It is obvious, however, that in the story, a character is created not in terms of any one method, but in terms of them all. No character can truly be said to exist if the writer merely tells how he looks and not what he says and does. It is true that the characters in certain short stories remain, in terms of their physical appearance, vague and shadowy while giving us, at the same time, a strong impression of their inward natures. Perhaps the least significant element of a person is his physical appearance—certainly that is so if one had to choose between the mere physical traits alone and those significant personal and emotional characteristics that make a person individually interesting. But it remains a rule, established by convention, that to give the principal characters of a story any vitality, the writer must try to suggest all four sides of his portrait, the general, personal, emotional, and physical. In doing so, he must inevitably combine the methods of presenting character that we have been discussing. Only in such a fashion can a character seem to have depth, which is only another way of saying that, on the basis of what we know of a character in a short story, we can rather confidently predict how he would act in other circumstances, confronting another dilemma. The repetition of a character's traits when variously given in terms of exposition, description, action (including dialogue), and narration, will lend a solidity to the portrait that any one of these methods, taken alone, cannot offer. Hence, it is unwise for the inexperienced writer to practice any one method separately from the main body of a story, for it is his function to imagine character so well as to involve the characters in a developing structure, which will call into use all four of the basic tools of composition.

There remain two things left to be said about characterization. What, in sum, causes the differences between characters in quality stories and those in commercial ones? And while we are on the subject of characterization, how do characters in short stories differ from those in the novel?

To discuss why there is a difference in characterization in commercial and quality stories, one would like to be able to discover some hard-and-fast rule covering the length of both types of short story. That is, it would be relatively easy if one could say that in the quality story a good deal more space is devoted to the characters, and that as a consequence these stories are longer as a rule than commercial ones. Unfortunately, even a superficial acquaintance with the various types of short story will disclose that many quality stories are quite as short as the conventional slick story and quite as long as the fifteen-thousand-word pulp confession story. One can only assert that quality writers tend to consider length as less important to their undertaking than do commercial writers. As a consequence, they feel a certain freedom in creating character, which leads them sometimes, though not always, toward lengthier descriptive and expository passages than commercial writers would feel safe in using.

One of the main distinctions between the characterizations of commercial and quality fiction appears to be the subtlety of shading in describing character. That is, the commercial story tends to draw rigid lines between the good and the bad, the hero and the villain, the sympathetic and unsympathetic character. The result is an increase in direct dramatic appeal and an absence of overtones or resonances that are set up and carry the reader along in a state of curiosity for some time after the story is ended. In quality stories, the shadings between the good and the bad character, the sympathetic and the unsympathetic, tend to break down. It is unusual, as we pointed out in discussing the off-beat story, to find an unsympathetic protagonist in commercial stories. It is not at all unusual in quality stories to find an unsympathetic character presented in such a fashion that, eventually, he becomes sympathetic. The quality story pleads for an extension of our sympathies at the risk of losing sheer dramatic excitement.

Thus, in one book devoted to an audience of would-be successful authors, we are told by an editor who has worked on several commercial magazines that whenever character threatens to overshadow action in interest, the writer must remember that action is more basic and that stories may exist in which our interest in character is almost, though not quite, negligible. In another book written for a literary audience, we are told that stereotypes of character exist only in commercial fiction, never in serious fiction, and that to read commercial stories with more than a superficial interest is to overlook gratuitously their great distortions of reality. It appears that the commercial editor desires stories of action rather than of character, and this critic then goes on to point out that commercial writers prefer stories of action rather than character. Isn't this a little like accusing an arsonist of being a firebug?

It seems useless to draw battle lines over the question, particularly if one is seriously interested in becoming a writer. The convention of commercial fiction, which prohibits subtle shadings of character, functions in a number of quality stories with telling effect, such as in Ernest Hemingway's "The Killers," Shirley Jackson's "The Lottery," or De Maupassant's "The Necklace." The most one can do is to point out that commercial stories do tend to present less tellingly drawn characters but it is no less possible for the commercial writer to fulfill the primary functions of the story than it is for the creative artist; and one can do no better than to again quote Somerset Maugham, using his words to express what those functions are: a good short story, he writes in his chapter "The Short Story" in *Points of View,* "is a piece of fiction, dealing with a single incident, material or spiritual, that can be read at a sitting; it is original, it must sparkle, excite or impress; and it must have unity of effect or impression." Many a commercial story of the present time certainly fulfills this prescription.

The really central distinction in characterization in commercial and quality stories, apart from the greater subtlety of character, lies in the fact that the noncommercial writer attempts to develop his characters by indirect, rather than direct, statement. In this chapter, we have already indicated this distinction, but it is by far the most important one and deserves further consideration. The pulp or slick writer may characterize an individual as methodical in his habits, fussily aroused when things are out of order, happy only when he has reduced his existence to a barren colorlessness. The purely creative writer attempts to establish such traits in terms of felt experience, as Henry James does of Marcher in "The Beast in the

174

Jungle," or as Joyce does of James Duffy in "A Painful Case." It is the attempt to render experience on the most immediate and concrete levels that modifies the quality writer's characterizations. Otherwise, he, too, would be forced to exhibit his character in terms of direct statement. The attempt is a very great attempt and deserves its exalted place in the art of the short story, for by avoiding overt statement about character, the writer often allows the more immediate perceptions of the reader to operate on character. By means of this technique, the writer does not ask the reader to imagine for him—he does the imagining for the reader. As a consequence, the writer can suggest the composite connections and interconnections of character with environment or with tangible fact in such a way as to stir up all kinds of reverberations, echoes, and nuances in somewhat the same way life does. To read a letter from a long-dead loved one in an attic where apples are stored, where perhaps the weak rays of a slanted wintry sun play over the wrinkling skin of the apples and a rich fermenting sweetness fills the air—is this not to combine objective fact with suggestion?

Because of his organized sensibility, the creative writer may be, and in fact is at times, an advance guard of the spirit of his age; such is Stephen Crane, whose war stories provide a tragi-comic view of human carnage, or Anton Chekhov, whose stories delicately spin out causes for violence. And undoubtedly because of this, in a kind of perversity, so far as writers themselves are concerned, critics have taken it upon themselves to erect flat rules about writing that make the more direct methods of commercial fiction seem unworthy of attention. It is interesting that both Stephen Crane in his Whilomville stories, and Anton Chekhov in the three hundred stories he wrote from 1880 to 1885, wrote potboilers. How much the practice of direct presentation may lead toward more subtle forms of artistry is outside the scope of this book, but that there is some connection is not debatable. For this reason it seems unfair to applaud the merits of characterization in the quality story and simultaneously condemn the hearty and robust directness of commercial fiction.

To turn, now, to the question of the difference between characterization in the novel and the short story, we confront something about which there is no difficulty in making a clear, positive statement. For with the exception of certain types of novel, such as mystery stories and routine westerns, without fully developed characters a novel cannot live. In a novel, one must show all four sides of a character, his general, personal, emotional, and physical traits, and with such a development that the reader is satisfied by the totality of character presentation.

For example, we mentioned a commercial story about a college girl who wished to seduce a man in order to get what she actually wished out of college, marriage. In the short story, it is sufficient to show her as a member of a group, as being headstrong and selfish, and not unattractive. To take the same character and put her into a novel would require a great expansion of this limited characterization. In terms of her general traits, we would have to know her childhood environment, her past education, her family's influences upon her, the crowd she was accustomed to running around with. We would have to expand the presentation of her personal traits. We know that she is selfish and obstinate, but what about the rest of her? Is she wise or foolish? Merciful or cruel? Passionate or frigid? We know that she is inclined to pout and to be resentful, but what other emotions belong to her? What are her hopes, fears, dreams, sorrows, joys, desires, hates, pet peeves? We know that she is attractive, but how do her physical characteristics link up with the rest of her? Has she had to battle unattractiveness in her childhood? Has her physical appearance set up any psychological barriers in her character? Or has it smoothed the way for too easy acceptance, not enough challenge?

These are questions that the novelist would have to ponder. In fact, it would not harm the short-story writer to ponder them in constructing his story, for a short story results from a deliberate whittling away of nonessentials. The novel tends to make such elimination less necessary; there are fewer nonessentials in the novel.

In speaking of characterization, we have given rules and techniques, and it might appear to some readers that a character, like a plot, like a short story, will be manipulated, invented, mechanical—a little like a jigsaw puzzle, a trifle like a machine. There is some truth to the assertion that a short story *is* exactly this, even a great short story; but the truth will be more apparent to a writer than a reader. In a way every story writer must be a bit of a magician, by dextrous sleight of hand making rabbits appear or disappear, or discovering a live person within a supposedly empty box. The audience, who suspends disbelief for the illusion of the show, may even become so enthusiastic as to think that magic actually does occur. The audience will then be in the same frame of mind as certain literary critics who hold that, in the final analysis, the art of the short story is too mysterious to be explicable. The true mystery is that the writer can believe so intensely in what he is doing as to make the illusion possible for the rest of us. The real success of the writer in creating a character will depend upon the intensity of his faith that such a person as he describes really could exist.

EXERCISES FOR CHAPTER 8

1. Read a pulp, slick, and quality story. For each one, underline the general, personal, emotional, and physical traits of the protagonist in any passages exposing his character. Determine which story is most concerned with fully developing the character. Do any traits predominate over others in the characterization; for example, does the author of the pulp story concentrate more upon the physical traits of his character than the author of the quality story? If so, why?
2. Demonstrate how the complication threatens the character of the protagonist in each of the stories you read for the first exercise.
3. Analyze the following characters and determine whether or not they are valid characterizations; i.e., that they are thoroughly consistent and probable: the Partner in Bret Harte's "Tennessee's Partner"; the Sire de Malétroit in Robert Louis Stevenson's "The Sire de Malétroit's Door"; the mother in D. H. Lawrence's "The Rocking-Horse Winner."
4. Take the formula story you wrote for one of the earlier exercises. Now go back and underline the general, personal, emotional, and physical traits of the protagonist. Which form of characterization predominates? If there is more characterization by action than by description, determine why.
5. Determine what traits the protagonist reveals in the moment of truth in each of the stories named above in the third exercise.
6. As we have discussed previously, an embryo plot develops when we exaggerate the complication facing a character. Is it possible to imagine a character first and then confront him with a complication? Discuss. If you come to the conclusion that you begin first with character rather than with complication, does this invalidate the method of developing a story by exaggerating a complication?
7. Which of the following implications can most logically be drawn from the statement that "the real success of the writer in creating a character will depend upon the intensity of his faith that such a person as he describes really could exist"?

177

a. A writer need not exaggerate the traits of his character.

b. To create a vivid character, the writer must exaggerate character traits.

c. Only writers of quality stories have the right to become enthusiastic about their created characters.

d. A character in a story is less real than a character in real life.

8. Discuss why it is unsound to practice only one method of characterization.

9

The Techniques
of Craftsmanship
and How Professional
Writers Employ Them

THERE ARE A NUMBER of technical elements that we have yet to discuss in the creation of a short story. Although compared to the development of a story line or plot, or the choice of the curve of fiction, or the point of view from which to tell the story, or experimentation in various ways of handling the complication, these elements are subsidiary, they are nonetheless very important. It is our present purpose to discuss and examine them in some detail, even though this means that in this chapter we are forced to skip from topic to topic.

SITUATION AND SCENE

Webster's New Collegiate Dictionary defines a situation as the "relative combination of circumstances at a moment; a critical or unusual state of affairs; specifically, in narrative and drama, a particular complex of affairs at a given moment in the action." A scene, on the other hand, refers to that "part of a drama or narrative presenting a single situation, dialogue, or the like"; and it may refer to "the place in which the action of a play, story, etc., is laid. . . ." In order to untangle these two definitions, we will begin by stating that a situation is the more general and abstract. It embraces, in statement form, the complex of issues, attitudes, and values involved in any encounter or conflict. We can sum up a scene in a sentence, such as "a boy meets a girl," "a farmer faces disastrous crop losses from frost," "a wife loses her husband's love"; the scene is a particularized method of presenting a situation. To state what a scene presents, however, forces one to describe it in terms of the situation involved in the scene; and it is obvious that in doing so, we desert the scene itself for the sake of the summary. A scene is, therefore, a method of making a situation concrete, particular, and visible; that is, we perceive a scene through our senses. We conceive of the situation, with our minds, however.

1. A short story is generally confined to not more than one statement and two restatements of the central situation.

As we have already seen in discussing the comic and tragic curves of fiction, and in discussing characterization where a protagonist moves from his general traits to a denial of them and then returns to his original characterization once again, there appear invariably to be three stages in the conventional short story. At times we call these three stages the beginning, the middle, and the end; but it is more helpful to call them, here, the statement and restatements of the situation; for the word *situation* denotes, as we have observed, a conflicting tangle of issues and values; and the words *beginning, middle,* and *end* imply steps along a chronological path, without any implication of conflict. In the linear story, the protagonist faces, generally, only one statement of a situation to which he is either blind or passive.

The issues that are involved in a situation of conflict may be sorted out in terms of certain questions. *Who* are the characters involved? *Where* does it take place? *What* exactly does take place? *Why* did the conflict arise? *When* does it take place? *What* exactly are the issues involved? Now it is obvious that in thinking about these questions, we are attempting to develop the situation in concrete terms and convert it into a scene or scenes. The conflict of a story emerges in terms of scenes. Though there are generally three statements of the situation in the conventional short story and one in the linear story, the author may find it essential to use five or more scenes to bring the conflict to life. We will see in a little while how

180

to choose the moments in the story that should be converted into scenes.

Now it is obvious that the forms of conflict, which can occur in short stories, is limited. Let us list the possible, and most generalized, ones:

Man against man	Man against nature
Men against men (war)	Man against disaster
Woman against woman	Man against himself
Woman against man	Man against his environment
Man against woman	

It is not through these generalized conflicts that a writer can be original, but principally through his language (style, figures of speech, vividness, etc.), through the management of scene, and through the restatement that he gives to his central situation. Let us, for example, take one of the oldest forms of conflict, man against woman:

Situation 1: Boy meets girl.
Situation 2: Boy loses girl.
Situation 3: Boy gets girl.

The ability to use originality in the restatements of a central situation is extremely important. To make a story salable the writer has to invent an original restatement of the situation for the boy to meet the girl, an original restatement for the boy to lose the girl, and an original restatement for the boy to win the girl. An excellent example of an author's creating original and entertaining restatements of the oldest situation in writing is contained in the slick story, "The Next to the Last Word," reprinted in the Appendix on page 349. Unfortunately, many short stories that find their way into magazines conform to classic situations, stereotyped characters, and unimaginative or imitative restatements. Perhaps one should rather say fortunately, for thereby a market exists for the originally inventive writer who uses talent and skill.

Now although a writer will think in terms of situations, he must also be able to desert the purely abstract sphere of thought and turn his abstract conflict into particular scenes. As the reader will recall, we remarked in dealing with the four basic tools of composition that only certain parts of a short story should be put into scenes of action. How, then, does one choose those parts that are to be portrayed in scenes? The principle to observe is the following:

II. Dramatize in scenes those parts of the story in which the tangle of issues becomes clearest and the conflict most dramatically forceful.

Now let us look at several examples of magazine fiction to illustrate the authors' use of central situation and conflict, as well as to give us clues about the construction of scenes:

1. A love story of the eternal triangle. Two men want the same woman —man against man—and the author produces conflict each time they meet.
2. A love story of the eternal triangle. Two women want the same man —woman against woman—and the author produces conflict each time they meet.
3. A young adult story of a couple heading for divorce—man against woman—and the author produces conflict each time they meet.
4. A story about a young city couple who buy a farm and face all kinds of trials—man against nature—and the author produces conflict as they fight nature to save their crops.
5. A western story about a cowboy and a wild stallion—man against nature—and the author produces conflict each time they meet.
6. A story about townspeople fighting a fire that threatens to wipe out the entire town—man against disaster—and the author produces conflict as they fight the blaze.
7. A mystery story about an escaped criminal who has gone straight for many years, is married, has children and a respectable job— man against himself—and the author produces conflict as the hero fights with his conscience.
8. A story about a woman who has a weakness for gambling ("Winner at Bingo," printed in the Appendix on page 285)—woman against herself—and the author produces conflict between the woman and her conscience.
9. A young love story ("The Next to the Last Word," printed in the Appendix on page 349)—man against his environment—and the author produces conflict as the man struggles to escape from his environment and take his girl with him.
10. A career story ("No Margin for Error," printed in the Appendix on page 331)—man against himself—and the author produces conflict between the man and his conscience.
11. A suspense story ("I Will Not Talk," printed in the Appendix on page 382)—man against man—and the author produces conflict in the constant clash of two men's wills.

And let us look in more detail at several examples of quality stories:

12. Somerset Maugham's "The Colonel's Lady": A story about pompous Colonel Peregrine, who faces, as he thinks, social disapproval over his wife's popular book of love poetry describing an adulterous affair —man against man as social beings—and Maugham produces conflict each time Peregrine faces a representative of the social world.
13. De Maupassant's "The Story of a Farm Girl": A story about an ignorant peasant girl whose search for love leads her to give birth to an illegitimate child and to face loveless social disapproval— woman against her environment—and the author produces conflict each time she faces her small world.
14. Mark Schorer's "Boy in the Summer Sun": A story about a young college graduate who in late summer discovers that he faces a new world in which change must be accepted—man against himself— and the author produces conflict each time the protagonist faces his changing world.

In even so cursory a glance at successful short stories, one notes that each situation results in suggested moments of portrayed conflict. As a result, one can see that there are certain elements that each scene must possess:

> *III. A scene must involve the following three things:*
>   *1. A meeting between two opposing forces.*
>   *2. An exploitation on the part of the writer of the inherent conflict within the meeting.*
>   *3. A suggestion as to the result of the meeting.*

If each scene contains these elements, then it follows more or less naturally that the scene will serve one further capacity, which we can state in the following fashion:

> *IV. The result of the meeting between two opposing forces in any scene must be the primary cause for what happens in the next scene, and must set up a transition to it.*

Inexperienced writers often get their scenes out of focus by overlooking the fact that the real justification for so close and meticulous a view of events will lie in an analysis of the elements of the conflict inherent in the situation. To outline a story in terms of the story's situation will often expose to a perceptive eye the points of conflict that deserve to be dramatized scenically.

It is worth a brief digression at this point to clarify a question which the reader may have about the construction of scenes. For he may have observed in numerous short stories that an author used the particularity and concreteness of scenic presentation for other effects than we have described. That is, he may use scenes to characterize or simply to convey information that the reader must know to understand and believe in the story. The best way to differentiate between scenes used for such purposes and scenes used to develop the conflict is to describe them by the words *small* and *big*. The big scenes in any short story always present a meeting between opposing forces, as well as all the other elements we have mentioned.

The sole purpose of the writer in bringing opposing forces together is to produce conflict. The result of the meeting in every scene must be that somebody or something wins, loses, concedes a point, is forced to make a decision, or just simply withdraws. Thus, in the love story about the two men who wanted the same woman (example 1, above), both men in one of the scenes ask the girl to go to a dance; she cannot go with both of them, and so one must win and the other lose. In the story about the city couple who bought the farm (example 4, above), a heavy frost in one scene destroys their fruit crop; nature wins and they lose. In the story about the townspeople fighting the fire (example 6, above), it appears that the townspeople have the fire beaten only for the wind to shift, and the townspeople lose ground. In one scene of "The Colonel's Lady," Colonel Peregrine meets a newspaper reviewer of his wife's book, dislikes the fellow intensely at first sight, hardly listens to the man's praise of his wife's poetry, and withdraws, wandering off to eat lunch in irritation. A study of the pulp and slick stories in the Appendix, also, will show that opposing forces meet in all the big scenes.

Though the writer exploits the conflict inherent in the meeting of opposing forces, this does not necessarily mean that violent action occurs. Yet if there is anything that distinguishes pulp, slick, and quality stories in the handling of scenes, it is in the relative physical energy of the participants. In most pulp confession stories, the protagonists weep, cry, shout, scream, slam things, call on God in extemporaneous passion, and in general act with little restraint. The pulp story writer is following a convention of his trade, which insists that conflict must have a demonstrable physical analogy. This is not true of slick or quality stories, and much less true of the latter than the former. There are two reasons: the situational conflict in quality stories tends to be representative of classes, social groups, mankind in general, rather than of some individual, passionate person; and the protagonists usually exhibit certain typical characteristics that we have noted a number of times in quality stories. They are to a certain extent blind or passive toward the conflicts facing them, and hence often act in a more confused fashion than do pulp or slick protagonists, who appear to know without a shadow of a doubt what the conflicts are that face them.

PANORAMA

We now turn to a way of presenting situations that is pre-eminently characteristic of the quality story, though it occurs now and again in commercial fiction. The pulp and slick writer is generally dedicated to the proposition that his story occurs in a particular time, a specific locale, and involves a recognizable and limited number of participants, who are individuals in their own right. The quality writer is inclined to make his story more universal in nature; his locale, though specific, more representative of a wider region, a historical consciousness, or the universal human condition; and he will almost always view his characters as representative of social, cultural, economic, historical, or any of a variety of other forces. None of this means that the quality writer does not employ scenes as do commercial writers, but frequently enough, in order to introduce a scene, the quality writer will use panorama. Precisely what is the meaning of panorama?

Panorama attempts to express the universal aspects of a situation rather than the strictly limited and specific.

It will be best to take a couple of examples to indicate the nature of panorama and its distinctive use in the quality story. The opening paragraphs of Hemingway's story, "In Another Country" serve as an excellent illustration of the panoramic view:

In the fall the war was always there, but we did not go to it any more. It was cold in the fall in Milan and the dark came very early. Then the electric lights came on, and it was pleasant along the streets looking in the windows. There was much game hanging outside the shops, and the snow powdered in the fur of the foxes and the wind blew their tails. The deer hung stiff and heavy and empty, and small birds blew in the wind and the wind turned their feathers. It was a cold fall and the wind came down from the mountains.

We were all at the hospital every afternoon, and there were different ways of walking across the town through the dusk to the hospital. Two of the ways were alongside canals, but they were long. Always, though, you crossed a bridge across a canal to enter the hospital. There was a choice of three bridges. On one of them a woman sold roasted chestnuts. It was warm, standing in front of her charcoal fire, and the chestnuts were warm afterward in your pocket. The hospital was very old and very beautiful, and you entered through a gate and walked across a courtyard and out a gate on the other side. There were usually funerals starting from the courtyard. Beyond the old hospital were the new brick pavilions, and there we met every afternoon and were all very polite and interested in what was the matter, and sat in the machines that were to make so much difference.

After the close of these two paragraphs, a doctor comes up to the narrator, and we have a scene; but first the two paragraphs have given us the whole panorama of the situation. It is a view that distinguishes between those who are in a world at war and those who are in another place, "another country," those who have been wounded and are now out of the war. The sweeping view of these first two paragraphs is closely carried by details. For the narrator, who is an American, we learn later, to be in another country is to be in Italy, rather than in the United States; but for the hospitalized soldiers, it is to be in the city and not at the front; they are visitants at the hospital—they walk from the city to the other country of the maimed; they are returned soldiers and not the civilian population; and of them all, the major in the story is in yet another country still, the country of the innately brave. Throughout, the details suggest separation, isolation, loneliness, death: the dead game hanging on hooks, the fall, the wind from the mountains, the politeness of each man to the other, the sense of the futility of their search for health.

As we suggested in discussing Gustave Flaubert's story "A Simple Heart," and as we observe in "In Another Country," a panoramic view of character is obtained by suggesting a view over all—the use of plurals to indicate habitual actions, a daily conformity to circumstances. While the scene is particular and timeful, panorama suggests that time is unimportant, for there is no concentration upon any one moment. Those who were "at the hospital every afternoon" are less individualized people than they are generalized outcasts, both from war and from civilian life. Thus, the characters represent a particular aspect of humanity trapped in limbo and describe one of the generalized results of war-making mankind.

Now let us look and see how closely the commercial writer approximates the use of panorama. That panorama appears infrequently in commercial fiction is certainly a safe generalization; but this is not to say that it may not be used at all. And a somewhat close approximation to panorama can be seen in the amusing slick story, "Precious Moment," printed in the Appendix on page 372. The first four paragraphs of that story serve to give an overall view; but it is noteworthy, in contrasting these paragraphs with the opening paragraphs of "In Another Country" that the panoramic effect confines itself chiefly to recognizable characters and to establishing the situation, rather than to extending the significance and inclusiveness of both. There is a much closer approximation to the use of panorama, which is found so frequently in quality stories, in one of Walt Coburn's fine Western stories, "Dynamite" (first published in *Adventure,* August 1928). In order to give us the significance of his protagonists, one of whom is an old-time freighter, the other a swamper, Coburn contrasts the old days with modern ones. The development of the West owed much to the rough-hewn, whiskey-drinking, mud-fighting freighter and his team-drawn cargo of dynamite, liquor, victuals, and so on, which struggles across the endless prairies in all sorts of weather. Modern times have brought highways, motor-drawn trailers, and the disappearance of a colorful breed of men. Coburn's story pauses to give in panorama the flavor of that rough era as a part of the past.

Panorama is an invaluable device for extending the story's central situation, making it more universal, abstract, and applicable to the widest possible range of significance. Its use in the commercial story is very limited, and justly so in terms of the rationale of pulp and slick writing.

MOTIVATION. MOTIVATION REVEALS TO THE READER WHY A CHARACTER DOES AND SAYS CERTAIN THINGS RATHER THAN OTHERS.

The fact that we have characterized an individual may not reveal the reasons why he acts the way he does in a particular scene. Perhaps such a statement may seem odd to the reader who imagines that action, of all the methods of characterization, is the most revealing way of establishing character. To illustrate the importance of supplying motivation, let us take an example:

"Will I see you tomorrow?" Matt asked.
"I'm going to the Johnsons' party," Phyllis said.
"And so am I," Matt said.

It is possible that we have shown Matt to be a basically kind man, but rather shy, perhaps overly punctilious in some ways, since he leads a bachelor's existence. And Phyllis is a young, charming woman who has an independent mind and a ready insight into the nature of other people. Even had we described the characters prior to the quoted conversation, would the reader have been able to experience the scene? It is doubtful, for both characters are used here as mere puppets to tell the reader that Matt wants to see Phyllis again, and their conversation merely provides a transition to the scene at the Johnsons' party. Let us rephrase the scene and supply the motivation:

"Will I see you tomorrow?" Matt asked, and found himself suddenly go tense as he waited for her answer. She was the most beautiful and charming woman he'd ever met, and he wanted to see a lot more of her. If she refused to see him again, it could only mean there was another man.

"I'm going to the Johnsons' party," she said, smiling as if she felt kindly toward him.

"And so am I," he said happily, reading in her smile more than just a promise to see him tomorrow.

A study of the stories in the Appendix will show that the protagonists have been given very strong motivation for everything they say and do. Marge Stark's gambling, in "Winner at Bingo," leads her to lie, cheat on her food budget, and even steal from her husband. Such an immediate motive often conceals others more deeply hidden that the characterization will suggest. In "No Margin for Error," Jack tries to cover up his mistake because he believes that if he admits the error he will lose his job, his future, and the home he and his wife have been planning to build. In "Next to the Last Word," Joe Douglas wishes to escape from his New York environment because of his selfish desire to have Sally all to himself. In Katherine Mansfield's "The Fly," the boss ushers old Woodifield out of the office because he wants to give vent to his grief over his dead son and is too proud to show emotion before Woodifield.

> I. If the motivation of a character cannot be directly established by what that character does or says, then use another character to speculate about the motivation.

In Hemingway's story "The Killers," for example, the reader is informed about Ole Andreson's motivation through the speculations of George and Nick Adams:

They did not say anything. George reached down for a towel and wiped the counter.

"I wonder what he did?" Nick said.

"Double-crossed somebody. That's what they kill them for."

We know that this is a mere guess on George's part, since but a moment before he had remarked, "He must have got mixed up in something in Chicago." The dialogue between Nick Adams and George is sufficient, however, to account for Ole's actions.

> *II. In first revising a story, check everything a character does or says in order to make certain that the motivation is clear and evident; it sometimes helps to provide merely an adverb.*

" 'It looks like Tom is going to lose his farm,' Jake said." Now in this sentence we do not know how Jake feels or why he makes the statement, but if we add the adverb *sadly,* then we start to establish his motivation. The inexperienced writer must be on his guard, however, not to let adverbs become too prominent, for the conventional *-ly* ending and repetitive pattern will eventually kill otherwise acceptable dialogue:

"Are you sure you would like to go?" she asked lazily.

"Of course," he answered slowly.

"You seem so positive," she sulked prettily.

"I am positive," he said assertively.

Great writers frequently use adverbs, but when they do, they place them so as to be relatively unobtrusive. Note, for example, D. H. Lawrence's adverbs in the following passage from "The Rocking-Horse Winner," which we have italicized to indicate how they help to establish the characters' motivations:

"Mother," said the boy Paul one day, "why don't we keep a car of our own? Why do we always use uncle's, or else a taxi?"

"Because we're the poor members of the family," said the mother.

"But why are we, mother?"

"Well—I suppose," she said *slowly* and *bitterly,* "it's because your father has no luck."

The boy was silent for some time.

"Is luck money, mother?" he asked, rather *timidly.*

"No, Paul. Not quite. It's what causes you to have money."

"Oh!" said Paul *vaguely.* "I thought when Uncle Oscar said filthy lucker, it meant money."

"Filthy lucre does mean money," said the mother. "But it's lucre, not luck."

"Oh!" said the boy. "Then what is luck, mother?"

"It's what causes you to have money . . . if you're lucky, you will always get more money."

"Oh! Will you? And is father not lucky?"

"Very unlucky, I should say," she said *bitterly*.

A thorough understanding of the motivation or motivations behind a character's actions will help clarify the situation of a story in a writer's mind and make it possible for him to visualize his story better in terms of scenes. In every story, we must ask again and again, why? Why did the woman who lost her only child refuse to adopt another? Why did the lonely old man accept a job as a lighthouse keeper? Why did the young and happily married woman leave her husband to accept a job as ticket taker in a circus? Writers continually ask themselves the question—and provide the answers. Why did Colonel Peregrine in "The Colonel's Lady" make a complacent remark upon first reading his wife's book of poetry, only to completely reverse his views later? Why did Pepé in John Steinbeck's "Flight" throw the knife, kill the man, and then run to the mountains?

No story writer of any kind can afford not to satisfy his own curiosity and that of the reader in the actions of his characters. But if there are no distinctions between commercial and quality writers in terms of the necessity to provide motivation, there are distinctions in the sorts of motivation they use.[1] Quality writers tend, by and large, to avoid normal, outward explanations for events and to search for deeper psychological and perhaps even subconscious explanations. We have already witnessed the phenomenon in D. H. Lawrence's "The Rocking-Horse Winner." Reflection upon the quality stories that we have already discussed will support the statement. Many of Hemingway's heroes exhibit a morbid dread of death and an intensified, hypersensitized appreciation of bravery in the face of death. Katherine Mansfield, Anton Chekhov, and Alberto Moravia all tend to take one trait of an individual—perhaps a concern for sex, a desire for love, a wish to retain youth, a sense of greed—and exaggerate that trait so much that it becomes the one compelling and powerful motivation for the individual's actions in life. The motivations of commercial stories

[1] For confirmation, see an interesting article by F. A. Rockwell: "The Why Behind the What," *Writer's Digest* (November, 1961), pp. 32–33; 74; 76–77; 80.

190

tend to be based upon the conscious mind—what a person does can have a very reasonable and valid direct explanation given for it. The motivations of quality stories are based upon the unconscious mind, the subconscious mind, or even on instincts normally hidden. The rapid growth of the science of psychiatry within the framework of an industrialized and highly mechanical age offers explanations for human behavior in terms even of automatically conditioned responses. Whatever motivations are used, however, the noncommercial writer tends to stress the more hidden, deeper, and often more melancholy reasons for action. As we have seen in the linear story, authors frequently base the behavior of the protagonist on his neurotic self-involvement, rather than upon his ability to perceive, declare, and solve his problem.

OBJECTIVE FACTS AND EMOTIONAL FACTS

Of what does the illusion of reality in a short story consist? The question is, in many ways, a difficult one to answer. When we put our finger on what strikes us as having most reality, we very frequently find it to be the result of a contrivance based upon an artifice and inflated by means of an exaggeration. Most of the secret is found to lie, however, in the fact that a reader believes what we have written to be the truth.

To test the validity of their stories, writers need the discipline of an audience, because they are all too ready to slip back into their own illusions, believing them as if they were actual.

The peculiar thing is that the illusion that one presents is not based so much on the objective facts of the story as it is upon feelings— emotional facts, let us call them. In other words, everything in a short story functions not to present reality, but to give an impression of reality. And this is an impression that brings into play the subjective or emotional personality of the reader. The writer can almost guarantee the reader's willingness to suspend his objective knowledge—he can swallow cabbages as well as underground tea parties if he is put in the proper frame of mind. But once let him read a writer who does not prepare the way by having his protagonist step through a looking glass, and one part of the reader's mind will be at war with the other; his objective knowledge of an ascertainable world will be at war, as it always is, with his subjective emotions. The suspension of disbelief, which Coleridge speaks about as constituting "poetic faith," is a paid suspension that must be purchased: the price exacted is a reader's acute willingness to give disbelief full reign whenever he encounters what goes against established facts. Thus we arrive at a paradoxical rule:

> *I. To increase the illusion of reality, which consists of a reader's subjective faith in what he reads, load the story with accurate objective facts.*

The paradox is observable every time one encounters a story with a verifiable background. For example, a murder mystery recently published in *Ellery Queen's Mystery Magazine* takes place in a hospital laboratory used primarily for sampling and typing blood. The objective facts of the story are there: mention of notes on refrigerators, enamel trays, gentian violet, crossmatching of blood, blood types, reactions of patients to blood transfusions under anesthesia, external symptoms of patients receiving incorrect blood types, identification collars on bottles, sera used for typing blood, aging dates of crossmatched blood, symptoms of shock. Because the facts are verifiable in the story, we grant a faith in and credibility to a story that would otherwise go down like an aspirin tablet swallowed without water. This is not to deny the author's skill; it is rather to affirm it, for the story functions, as all stories must, in terms of a valid and probable exaggeration of character and action against the background of a verifiable world.

Thus if the story writer is to convince the reader of the reality of what he writes, he must command many outer facts, facts of things, places, processes, appearances, machines, locales, looks, prices, colors —the myriad and one things that make up an objective world—a world whose nature and qualities we can all of us agree upon as existent, verifiable, and external to us. The external world is very important to a writer, but of course it is no more the world of the written story than a cat is a drawing. The objective world is always in motion, endlessly at work—surfaces grind against surfaces, the sunlight shifts and changes over the wheat field, the very wheat grains themselves twist within their husks and grow and ripen and then are subject to the grinding wheel or a gentle rotting in the ground. The writer arrests the manifold changes, projects them through his imagination and skill into form, implores the reader by the very presence of that world to accept other things on trust—and then in time, he too becomes dated, and the very solid substance of his outer world will vanish into the limbo of the past. It is a manifest irony, in the last analysis, that the substantiality of the story writer's art—in terms of the future—must rest not upon what is so readily ascertainable as upon the insight into human motivations he reveals, while using factual objects and bits that reflect the material world—like paving blocks and sky-scrapers, eyebrow pencils, and stock quotations—to convince the reader that he knows what he is writing about. Thus we arrive at an-other paradoxical rule:

II. To increase the illusion of reality load the story with accurate emotional facts.

A story must communicate emotion to the reader. The more emotion —without sentimentality—the better the story. Here, too, the story writer halts and arrests time in its passing. Human nature may not change over the centuries; but the things that human nature surrounds itself with change vastly, and hence human responses alter and shift. We are not living like the people of classical Greece today; we have television sets and intercontinental ballistic missiles. The proportions of our feelings have undergone remarkable shifts. We can understand the classical Greeks because they are our intellectual ancestors, but they would have some difficulty in understanding us. The new writer must be aware of the feelings he creates and must endeavor to make the reader feel the way a character feels when he does or says some-thing. Part of the art will be to suggest a dominant emotional tone, part will be to suppress overstatement about emotion, part will con-sist in telling the reader directly, part will be to avoid directness by the use of symbols. Let us look at some examples:

Chekhov's "The Kiss" (direct statement about emotion):

There were times when he envied the boldness and swagger of his companions and was inwardly wretched. . . .

Dostoevsky's "An Honest Thief" (direct statement about emotion):

I began to get frightened; I was so worried, I couldn't drink, I couldn't eat, I couldn't sleep. The fellow had quite disarmed me.

Stephen Crane's "The Open Boat" (direct statement about emotion):

The correspondent, plying the oars and dreaming of the slow and slower movements of the lips of the soldier, was moved by a profound and perfectly impersonal comprehension. He was sorry for the soldier of the Legion who lay dying in Algiers.

Thomas Mann's "Disorder and Early Sorrow" (direct and indirect statement about emotion):

He holds his darling on his lap and her slim rosy legs hang down. He raises his brows as he talks to her, tenderly, with a half-teasing note of respect, and listens enchanted to her high sweet little voice calling him Abel.

Hemingway's "The Killers" (indirect statement about emotion):

"I'll go see him," Nick said to George. "Where does he live?" The cook turned away.
"Little boys always know what they want to do," he said.

Herbert Gold's "Where a Man Dwells" (direct and indirect statement about emotion):

Before he could speak, the girl's hand started in a stiff painful gesture towards the weeping child. Abruptly it jerked out wildly—"For Christ's sake!"—and struck the child's cheek, staggering him, catching him in the middle of a sob. "Shut up, brat!" she cried in a high shrill voice.

If a reader cannot feel emotion in a story, he cannot possibly believe it. To communicate feeling in words requires many technical skills; but it requires pre-eminently that the author himself feel more than ordinarily strongly the way his characters feel. Half or more of the genius of a story writer consists in finding out what his characters' feelings amount to; the other half in bringing the reader out of a state of torpor into feelings that he ordinarily does not experience. Thus, a writer must practice until he acquires a range and subtlety of his own, being aware that for any action the character performs, there is some emotion accompanying it. If he must, let him label his character's acts and emotions in terms of what might be perceptible, what might be felt, striving always to bring the two together into one:

He crossed the room [fact], feeling as though he had just conquered a shark [emotion].
She wheeled around [fact] in panic [emotion].
"Please go away," [fact], she cried pathetically [emotion].
He smiled [fact] like a rodent in a cheese factory [emotion].

The inexperienced writer need not be afraid to make the emotions of his characters quite openly apparent to a reader. To fail to do so will be to ask a reader to guess what is going on in the minds and hearts of the people he is reading about, and ordinarily the novice at writing will not have yet grasped the more indirect ways of conveying emotion. The error of overstated emotion leads to melodrama rather than drama. But better melodrama than no drama at all; and the overemotionalism of the early story very often only precedes, if a writer perseveres, the controlled emotion of later ones.

THE NARRATIVE HOOK

No significant emotion is possible in a story unless there first is a complication. To increase the illusion of reality in a story by loading the story with accurate emotional facts depends upon there being a story to begin with. Thus, though we have just suggested to the reader that he must load his story with emotion, let him remember that his emotional display must always lie under the restraint of structure—and, paradoxically, the emotions of his characters will actually be only sharply and clearly felt because of the structure. When a writer becomes able to suggest by more indirect means what his characters feel, it will be only through the fact that his complication and the structural way he puts it to use allow him such indirection. The clearest example is in a number of Hemingway's stories, for it seems necessary in the Hemingway structure that his hero admire the man who did not grouse about his own feelings.

At any rate, in speaking about the necessity for emotion in the short story, we wished to return to the only principle that can give unity to the emotions that occur in the story, the complication itself. And there is a moment in the story in which it is necessary that this principle of emotional unity be the device that causes the reader to continue reading. Obviously such a moment occurs early in the story, either right at the very beginning or immediately afterwards as the sequel to the complication presented in the beginning. Since one can abstract such a moment from the rest of the story, it has acquired a name: the narrative hook. We have previously mentioned the narrative hook in Chapter Three. Its pre-eminent quality is that it should arouse so strong a feeling of interest in the reader that he must continue the story to see what happens.

If the writer cannot discover a narrative hook in the story he is plotting, this simply means that the complication is not yet deep enough.

Let us look at several illustrations of the narrative hook: W. L. Heath's "No Margin for Error" (which is found in the Appendix on page 331), gives us a narrative hook in paragraph 35, following the introduction of the complication proper. Here, the narrative hook consists of the protagonist's decision to try to cover up his mistake in computing the cost of a rug—a mistake that would cost the company a lot of money, lose the protagonist his job, and also endanger the job of the protagonist's boss whom he likes a great deal. The decision the protagonist makes interests the reader because it indicates directly how much emotional involvement the hero has in solving the complication: he wishes to protect himself, his boss, and his wife's dreams of the future. Following the protagonist's decision to make up for his mistake, the author capitalizes on the narrative hook he has used by making the complication even more serious, as we discover in paragraph 101, when the protagonist realizes that in deciding to conceal his mistake, he is endangering the very basis of his marriage.

The description we have just given of the narrative hook differs from the way some authors use the term, for they consider it to be the opening scene of the story in which the complication is initially presented, the main character and his dilemma are clearly and vividly portrayed, and in which the exciting circumstances that the reader is thus made to visualize will cause him to continue reading. Whether one considers the narrative hook as a sequel to the complication or the initial dramatization of the complication itself, however, does not lessen the necessity to arouse the reader's interest through the principle by which the story gets its main structure: the involvement emotionally of a character in a complication.

There are both physical and literary distinctions to be drawn between commercial and quality stories in the use of the narrative hook. As far as the physical aspects are concerned, a mere glance at the stories published in pulp, slick, and quality magazines will show a significant difference. In pulp magazines, such as the confession magazines, there occur photographs of professional actors or models posed in a scene or situation to suggest the story's nature and interest. Captions, or even quoted statements from the story itself, serve to alert the reader. In slick magazines, the attempt to interest the reader by photographs of real people gives way to illustrations, drawings, and sketches, though they, too, are always accompanied by captions. In quality magazines, though one may find sketches, line-drawings, or the like, an attempt to embody the story directly is rarely made—rather the tendency is to use the sketch as a symbol of the general subject of the story—and frequently the story is presented only in terms of title, author's name, and text. Whenever some opening attempt is made to represent the content of the story, however, we have another instance of a hook being used to snare the reader's interest.

The implicit suggestion in the variations of the physical appearance of the story leads one to suspect that the quality writer is less concerned than the commercial one in the use of hooks, narrative or otherwise. In the main, this is true, if one considers the narrative hook to consist of the initial presentation of the complication or the minor complication leading to the major one. One can think of examples that are exceptions, such as the arresting beginning of Heinrich von Kleist's "The Earthquake in Chile," or Ilse Aichinger's "The Bound Man." But actually, all stories, quality and otherwise, which depend upon a necessary exaggeration of the complication, involve the use of the narrative hook in terms of the first definition we have given it. Thus, on the perfectly literal level of Hemingway's "The Killers," we have a hook in the reluctance of one of the killers to state what they will do to George, Nick, and Sam if Ole does not show up.

TRANSITION. A TRANSITION CAN BE USED TO BRIDGE A LAPSE OF TIME OR TO MOVE FROM ONE SCENE TO ANOTHER, OR BOTH.

Not all short stories proceed in a regularly unfolding action, following the classic requirement of unity of time—though that principle does indeed provide for a maximum of dramatic interest and excitement. As we have seen, complications consist of events that may not be readily solved—if, indeed, they are solved at all—and may involve more than cursory effort on the part of the protagonist or more than superficial effects upon his character. To insist upon a unity of time in the classic sense would seriously weaken the complication in many a story, by driving it solely into timeful action and hence away from depth of characterization or suggestiveness. Indeed, some short stories suggest events over a period of many years—such as D. H. Lawrence's story "Things," in which the protagonists are shown following a given pattern for some fifteen years. The unity of that story, in effect, proceeds from the fact that time, among other things, really means nothing at all to the characters; and the transitions are very skillfully handled, indeed.

The faults that beginning writers display in writing short stories are to make overly abrupt transitions, or to go to the opposite extreme and make long-winded and self-conscious transitions. There are certain ways to avoid both errors; let us look at them:

> *I. In writing, it is sometimes effective to indicate a transition merely in terms of the physical appearance of the manuscript. One accomplishes this by leaving a space between the paragraphs twice as great as the customary one.*

> *II. Again, transitions can be indicated by using standard phrases.*

In making transitions, it is nearly impossible nor should the writer necessarily try to avoid the use of certain standard phrases: "The next day . . . ," "A month passed . . . ," "Winter came to the valley. . ." can be invaluable, when rightly placed.

> *III. To avoid any abruptness in transition, however, give the reader a clue that the transition is going to take place. The reader's own anticipation of a leap in time will help bridge the gap.*

A failure to allow the reader to anticipate a sudden break in the time of a story may result in the story's failure. A reader is too suddenly jarred out of his dream world by a faulty transition he did not anticipate. Let us take an example:

Jane let Helen off at her apartment and then drove on home.
The next day when they met for lunch at the Biltmore, Jane noticed that Helen didn't look well.

One moment the reader is with Jane and Helen in the car; the next moment, he is having lunch with them in a hotel dining room. A faulty transition of this sort is sufficient to make many a reader lose interest, and many an editor stop reading. How can one avoid the mistake?

> *IV. Let the reader anticipate a transition through the use of dialogue.*

Jane stopped her car in front of the apartment house where Helen lived. "Don't forget our luncheon engagement at the Biltmore tomorrow," she reminded Helen before driving home.

198

Jane couldn't help noticing that Helen didn't look well, when they met for lunch the next day. She frowned as the discreet headwaiter showed them through the snowy dining room of the hotel.

Notice this example from Somerset Maugham's "The Colonel's Lady":

"I expect it'll be very dull, but they're making rather a point of it. And the day after, the American publisher who's taken my book is giving a cocktail party at Claridge's. I'd like you to come to that if you wouldn't mind."

"Sounds like a crashing bore, but if you really want me to come I'll come."

"It would be sweet of you."

George Peregrine was dazed by the cocktail party. . . .

V. Let the reader anticipate a transition through the use of narration.

Here is an illustration of this method, using our friends Jane and Helen:

Jane stopped the car in front of the apartment house where Helen lived. After reminding Helen of their luncheon engagement at the Biltmore the following day, she drove on home.

And here is another from the story "Things" by D. H. Lawrence:

However, New York was not all America. There was the great clean West. So the Melvilles went West, with Peter, but without the things. They tried living the simple life, in the mountains. But doing their own chores became almost a nightmare . . . A millionaire friend came to the rescue, offering them a cottage on the California coast . . . With joy the idealists moved a little farther west. . . .

VI. In giving a reader a clue that the transition is going to take place, also let him anticipate the setting of the next scene.

The scene will ordinarily change not only in time but in place. As may be seen in the above examples, the place of the next scene is mentioned; and the writer makes his transition more subtle to a certain degree by giving descriptive details suggestive of the new place to which the action will move:

"Are we going tomorrow? Are we really going to the circus?" Peter asked with his eyes as big as silver dollars.

"Yes," his Dad said, reaching down and patting the shiny brown hair with an affectionate hand.

Lights danced. The trumpets blared. Horses wheeled in the circle. Overhead, in what seemed a vast new sky, aerialists casually clutched at thin lines of steel. Peter sat without making a sound.

If the effort is to capture a mood of excitement in the boy, then such a use of transition will sustain the mood, suggest the boy's own anticipation of the event—perhaps even his dreaming about it during the night—and these suggestions may compensate for any slight abruptness one finds in the transition.

To illustrate faulty transition, here is a representative passage from a student's story:

Frank Smith ordered his secretary to get him a reservation on the eleven o'clock plane for Washington and to wire Senator Davis he was coming. He wondered what the Senator wanted, as he rode in a taxi from his office to his apartment. After packing an overnight bag, he took a taxi to the airport. Upon arrival at the Washington airport, he took a taxi to the Senate Office Building. The Senator's secretary told him the Senator was waiting for him and to go right in.

"I appreciate your coming at once," the Senator said as they shook hands.

The student's reason for making such a circumlocutory transition was that he wished to increase suspense. But what suspense can there be in irrelevant detail? The reader is only interested in what Senator Davis wants with Frank Smith, and the sooner the author gets Frank into the Senator's office, the better. The transition may be shortened and made more effective by the use of dialogue:

Frank Smith pushed down the intercom button on his desk. "Miss Jones, get me a reservation on the eleven o'clock plane for Washington, and wire Senator Davis I'll be in his office by one o'clock."

"I appreciate your coming at once," Senator Davis said as Frank entered the Senator's office.

We can make the transition even shorter by using narrative:

Frank Smith asked his secretary to get him a plane reservation for Washington and to wire Senator Davis that he would be there at one o'clock.

"I appreciate your coming at once," Senator Davis said as Frank entered the Senator's office.

200

Students frequently are excited about using methods that are now no longer new, but which still remain under the sanction of the experimental rather than the traditional. We have had occasion before to remark upon the technique of stream of consciousness, which was brought to whatever values it may have for the writer by James Joyce and Virginia Woolf. In such a method of procedure, verbal association plays a large part, the innermost recesses of a character's many experiences being crowded together, in frequently fantastic, or at least fanciful, ways, as a substitute for external causal relationships, grammatical syntax, time distinctions, and the other ways in which we usually separate experiences or bring them together logically. The net effect of the stream-of-consciousness technique is to break down all patterns that we normally think of our minds' using and to replace them instead by patterns—if, indeed, one can call them that—that are pre-eminently private and subjective within each individual. One of the chief things to wither under such a technique is the logical nature of the transitions one makes—for logic has nothing to do with the leaps, the skips, the jumps, the sudden shifts in idea, in imagery, in sound, and in rhythm caused by peculiarly private meanings. It is, of course, supernally useless to argue against any new addition to the techniques a writer may use, but we think it wise to voice the warning that the technical advances that a writer makes will depend upon his own growth, rather than upon experimenting with changes that alter the form and structure in the whole field of literature. Hence, as we have indicated before, in discussing the work of great writers, the first steps appear very frequently to be crude, unpolished, largely imitative, and original work emerges through practice in writing—depending upon an author's talent and ability. It certainly will not hurt a beginning writer to attempt lucidity, clarity, and simplicity; he may even find that such an attempt is more difficult than it first appears.

PLANTING. PLANTING GIVES THE READER A CLUE THAT MAKES SOMETHING THAT HAPPENS LATER IN THE STORY BELIEVABLE.

Chekhov's statement about this device is famous, and the point he makes, that the gun that goes off later on in a story must be mentioned in the beginning, reminds us that not only all details function for a net impression, but that certain details have an evident later usefulness in the story line. All too frequently, beginning writers fail to arrange successful "plants" in their stories so that later events, instead of being believable, are more nearly incredible.

Let us discuss some obvious plants first. In a motion picture or television show, the viewer is very frequently shown an event that exactly echoes Chekhov's statement: a character approaches his desk and opens a drawer; within, there is a gun; the character takes the gun out and puts it in a pocket or purse. It is quite believable, then, that the character will shoot someone later. Another rather obvious type of plant in the short story is the threat uttered by one person and witnessed by another. Often such a situation occurs in mystery stories, and the implications are obvious: the threatener will be blamed for the murder or the robbery.

Less obvious than clues of so direct a nature are those that function in terms of character. Here planting can be exceedingly useful in maintaining consistency of character. To have a character who is not known to be mean or despicable perform a mean and despicable act will cause the reader to lose faith in the story. If the writer makes certain that such a character has been seen to perform some mean, but relatively minor act, early in the story, then the later action becomes credible. An illustration of planting occurs in "Precious Moment," the slick story printed in the Appendix on page 372. Mrs. Billingsley accepts with cheery good humor Dave's inebriated introduction of her to his friends as "Boo-Boo," and this is consistent with her character and with the story's tone; because we have already seen Mrs. Billingsley using the word *boo* in playing with the children, we realize that she is warm and motherly without primness or a false sense of dignity, and she has been characterized previously as a person with a sense of humor.

In effect, material can be planted by one direct mention of it, the writer relying upon the reader's concentration to remember the detail later; or a plant may require repetition. Certainly, if the writer is to have some characteristic function importantly in either the success or failure of the protagonist, the trait must be planted in the reader's mind by repetition. If, for example, the heroine is an ambitious woman who drives her husband into a heart attack by trying to keep up with the Joneses, the writer must plant such a character trait early in the story and make it significant by repetition.

De Maupassant's short story, "A Piece of String," has several examples of how the device of planting is used successfully. A Norman peasant, toilworn, economical, and of an obsessive cast of mind, stoops to pick up a piece of string along the road. He is observed by his enemy, the harness-maker. A little later, notice is given that a pocketbook has been lost on the road. The peasant is accused and searched. When he explains that he was only picking up a piece of string, nobody will believe him. He is rebuked by his countrymen as a rascal, a sharper. The pocketbook is found by someone else and returned, but still the peasant's story is not believed. He insists, and people turn away from him. He grows ill, wastes away, and in the delirium of his death, keeps claiming his innocence.

How exactly is planting used in the story? First, there is the mention of the enmity between the peasant and the harness-maker, who witnesses the peasant pick up the piece of string, for later the harness-maker is the one who accuses the peasant of stealing the pocketbook. Second, there is the description of the peasant's character as thrifty, practical, tenacious, and a "good hater"—the mark of an obsessive mental disposition—for all these traits could lead logically to the conclusion that he would pick up the pocketbook as he had the string, that he would hide it through his thriftiness—he was "economical like a true Norman"—and that he would be obsessed by his sense of injured innocence upon being accused by the individual he hated. But there is a third way in which planting is used in this story; it gives the story added depth and contributes to its ironic effect. For De Maupassant has been careful to plant in the reader's mind the fact that all of the peasant's countrymen are like himself: toilworn, thrifty, tenacious, good haters. By making the peasant absolutely typical of his milieu, we arrive at the fundamental irony of the story, carefully planted within it: the doubted innocence of the peasant which leads to his ruin emerges from the same character sources as the obsessive accusations the others level at him.

When material is planted in the commercial story, it functions primarily in terms of the actions and characteristics of the protagonist. The abstract significance of the complication in the quality story may lead a writer, as it does in De Maupassant's "A Piece of String," to plant the same traits as the protagonist has in those around him. In this way, the complication, ceasing to be individual and personal, acquires ramifications on the social level.

NOMENCLATURE. THE PROPER NAMES GIVEN TO
CHARACTERS MUST FUNCTION IN TERMS OF THEIR
CHARACTERIZATION; THE PROPER NAMES GIVEN
TO PLACES MUST FUNCTION IN TERMS OF
THE DESCRIBED SETTING.

By such a statement we are not prescribing what was once so popular in the hands of earlier novelists, such as Laurence Sterne, Trollope, and Dickens, the selection of a name for a character that implies the author's overt attitude toward that character: Dr. Slop in *Tristram Shandy,* Mr. Slope in *Barchester Towers,* Fagin in *Oliver Twist,* for example. Writers have tended to get away from such directness, a directness that undoubtedly extended from the great medieval tradition of nominalism—each vice or virtue represented by an allegorical name. At present we are more concerned with what might be called the negative aspects of selection: a person's name should not detract from the given characterization; a place name should not jar with the described setting. To name a heroine Sadie Gluck destroys the illusion of a story. To name a romantic seaside resort Bogg's Junction is to bring the writer's idea of romance into question.

Without becoming overt, a writer can select names that help in the characterization. To call the miserly, sharp-dealing real-estate broker by the name of Cyrus Pickering is to reinforce the characterization. We are dealing here with the problem of word associations, a problem of which a writer must be intimately aware—his awareness taking into account not only what words denote and connote, but also those vaguely felt associations that may make or destroy the effect for which he searches. How apt, when one considers it, is such a name as Miss Pearl Fulton in Katherine Mansfield's story "Bliss," with its ambiguous suggestion of fulsomeness, ripeness: the name does not jar us but seems entirely appropriate when we see her conducting an illicit affair with Bertha's husband.

I. Avoid the too frequent repetition of a character's name in a story.

It is a common fault for the inexperienced writer to assume that using the character's name will evoke that person for the reader; and having once made the error, he will continue to compound it past endurance by repeating the name, page after page, throughout the story:

"I want a divorce," Matt said.

"Matt darling," Phyllis cried with alarm, "you can't mean it."

Jarl looked up at his brother. "You do mean it, don't you, Matt?"

"Matt," Zack said solemnly, "if you divorce Phyllis, you and I are through."

If a writer wishes the reader to slash his wrists, all he has to do is carry on this sort of thing long enough and at the same time interest him—if he can!—in the story.

That a name does not jar with the characterization, that in fact it may represent character on the associative levels of language, is not the same thing as to say that it will replace characterization. First, then, think in terms of the character, only secondarily in terms of the name. A writer also can make good use of the fact that we are known to different people by different names. With some people in the story, characters will be reserved, polite, slightly elevated; with others, clannish, amiable, perhaps even too relaxed; with yet others, dour, pompous, and a bit too cold. The variety of names by which we term them reflect in many ways these varying emotions: Dick, Richard, Dickie, D. J., Rick, Rickey, R. Janson, etc.

II. To avoid faulty repetition of a character's name, identify the person by a pronoun, by a different name to represent another shading of personality, by his profession, by his appearance, or by his nationality.

Yet here again, the reader is warned not to fall into the error of circumlocution to avoid repetition, a warning that is underlined by the following example:

Matt slowly swiveled his grizzled head to confront the scene. He was a bulky man with a large chest cage, long hairy arms ending in thick wrists and massive fingers. The large-chested man watched the scene intently. He worried about the fact that his brother had not come. It was not usual for the gray-haired man to worry. When he had practiced law regularly, he had been known for his icy calm. But now the big-handed lawyer displayed in tiny but revealing ways the fact that he was worried.

STYLE

Of all the elements of writing, style is perhaps the most difficult to teach, and yet the fact that good and great writers have recognizable styles—in fact, use their style in the most functional and organic ways to tell their stories—provides a constant incentive both to think that style is teachable and to make the attempt. Nothing could be more futile. The only things that can be taught about style lie in other realms as much as in writing. That a man should be an accurate observer, that he should avoid sentimentality, that he should be direct, simple, and lucid in thought as well as feeling—all these qualities, perhaps one could call them moral attributes, even, have to do with a person's character as well as his style. For what they are worth, here are some precepts that make sense as far as character is concerned—and they make sense for style, too, granted that the writer will have the perseverance to master the rules in his own personal fashion:

1. Avoid turgidity. Heavy prose comes from heavy personality, muddiness of thought and feeling. The language is full of euphemisms which make for turgidity: *passed away* for *died; social control* for *discipline.*
2. Cultivate simplicity. Prefer simple things to the ornate and showy, which dissipate the emotions by distracting them.
3. Feel accurately: emotions have a habit of running away with the reason. To feel accurately is to know why one feels any sort of emotion.
4. Learn to discriminate in terms of the value of things. War is never a joke for the man who dies in it.
5. First comes clarity; after that other things may follow.
6. Learn the secret of freshness; it is to be awake constantly to shifting values.
7. Value the truth in yourself, and respect it in others.
8. Avoid elaborate approximations; a bed bug is not an unclean nuisance; it is a savage little insect that bites.
9. Value action; it teaches one how to be impatient with meaningless things.
10. Place experience before books, books before thought, and thought in front of feeling.

The above rules have to do with character under the assumption that Buffon's maxim, *le style est l'homme même,* gives an accurate view of the relationship between what one is like and the way that one writes. But, of course, their direct application to writing involves several other prescriptions, which we have phrased in the following way:

1. The best way to write is to write naturally, just as it comes to you.
2. The only way in which style improves is through the perseverance to improve what one has written.

3. Young writers begin as imitators of other styles before they discover their own. Dissatisfaction with the way one writes is the opportunity for change and growth.
4. More can be gained from crossing words out of what one has written than from putting many more in.
5. Short sentences, like silence, can be more evocative than roundabout phrases and much noise.
6. For a style to be meaningful in a story, it should never attract attention to itself. If we fall to exclaiming in admiration about the style of an author, it is certain that we are not paying any attention to the illusion of reality he is trying to create.
7. Cultivate active, crisp, direct expressions. Begin with verbs as the most important words; avoid extravagant adverbs and adjectives.
8. Learn to experiment with words and statements. Eventually a man's style crystallizes, and he will have difficulty changing the way he writes.
9. Never use style to create an impression that is not functional in a story. Many authors treat serious subjects with a tone of religiosity, which makes it certain that they little value the seriousness of what they are saying.
10. To be known only as a stylist indicates a weakness in what a man has written.

SLANTING

We come now to a subject that has gained a debased currency from those who think of professional or commercial writers as money-driven. The word is used in a pejorative sense to imply the bastardization of the creative process by a concern for the cash register. We agree that for those who value their own creativity—and this statement applies not alone to the purely literary writer but to the commercial writer as well—to slant stories is, in fact, to sell out the imaginative drive. But the term *sell out* applies here not necessarily so much to money as it does to the giving away without adequate recompense—what, in fact, can never be recompensed—of a sense of satisfaction in producing one's own work. We have taken occasion before to refer to Somerset Maugham's statements concerning the short story. There is one paragraph in his book *Points of View* that makes eminent sense on this subject, and we hope the reader will forgive a long quotation:

It is fitting now that I should tell the reader something about literary composition of which, so far as I know, the critics, whose duty it doubtless is to guide and instruct him, have neglected to apprise him. The writer has in him the urge to create, but he has, besides, the desire to place before the reader the result of his labour and the desire (a harmless one with which the reader is not concerned) to earn his bread and butter. On the whole he finds it possible to direct his creative faculty into the channels that will enable him to satisfy those modest aims. At the risk of shocking the reader who thinks the writer's inspiration should be uninfluenced by practical considerations, I must further tell him that writers quite naturally find themselves impelled to write the sort of things for which there is a demand. That is not surprising, for they are not only writers, they are also readers, and, as such, members of the public subject to the prevalent climate of opinion. When plays in verse might bring an author fame, if not fortune, it would probably have been difficult to find a young man of literary bent who had not among his papers a tragedy in five acts. I think it would occur to few young men to write one now. Today they write plays in prose, novels and short stories.

Somerset Maugham would be the last to regard himself as godlike, nor do we wish to deify him; but of the many words written on the subject of professionalism, his seem to strike that happiest of balances —one in which the paradox of the creative urge and the necessity to cater to public taste comes out without that suborned sense of moral virtuousness that marks the words of so many other writers on the subject. In short, it is not the desire to earn fame and fortune that is reprehensible in a writer, for what writer has not dreamed of both? It is the willingness to falsify feeling, to pretend plot, and to manipulate character that is bad.

Having said so much by way of preface, let us now see how writers can slant their stories to fit a particular market. We do not recommend the procedure; it does put a handicap on creative ability. The writer should write what he feels like writing and then find a market for it. But nonetheless, the technique is of interest—if for no other reason than that describing it exposes editorial preferences and readers' tastes in the short-story market.

To find out the formula of a particular magazine:

1. Make a list of all the settings used in the stories. Let us say that you make a list of forty stories and discover that the settings for half of them are in the suburbs of large cities. This will indicate editorial preference for a particular milieu.
2. Make a list of the general traits of the heroes and heroines. Let us suppose that the predominant groups discovered are professional people: advertising executives, doctors, lawyers, bankers, etc. By

making the hero one of these, the writer will have a better chance to make a sale than by using a vandal, rascal, vagabond, or picaresque type for his protagonist.

3. Make a list of the personal traits of the heroes and heroines. Again, let us suppose that the majority of the heroes are dedicated to their profession and are friendly and sociable. If the heroines are predominantly ambitious, then make the heroine of your story ambitious.

One hardly has to proceed further to know how to slant a story for this magazine. The editor prefers stories set in the suburbs, dealing with advertising executives, doctors, and lawyers who are dedicated to their professions, sociable, and married to ambitious wives. One has therefore a formula for slanting.

It is obvious that there are other matters also to consider. What are the complications like? Do they concern marital problems? Education of the young? Getting along with the boss? Social advancement? Community projects? Rivalry between husbands or between wives? And of course there are other things, such as the slant toward a masculine or feminine audience, the use of tone (humorous, optimistic, etc.) to establish the nature of the complication, and so on. By and large, however, if a reader of forty stories cannot discover a common denominator in them, then he perhaps should turn to other things than writing. The mere fact that one can successfully slant a story does not, of course, guarantee its acceptance. Perhaps it will lack verve—and very probably will; besides editors have a way of changing jobs or of dropping dead, and then where are you?

REVISION

Can a flat rule be made about revision? If one reads the variety of statements which professional authors make about revision, he will end up concluding that in terms of this subject, individualism finds its greatest support. Every writer will have to decide for himself how he is to go about revision. Erskine Caldwell has remarked that he revises every story he writes at least fifteen times before sending it to his agent. Some authors, like Katherine Anne Porter, state that their first draft of a story is their best draft, and never or rarely revise what they have written. Dorothy Canfield Fisher's method was to go over a story numerous times, checking the story in terms of categories of error: errors in grammar, in punctuation, motivation, probability, sound, action, suggestiveness, and so on.

It matters little whether one is writing commercial or noncommercial fiction, the necessity for revision will usually be apparent. It is true that some stories seem to write themselves, and the writer may find himself in that happiest of situations in which the most careful re-reading of a story reveals that little need be changed—or, in fact, can be changed. But for the most part, it seems quite probable that as one progresses toward purely creative writing, he will have greater need to revise his stories in order to attain the more subtle effects toward which he aspires. That is, the more literary the story, the greater the care must be in the selection of words, the rhythm of statement, the suggestiveness of detail, the nuances of characterization—in the full range, in other words, of the tools, devices, and techniques that such a writer uses.

The matter of revision is an important one, and it deserves to be stressed as much as possible. And this, of course, makes the subject somewhat frustrating, for one is able to speak more about its importance than to give a strict methodology. Nonetheless, here are some useful and practical hints about revision.

I. Effective revision depends upon the critical ability of the writer.

Such a flat statement seems so obvious as to hardly need much underlining; yet like a good many other open truths, its significance may be overlooked. How does one develop a critical ability? First, it never harms a writer—although paradoxically it may not be necessary—to know the names of the various tools of his craft: grammar, spelling, punctuation, the rules of the mechanics of writing, which belong to the primary level of knowledge; and the devices of language, characterization, symbolism, rhetorical techniques, and so on, belonging to a more advanced level. In other words and to a certain extent, critical ability may depend upon one's having mastered a certain amount of objective knowledge. The reader may be puzzled by our reluctance to state that it definitely will, but we must reserve for some writers the right to make their way through revision without necessarily being able to name professorially what they are doing. In any case, as we have said, it will not harm a writer to know the technical terms of his craft, and it may even do him some good.

Far more important to a writer is the knowledge of how best to use his critical powers. Again such a statement may appear absurdly simple, but a view of the creative process will show that certain moments, rather than others, are more favorable to revision. The creation of a finished story is a combined subjective-objective process. That is, during composition, the writer is, in fact, engaged in the actual selection of words, choosing to use certain ones and to avoid others. The process, however, which is at times lightning fast, involves, in the best and most productive moments, a siphoning upward of words and patterns of expression from the innermost recesses of the mind, which have seemed to lie there awaiting such an opportunity. At such moments, the writer's critical powers are almost completely suspended, though this is never true entirely. At other moments, when the energy of the writer flags, he appears to be much more consciously choosing and rejecting, attempting to evade a difficulty or master it. As a whole, the process remains, nonetheless, more subjective than objective, and it appears to be usually accompanied by a sense of release, a feeling of warmth, an exuberance of the emotions, which can frequently deceive the writer into believing that he is producing a masterpiece. This attitude will sometimes persist for many hours, even days, after the act of writing ceases; and it suggests that the best place to stop work— the demands of time, hunger, family, and other matters being what they are—is at that particular moment when the work seems to be going swimmingly. The writer who pauses at such a moment will when he returns to his story generally have some traces of his elation remaining, while if he stops at an impasse, he must come back to an impasse, finding it much more difficult to get going again. Such a fact testifies to the predominantly subjective nature of the creative process, as well as to the fact that for the writer to exercise objective criticism, called forth by facing the impasse, causes a lowering in creative intensity.

Despite the fact that a writer may persist for a length of time in a heightened sense of pleasure or excitement, inevitably there will come a cooling-off period. There are certain psychological dangers in such a moment. It is a return from an illusion to the cold world of actuality —the same kind of painful return, perhaps, that Keats experienced and described in his "Ode to a Nightingale," a languishing of ardor, a frightening and sickening view of the sorry alternative one faces, robbed of the warmer colors of the fancy and imagination. One of the great hazards of such a phenomenon is that it tends to undermine the writer's confidence. The devices he has used seem cheap; the illusion he has attempted to maintain seems staged; his characters appear dead —not those glowing characterizations he had envisioned but merely puppets. There are three ways of solving the predicament. One is simply to lay the story by a sufficient length of time so that the trough of depression lessens. Another is to prepare oneself in advance for the difficulty by recognizing that the experience is normal and very frequently, by exaggeration, deceptive as to the real worth of what one has written. Just as a writer's moments of elation are deceptive, so are his moments of melancholy. So prepared, a writer can tackle the task of revision with some faith that the act of criticism in itself will reveal a truer appreciation of the worth of what he has written than his mere emotions provide. The third way is to lay the story by and start another, and then in the midst of another creative surge, return to the first story again, using the renewed enthusiasm to spark one's flagging critical energies. Of the three methods, the last is the most dangerous since it may occur that a return to the first story will completely crush all enthusiasm to continue writing it; but the method works sometimes.

When should a writer commence revision? Ordinarily, it is better to lay a story by and let it rest than to begin revising immediately. If, as one should, a writer works as rapidly as possible in creating a story, his immediate revision will most likely have to do battle with his sense of achievement. A writer sometimes produces more than he intended —that is, he may have suggested a good deal more in his story than he could have expressed in any direct statement—and to realize this it is necessary to gain an attitude of detachment, rather than to persist in the emotion that his story inspired in him. Revision, like creation, is a combination of the subjective and objective, but in revision there is a reversal in the subjective-objective proportions. That is, the critical process is by far the more objective of the two, but if his revision appears successful and the writer regains confidence, he will find a renewed enthusiasm for what he has written—not the same kind of subjective enthusiasm, which has led him daringly to cover a barren piece of paper with black and supposedly meaningful lines, but an enthusiastic perception that what he has written will have meaning for a reader. In other words, while creativity is a highly selfish, ego-oriented process, revision implies a social extension to what has been created, for it aims at the understandings and emotions of other men. Revision is, thus, best performed in those moments when the writer can cease thinking of himself and can, with some candor, consider the demands that a reader might make when he reads the story. That such an activity is frequently carried on while the writer is undergoing a black fit of melancholy about his own presumptuousness in planning to offer what he has written to the public is only a healthy manifestation of renewed humility. Writers are, indeed, a strange lot.

One method of revision which the authors have found exceedingly effective is the following. After having written the first, perhaps even the second draft of a short story, the author should resolutely put it aside in a folder for at least a week. The use of the word *resolutely* is meaningful here, for it frequently happens that a writer will become so enamored of his creation he will write and rewrite, only to produce eventual dissatisfaction and, worse, confusion. Having resolutely put his story aside for a week, the author will find a strange thing happening. During that period, while he is hard at work on a second story, his subconscious mind will be working upon the first. He will find himself waking up in the morning with an idea about improving the story, perhaps with a bit of dialogue, elements of characterization, a new slant on working in necessary exposition, etc. He should make notes of these random, subconsciously induced suggestions and place them in the folder. At the end of the week, he will generally find that not only has the story been put aside sufficiently for him to see it in better perspective, but he will also have at hand a number of valuable suggestions for carrying out improvements.

Having said so much, however, does not finish the question. If there is one thing to avoid in the matter, it is dogmatism. Often it is better for a writer to lay a story by and let it rest than it is to tackle revision immediately. But the statement seems somehow more applicable to the beginning writer than to the competent professional. With greater experience and familiarity, a writer begins to discover his creative intentions much more certainly as he writes. There is a tendency that grows with experience for the writer's mind to bring about a fusion of the creative and critical processes when he first composes a story. The overly optimistic glow of the neophyte becomes more sober—the exaggerated sense of despair and gloom of his critical self is alleviated by more mature insight. It begins to be possible for him to revise and alter as he writes. What would be fatal for a novice to attempt, the meticulous picking and choosing of words, the endless fretting to write a finished product at the first sitting, becomes more possible for the experienced professional. Mrs. Gertrude Hecker Winders, for many years a writer of commercial fiction and now a successful author of numerous children's books, remarked to a story group that she writes and revises as she goes along, so that what she has first written is close to the final form.

To escape revision is never entirely possible, but its combination of the critical act with the creative suggests that our ordinary use of these terms may be more than slightly erroneous. The deceptive ease of composition must face the relatively arduous second view, the agonizing reappraisal of a mind aware of an intention and partial failure. As a result, it is no empty phrase to say that most writing is rewriting; and, in fact, revision, when it comes closer to the carrying out of an intention, is actually more creative. Thus, the peculiar hell of the writer, who very frequently is regarded by nonwriters as somehow having escaped into a kind of imaginative freedom, consists of a constant attempt at escape, only to bring himself back in terms of a teeth-grinding admission of inadequacy and a stubborn will to mastery. If most writing is rewriting, then the whole subject of revision is certainly as important as discussions of how to exaggerate a complication in order to make it seem more interesting than life. The critical act of revision must make good the creative attempt.

It is the experience of most authors that when they write they overwrite. As a result, it is a safe rule to state that revision consists far more often of cutting out things than of putting them in. In order to learn what to cut, a reader will do well to read his story aloud. For several reasons, the mere act of turning a story into sound serves to reveal the errors, the flatness, the awkwardness, the lack of suspense or dramatic excitement, the over-lengthy descriptions, the lack of verve in a story far better than any number of silent readings. Does the dialogue race along with an illusion of immediacy and reality? If not, a spoken rendition will certainly disclose the failure. Does one wonder, as he reads, "Now, I have forgotten just exactly what I am building up to in this scene"? Perhaps the important fact is that in reading aloud, one must read much more slowly and pay more attention to each individual word than one does in reading silently. Silent reading makes it possible to skim over familiar material, to lose the individual word in the meaning of a whole sentence, and thus to impose an artificial rapidity upon what is actually dense and tangled. The eye can grow accustomed to the look of a sentence. It is much more difficult for the organs of speech, the tongue, the lips, the jaw to deal with what the eye has already accepted readily. It may be, in part, the matter of more muscular exertion in reading aloud that

214

makes for greater clarity and impact. It is certain that the ear is a more astute critic of awkward sounds and tangled rhythms than the eye that takes in everything at a glance, so to speak.

There is another matter in the problem of revision that deserves attention. This is the question of who stands in the position of authority in revising a manuscript.

II. Prior to acceptance for publication, the writer must learn to become his only valid critic. Afterwards, the author must accept the criticisms and revisions of his editor.

Young writers need the advice and aid of competent critics, but they would do well to ascertain the competence of the people they consult, for nothing is more disastrous than to decide to revise a story in the light of criticism—one should better say, the darkness of criticism—given by someone who has a secret unfulfilled ambition to write. For those with such an ambition, who have never actually written a jot, usually have one story that they have thought and thought about; and invariably they will want to alter the manuscript they are given in terms of the unwritten story that they secretly feel is so much better than the miserable thing they are holding in their hands. Envy, as well as ignorance, plays a part in poor criticism; but there are hosts of other things as well that make the nonprofessional person inadequate as a guide and critic: the little learning, which blinds both reader and writer to the lack of real intelligence; the awe and astonishment, which blind the writer to any faults in the story; that species of kindness, which will not let acknowledgment of a story's flaws come between friends; or the whole host of prejudices as to what constitutes good writing, the amateur critic rarely seeing that good writing is the result of many attempts. Young writers need competent advice and aid, but this advice and aid should be given in the form of the tentative, and it should be so taken.

In short, if there is anything that the beginning writer must cultivate, it is a sense of his own standards of taste and value. It is impossible, frequently, for anyone to act upon good suggestions if he has not arrived at them by himself. It takes a proud man to see the stupidity of a haughty man. The writer, to be worth his salt, must understand that he is, in fact, all alone before what he is doing. It is his; it belongs to no one else. He must have the faith in himself to cast away what others might perhaps admire, to alter what he might treasure in the face of an intention that cannot use it, and to avoid the self-pity that constantly edges him into thinking that he does not have it within himself to become what he hopes to become.

A writer must have faith in himself, and such a faith comes—not too easily, a bit intermittently—through perseverance, a little at a time; but that little helps increase the store. The act of submitting one's work for publication leads more often, in the early years, to the possibility of frustration and disappointment than it does to facile acceptance and success. The young writer must prepare himself to face, at times, many long and lonely years of striving. He works, he revises, he has done his best—and he cannot sell. The writer's pride in the act of creation may hold off, with a sweet smile, disappointment to the critical faculty, and the critical faculty may come back, with a dour grimace, holding out a rejection slip and a grinding sense of uselessness. The experience is so common to all writers that one would think the classic pattern should serve as a guide to the neophyte. Happily the dogged folly of some keeps insisting that disappointment does not matter.

Having revised his story to the best of his ability, with a faith in the story's intrinsic values—and he can test such values in objective terms—a writer should offer it for publication at least fifteen times. He should have the faith to submit what he has written, no matter the disappointments, and he should not yield that faith too easily—fifteen times is in a sense merely arbitrary, but it must never be a matter of easy yielding. If he cannot find a market for what he has written, then he should revise the story again. After the revision, he should then feel free to submit his work all over again. If he cannot have sufficient faith in his revised story, then a careful review of his folly in sending out what was not particularly valuable will provide several interesting lessons in self-control, as well as a resolution to avoid in the future some of the errors that have caused him such heartbreak. Any salve for a wound is preferable to none; and it is a happy fact that when a writer sends out his stories, his expenses in postage are tax deductible.

Now what if the story is accepted? One of the best ways to learn how to revise is to study the edited version of a story. This may seem both paradoxical, and for the romantic, a trifle nauseating. After all, does one not revise his story in order to get it accepted? True, but magazine editors frequently go on from where the writer left off. Very rarely does it happen that a story will be published in exactly its original words. Frequently editors change a statement, eliminate a passage, alter a construction. The writer should make carbon copies of everything he writes, and if he is successful in selling a story, he should check his carbon copy sentence by sentence against the published version. The process will immediately point out the weaknesses the editor found in the writing. Perhaps what the editor has regarded as unnecessary will have seemed to the writer to be absolutely essential; and, in fact, editors being human and fallible, what they have destroyed may well be essential. But by and large, editors are highly qualified to recognize deadwood, meaningless amplification, awkward constructions, and so on. The beginning writer, at any rate, will do well to make such an assumption, until he has arrived at an eminence that will allow him to dictate to the man who is providing him with his bread and butter.

In the most absolute sense—that is to say, the most romantic—a writer should view his own finished work as established in somewhat the way scientific law is established: proved, incontrovertible, solid, and absolute. Yet every writer will admit dissatisfaction with what he has written—some slight, sneaking dissatisfaction that gnaws at the spirit, wakens him at night, and causes a pulse to jump somewhere in his being. It may not be far-fetched, therefore, to recall, at this time, the hopes of the founders of a democracy, that the public (in this case, represented by the writer's editor or readers) will have sense enough to accept what is acceptable and taste enough to reject what means very little for humanity at large.

EXERCISES FOR CHAPTER 9

1. Provide both outwardly normal and psychological motives for the acts of the following characters:
   a. The failure of a truck driver who is normally conscientious to stop after a hit-and-run accident. (Read Alberto Moravia's "The Secret.")
   b. The desertion by a man of his dearly beloved brother who is therefore killed by their enemies. (Read Joseph Conrad's "The Lagoon.")
   c. The embezzlement of a sum of money from his own bank by a rich and prominent banker.
   d. The attempt of a cowardly soldier to get water from a well that is exposed to withering fire from the enemy. (Read Stephen Crane's "A Mystery of Heroism.")
   e. The destruction by a kind father of his son's chemistry set.
2. Study any scene in a short story, rephrase the scene in terms of its

inherent situation, and point out how the conflict is dramatized in the scene.

3. Turn to page 331 of the Appendix and determine what objective facts the author of "No Margin for Error" must have known in order to write the story.

4. Check your most recent story for transitions in time or place. Are the transitions smooth, or do they cause an abrupt shift in the reader's attention? Can you determine whether or not you normally use the method of leaving a space in the text to indicate a transition? Is there any other way in which you can accomplish the transitions? Read D. H. Lawrence's story "Things," and discuss his method of making transitions. Does beginning a story in the wrong place—i.e., prior to a dramatic moment in the complication—aid or hinder in making smooth transitions?

5. Read the opening paragraphs of Edgar Allan Poe's "The Fall of the House of Usher," and underline his verbs, adverbs, and adjectives. Do you consider his style effective? How much does the story depend upon his style? Reread Hemingway's "The Killers," and underline his verbs, adverbs, and adjectives. How do you account for the differences between Poe's and Hemingway's writing? Is Hemingway's style significant in the telling of his story? In terms of the prescriptions given the reader about style, to which author would they best apply, Poe or Hemingway?

6. What material has been planted in the story "No Margin for Error," found on page 331 of the Appendix, that makes it probable that Stanley Gibbs could have made the error to begin with?

7. Take any paragraph of your writing and see how many words you can cross out of it and still retain its meaning and effect.

10 *How to Avoid Clichés, and the Use of Types and Stereotypes*

IT IS ALMOST IMPOSSIBLE in a discussion of writing to state the exact methods that will finally yield the effects one feels in a very good short story. For there is, quite apart from technique, the question of vitality, *élan,* drive, freshness—those things that flow from a spark in the writer and that are, since so wholly the writer's own, inimitable. The difficulty is always greatest in the question of originality. Here is a story that one picks up and reads breathlessly and cannot put down again until it is finished. Perhaps not everything in the story has made sense to the reader; perhaps some things about it seem highly puzzling; but he has read it through with a sense of wonder, simply because he could not help himself. And now we must try to tell the reader how to be original; it is a little like Miss Havisham, in *Great Expectations,* pointing her bony finger at Pip and Estella and saying, "Play!"

Can originality be taught? There is a point at which it cannot be taught; yet something can be done to start the new writer on the path toward it. In considering the subject then, let us begin with plotting, next look at characterization, and then finally, consider language itself again as a stylistic medium.

In its general nature, the trite or hackneyed in any one of the areas mentioned results from overimitation. The word *cliché* in French means in its literal sense either a photographic negative or a stereotype plate, by means of both of which, obviously, the same image can be reproduced countless times. Here, then, is the quandary the new writer faces. As a fledgling, he watches, as he must, the flights of other birds—it being the general experience of practically all writers that they go through an early phase of imitation. Yet imitation produces only the trite. Trite imitation is, therefore, the young writer's boon companion, the ghostly marcher in sleepless thoughts at night, daylight's dull and stale friend, limned in overgreat enthusiasm but too, too easily reducible to an acquaintance whose brain is not of the best, whose heart is on his sleeve, whose mere visage produces that final surfeit of slow boredom, a yawn. And no matter what the enthusiasm of the young writer for his own story, if it is trite he has as much chance of getting past an editor's desk and into print as the squall of an infant can allay the voracious passions of a crouching tiger.

Hence, in this chapter, we propose to deal with the reasons why nine out of ten commercial short stories submitted to magazines by new writers are rejected. And, as usual, we will examine whatever distinctions we find between commercial and quality stories in the use of clichés. It strikes one almost immediately that quality stories should be practically free from the hackneyed for the simple reason that they are wholly creative in nature. Yet strangely enough one can find many quality stories that use conventional and trite complications, stereotyped characters, if not actually caricatures—and they manage to become fresh and original. How? We shall see in a moment after looking at the possibilities for using originality in the plots of commercial stories.

Since there are only three basic plots used in commercial fiction one could say immediately that all pulp and slick plots are based on clichés. For example, let us take the generic plot of conflict to eliminate an opponent in order for the protagonist to solve his complication and reach a worthwhile goal. One of the oldest uses of this plot is the story where boy meets girl, boy loses girl, and boy finally gets girl. We find such a plot used at least once in every issue of any magazine that publishes pulp or slick love stories. But we also find that the authors have given this hackneyed plot a new treatment that lifts it out of the realm of triteness. Whether or not any story seems hackneyed depends entirely upon the originality of its presentation. The test is a very simple one: are the restatements of the central situation boring and familiar? If they are, then one will have produced the hackneyed. For example, a boy meets a girl as she comes out of a department store's revolving door with an armload of packages. He bumps into her accidentally. She spills the packages to the sidewalk. He helps her pick them up. Their eyes meet—a flash of lightning goes off, as it has for legions of lovers who have already been doomed to oblivion—and the story races along with all the aplomb of a seventy-year-old who almost made the four-minute mile when he was twenty.

The moment anyone writes such a restatement of a central situation, he must recognize that he has produced what is trite: he has read it many times in short stories, he has seen it on the late show, where television dramas grind themselves out too frequently in terms of what was once acceptable in magazine writing but is now out-of-date. There is no excuse for any would-be writer to produce such a hackneyed opening.

1. To create original situations, make them result from the dominant traits of the central characters.

The trite situation described above virtually depends upon a mythical statement somewhere in the background that runs like this: young love happens, and it happens by accident; there is a kind of providence in the affairs of the heart that will bring young lovers together anywhere, even when they least expect it. What such a myth can do to character is to dehumanize it completely. The myth implies that the characters involved in the episode are about as fascinating and individualized as the two poles of a magnet. Brought into any kind of accidental conjunction with one another, they must cling together by fatal law. And it is fatal—it is deadly. The principle stated above simply reasserts what we already have set forth in the chapter on characterization: the amount of interest a story holds depends on our being able to identify ourselves with the characters. When we make the situation result from, or hinge upon, the dominant character traits of the central characters, we are back on the path toward original statement. To let accident rule here is to resort to the questionable belief that interesting conflict can come about through chance or accident occurring to a person whose humanity is not, in fact, at issue in the accident.

Since the fundamental purpose of the short story—there may be other purposes, of course—is to arouse emotion in the reader, it follows that unless we produce emotion we cannot arouse interest. The story that seems a cliché inevitably drifts toward the realm of accidental event occurring to people whose humanity the writer has not felt. In the story "Russian Roulette," we have a familiar pattern: hero and villain. Whether or not such a familiar arrangement interests the reader will depend precisely upon his ability to sympathize with a boy whose fatness has had such effects upon him as to make him choose friends at any price, and in the total irony of the search for friendship to discover that he has chosen a weak coward whose desire for admiration leads him into robbery, and potentially far more serious crimes. The situations grow from the characters, or attack the characters of hero and villain, and if character and situation are, in effect, so strongly relevant to each other as to make the reader realize with a sense of sick anxiety the actual possibility of disaster, then one will have avoided to a great extent the dangers of the stereotype.

The importance of such a point cannot be overstressed. Merely for practice, let us take the most used form of story-plot, place it in a typical setting, construct a complication that borders upon the conventional, and save it through the dominant traits of its hero and heroine.

It is a coeducational college campus on the day of a big football game. We will avoid the big college football hero, who is too dull a character in fiction to be worth our interest. Our hero is a studious young man, intent on getting all he can out of a college education. Athletics for him resemble what a fox hunt did for Oscar Wilde: the unspeakable in full pursuit of the uneatable. Our heroine will not be the college campus queen, either. Let us make our heroine a shy girl, whose very shyness prevents her from entering into social life at college. So, on this particular day, everybody else sets off for the stadium for the first big game of the season. The hero does not go, however; neither does the heroine. Being studious, the hero prefers the library. The heroine does not go to the game because all the other students mistake her shyness for snobbishness, and nobody has asked her to join them.

Now we can make the heroine's plight worse by making her a hometown girl with parents who have scrimped and saved to give her a college education with all the trimmings. Would not these same parents want her to enjoy the college life neither of them ever knew? They expect her to go to the game. What can she do? She does not want to hurt them by telling them nobody asked her—not even the coeds in her classes who did not have dates and went in a group. There seems only one thing for the heroine to do. She dresses for the game and leaves home, wearing the school colors and carrying a pom-pom. She lies to her parents and says that some of her friends are going to pick her up at college.

Where can she go when she leaves home? The movies do not open until evening. Where can she hide? In the college library, of course; and that is how we bring the hero and heroine together in an original way for boy to meet girl.

The very same traits that brought them together will produce the fashion whereby the boy loses the girl. After a few dates, the hero becomes forgetful of the heroine. He buries his nose in a textbook, or he involves himself in research and forgets that he has a date. Our heroine believes that she is being taken for granted. That a girl is shy does not mean that she has no feminine heart—and that is how the boy loses the girl in an original situation. And further, once having been discovered and apparently appreciated—what a blessing to the shy person—and then just as wantonly abandoned, she begins to cultivate wounded pride quite naturally.

With a little concentration upon the girl's predominant characteristics, we can create a situation in which the boy finally gets the girl. The quarrel and parting force the girl to make an agonizing decision. She decides to show the hero that he is not the only man on the campus. She becomes determined to overcome her shyness and court popularity. After several attempts that only meet with failure, she is finally asked by a coed to go on a double date, the coed's girl friend having gotten a bad cold. The heroine goes on the double date only to discover that a girl has to pet and neck in order to be popular. This so revolts a shy girl like the heroine that she realizes she will never be popular. Here is her moment of truth. She sees herself as a person sensitive and unfortunately shy, but not without value—and her greatest value is self-honesty.

Now it is the day of the big final game. The hero is again in the college library, studying. The heroine, again under the desire to make her parents happy—a desire that does not in the least conflict with her new view of herself—tells her parents that she is going to the game. We see her, again wearing the school colors and carrying a pom-pom, enter the school library. She tells the hero that she now understands how important his studies are to him and why they must come first. She also tells him, breaking down a trifle, that she feels herself to be a stick-in-the-mud and that she will never be popular. The hero takes her in his arms; he tells her he loves her just the way she is. The resolution, therefore, comes out of the dominant traits of the characters; and that is how boy gets girl in an original situation.

An excellent example of original situations in the boy-meets-, loses-, and-finally-gets-girl type of plot is the slick story "The Next to the Last Word" which is printed on page 349 of the Appendix.

Now as we observed before, as the student learns to write a short story, he will learn how to bypass making an outline of the complication and then turning such an outline into a formula or chronological plot. He will tend naturally to plot a story in terms of the dominant traits of his characters, as we have just done, producing conflict, scene, characterization, in terms of the way he conceives his characters.

This is to state that the first step toward writing an original story must inevitably lie in the writer's making his complication function in terms of character traits. Yet as we are all aware, though such a story may generate interest, and must generate interest if the characters have been made vivid to the reader—there still remains the possibility, even so, that the story will end up by being considered trite. Why is this so?

Professional writers, aware of the significance of making their stories result from the dominant traits of their characters, will already have tended to create characters who are the opposite of the conventional. If one were mathematically inclined, he could phrase it in terms of a formula. Let A represent the stereotype. Therefore, Z represents something fresh and original. But the problem is that Z repeated frequently enough begins to have all of the stereotyped qualities of A. A may, therefore, become fresh again in the public consciousness merely because A has been forgotten—or if remembered as dull, then both A and Z have become useless to the writer. He must move to B. B repeated frequently enough may make both A and Z original, or if not succeeding, must give way to C. The series can be repeated ad infinitum using subnumbers.

Now there is a way out of the dilemma. The new writer will already have taken the first step when he makes his stories function in terms of character traits. But the feeling for a character will avoid triteness only partially. As a result one can see that the restated situation itself may seem stereotyped even if based upon character traits. What to do then? An important corollary to rule I gives the answer:

224

IA. Recognizing that one's story is trite, even though it is based on the central characters' dominant traits, try to use a different structure in developing the complication or tell the story from another point of view.

Now, there is a danger in such a corollary for the inexperienced writer. He must have read sufficiently to know whether or not his story is trite, and he must have experience and talent enough to be able to master the different ways to handle a story's structure and point of view. An illustration of the method by which a creative writer can take an old stereotyped conflict and turn it into something highly original may be seen in Jean Giono's "The Corn Dies," which is found in the Appendix on page 437.

It is familiarity and not formality that often makes us dull. And the striving after a new familiarity is but a striving after a new dullness. Yet there are rules that have been compounded out of the experience of the craft of writing. Rule I in this chapter states the fundamental. Put simply, nine times out of ten what makes a story trite can be traced to flaws in the characterization. Why is this so? No matter how well one exaggerates the complication facing a recognizable character, unless that character has an initial reality, then the story will lack verve. The complication and its exaggeration —what in essence becomes the plot of the story—function only to show the protagonist's character. Certainly this is true on the basic levels of the art of the short story, for the resolution of the story is made to hinge upon some discovery and change in the protagonist himself. If the protagonist is as dull as dishwater, how can his story excite a reader? Further, since there are only a limited number of plots possible in any form of fiction, certain situations must, of necessity, occur and reoccur many times in short stories. One of the first ways to prevent such a reoccurrence from having a paralyzing effect upon the story is to interest the reader in the characters involved. The interest can be accomplished only by the insight of the writer.

We did not begin this book with the position we are now advocating in relation toward the story, because it is essential that a novice learn first all the rudiments of plotting. When someone is just starting to write, he will have all sorts of characters in mind. For the most part, he will not know what to do with them. They exist there in the imagination, whipping out neat little snatches of dialogue, posturing before the mirror of one's thoughts, usurping one's time in the oddest situations—frenetic moments of a religious crusade aimed at saving people from themselves, or during an idle walk while one stares at beech trees and wonders about old Mrs. Popinjay down the block. Plotting, quite simply, reveals what may happen to these figments of one's imagination. Otherwise they remain as figments. For this reason, we began the book with the problem of plotting. Now, however, we make the assumption that the reader has gone through exercises aimed at strengthening his ability to plot, and still his stories do not appear successful to him. For all his excitement in writing them, they remain hackneyed. The first and most important remedy for the trite story is to discover whether or not there is a necessary relationship between plot and the dominant traits of the characters.

With experience the reader will find that he will get an idea for a story, or perhaps merely for a character, and without thinking, except subconsciously, about exaggerating the complication or developing the plot of a formula or chronological story, he will write the story in terms of the characters. But after writing it, if he checks himself, he will find that he has used all the techniques of making a complication as serious as possible, including the principle of discovery and change—that in other words, what we have stated as the development of a plot through the dominant traits of the characters does not violate what we initially stated. For example, in the story about the two college students that we recently sketched, the heroine's complication is that she is shy. The complication is increased by the fact that other students take her shyness for snobbishness. Again, the complication becomes deeper since her shyness prevents her from entering into the social life of the campus. The complication grows even more major the day of the first big football game when she is forced to lie to her parents. The complication appears to be solved when she meets the hero in the school library. They begin dating, but this apparent solution ends in disastrous failure, after she and the boy quarrel. This then forces the heroine to make the agonizing decision to try to overcome her shyness and become popular. Out of the agonizing decision comes the solution when she goes on a double date and discovers that to become popular, a girl must pet and neck. She changes her mind, and through the change, the actual solution comes as she realizes that the hero is the only boy for her and that his studies must come first.

Granting that there is such a relationship, nevertheless, as we have pointed out, may not save the story from triteness. Hence, our corollary to rule I on the subject of originality. One must not venture to invoke the corollary too lightly. New writers have a way of wishing to avoid the disciplines that they must necessarily learn before they are capable of advancing beyond initial rules and principles. In an impatience with their stories, they leap to experimenting with the refined techniques of the quality story without knowing exactly what they are doing. If they are successful, they will, to escape their own triteness tend to move away from the rewards that the commercial artist can reasonably expect from his work. But it is far more likely that they will fail and hence produce shapeless lumps, which might cause the equally deficient in critical skill to admire what in the last analysis is only novel without being really and truly original. That this distinction exists may be seen in the subject of painting: Rembrandt will forever be original without being novel. The experimental modern painter may drop his pigments from a height of ten feet above his canvas, while swinging over it suspended by a rope—and one could wish for his lack of originality he had the rope around his neck instead of around his waist. Novelty is of the moment; originality can last for centuries. Hence, the importance of our first principle.

Yet granting that the writer has sufficient ability, let us look to see what he might gain from using the corollary. To use multiple examples at this point is possible but not practicable. Of the three stories we have chosen, two use the boy-meets-girl situation and do so imaginatively. They are Mark Schorer's "Boy in the Summer Sun," and Alberto Moravia's "Appetite." The third story, one that we have already discussed several times, is Ernest Hemingway's "The Killers," an endlessly fascinating story in terms of technical, as well as artistic, achievement.

Because in Chapter Nine we previously mentioned Mark Schorer's "Boy in the Summer Sun," we need not go into the story at great length. It concerns, as we pointed out, a young college graduate who, in the waning days of summer—a time of melancholy in its last moments of lingering warmth—faces having to return to the city and an unwelcome job. But it is not strictly this that plagues him. It is the recognition of change. Each little change in life is a kind of death, and he realizes, however vaguely at first, but with growing certainty, that the greatest change he faces is the loss of his girl to another. His college girl friend, so visibly present and lovely to him

227

in the story, nevertheless already belongs to a past that is now gone, that goes as summer goes, with a sweetness that is like a sob in the throat and an ache for its loveliness.

Mark Schorer's story, like the hypothetical story we constructed about the shy college girl, depends upon an implicit recognition of the character traits of protagonist and heroine. Yet it does several other things. First, it changes the values of this most conventional of plots. Instead of boy-meets-girl, boy-loses-girl, boy-gets-girl, we now have boy-has-met-girl, boy-loses-girl; that is, a shift in time perspective has taken place. The time of the story and the time of the complication are the same so that the story falls within the forms of structure discussed in Chapter Four. Nevertheless, in focusing the story, not upon the meeting between boy and girl but upon their separating, the author suggests a deepened complication—the dying of love is like the dying of life—through the inability of the protagonist to change it. In altering the time perspective, the author has been enabled to end his story, as some other quality stories do, with the moment of truth. (See Chapter Eight.) So in "Boy in the Summer Sun," the protagonist realizes that he has been clinging to his college life and love as the very young treasure any illusion, not wishing to face the new reality and accept it. So harsh and painful is this realization that he returns to himself and his traits with a sense of having been injured: "he thought then that this aloneness would never entirely leave him again, but . . . finally anyway, it would have left him somewhat less empty, less deadly calm. . . ."

Now, though there is nothing wrong with our story about the college girl, as it stands—its effectiveness depending, as every story's must, upon the vividness with which the central characters are established—it is possible to follow the same device that Schorer has used in his story and, thus, to present the story in a different fashion. Let us try, then, beginning with the assumption that the girl has already met the boy, and that she is made aware, through his own scholarly pursuits, of his inattentiveness to her. Left out of things through mistaken shyness, the girl faces a decision. She wishes to prove to herself that she is not truly the kind of person so many students mistake her for, a social snob. As a result she accepts a blind date only to discover that popularity is the same thing as the hell of the Victorians—sex blatantly displayed as a routine ritual. The net result is that in her meeting with the boy in the library on the day of the big final game, she discovers, in that moment of truth compounded, that her shyness leads her only into equivocal situations, that she values her own honesty above his, that she will not be a party to the mating game until she can find someone who will value her as more than an odd moment, and she leaves.

We have deliberately added a tone of comedy to the facing of the moment of truth on the part of the heroine, for such a tone captures the rarity in the character, accounting for her shyness as a kind of latent Victorian naïve that becomes aware of itself and, also, of an unwillingness to compromise. The character, thus, shows a sense of real values in the midst of a world of conventional, social hypocrisy.

Or yet again, looking at the same structure and emphasizing the serious cast of the girl's mind, the moment of truth that she faces could be given all the elements of the pathetic. The heroine discovers that for her to achieve popularity would practically mean she must give up her chastity; wounded by the recognition, she goes to the library to confront the hero. Her shyness is a mask for pride and honesty, but now there is no point in maintaining it. She cannot accept him if he is unwilling to accommodate her values into his course of things. He is bewildered by finding a woman who values herself as much as he values his studies. And she leaves, crushing the regret in her mind at finding herself facing a life of loneliness on a college campus, yet at the same time aware of the impossibility of yielding too easily to the very things that attack her spirit.

Whatever dominant traits of the heroine the writer might emphasize —and he can do so only through an acquaintance with his subject!— there is a certain benefit in making such an attempt. And it is this: being able to give a story different structures as a way of getting rid of triteness suggests that the attributes of character, which the writer might otherwise take for granted, have a vital function in the complication. As a result, the attempt to use a different structure will tend to deepen the writer's understanding of the things at stake if the protagonist cannot solve his complication. As a further result, the character will become heightened in interest, the complication will seem more significant, and the attempts to resolve it will acquire— as in every comic plot—those essential hints of possible tragedy that will turn the comic resolution into a true release. The hackneyed story comes from taking a character for granted.

In Alberto Moravia's story "Appetite" we have a stereotyped plot the staleness of which has been negated by using an original point of view. Let us tell the story first as a formula story, next in terms of what Moravia deletes from the formula before adding the different point of view, and finally in the terms Moravia told it.

The formula story would go something like this: A fat young man by the name of Carlo falls in love with an attractive girl, Faustina. He is immensely attracted to her. Yet at the same time, he cannot control his desire for food. His mother is a florist who makes her living by selling flowers near the Policlinico hospital. She earns enough for a livelihood, but she earns no more than enough; certainly not enough to support a glutton. Poor Carlo falls in love, and yet he must eat. He besieges his friends with suggestions that they buy him food in order to marvel at his great ability to dispatch it. Faustina, subjected to this aspect of Carlo's character, grows cold, understandably enough. Poor Carlo thus faces an agonizing decision. Either he must give up his self-indulgence in eating, or he must give up Faustina. He elects to give up the eating and undergoes the tortures of the damned, trying to do so. He finds that he cannot easily quell his appetite or avoid the importunities of his friends to indulge in a bit of social conviviality. But so manful is his decision that, at length, after refusing in Faustina's presence a particularly inviting meal, he eventually wins her. His appetite is less important than his love.

Now this is not the story that Moravia has given us. Aware that such a plot violates the integrity of his protagonist's character, Moravia has Carlo not even attempt to reduce. Carlo becomes the true glutton. He is in love, true enough, but at the sight of food, he is a mere weakling. We, thus, have a linear character unable to cope with his complication, although he is aware of it. Told in such a fashion, and omitting the use of a different point of view, the story would go like this: Carlo, a glutton, meets Faustina, a girl who is close to being his idealization of woman. He discovers that she is interested in him, but the realization conflicts with his abnormal craving for food. He sentimentalizes his relationship with Faustina— but no matter how much he adores her, at the sight of food, he invariably weakens. At a critical moment, a great dinner given by Faustina's mother for guests who at the last moment have been unable to come, Carlo falls upon the food with ravenous appetite, and he thus loses her. She is revolted by his gluttony.

This, also, is not the story as Moravia has presented it. In both the versions which we have suggested, the point of view has been

Faustina's. At least, her reaction to Carlo has made her the focus of interest. As such, the story has made the situation yield a fairly unequivocal conflict, that between base gluttony, on the one hand, and love on the other. Carlo, as a linear character, might have an interest for a literary audience if his predicament were of a more intellectual nature: if his refusal to face his complication, or his blindness and passivity toward it, were significant of more than a mere craving of his stomach. But since Carlo is unintellectual, since his reaction to life is babyish, the conflict produced between his gluttony and Faustina's significance for him is, apparently, too severe, too much in the nature of a token opposition, to be interesting and provocative. Even the linear character becomes uninteresting to the contemporary writer if his character's passivity has little significance.

Thus, Moravia tells his story from the point of view of a narrator, a former friend of Carlo's, interested in him and amused by him, but aware at the same time of Carlo's great failings:

Take note of him, have a good look at him; he has a flat face all covered with freckles, he wears strong glasses, being short-sighted, and his red hair is cut in a brush. His chest shakes at every movement, like a woman's; he has a paunch that sticks out, and a pair of monumental legs. He always dresses in the American style, with a wind-jacket and striped trousers: the jacket fits him as closely as an undervest; and as for the trousers, every time he bends down you get the impression that they are going to split up the back. Carlo and I were friends but no longer are, and I am sorry for this, if for no other reason than that, with his remarkable physical appearance, he banished all sign of gloom. If you were feeling melancholy, you had only to watch Carlo eating. . . .

Here the former comic character of the formula story, the former passive character of the linear story, has once again become, by virtue of his passivity, a comic character. But the comedy depends upon the point of view, now the point of view of the narrator, who capitalizes upon the passivity of Carlo by stealing Faustina away from him. With this addition, Moravia saves his story, for in contrast to the abysmal weakness of Carlo, we get the aggressiveness of the narrator. Opposed to Carlo's almost feminine character—the weakness of a male always seeming to suggest the feminine, the aggressiveness of a female always seeming to suggest the masculine—are the masculine aggressiveness of the narrator and the feminine aggressiveness of Faustina.

As Moravia tells the story, Carlo invites the narrator to accompany

231

him to Faustina's home in order to aid in effecting a reconciliation between himself and Faustina. Faustina's mother has cooked a grand dinner, but the guests do not arrive. We learn that the narrator has been included because of Faustina's urging, and as a consequence, while Carlo is rejected for his gluttony, the narrator and Faustina exchange significant glances, and eventually arrange a tryst. At length, Carlo is through eating—he has been rejected by Faustina, but manages to consume a vast quantity of food at the very time he is weeping—and he and the narrator leave together. Once outside, the narrator bids Carlo good-bye and goes off alone to meet Faustina. But as luck would have it, after he has met her and is walking down the street with her, they pass a pastry shop where, in the doorway, appears the hapless Carlo, "his face all smeared with vanilla icing." Faustina is not in the least put out, and she calls goodbye to Carlo as she and the narrator continue down the street "arm in arm."

The shift in point of view, which we have suggested that Moravia made in first casting his story, has allowed him to deepen his characters' traits, rather than to alter them. Thus, the corollary to rule I urges the writer to utilize other structures and points of view so as to develop his story in terms of the way he really might view his characters if he finds that his initial effort is flat and stale. This is not to suggest, however, as we have from time to time observed, that the comic plot is necessarily lacking in originality. It seems constantly necessary to remind the reader that all too frequently—and particularly in view of the prominence of the linear story in contemporary fiction—the young writer will assume that comic plots are banal *ipso facto*. If a writer assumes this, he will have overlooked many things which this book has attempted to teach him, but even more seriously he will have overlooked the presence of latent comedy in actual experience—a most serious neglect, indeed.

Now the mere fact that a writer will shift the point of view of his story in order to capture a different and more original aspect of it should not mean—and in practice, does not mean—that the writer need necessarily deepen the traits of his principal characters. In fact, he may change one, some, or all of his characters from types to stereotypes, perhaps even caricatures, purposely. Such an alteration is partially evident in Alberto Moravia's presentation of Carlo. So gross does he make the protagonist become that he seems but a mere caricature of a man, and in this way Moravia heightens by contrast the different, more refined animality of the narrator and Faustina.

At this point, Hemingway's "The Killers" becomes of interest; and in order to look at Hemingway's story again, let us begin with several important definitions. How do we classify human beings as we meet them in short stories? Let us construct a ladder, at the topmost rung of which stands the individual human being. Farther down the ladder, which for the sake of convenience let us name the ladder of dehumanization, stands the type. Below the type stands the stereotype. And at the very bottom stands the caricature. Hemingway's "The Killers" serves as an illustration that the use of the almost thoroughly dehumanized caricature or the slightly less dehumanized stereotype may nonetheless be utilized to tell a gripping story.

An individual, we may take it, is a very complicated organism in every aspect of his being. In fact, he is so complicated that, as we have noted before, he is not really valuable as he stands for short fiction at all. He is the full, the complete man, nothing in his being actually escaping our examination. He is full of such a set of contradictions in character, in emotional nature, in ideas, as to be overlarge for the canvas on which he is to be drawn. Below the individual, and much more manageable for the short-story writer, is the type— the individual compartmentalized in terms of certain dominant characteristics. The short-story writer works with types in his stories. The type overdone, so compartmentalized indeed as to have become mere puppet, is the stereotype. The types, which short stories present to our view, are cranky old maids, fussy, middle-aged bachelors, the college-athlete hero, the wild-eyed young revolutionary, the dumb blonde; but these are, if types, also stereotypes. A stereotype is, in fact, a repeated type, described so frequently as to become hackneyed. The step that is farthest down is the caricature. While it is true that the exaggeration of a given trait aids one in characterization, if only one trait and a minor one at that becomes exaggerated as the only identifiable mark of the individual, we produce a caricature. The caricaturist draws Jimmy Durante's nose out of all proportion to his face. What is left is not the real Mr. Durante, but simply a suggestion of a man, which leaves out of consideration all the warmth and humanity of the real person. We all have a maiden aunt who feels faint once in a while. On rare occasions she uses smelling salts. If we put her into a story, exaggerating this one characteristic, and show her fainting at every small thing that upsets her we will have produced a caricature. No editor would buy the story, for the caricature is unbelievable.

It will not do to generalize overmuch as to the relative usefulness of the individual, the type, the stereotype, or the caricature. One can only say that the usefulness of the extremes—either of the individual or of the caricature—is much more limited than the usefulness of the type and the stereotype. To put the individual human being in the short story is an impossibility; the caricature, a possibility, but a dangerous one unless a writer knows really well what he is doing. Certainly, novelists make use of individuals and caricatures, as does Dickens in so many of his books, but the short-story writer is much more limited in his range of view and must ordinarily use types and stereotypes in order to produce his story.

Now such a statement may bring the wrath of a number of people down upon our heads. First, those who are mindful of F. Scott Fitzgerald's widely quoted statement will feel that we have here recommended what in fact we are anxious to get rid of: clichés. Fitzgerald said, roughly, that "when one begins with an individual, he finds that he has created a type. When one begins with a type, he finds that he has created . . . nothing." The statement is often used to indicate that the writer must use individuals in his stories rather than types; and having described an individual thoroughly enough, he will discover, somewhat to his amazement, that he has ended with the typical person. Second, it would appear that in making allowance for the use of stereotypes within the story, we are once more giving the writer liberty to produce the hackneyed.

The truth is that a writer by thinking in terms of individuals may blind himself to the way the characters work in a story and fail to emphasize his protagonist's general traits sufficiently, so that they no longer function organically in the plot he is constructing. And it seems just as obvious that, in the same way, many stories of a purely creative nature must make use of stereotypes to gain their effects. What seems most pertinent in both situations is that the writer, in characterizing, thinks in terms of the whole effect he wishes, rather than in terms of some abstract prescription coming from the outside, as it were. For example, in story structures of type VIII that we discussed in Chapter Five, the purpose is to minimize the role of the protagonist and to show the effects that the protagonist's complication has upon peripheral characters. In the following chapter, we discussed such a story structure in terms of the question of point of view, there again determining that the author's interest in character would be held to a minimum since it seems that, in stories told from this viewpoint, the author is less interested in character study than he is in showing the effect of certain forces meeting and colliding in the story: the least personalized characters serve best to portray these forces. Hence, in such a story as Hemingway's "The Killers," the gangsters are no more than stereotypes: they wear tight-fitting black overcoats, derby hats, and they conceal their weapons in characteristic gangster fashion by sawing the ends off the barrels and sticking the remnants inside their coats. George and Sam are stereotypes, also, one being the small-town entrepreneur, not at all anxious to meddle, and the other a Negro fearful of showing any concern at all in the affairs of white men. The only character who moves away from the stereotype into a type is Nick, for he is the only one who is allowed to show any emotion at the horrible plan underway. The inexperienced boy about to be wounded by a view of the callous, brutalized world is here portrayed. Such a type is standard in the Hemingway repertoire.

What is, of course, thoroughly functional is that Hemingway's use of stereotypes forms the very heart of the story. The pain of the individual is produced, in fact, by the callously efficient fashion— whether economic or political—with which society decides the fate of others who have moved outside its pattern. Nick Adams faces a world the values of which have become frozen through repetition and a too narrow concern. The elements of human personality have been forgotten by means of mere repetition: a repetition of loyalties, roles, choices, duties, functions. To be capable of eating a dinner as a forerunner to killing a man—such a loss of humanity follows from our descending scale of values that life itself is a stereotype. How can George and Sam escape? The one arranges a menu that will function up to a certain time, and the other cooks it. The killers try to change the menu, and end by accepting the stereotyped substitute.

Having dismissed both the individual and the caricature as being more or less nonfunctional in the short story, and having suggested that the story writer must make use of types and possibly of stereotypes, depending upon the kind of story, we now come to the crux of the matter. In the use of types—and the possible use of stereotypes —where is the newness, the freshness, the originality? It lies in this: originality consists in suggesting the perennial human problem beyond the façade of what must inevitably be simplified in terms of form. With Hemingway's stereotypes in "The Killers," as with the endless types of every good short story, originality will consist in a rediscovery of the obvious, the new forces at work to explain the changes in old or typical characters.

We moved our discussion away from the commercial to the quality story as a way of suggesting to the reader, as he gains experience, some of the methods he might use to rescue his story from the hackneyed. Let us now return to the commercial story and the development of its characters. For if the purely creative writer can convert stereotyped characters and even caricatures into something valuable for the reader, the commercial writer is much more limited. It is necessary for the commercial writer to use types, to make them believable and vivid characters to the reader, to make them say something meaningful as personalities in the story. Less than this will hardly do, and more than this would be impossible, virtually, for any short-story writer. As a consequence, the pulp and slick writer must avoid the stereotype. Unless he alters his structure, he must fashion his story, according to rule I, in terms of the dominant character traits of his principal characters. Now what if his protagonist seems to be a stereotype and yet the writer wishes to use the formula plot that belongs to commercial fiction?

II. *The commercial writer avoids stereotypes by creating their opposites.*

We are all quite familiar with stereotypes because we have seen them daily on television. The bewhiskered, tobacco-chewing, old sourdough is an illustration. He has darkened the cathode tube so frequently that it is not even startling to see him doing the commercials from time to time. But such a character in a short story makes the story unsalable. No editor will touch it, primarily because such a character, lacking the visual reality he has on television, has certainly lost the fictional interest he had many years ago. If one needs a prospector for a character, he might search out an opposite, such as a former professor of philosophy who gave up his university position and is now bent on striking a bonanza. At retirement age, what else might he do?

III. *One may avoid stereotypes by assigning conventional roles to minor characters.*

The word *conventional* here has a slightly different meaning from the way we have previously used it. Frequently stereotypes have been created through the writer's natural process of exaggerating character traits. Thus, the casual, gum-chewing, wise-cracking chorus girl with a heart of gold may never have existed on sea or land—and what naïve young imitators she has had illustrate perfectly another of Oscar Wilde's observations that "life is an imitation of art." To deflate the usual exaggeration that has been made of the chorus-girl character is but another way to secure a different exaggeration, for if we make our stereotype into a sincere, hard-working, ambitious girl who wants to get ahead in show business, we will gain the reader's surprise and interest. It is the same surprise that one might experience upon discovering the most glamorous woman in the world dressed in her apron and opening a can of beans in the kitchen. A conventional role for a character who has not been associated with such a convention is a way of avoiding the stereotype. We are all familiar with the stereotyped private eye, who does more love-making than he does detecting. Such a character can become more readily believable if we make him a married man devoted to his wife and children.

IV. To avoid the stereotyped character, the writer should use his own experience.

Frequently enough, the new writer, who is stimulated by his reading and writes stories on his own, may use as his models characters from stories that have been a source of interest to him. The only way to avoid such a pitfall, for a writer who has not had much experience, is to look at the people one knows. The character refashioned from another tale will ordinarily be a shadow of its original, a mere duplication. In writing a story about a school teacher, for example, the writer should ask himself to recall whatever school teacher he has met in his life who has most vividly impressed him. To answer why the teacher made the impression will help to avoid the stereotype.

Now let us turn to the actual words that the writer uses in his story. It seems a safe assertion that if the prose of a story is cliché-ridden, we will have a more than mere superficial clue that the story itself in terms of characterization and structure will also be hackneyed. For it seems likely that a person whose imagination does not use words as the instrument of his illusion will not create a story original in all of its other parts. However that may be, it is certainly true that a story written in stilted prose will not tempt the reader into the kind of interest that the writer aims to excite—no matter how fresh it is in terms of structure and characters.

Now it happens that many writers in their first drafts—unless they revise as they go along—tend to use clichés. The new writer should not worry too much about their occurrence as he writes his story, for he should try to carry the story along swiftly in its initial stages. Creative excitement seems to build on itself and to dwindle if one writes—to use a cliché—in fits and starts. The time to get rid of clichés is in revision.

How, then, does one recognize clichés? If the novice is in any doubt, he can consult a list of clichés, which practically every college English textbook will enumerate. And he will, doubtless, recognize a cliché in his work anyway by its familiarity. Here are several: at a loss for words; better late than never; budding genius; easier said than done; the irony of fate; psychological moment; sadder but wiser; with bated breath.

Some clichés can simply be deleted. For example: " 'I'll get you for this *come hell or high water,*' Hartley threatened." All we need do is cross out the italicized cliché. Other clichés we can replace by another word or phrase. " 'You can *bet your sweet life* Frank will be convicted,' Ben said." It is obvious that the cliché hides Ben's confidence in his assertion. What we need to do is to cross out the cliché and use an adverb to indicate the character's confidence: " 'Frank will be convicted,' Ben said confidently."

Clichés of the sort mentioned above are obvious and easy to eradicate. But those clichés that occur in writing and help to characterize should be retained. For example, " 'It's dollars to doughnuts it ain't going to rain,' Jess said." If the cliché happens to be a favorite expression of Jess, an expression he uses to preface any positive statement he makes, then it is not actually a cliché in the accepted sense of the word; it becomes a character tag. There are two other reasons for the use of such clichés in a short story. When the cliché is a common expression used by a certain group in society, it is permissible to use it. For example, in a story about teen-agers, it is all right to use such an expression as "He's a square," because it is an expression commonly used in such a group. And again, when the cliché is part of the regional speech of the story's characters and setting, it is certainly necessary to use it. For example, in a story laid in the South, the sparing use of the expression "You all" is quite permissible.

Frequently clichés are the result of a writer's using stereotyped characters in his stories. Clichés redound in the work of students when it comes to characterizing heroes and heroines. Here are some examples: "Her eyes were limpid blue." "He stood straight as an arrow." "She had a cute smile." "He was tall, dark, and handsome." Or if the protagonist is not stereotyped, a cliché can occur from the failure of the inexperienced writer to let the reader understand a character through scenes of action.

An expression that is now a cliché often started as an expression, usually metaphorical, that stated something with wit, humor, or cogency. Its original user applied his eyes, his other senses, and his imagination to grasp significant comparisons or to convey a bit of sharp crispness. What was once an evidence of vision is now a cause of blindness; and if the writer is to rid himself of clichés, he must work at letting all of his senses operate upon his subject. That a genius *budded* was once an expression that conveyed something. Now, *budding genius* is so tired an expression that it has been drained of meaning. The expression *genius in full flower* only recalls the cliché. In order to get rid of clichés in describing genius, one might do as Aldous Huxley did in "Young Archimedes" and describe the half-man, half-boy in young Guido, abstracted in moments of play, his eyes seeming to focus on a world apart. Only in such a fashion is it possible to get rid of clichés.

We would like to conclude this chapter with a reminder to the young writer that he need not feel that his work is dull if it states something about the way the human heart behaves in a sincere and moving fashion. For the true essence of originality will be to re-discover the very old dressed in its new garments. Not everyone is able to produce what has been described, in a memorable phrase, as "a timeless creation on a time-conditioned stage," but to look within oneself at the causes for his own emotions, and to be able to re-produce those emotions in others will be to overcome to a great degree the turgidity that rests in the trite and the hackneyed.

EXERCISES FOR CHAPTER 10

1. Pick out those stories you have written that strike you as being most subject to the charge of triteness. Does the story's action devolve from the traits of the major characters? Have you made use of stereotypes? Try to alter the complication of a story through the use of one of the plot structures discussed in Chapters Four and Five, or tell the same story by using a new point of view.

2. In discussing the handling of a complication, we mentioned that certain tonal values in the story can be emphasized—comic, tragic, pathetic, wry, or what have you. What would the effects be upon a trite story if it was deliberately shifted in tone, from say, romantic seriousness to deft satire? Is it necessary to alter the plot and the complication if such a shift is made? Why, or why not?

3. What physical types do the following stereotypes suggest? The pompous Britisher? The Latin lover? The old-maid school teacher? The shy, young girl? The college professor? The gunrunner? What is the effect of shifting from stereotyped physical characteristics to new ones in terms of the triteness of the characters?

4. Make a list of five or more persons who have had the strongest influence on your life. Then give a series of specific reasons for their influence. Could you consider these persons in terms of types?

5. Discuss the following statement in terms of any story that has struck you as being vivid in characterization: "The art of creating moving characters is to suggest the complexity of the individual lurking within the type."

11

How to Select a Reputable Agent, Critic, or Consultant

IN DISCUSSING the subject of revision in Chapter Nine, we deliberately avoided a digression that would have been natural there, for it would have introduced an imbalance in a chapter already burdened by subject matter. And this digression concerns the value of literary agents, critics, and consultants for the writer, neophyte or not. Although a new writer can produce competent work on his own and find a market for his writing, yet he must consider the advantages of professional help in both writing and selling. Needless to say, there are pitfalls to avoid in securing such help, and we wish therefore to canvass the subject.

AGENTS WHO ADVERTISE:

In every writer's magazine one finds advertisements by literary agents who would like to increase their clientele. All of them charge a fee for evaluating a manuscript, and this is a perfectly reasonable practice; any agent pledged to evaluate manuscripts for nothing would go bankrupt in a hurry. The agent charges a fee for two main reasons: one, he wishes to discourage freeloaders; two, he wishes the new writer to indicate through the payment of a fee that he has serious intentions professionally. Unless a writer has already sold at least five hundred dollars of his literary output to magazines, he must pay a fee to these agents.

The selection of a reliable literary agent may be one of the most important steps in a young writer's career. There are certain ways of knowing whether or not an agent is reputable. Let us examine the advertisements that agents use in writers' magazines. Here for example is a full-page advertisement by an agent. We know that he is reputable because he lists the names of a dozen hard-cover publishers to whom he has sold books during the past year. If the writer has a novel that he wishes evaluated and hopes to market, this would be a good agent to select. The nominal fee charged is well worth it.

Again, we discover another full-page advertisement in which an agent shows photographs of checks he recently received from all types of magazines. It would not be possible for an agent to fake such evidence, and consequently one knows that the agent is reputable. If the writer has an article or a short story he wants evaluated, and an agent to handle it if the writing is salable, this would be a good agent to select. And here, again, is another agent whose advertisement consists in part of a photograph of perhaps a dozen magazines with the titles of stories or articles in them written by his clients. He, too, is reputable.

In other words, the thing to be careful about is to select an agent who gives, either through his advertisement or by personal evidence to the client, proof of his reliability. Most agents of good repute lose money by evaluating manuscripts for the fees they charge. They are anxious to develop steadily selling authors, for whom they can act as agents, and hence they tend to keep their fees down. If they can see no possibility of developing a new client into such an author, they will state as much quite frankly and refuse to evaluate any more of the client's manuscripts. On the other hand, if a submitted manuscript shows the least promise of a future career for the client, the agent will work with him like a devoted brother.

The inexperienced writer should not feel ashamed to pay a fee to a good agent to evaluate what he has written. Most young writers are the world's worst judges of their own work, and it frequently occurs that established authors require the services of an agent for criticism and marketing. Too frequently, a writer lacks what the agent has, the ability to read the work objectively. A writer's unconscious mind and imagination can trick him into seeing, hearing, and feeling things as he reads that simply are not in the manuscript. An agent reads objectively, and will see, hear, and feel only what the written words tell him. After an agent has made two or three sales for a client, he will drop all reading fees and work with the client on a straight ten per cent commission on sales.

Unfortunately, there are many unreliable agents. They operate out of small offices or their homes. Their major interest in a prospective client is in the reading fee, rather than in the career of the person whose writing they are supposed to evaluate. Since most beginning writers make the same mistakes, one of these agents can skip-read the manuscript and simply tell his secretary to mail back to the client a copy of form letter number five.

Usually one can identify unreliable agents through a study of their advertisements. One never sees actual photographs of the books they claim to have sold or the actual names of publishers. They may advertise credits from magazines they have sold to, but never the names of their clients or their clients' stories. At times the reputable agent does not bother with specifics in advertising; but a prospective client can protect himself by requesting evidence from the agent about his sales before he sends in a fee.

CRITICS AND CONSULTANTS WHO ADVERTISE:

Selecting a professional critic or consultant who charges a fee is somewhat more difficult than selecting a good agent. One would think that a man who proclaims that his OWN WORK has appeared in the *Saturday Evening Post, Good Housekeeping,* and so on, would be reliable. Such, sadly enough, is not necessarily true. An instance like this once came to our attention through a beginning writer. Investigation revealed that the critic had not lied. His work *had* appeared in these magazines, but what he had gotten accepted consisted of fillers and short poems. This apparently did not stop him from setting himself up as a critic of short stories, although he had never sold one in his life.

The best and safest way to select a reputable consultant or critic is to choose one who has written one or more textbooks on writing. In a copy of the *Writer's Digest,* for example, there is the advertisement of a critic who claims that his book on writing has sold 40,000 copies. Each issue of the *Writer's Digest* lists recommended textbooks on writing. This consultant's book is listed there, and one has, therefore, extremely good evidence that he is reputable.

Another advertisement establishes as a literary consultant a man who is the author of four textbooks on writing, who is a member of the Authors' Guild and the Authors' League of America. His reputation is secure through his achievements. And again, another author advertises herself as a literary consultant on juvenile stories and novels. She is the author of textbooks on the subjects, and she is a reputable consultant.

Unfortunately, there are many disreputable consultants and critics. Most of them advertise that they do not charge reading fees, which is a come-on. How much they can extract from a prospective client depends upon what he writes them about himself. If the client remarks that he is on relief, the chances are that his manuscript will come back via the Atlas missile. If the prospective client writes that he owns a sixteen-hundred-acre farm, he may foolishly spend as much as a thousand dollars or more for evaluation or ghost-writing.

The disreputable consultant and critic, like any disciple of Satan's, knows how to equivocate in such a way as to arouse the expectations of a writer in order to rob and cheat him. They will promise the client that, after he has met their price for putting the manuscript into shape for market, he will have no trouble selling it to the *Saturday Evening Post*. This is not a guarantee. It is a promise. The same goes for a novel or other book-length manuscript. After being given a thousand dollars, they will pay a hack writer five hundred to rewrite the manuscript; they promise that the publishers will fight one another to buy it, but they will not guarantee that this will be the case.

The best thing to do in the event any literary consultant or critic wants an additional fee to do what he first indicated he would perform for less money is to write and tell him to send the manuscript back immediately. There is an exception to be noted here. If the prospective client has a clear understanding with a literary consultant or critic that the initial fee is a nominal charge for the express purpose of evaluating how much work needs to be done on a manuscript, then the client can feel reasonably secure. In any event, the reputable consultant or critic will return the manuscript if in his opinion the work is unsalable. Reliable consultants have a reputation to maintain, and they maintain that reputation only by helping to revise novels they believe are salable and from which they can later gain credit.

AGENTS WHO DO NOT ADVERTISE:

Such agents are listed in the *Literary Market Place,* published annually by R. R. Bowker Company, a copy of which should be in every writer's library. If a prospective client has not had at least one novel published or sold at least a thousand dollars of his work to magazines, there is little use in applying to these agents. If one sends in a manuscript not previously requested, it will be returned, marked DELIVERY REFUSED.

A great many agents who start out by advertising stop advertising after they have gained a stable of successful writers. Some of them are former editors of magazines and publishing houses. One may even find an author or two among them.

Even if a writer has published a novel or two and has credit for a thousand dollars or more in sales, selecting one of these agents at random is a chance affair. It is not risky in the sense that any one of them is not reputable, but most of them specialize in a certain kind of writing. For example, if one writes mystery stories and selects an agent at random, he may find that he has chosen one who specializes only in juvenile fiction.

The best way to select one of these agents is to ask the advice of an editor. If a writer has established a relationship with a magazine editor through sales, he can write and ask him to recommend an agent; the editor of any publishing house that has published a writer's work will normally be happy to recommend an agent.

The editor most familiar with a writer's work will know all his weaknesses in writing. If he has to do considerable editorial work on the writer's manuscripts, he will recommend an agent who has editorial talent, one who can help the writer overcome his weaknesses. If the editor has to do very little editorial work on the manuscript, he will recommend an agent who is strictly a selling agent, one who expects manuscripts that need no revision or editing.

We do not believe that there is a magazine editor in the business who would not prefer to do business through an agent. Editors expect agents to submit stories to them that meet immediate editorial needs. An agent can determine these needs by a telephone call. A writer living in a small town has normally only a market letter, stale by some three or four months, to guide him. Editors expect an agent to act as referee in any dispute between themselves and an author, especially in the matter of revisions. They regard the agent as the person most suitable to influence the author to make necessary changes, to meet established time schedules, and to produce work on demand. For example, let us assume that an editor is setting up a future issue of his magazine and needs a mystery story to round it out. He picks up a telephone and calls an agent who, as he knows, handles mystery writers. He tells the agent how many words he wants. The agent gets in touch with one of his authors, and tells him to work up a mystery story and have it in the agent's office by a certain date. Editors normally prefer agents to handle such assignments, rather than to have to take time from their own busy schedules.

At the very beginning of this chapter, we asserted that the proper choice of an agent might be one of the most significant things a young writer can do in furthering his career. The advantages for a writer who has managed to interest a good agent in his work are manifold: an agent can relieve him of a number of cumbersome details, such as keeping a file, selecting markets, mailing out scripts, keeping informed of new and significant changes in markets, and so on. Again, a writer can depend upon an agent to get him an increase in word rates, after selling a few of the stories to a particular magazine. In addition, a writer can rely upon an agent to direct him into the best field for his work. An agent may see in the writing of a woman client, who writes confession stories, the talent and ability to write good slick stories. The agent performs an invaluable service in encouraging the growth of the writer. Then too, there is a saying among writers that no agent can sell a story that a writer cannot sell himself. All things being equal, this may be true. But all things are not equal. The agent, usually located in the heart of the publishing world, has his fingers on the pulse of editorial requirements. He is personally acquainted with editors and in daily contact with them. The writer may submit his story to a magazine that is overstocked and is cutting down on its inventory; he cannot make the simple phone call that the agent can and talk to an editor. An agent, frequently, may practically sell a story over the telephone before calling a messenger service to deliver it.

In sum, a good agent is a blessing, for he provides guidelines and discipline, aid, comfort, advice, and encouragement. With the exception of agents who advertise, most writers will agree that it is more difficult to sell a story to an agent than it is to an editor. An agent's entire income depends upon the ten per cent commission he receives. He can only allocate so much time to each manuscript he handles. An off-beat story that he knows will take a lot of time and work to place is not, for him, worth handling. Each agent sets his own standards, but generally if he cannot see at least a two hundred dollar sale for the story, he will not bother to try to sell it. Looked at in the light of common sense, such a principle gives the writer an assessment, which it is necessary for him to know, of how his own individual talent may function in terms of what exists. It is no strange phenomenon that writers adapt themselves to the world in which they live, with a curious combination of practicality and talent, insight and method, imagination and coolheadedness. It has been the perennial task of great writers and imaginative tellers of tales to do so from the very earliest times when an audience awaited the sound of a narrator's voice. Of what can writers sing if not of humanity? Humanity is both the stage and the audience; it demands to see itself in the guises and roles it plays. Like any audience, it plays out its own tyrannies with a sense, nevertheless, of justice. It may be the role for some to chant in cool, small voices under a forest leaf, to sing the aphid's song, tiny, integral, and distinct. But the writer belongs to general humanity or else his nature founders in isolated self-absorption; and an agent is a means whereby the writer may discover within himself what common meanings he can share with others.

Literary agents who do not advertise will generally return a manuscript to a writer if they imagine that the story will take a lot of time to find a home, or if it will not fetch enough money. Their comment will be that the manuscript is unsalable. Writers long ago learned that what the agent really means is that the story is not profitable, so far as the agent is concerned. Such an evaluation may be true; it may be false. The writer can either try to market the manuscript himself, or send it to a consultant who charges an evaluation fee to find out if the story is not, in fact, one which does say something and is salable. Yet we must always consider that the agent tells us his opinion. Agents like everyone else are fallible; but they have standards and values, neither of which are to be taken lightly. No man can scorn the considered judgment of any other without facing the perils of his own pretentiousness. No one can say that his own opinion must be correct.

To acquire an agent means that the writer commits himself to the opinions, perhaps even the prejudices, of another who is more knowledgeable than himself in certain ways. The writer, therefore, must consider that being accepted by a reputable agent is already a mark of success. He may never produce what is marketable in terms of the many, but the chances are that he will, for the agent will have seen in the writer a source for his own existence. Let us not think of this only in the economic sense; what one lives on is far more complex. One may be certain that an agent will take pride in a writer who has succeeded, for the success is often the product of the agent's own sympathy and encouragement. Certainly the intangible goals of life must have meaning for anyone who considers the creative life worthwhile. An agent is an alter ego, a voice that keeps continually prodding the individual into saying something valuable. If he puts a price upon what he does, he does no more than others who put a price upon what they do. All in all, a beginning writer can consider himself blessed to have a person speak for him who considers that what the writer says must have value for others to read. In what other way can a writer feel significant?

12

How to Prepare
a Manuscript
for Submission

THE OUTWARD APPEARANCE a man has will either command respect or disapproval. It is the same in trying to sell stories. Certain forms and conventions are used in the preparation of manuscripts that enlist approval. Rather than ask whether or not this should be so, it seems the better part of social prudence to think that no man is free of judging anything in terms of how it looks. If a writer wishes to gain professional standing, he must submit manuscripts that follow professional forms. Otherwise he stands the chance of having his manuscript rejected before it has even been read.

We shall describe for the reader a format that has become conventional in the preparation of manuscripts. It is not the only one, but it is in general usage among professional writers. There can be other conventions, a result of the fact that we are dealing with matters established by tradition; for example, manuscripts of a scholarly nature require a different treatment. But in the main, a writer will not go wrong who accepts what is given here as established and as satisfying the editorial requirements made of all manuscripts: neatness, legibility, form.

Let us begin by listing certain tools that any writer will find invaluable in the preparation of his manuscripts:

1. A good dictionary.
2. *Roget's Thesaurus* in dictionary form.

3. A good typewriter, preferably in pica type, although editors will accept manuscripts in the smaller elite type so long as the keys are clean and do not clog.
4. White bond paper, preferably 20-lb. bond, $8\frac{1}{2} \times 11$ inch for original copies.
5. Newsprint yellow second sheets, $8\frac{1}{2} \times 11$ for carbon copies.
6. Carbon paper, $8\frac{1}{2} \times 11$.
7. Manila gummed-flap envelopes, 9×12, for returns.
8. Manila gummed-flap envelopes, 10×13 (although for relatively short manuscripts the $9\frac{1}{2} \times 12\frac{1}{2}$ size is adequate) for outgoing manuscripts.
9. Gummed first-class-mail address labels.
10. Gummed first-class-mail stickers. (Although short stories may be sent book-rate, $9\frac{1}{2}\cent$ for the first pound, $5\cent$ for each additional pound, according to Sec. 135.13 of the Postal Manual, it is wiser to send such materials first-class. Manuscripts sent as educational materials may take two or three weeks in transit time.)
11. A postage scale, invaluable for a writer if post-office windows are usually busy.
12. A subscription to a writer's magazine. The three most useful are the following:

Writer's Digest	*The Writer*	*Author and Journalist*
22 East 12th Street	8 Arlington Street	3365 Martin Drive
Cincinnati 10, Ohio	Boston 16, Massachusetts	Boulder, Colorado

We will now give a list of "don'ts" that, unless they are heeded by the writer, may betray his story as the work of an amateur to a magazine's mail boy. The mail boy in some magazine offices is the first judge of manuscripts, and if a manuscript appears amateurish, he has the authority to place it unread in the return envelope with a rejection slip.

1. Do not submit a manuscript in longhand. A typewriter can be rented at reasonable rates, or if necessary, one can mail his handwritten manuscript to one of the typists who advertise in the writer's magazines. They will perform a professional job for a reasonable fee.
2. Do not submit a manuscript in single-spaced typing.
3. Do not use any other color except black for the typewriter ribbon.
4. Do not mail a manuscript rolled, folded, or in any other way than flat.
5. Do not decorate the manuscript with any form of scroll, sketches, or other art work.
6. Do not tie the manuscript up with a ribbon or string; do not staple

it or use paper clips to hold it together. A manuscript consists of a number of separate sheets placed in proper numerical sequence.

7. Do not turn any page upside down intentionally in order to determine if an editor has read the story. The mere fact that such a thing has been done is sufficient to infuriate him.

8. Do not forget to paste stamps on the return envelope. It is not up to the editor to see that one's manuscript is supplied with postage. Stamps enclosed loosely in the envelope may get lost, and if so, the manuscript will not be returned.

9. Do not send a letter along with the manuscript telling an editor how good the story is, or asking him to join in the chorus of approval that an aunt, a friend, or one's minister has raised about the story. Let your story speak for itself.

10. Do not offer the story for nothing.

11. Do not forget that the editor is the buyer and that you are the seller. If he asks you to do a revision on a story, do it gladly.

12. Do not inquire about a manuscript until two months have elapsed after sending it. Then, in writing an editor, be brief and polite. For example:

Dear Editor:

      Would you please let me know the status of my story entitled _____, submitted to you on _____(date)? I am enclosing a postal card for your convenience.

                               Yours truly,

With the tracing letter, enclose a self-addressed post card, after typing on the back of it the following:

      Status of _____(title of story). Would like to hold this _____ more weeks before making decision. Sorry, can't use this one. Returning to you at once. ( ) check. Putting story up for acceptance. ( ) check.

                        Name of editor and magazine.

13. Never lie to an editor if you make a first sale to him. When a magazine editor accepts a first sale, he sends a letter something like the following:

Dear _____:

     I have read your story HIGH ON A HILL and like it very much. I will put it up for acceptance at two hundred dollars as soon as you send me an editorial reference.

Yours truly,

To claim to an editor that one has sold stories before to other magazines will result in the writer's being black-listed. No editor ever accepts a story without an editorial reference from any writer who has not sold to the magazine before, unless the manuscript was received through a literary agent. All editorial references must be checked before a story can be accepted.

Thus, in answer to the editor's letter, one can simply inform him that the story was a first sale. State how long you have been writing —so many months, so many years. Send along an affidavit that you are the original writer of the story. And it would not hurt to enclose a letter from your minister or some other reputable person, attesting to your good character. Editors do not reject stories they like merely because they are first sales. Why should they? They know that they do not have to pay as much for a new writer's story as they would have to regularly contributing and established authors. And quite frequently editors are prone toward self-congratulation at having discovered new talent.

14. After making a first sale to an editor, do not write to tell him about an idea you may have for a new story and to ask his advice. Go ahead and write the story. It is the written story that counts.

15. In submitting a new story to an editor to whom one has made a sale, it is permissible to send a short covering letter, such as the following:

Dear Mr. _____:

     Thanks again for accepting HIGH ON A HILL. I am enclosing another story entitled THE PAGAN. I hope you like it. If not, I'll try for a better yarn and better luck next time.

Yours truly,

Since a manuscript must have a professional appearance to get read in an editorial office, the first page should look like the sample that follows. (Note: We are assuming that the writer is submitting the manuscript on his own, rather than through an agent. In the event that he has an agent, his first page will contain several slight changes from the one that is given here, which we will mention in a moment.)

252

Your legal name here
Your street address here
City (Zone), State here

Approx.   words
Usual rates-Usual rights

CENTER YOUR TITLE HERE IN CAPS

by Your name as author here

Drop four spaces below your name as author and begin your story. This is the way the first page of the manuscript should look. Indent five spaces for each paragraph and leave two spaces between sentences. It is conventional to double-space between lines.

Leave a margin of at least fifteen spaces on the left side of the sheet, and try to leave at least an inch on the right side. Leave a margin of an inch and a half at the bottom of each page and at least an inch at the top.

Do not specify what serial rights you are offering in the upper right-hand corner of the first page. Some magazines buy only first North American serial rights. Some buy all serial rights. The phrase "Usual rates-Usual rights" can be used for all magazines.

In arriving at the number of words in a manuscript, one can use several methods. For example, one can count the number of words on the first three pages, take the average per page, and multiply by the number of pages. Again, one can count the words of perhaps a dozen lines, compute the average number of words per line, and arrive at an average number of words per page.

In making transitions of an abrupt nature, drop down four spaces as has been done here. It is not wise to number each separate section of a story in the way that is frequently done with an essay.

This is the way the second page and each succeeding page should look. Place the title of your story in capital letters in the upper left-hand corner of every page after the first one. Directly opposite, in the upper right-hand corner, place the page number. Drop four spaces below the title and continue with your story.

On the last page drop four spaces below the last line and type the word "END" in the center of the sheet.

After you have made a sale and wish to submit a manuscript to a magazine you have never sold to, make a masque for your manuscript like the one that follows. List all your writing credits, even if only a filler, as long as you got paid for it. Assume that you have sold to *True Confessions,* a filler to *Parents' Magazine,* and a juvenile to *Calling All Girls,* your masque would look like the sample on page 255. (You list the name of the magazine and of the publisher under editorial references until such time as you have accumulated several writing credits. At such a time, you list only the publisher.)

Even when he uses a masque, the writer continues to prepare the

Your legal name here   Approx.   words
Your street address here   Usual rates-Usual rights
City (Zone), State here

CENTER THE TITLE OF THE STORY HERE

by Your name as author here

EDITORIAL REFERENCES:

True Confessions, Macfadden Publications, Inc.
Parents' Magazine, Parents' Institute Publications
Calling All Girls, Parents' Institute Publications

first page of his manuscript in the form we have given on page 253.

In the event that the writer has an agent, however, he makes two slight changes on the first page of his manuscript. The upper left-hand corner of the manuscript's first page he will leave blank, for the agent will fill in the blank space since he is submitting the story. And at the upper right-hand corner of the manuscript's first page, the writer will omit the phrase "Usual rates-Usual rights," for it may happen that his agent can obtain for him better than usual rates and rights.

Now let us follow a manuscript into a magazine office. The manuscript does not go directly into the hands of an editor unless the office is extremely small and the publication a relatively minor one. Let us assume that the manuscript has been sent to the editorial offices of a magazine with a mass circulation. It arrives in the morning's mail with perhaps a hundred other manuscripts. And now we can understand why it is important that a new writer make a professional impression with his submitted manuscript; it is the only thing he has to plead for him. In large editorial offices all incoming manuscripts will be handled by a mail boy who works with three baskets marked RETURN, SLUSH, or RUSH. Let us examine the type of material in each basket.

In this pile, the mail boy places any manuscript that betrays the writer as an amateur. The manuscripts may be typewritten in red ink on paper of an off-shade of green; they may be tied fancily in pink ribbon; they may be handwritten; they may, in other words, demonstrate one or many of the errors we have already listed as marks of the rank nonprofessional. The mail boy places a rejection slip along with each manuscript in the return envelope, and sends it unread on its way back to its hopeful but imprudent owner. The mail boy is the only person in the office who has glanced, however briefly, at the fond missive; and it is his job to weed out, thus, those manuscripts whose appearance at first glance most frequently states the truth about their inner contents. Of course, it is possible for an unknown writer to pen words of gold on the backs of old envelopes, but if he wants those words read, he must adopt certain conventions.

THE SLUSH PILE

The mail boy places in this pile all manuscripts that have a professional look about them and all manuscripts by authors who list any editorial credits through a masque or covering letter. He does not put into the slush pile the manuscripts of authors who have sold to this magazine in the past, since he has a card index which lists the names of all such authors. Essentially, then, the manuscript of the novice, professional in appearance and following the conventions, will go into the same pile as manuscripts received from authors who may have published fifty or a hundred stories in other magazines.

Now every manuscript in the slush pile gets at least a partial reading by what are called first readers in the editorial offices of the larger publications, or by an assistant editor in the smaller ones. A partial reading may be an entirely fair reading. The reader will judge the manuscript in the only way in which an editor can judge it, in terms of its suitability for his office's own needs and publication. Thus in a partial reading, the assistant editor will read the beginning. If that is suitable, he will read the ending; and if he likes it, then he will read the entire manuscript. The novice can gather from this procedure that the way his story opens has vast importance, for unless the beginning captures such an editor's interest he will leave the rest of the story unread.

The assistant editor has the authority to reject any manuscript he chooses. Those he rejects are returned to their authors with just a printed rejection slip. It does not make any difference, usually, who the author is. If the story is unsuitable, the assistant editor will reject it. In a large office, an assistant editor may reject as many as ninety per cent of the manuscripts he reads. Now this rejection does not mean necessarily that the assistant editor does not like the story. For one thing, the story may be a corking good one and yet not fit the editorial requirements of the magazine. For example, if the magazine publishes only adult fiction and the story concerns teen-age love, the assistant editor will reject the story. Many inexperienced writers just do not pay enough attention to marketing their work.

Again, an assistant editor may reject a basically good story if the craftsmanship is faulty. The story may have good characters, a strong plot line, and yet its style may be stilted and full of clichés. And it is obvious that no matter how effective an opening a story may have, it may not hold up throughout. Stories with a weak plot are often rejected. The most unfortunate type of rejection for the new writer will be when a story is too similar to one recently published or to one scheduled for future publication. Such a writer will not be able to gather from the rejection slip why his story was not accepted; if he has been faithful in studying the market requirements, he may have written a fine story, adopting the very tone and technique of the magazine. If he has the faith in his work that he should have, then he can perhaps imagine that his story was rejected because it was good enough!

Manuscripts that the assistant editor approves of he sends to the editor with an interoffice memo. On this memo he may state briefly why he thinks the story merits acceptance: "good plot"; "original situations"; "filled with suspense." Now although an assistant editor's recommendations are very important, nevertheless, the story may yet be rejected. (But the chances are that a story that gets this far in a magazine office will usually be accepted.) The editor may reject a story for any one of half a dozen reasons, although personally he may like the story. In turning a story down, the editor will usually write a short letter saying that he is sorry he must reject the story. He does not have the time to give his reasons. More frequently, instead of a letter, he will use an ordinary rejection slip, but pencil on it the word "Sorry" and his initials. When this occurs, the new writer can be certain that his story is salable if he just keeps trying. It also indicates that the editor liked the story, but for reasons beyond his control had to reject it. And it indicates as well that the editor liked the writer's work and would like to see more of it.

THE RUSH PILE

We come now to the rush pile. In this pile, the mail boy places all manuscripts received from literary agents; all manuscripts that are the work of authors who have sold to the magazine before; all manuscripts with a sticker (some magazine editors supply such stickers: "Rush to the desk of such and such an editor"); all manuscripts with a covering letter indicating that the story has been revised in the light of the editor's previous request. It sometimes occurs that an editor will ask a writer whose manuscript he has liked to make a few changes in the story. The story will be returned, and with the revision, the author will write a short note to the editor saying: "Here is the revision of _____, which you requested me to make in your letter of July 10, 1962."

Obviously, all manuscripts in the rush pile go directly to the editor for his reading and his acceptance or rejection. If the editor rejects manuscripts that have been submitted by literary agents or previous contributors, he will dictate a short letter of rejection. If he rejects a manuscript by a writer who has not previously sold to the magazine, he will generally use a rejection slip, writing the word "Sorry" and his initials on it.

If an editor accepts a story, he will write the author and state what payment will be made for it. How long the author will have to wait to get the money depends on the magazine. Generally a check will come through in about two weeks, following the letter of acceptance. There are some few magazines that are not at all prompt with their payments, and there are some that do not pay until after the story is published. But most magazines that list their procedure in such a book as the *Writer's Market* as "payment upon acceptance" will send a check to the author within two weeks.

Most editors have complaints, and they are legitimate ones, about a beginning writer's fretting over the time it may take for his story to be accepted or rejected, about a young writer's willingness to think that one sale forms a guarantee of future sales, about nasty letters that new writers sometimes send in for having had a story rejected. If the beginning writer wishes to be blacklisted by an editor, all he need do is to show rancor, suspicion, and ill will to the editor who has rejected his material. It is true, however unfortunate it may be, that young writers must learn to accept disappointments and frustrations, even for relatively good stories. But if there are disappointments, there are rewards, too, and the greatest one is that the writer is doing what he feels compelled to do. He is satisfying some inscrutable demand in his being that urges him to regard his work as ultimately rewarding for the stature it gives him in his own eyes. Not to regard the profession in this fashion is to be a dilettante, a dabbler.

Perhaps the following incident will serve to drive home our meaning. One of the authors of this book was sitting in the office of the editor of a mystery magazine. The editor showed him a letter from a very well-known New York physician and surgeon who was a mystery fan. The doctor had submitted a mystery story to the editor, and the editor had rejected it. The doctor then took it upon himself to write the editor a nasty letter to the effect that his story was superior to all those published in the magazine.

The editor broke with tradition and replied to the letter as follows:

"Dear Doctor:

I would be happy to accept and publish your mystery story the day after you let me take out your appendix. . . ."

Conclusion

SEVERAL FINAL WORDS of conclusion seem appropriate for a book that has presented a variety of materials on the art of writing the short story. Though it may seem to a reader reviewing what he has learned that we have laid down flat categorical rules, we must once more explain that such a procedure is merely the most practical way to handle a difficult subject. We believe that what a reader has learned about the techniques used in the pulp, slick, and quality story will enable him to find his own level in terms of his own individual talent.

In addition to the blood, sweat, and tears of creativity, there is also pleasure. And the element of pleasure gives a clue to one's ultimate development as a writer. If the reader enjoys pulp stories, he should try his hand at writing them, knowing that he can always move up and write better fiction if his talent allows him to. If he enjoys slick stories he should try his hand at writing these, knowing that any experience will be helpful if he wishes to write quality stories later. If he enjoys reading off-beat stories, he should try his hand at them. There is no better way to move on up to writing literary stories.

But the student or reader who may become a very successful pulp writer may discover with experience that he will never sell a slick or quality story no matter how often he tries. He may become a successful author of slick stories and find it impossible to write stories of either a pulp or quality nature. He may become a successful author of off-beat stories, but never sell a quality story. On the other hand, he may discover that he can cross the bridge, moving with ease from pulp to slick to quality stories.

We have scanted the very long short story or novelette in this book because the new writer's chances of finding a market for the novelette are practically nonexistent. Some editors make it a practice of assigning the few novelettes they publish only to authors who are regular contributors to their magazines. Some editors will not publish novelettes unless they are written by well-known authors. Some magazines do not publish any at all. If the story writer is persuaded that he must try a longer form than the short story, he should try to write a novel; it is far easier to get a novel published than a very long short story.

What can any book for the would-be writer offer in any serious vein, facing as it does such a variety of talents and aptitudes, other than to encourage whatever elements of creativity there are present? Ours is a fluid society, and this book is designed to capture, without prepossession in favor of any one form, the varied techniques of the short story. Only in such a way does it seem possible to allow all the different forms of story to be representative of the widely different sensibilities, imagination, and tastes of the reading public. For those who may object that such a point of view denies the ultimate values of literature, one can only say that the command, "Be Shakespeare!" is less realistic for a would-be writer than the command, "Be as creative as you can."

We repeat once again that what any writer will produce depends upon his own talent. We have provided the techniques to enable the reader to grow and experiment with his talent. If money is a primary consideration in his desire to become a writer, he should confine himself to the commercial forms. If money is secondary, and if he believes he has something to say, he should experiment with off-beat and quality stories, excellent preparation for the novel he will, perhaps, some day write.

We have expressly aimed at integrating the various techniques of writing, rather than driving them farther apart. Our ultimate hope is that this will contribute, from the point of view of professional writers, to a freeing of a would-be author's imagination in a practical, immediate way. We hope that those who read this book will discover a level upon which they can base professional growth. If, in our private capacities, we wish all writers might write quality stories, such a wish is in no way to be taken as a detraction of the basic techniques the writer must learn in his art. And it is not our private concern that matters, in the last analysis, for the tastes and judgment of the reading public itself will demand from any writer an interesting performance. Let him who dares scorn an audience.

There are a number of reasons why the reader can do no better than to learn to utilize the short-story structures we have described. To grasp the elements of structure is, in fact, the only general way to make meaningful the relationship between one's creative ideas and one's statements. Structure exhibits the nature of the relationships of all parts to the whole, and practice in synthesizing these relationships will be the very best method the amateur writer can use to further his professional creative ambitions.

Appendix

Contents of Appendix

Foreword

To HAVE INCLUDED in this section all the pulp, slick, and quality stories that we regard as models was obviously out of the question. We have used as a substitute for such a grandiose scheme a limited number of stories to illustrate the various forms, methods, and techniques used by the professional story writer. The pulp and slick stories were selected for us by a literary agent, whose business it is to know a salable short story. These selections were made from among the published stories of her own stable of authors and from among current magazines. The quality stories represent our own personal choice.

Following each story is a commentary. In these commentaries we have tried to show each story's structure, so that the reader can discover for himself how the authors of each story used the elements of point of view, characterization, exposition, description, action, narration, and craftsmanship. Our emphasis in the book has been a formal, structural emphasis. To fail to convince the reader that the authors of these stories have employed the methods we have suggested as essential would be a singular omission indeed.

The reader should have already memorized all the steps in the plot structures of the chronological and formula story, but to provide a ready reference, we have repeated them in the Appendix. And to aid the reader again, all paragraphs of the stories are numbered so that he can readily locate the allusions made to particular parts of the stories.

As the reader will have already seen from the contents page, the Appendix contains three pulp stories; one juvenile, one confession, and one mystery story. These three types of pulp story make up perhaps ninety-five per cent of all pulp fiction published. We did not include a science-fiction story for two main reasons: the market for science-fiction stories is a much more rigorous one than the other pulp markets we have mentioned; and we feel that one of the primary purposes of this text is to enable the new writer to break into print as rapidly as possible. In addition, the novice who wishes to write science fiction will find that the established authors in that form use all the same techniques that other professional story writers use and that we have described in this book.

The Appendix contains five types of slick story. These are the career story, the young-love story, the young married-adult story, the suspense story, and the off-beat story. Again, these types comprise practically all of the slick fiction published.

With the exception of the pulp mystery story entitled "Isn't It a Perfect Crime?" all the stories are the work of professional writers who are topmost in their fields. "Isn't It a Perfect Crime?" was written by a young writer still learning his craft. In discussing this story, we have pointed out certain weaknesses, which may serve to help others locate and correct weaknesses in the plot structures of chronological and formula stories written by themselves or others. All stories, to a truly discerning eye, exhibit certain weaknesses. If we have chosen one for such an appraisal, we have done so only in appreciation of the story's other values, which made it salable.

The quality stories we have selected indicate the great sweep of fictional curve and structure available to the short story as a creative form. Certainly, three quality stories cannot exhibit all the subtle lights and shades that great writers impart to their stories; but to indicate something more of the richness possible, we have expanded the commentaries to include a somewhat more critically appreciative type of analysis than of plot structure alone. If we seem to have scanted the representation of real literature here, the reader may readily make up the deficiency by purchasing any one of a number of good current anthologies.

THE PLOT STRUCTURE OF THE FORMULA STORY

BEGINNING

1. The beginning must be placed in time as close to the ending as possible.
2. If the complication itself is not immediately presented, a minor problem leading to the complication must be given.
3. The scene must be set.

4. The principal characters must be introduced, with an indication of their approximate ages, and the point of view must be established.
5. The tone of the prose must let the reader know what type of story he is reading.
6. The beginning must imply what ending is desired.
7. The reader must be trapped into reading the story by the use of a narrative hook.

MIDDLE

1. The middle must give the background of circumstances that produced the complication.
2. The middle must present a series of efforts (usually three) in which the protagonist attempts to solve the complication, only to meet with failure.
3. The middle must present, therefore, a situation of ante-climax in which it appears that the protagonist will finally solve the complication, only to meet with such disastrous failure that the reader is convinced that there is no hope of a satisfactory solution.
4. The middle must force the protagonist to make an agonizing decision that will point to the solution of the complication.

END

1. The solution to the complication must be satisfactory and believable to the reader.

THE PLOT STRUCTURE OF THE CHRONOLOGICAL STORY

BEGINNING

1. The beginning must set the scene.
2. The principal character or characters must be introduced, with an indication of their approximate ages, and the point of view must be established.
3. The tone of the prose must let the reader know what type of story he is reading.
4. The beginning must give the background of circumstances that eventually lead to the complication.
5. The reader must be trapped into reading the rest of the story through a minor problem that later results in the complication, or by arousing his interest in the protagonist's welfare.

MIDDLE

1. The middle must present the complication.
2. The middle must present a series of efforts (usually three) in which the protagonist attempts to solve the complication only to meet with failure.
3. The middle must present, therefore, a situation of ante-climax in which it appears that the protagonist will finally solve the complication, only to meet with such disastrous failure that the reader is convinced that there is no hope of a satisfactory solution.
4. The middle must force the protagonist to make an agonizing decision that will point to the solution of the complication.

END

1. The solution to the complication must be satisfactory and believable to the reader.

Maggie Mix-up

by VELA DE PEUGH

1   We were in the middle of dinner when my brother Bob, who's seventeen and a senior in Latigo High, found out I was going to help serve at Mom's tea the next day.

2   "Maggie? The PEST? She'll wreck things for sure."

3   His mostly baritone voice shot up into a high squeak at the end. The reason he was interested in the tea party was because it honored Thea Murray's visiting aunt.

4   "I promise not to scald the Murrays." I tried to imitate Thea's cooing drawl. "Don't worry, l-o-v-e-r."

5   Bob turned red and almost choked. He was sure gone on this blonde, Thea. She was pretty, all right, but the way she cooed and clung was enough to make you bilious.

6   "You rotten little eavesdropper!" Bob positively roared.

7   "Bob," Dad warned in a quiet voice.

8   "Oh, don't mind him," I put in airily. "His mad passion for Thea has driven him right out of his mind. Not that he had far to go."

9   Bob roared again. And it all ended up by both of us getting done out of dessert. It was my favorite, too—spice cake with whipped cream.

10   I snitched a banana in the kitchen as I went to my room. There I got my dog-fund box off the chest to count it up, not that I didn't know to a penny how much there was in the old candy box I'd pasted over with pictures of cockers. Sixteen dollars and thirty-two cents had gone through the slit.

11   When Bob's old terrier, Rip, died, I started begging for a dog. Mom said I was too careless to take care of it. Then she finally said O.K.—if I'd save twenty-five dollars.

12   That was to prove I was getting responsible, but I don't think she ever expected me to do it. I didn't really expect to, myself; I just hoped. But I wanted a black cocker more than anything in the world. She would have white feet and a white chest and love me and be all mine and I'd call her Lucky.

13   For months I'd been a regular miser with my allowance. Almost-thirteen is too young to baby-sit except for a little in the afternoon. It was sure hard to make extra money, but I'd tried everything Jinx and I could think of.

14   Jinx lives next door and has red hair and freckles, but for a boy he isn't half bad. He thought of the frogs and toads—fifty cents each—for rock gardens and pools. I'd get orders and he'd catch them, and we'd split the money.

15   Suddenly Bob's trumpet broke into my thoughts, coming from the living room across the patio. I'd never admit it to him but he's really good.

16   The next day, Saturday, was one of the foggy mornings we have in California, but it burned off by noon. I helped Mom and didn't forget or break a thing. I was feeling quite proud of myself as I dressed in blue linen with matching socks and white flatties. The color made my blue eyes darker and my light brown hair almost blonde.

17   I hurried to the living room where I was supposed to answer the door and make myself generally useful. Mom was giving things in the kitchen a last-minute check when I looked out and saw Mrs. Cleave coming up the walk. I would have bet she'd be the first, nosy and gossipy as she is.

18   I smoothed my dress and glanced down at my feet—and couldn't believe my eyes! Plain as anything, one of my blue socks was a bright green! I could just hear Mrs. Cleave pointing it out with her knowing titter, and Mom would be embarrassed again for having such a mixed-up daughter.

19   For the moment I felt almost frantic. Then I slipped off my flats and jerked both socks off, and put the shoes back on. But I didn't have any pocket, and the socks made too big a lump in my hand to pretend to be a handkerchief. If I stuck them behind a pillow or under a chair cushion, snoopy Mrs. Cleave was sure to notice a lump and find them.

20   The sound of the door chimes hit me like an electric shock.

My eyes lit on Bob's trumpet lying on top of the piano, and I jammed the rolled socks into its bell.

21   There were ten ladies counting Mom, and they seemed to have a fine time, talking about gardening and vacation plans mostly. I finally got a chance to slip across to my room and put on white socks. Then it was time to take in the refreshments— fancy little sandwiches and cakes too pretty to eat but too good not to.

22   I had to get a refill for the teapot at last, and that took a while. The cakes were melting away like snow on Mt. Baldy in a spring thaw, so I dawdled as long as I dared, hoping they'd begin to leave. There was a burst of laughter as I got to the living room door. I almost dropped the tray.

23   Thea Murray was sitting on the piano bench, looking up at Bob and trying not to join in the laughter. His star-basketball figure looked plain, tall, and skinny as he stood there with his trumpet in one hand and my socks dangling from the other. His bony face was going from red to white, and there was a look in his hazel eyes I'd never seen before.

24   I've played plenty of tricks on Bob, and never cared how mad he got, but this was somehow different. He looked more hurt than mad. All of a sudden I just hated those women for laughing, especially Thea. I shoved the tray at the nearest one and ran across and jerked the socks out of Bob's hand.

25   "I was trying to play a tune without anyone hearing," I stammered. It was the only excuse I could think of.

26   Later when I admitted what had happened, Mom only shook her head as if I were a great disappointment.

27   "Get lost, Pest," was all Bob said, in a bitter voice.

28   But, gee, how was I to know he and Thea would decide to come by and give the ladies some music? I tried to think it was really a funny joke, but somehow I just couldn't feel that way.

29   I kept trying to make him see I was really sorry, but everything I did turned out wrong. When I cleaned his room, he said I'd thrown away a theme and he had to do it over. And when I ironed his best shirt, I scorched it.

30   "Don't do me any more favors!" Bob yelled. "Just stay away from my things and keep out of my room!"

31   "Now, Bob," Mom said. "Maggie did mean well."

32   "That's what you think!" he growled, stomping out to wait on the curb for Tom. Bob was saving up for his own car, and he and Thea and Tom and Linda usually double-dated.

33   Things went along pretty well for the next week. I did offer to do an errand for Bob, and didn't even mention pay.

34   "What's the matter, Maggie?" He pretended to be stunned. "You must be coming down with something."

35   I kind of thought I must be, too. I couldn't understand the way I seemed to feel about Bob now—hardly jealous at all, and wanting to be friends instead of playing tricks on him.

36   I was pretty busy with all the work at school, and taking care of little Billy Moore later afternoons, and finding customers for our frog business. I got orders for four. I began to hope I would have my cocker soon.

37   Jinx caught the frogs down in the river bottom next Saturday, and they were rather small but plenty lively. He had them in a bucket, but we fixed them up in a florist's box I'd saved, and tied the lid on with the lavender ribbon. I planned to deliver them after church.

38   Just as I came through the front door the phone rang, so I dropped the box on the hall table and dived for it. It was for me all right—Katie Lu who can talk longer than anyone I know. Mom had to call me three times for dinner.

39   While I did the dishes, Bob got ready for the party Lil Howard was giving for the senior class. He was wearing a dinner jacket, and he had broken into his savings for an orchid corsage for Thea. It was going to be a real snazzy affair. He was still fussing with his tie when Tom rolled up and began to pound the horn on his old convertible.

40   After the door slammed and the car roared away, I went into the living room to see whether I wanted to watch T.V. with Dad or read my new book. Mom came in holding a square box.

41   "It was under the paper, and he forgot it," she said. "But I suppose they'll stop by on their way to the Howards'."

42   I bounced out of my chair with a gasp. Good grief! How could I have forgotten those frogs?

43   "That's mine!" I yelped, afraid she would open it. But by the time I was reaching for it, I knew it wasn't. This one had a pink ribbon, and it was a lot wider and fancy-fresh.

44   I lifted the lid, and sure enough it was flowers instead of frogs. A beautiful spray of tiny white orchids.

45   I felt sick-scared, and could hardly make my legs carry me into the hall. I prayed that the frog-box would be there.

46   The folded evening paper was alone on the table. In his hurry Bob had grabbed the wrong box. I must have looked wild-eyed, because Mom put her hand on my forehead to see if I was hot.

47   "Maggie!" she said quick and sharp. "What's wrong?"

48   "My frogs!" I wailed. "Bob took my box of frogs! If Thea opens it . . . !" The thought made me really howl.

49   I guess I didn't make much sense for a while, and by the time Mom and Dad had the story it was too late. Much too late.

50   Mom phoned the Murrays and was coldly informed that Bob had left. Thea was in hysterics, and her aunt had nearly had a heart attack.

51   Even in my room with my head under a pillow, I could hear Bob's roaring voice when he came home. I shivered, seeing in my mind what must have happened. Thea and Linda in their new party dresses, long and full-skirted. Thea opening the corsage box—and having a bunch of frogs jump out practically in her face!

52   The frogs leaping all over, the girls screaming, the boys yelling, and the older women fainting. Then everyone getting mad at poor Bob, and no party that night, and no girl any more, either, because Thea broke up with him, too.

53   I didn't know that until next day. Dad had calmed Bob down, but he wouldn't even look at me, or speak if he didn't have to. He looked so miserable the next few days that it just made me sick to see him.

54   By Thursday I couldn't stand it any longer. I knew I'd have to do something, but I was a long time working up courage enough to do it. Finally I got down my dog-fund and counted it again. Eighteen dollars and seventy-six cents.

55   I couldn't look at the pictures of cockers as I put the box out of sight. But I had been careless about the frogs, and if someone had to suffer it was only fair that it should be me.

56   The florist was very nice and sympathetic when I told him what I wanted and why. He gave me red rose buds for Thea, and pink and white carnations for her mother and aunt. With

the three boxes in my arms I sort of stumbled up the steps and leaned against the Murrays' bell.

57   "Well, what's all this?" It was Thea who came to the door.

58   "I'm Maggie Davis, Bob's sister. I want to apologize and explain about the frogs—it was an accident but my fault. And I've brought some flowers to say how sorry. . . ."

59   I was talking as fast as I could to get it all out before she shut the door. I had stepped inside and was pushing the boxes at her. Then the words clogged up because Bob had suddenly loomed up in the shadows behind Thea.

60   "Don't touch them!" he told her, angry and suspicious.

61   It was just too much. Why couldn't he ever believe me? The boxes fell on the floor and the flowers spilled out, but I didn't care.

62   "It was an accident!" I cried, my voice loud and trembly. "You don't need to be so mean about it! I suppose you think I'd spend all my dog-money just to play a corny old trick. Well, I wouldn't!"

63   I whirled out the door and started to rush away. But with my eyes all bleared up, I missed the top step and went headfirst down onto the walk.

64   The next thing I remember was Bob putting me down on the couch in the Murray house.

65   Then I tried to say I was all right, but they wouldn't even let me open my mouth or wiggle. I was horribly embarrassed, but pleased too, about all the fuss. Thea and the older women made a great to-do, and I found out being cooed at was really nice.

66   I found something pretty wonderful, though—my big brother. We still kid each other, but it's different now.

67   A few days later Mom said that since I was really trying so hard to be responsible, she thought maybe caring for a dog would be a help to me.

68   So I have my cocker, Lucky. Only it's really me that should be called Lucky, isn't it?

COMMENTARY ON THE JUVENILE STORY

There are approximately one hundred juvenile magazines published monthly, which buy short stories. They provide one of the largest and easiest markets for the unknown new writer.

We did not include a chapter on the juvenile story in the text of this book, because all the techniques learned in plotting complications, in structuring the plot, and in employing the techniques of craftsmanship are used in writing juvenile stories, except for the very youngest age group. Since we have not previously considered the juvenile story, then, let us look at it first in general terms before we consider the model we have reprinted.

The markets for juvenile stories are divided roughly into four age groups. The age group for which a juvenile magazine is aimed is always designated in its market requirements.

GROUP I. TINY TOTS FROM THE AGE OF FOUR TO SIX

The methods used to plot stories for this group consist of the following:

1. Use a copy of *Aesop's Fables* and a book of proverbs to provide the theme.
2. Stress the theme strongly in telling the story.
3. Broadly point out a moral or teach a lesson.
4. Keep your sentences short.
5. Avoid using words children of this age might not understand.
6. Tell the story in chronological order.
7. Tell the story as you would tell it to a child of your own in this age group.

Let us assume that you have a son who is five years old and he asks you why honesty is the best policy. Often questions of this sort are completely disarming, and there is a temptation to start out in left field with a philosophical disquisition on morality, as well as a dissertation upon law and order, the courts, juvenile delinquency, and so on. What one should do is to make up a story that a child of five years old can understand. You might talk about a bunny rabbit who got lazy and decided to steal carrots from his friend only to get caught by the farmer who had discovered friend rabbit's secret storage place. A story written for this age group should be simple and straightforward, couched in terms the child can understand, and quite strong in its stress on the lesson to be learned. The writer must rival most parents in his ability to tell such a story, for most parents have had to rephrase their ideas in such a fashion.

GROUP II. JUNIORS FROM THE AGE OF SEVEN TO TWELVE

In plotting stories for this age group, use the following methods:

277

1. Use a book of proverbs to help provide the theme.
2. Though the story must point out a moral or teach a lesson, you must be more subtle than for four- to six-years-olds.
3. Construct the story in chronological order.
4. You must let the child protagonist solve his own complication without any adult help.
5. You must make the complication similar to one children in this age group conceivably face—unless the story is based upon fantasy.
6. Do not write down to children.

One of the biggest mistakes made by inexperienced writers, trying to write salable juvenile fiction, is in writing down to the juvenile audience. It is the sort of error that many adults make when writing for adults, in fact, but it is fatal in writing stories for children. Children are very alert and immediately resent condescension. Editors of juvenile magazines are well aware of this and will reject any story in which the author assumes a mantle of superiority.

GROUP III. TEEN-AGERS FROM THE AGE OF THIRTEEN TO SEVENTEEN

For young people of this age group, use the following guidelines:

1. Employ a book of proverbs and a book of epigrams to help provide you with theme.
2. You can also plot for this group by taking a minor complication and making it major enough to become a short story.
3. Though theme is still important, you must be more subtle about it than for the previous two groups.
4. Write the story as a chronological or as a formula story.
5. Allow your protagonist to solve his complication without adult help.
6. Again, do not write down to these young people!

Let us take an example of the way in which a book of proverbs or epigrams will help in plotting stories for the juvenile market. We have at hand a book entitled *Thesaurus of Epigrams,* by Edmund Miller. Let us flip open the book and put our finger on an epigram: "Knowledge is a treasure, but practice is the key to it." This is a rather difficult one, but let us see if we cannot make a salable juvenile story out of it. Knowledge suggests a school, and since we are writing for the teen-age group, let us make our protagonist a high school student. We must find some way of making him realize that knowledge is a treasure. Let us give him a name, such as Charlie Granger. The fact that Charlie does not know what is contained in our bit of epigrammatic wisdom implies that he is not interested in learning. This suggests that we make him a football hero who is taking all the snap courses he can and is going to school just to play football and to have a good time. Or perhaps we can make him vitally interested in being in the high school dramatic club, but in nothing else. Let us take the latter and ask what sort of complication could Charlie face in a situation like this? The answer is obvious. Charlie learns that he is going to be disqualified from playing the lead in the school play unless he can bring his grades up in some required courses.

Now the reader must recall that in the second step of the middle in the chronological and formula story, the protagonist attempts to solve his complication only to meet with failure. Charlie tries to solve his complication by getting other students to tutor him so that he can bring his grades up, but he fails. He tries cramming, but this does not work, either.

Now for the ante-climax in step three of the middle. It practically writes itself. In desperation, Charlie cheats during a term examination and gets caught by a teacher. This forces him to make the agonizing decision, in step four, to quit school before the other students find out about it. This decision must point to the solution.

Charlie tells the teacher who caught him cheating of his decision. She tells him that she will give him another chance if he will give up all dramatic activities for the remainder of the school year and let her tutor him after school. Charlie reluctantly agrees, but in the months that follow, he discovers the joy of learning and discovers that knowledge is a treasure, but practice is the key to it. One can solidify the theme by having him discover the truth of the epigram, by having him get a part in the school play the following year, and by having him realize that his enforced pursuit of knowledge has made him a better actor.

From an epigram, we have plotted a salable juvenile story. Once the reader has practiced doing this for some time, he will find the mere reading of a proverb or epigram will stimulate his imagination to such an extent that the story will practically write itself. But let him remember, in addition, that it will be helpful for him to acquaint himself with people of the age group for which he is writing, to observe their dress, their behavior, their language, their looks. The juvenile reader wants to recognize himself.

For this age group, use the following techniques:

1. Use all the methods you learned for plotting an adult complication outline.
2. The complication must be sympathetic to the age group. The really important thing to remember in writing for young people of this age group is that they are facing the first adult decisions of their lives.
3. Write the story either as a chronological or formula story.
4. Allow the protagonist to solve his own complication.

Let us take a complication that faces many in this age group and make it bad enough to become a salable juvenile story. Many young people on their graduation from high school are unable to attend college because their parents cannot afford it. Danny Forester, our protagonist, faces just such a situation. In high school he has made above-average grades, and he has done brilliant work in certain of his studies, such as in biology and chemistry. Danny wants first to take the premedical course in college and then go on to medical school. He has the aptitude to make a fine doctor, but he faces the prospect of having no further education.

Danny tries to borrow the money from his uncle, who is himself a doctor. But the uncle refuses; he and his brother, Danny's father, are not on speaking terms because of a quarrel they had years before. Danny tries to get a part-time job at a local college only to meet with failure. And a scholarship application he had made was turned down in favor of a classmate of Danny's, whose father is very important in state politics. These attempts on Danny's part force him to make the agonizing decision that he will have to take a job in a drugstore after he graduates from high school. He tells his father of his decision. Then, in bitter frustration, he writes to his uncle and tells him how much he had hoped to go to medical school, but he cannot because of his poverty and the fruitless fighting between two brothers.

Danny is named valedictorian of his class. At the commencement exercises, he sees from the stage his uncle sitting on one side of the auditorium and his father on the other. Because of his deep disappointment at having his talents apparently scorned by his rich uncle, and through a sense of compassion for the humiliation his father must feel in not being able to send him to college, he discards the address he has prepared. Instead, he makes an eloquent plea for the brotherhood of man, urging his fellow graduates to devote their lives to brotherly love and understanding, so that they will not leave their children the legacy of fear, hatred, and possible annihilation of the human race which his generation have inherited. The address has the effect of bringing his uncle and father together, and Danny solves his complication.

Juvenile magazines, like the confession magazines, contain some stories that violate the plot structure of the chronological or formula story. The juvenile market is the easiest market for a beginning writer to sell to, and consequently it attracts a great number of submissions by those who are still learning their craft. The editor of a juvenile magazine knows he can publish stories with faulty craftsmanship, provided that the author has a story to tell, without fear of criticism from his juvenile readers. However, the best stories in juvenile magazines, like the best stories in confession magazines, are written by professionals and faithfully follow the plot structure of the chronological or formula story for all except the four-to-six age group. Such a story is "Maggie Mix-up."

COMMENTARY ON "MAGGIE MIX-UP"

The author of "Maggie Mix-up" has written a very good story aimed at the third age group of juvenile readers. She has obeyed the rule of not writing down to her audience. The complication is *en rapport* with teen-agers, thirteen to seventeen years old. The protagonist solves her own complication. The theme is more subtly expressed than in stories for the two younger groups. Let us, then, look at "Maggie Mix-up" more closely to see how the author has structured the story.

BASIC PLOT

The basic plot used in this story is conflict to overcome an obstacle in order to solve the protagonist's complication and reach a worthwhile goal. The obstacle Maggie must overcome is her own awkwardness, carelessness, and irresponsibility, which make her a pest in her brother's eyes. She wishes to prove to Bob that her intentions are good in order to reach the worthwhile goal of healing the breach in their love and affection for each other.

A dozen proverbs come to mind that could apply to this story. For example, the story proves that "blood is thicker than water." But the lesson the author wanted to teach is that no matter how much teen-age brothers and sisters fight, beneath it all there is a very deep bond of love between them.

COMPLICATION

Maggie faces the minor complication of being awkward, careless, and irresponsible. This minor complication consists of unpleasant attributes that, had she the freedom of choice, she would choose to be otherwise. She would choose instead to be graceful, careful, and responsible.

The complication is made more interesting than it would seem in real life by means of certain exaggerations. In real life it is very unlikely that Maggie would have stuffed her socks into the bell of her brother's trumpet. It is even more unlikely that her brother could not tell the difference between a box containing a corsage and one containing frogs. On the basis of the truth about Maggie, that she is a normal teen-ager at the awkward age of thirteen—which makes her careless and irresponsible—the author proceeds to develop a series of exaggerations, which make the truth amusingly evident:

1. Maggie, wanting to look her best, dresses carefully only to discover as the first guest arrives that she has on one green and one blue sock.
2. Maggie, taking off the socks, is unable to spy a place to hide them.
3. The only place Maggie can see to hide the socks quickly is in the bell of her brother's trumpet.
4. Maggie does not know it, but her brother Bob is scheduled to play his trumpet at the tea with Thea, his girl friend, accompanying him on the piano.
5. Maggie's carelessness causes her brother great hurt and embarrassment when he picks up his trumpet and finds her socks in the bell.
6. The complication is made more serious by Maggie's attempting to make amends by tidying Bob's room, only to throw out a theme, which he then has to do over, and by scorching his shirt.
7. The complication becomes so deep that something of importance is at stake when Bob picks up the box containing the frogs, instead of the box containing the corsage. As a result of Maggie's carelessness, Bob loses his girl. The important thing at stake, if the complication

remains unsolved, is the happiness of Maggie and Bob, the normal bond of love and affection between brother and sister.

8. The author uses the principle of discovery and change to make the complication so serious that it appears to be beyond solution. During Maggie's moment of truth in paragraphs 54 and 55—this moment is implied and not stated—she discovers she loves her brother so much she just cannot stand the rift between them any longer, which makes her change her mind about buying a dog. As a result, she uses the money to buy flowers and goes to the Murray home with the best of intentions, only to have Bob mistakenly think she has come to play another joke on him and Thea. Thus it appears that the rift between Maggie and her brother will never be healed.

9. The agonizing decision made in the pulp or slick story must point to the solution. In paragraph 61, Maggie makes the agonizing decision that her brother can never believe in her no matter how good her intentions, which leads to her running out of the house so blinded by tears that she misses a porch step and falls. This points to the solution since Bob, believing she has been hurt, becomes very solicitous about her welfare. The rift between them is healed.

The complication is made believable through Maggie's characterization as a teen-ager at an awkward age. And the solution is made believable for girls in Maggie's age group who have teen-age brothers of their own or are acquainted with their friends' teen-age brothers. This group will accept the idea readily that no matter how much teen-age sisters and brothers argue, underneath it all they feel a good deal of affection for one another. Finally, the complication is the device the author uses to communicate emotion to the sympathetic reader, since the reader will identify himself with Maggie and experience all her emotions as she tries to solve her complication.

PLOT STRUCTURE

"Maggie Mix-up" follows the plot structure of the chronological story.

BEGINNING (Paragraphs 1 through 22)

1. The scene is set in Maggie's home.
2. The principal characters, Maggie and her brother Bob, are introduced, with an indication of their ages. The point of view is established: this is Maggie's story.
3. The reader knows from the tone of the prose that he is reading a teen-age juvenile story.

283

4. The circumstances that produced the complication are presented. The reader learns that Maggie is at an awkward age, which makes her careless and irresponsible.
5. The reader is trapped into reading the rest of the story by having interest in Maggie's welfare aroused.

MIDDLE (Paragraphs 23 through 62)

1. The complication is presented in paragraphs 23 through 28. Maggie's carelessness in placing her socks in Bob's trumpet results in his embarrassment. As a further result, then, a rift develops between Maggie and Bob.
2. In paragraphs 29 through 53, we get a series of attempts on Maggie's part to heal the split between herself and her brother, only for her to meet with failure: the rift between Maggie and her brother grows wider.
3. Paragraphs 54 through 59 present a situation of ante-climax in which it first appears that Maggie will solve her complication. She uses the money she has been saving to buy a dog in order to buy flowers for Thea, Thea's mother, and Thea's aunt. When she goes to their home to apologize, explain about the frogs, and take all the blame, she meets with such disastrous failure (paragraph 60), the reader is convinced that the breach between Maggie and Bob will never be healed.
4. Therefore, in paragraphs 61 and 62, Maggie is forced to the agonizing decision that Bob can never believe in her or in her good intentions. These paragraphs point to the solution.

END (Paragraphs 63 through 68)

1. The solution of the pulp and slick story must be believable and satisfactory to the reader. The solution is satisfactory to the reader because he sympathizes with Maggie and wants to see the rift healed between her and Bob. The reader knows from paragraph 66 that there will never be another serious breach between Maggie and Bob because Maggie is now going to try very hard to outgrow her faults of carelessness and irresponsibility. The solution is also made believable through the unstated assumption made about Bob in the story: like any other teen-age boy, what he shows to the world and the way he feels are frequently two different things, and the truth is that he is devoted to his sister.

Winner at Bingo—
Loser at Marriage

by (AUTHOR'S NAME WITHHELD)

1   Six months after our marriage, Roger and I moved. Roger was with an insurance company and had just received an important promotion. I was so much in love with him that I was more than willing to follow him wherever he might go. But after the excitement of getting settled in a large city died down, loneliness closed in on me. I didn't know anyone and I didn't have anything to do. Roger worked very hard; half the time he'd be in bed and asleep by nine o'clock. I hated to complain to him, but I was bored to tears.

2   "Honey," he'd say, "there are lots of people around here. Can't you make friends with any of them?"

3   "How?" I'd demand. "The young ones all have babies, and that's all they talk about. Now if we had a baby. . . ."

4   "Marge, you know we agreed not to start on a family for a year. I want to get a foothold here first, some money in the bank." Roger was stubborn about that. He had made his plans and was sticking to them. While I liked the security that this gave me, I couldn't help feeling restless, even yearning. He just didn't understand how lonesome I was.

5   Back where we'd come from, I hadn't lacked friends; I'd grown up with them. I hadn't realized that starting over and making new ones would be so hard. I was from a small town and this was a big city; everyone seemed to know more than I. So there I was, twenty-one years old, pretty enough with my wavy, light-brown hair and my size-ten figure, married to the

285

man I'd loved ever since I was sixteen, but just miserable because there was no place I could fit in.

6   That was the way matters stood one morning when I met Amelie Price. I was sitting on a bench not far from the apartment house, watching the preschoolers at play and the mothers sitting with their baby carriages, when a middle-aged woman settled on the bench beside me, her arms filled with groceries. She turned to me. "Whew! I should know better than to stop in to the supermarket without a cart. Actually, I just went in for a quart of milk. And look at me."

7   I smiled. The packages were certainly bulging with more than milk. "They do look heavy," I said.

8   She nodded. "I shouldn't buy so much, but I had some extra money and I do love delicacies, bad as they are for my waistline!" She looked at me with friendly curiosity. "I've seen you around before, haven't I? You and your handsome young husband? My name's Amelie Price—we live in the same building."

9   "I'm Marge Stark," I told her shyly. We sat there together in the spring sunshine for about half an hour. Amelie was so easy to talk to, before I knew it I was pouring out all my woes. She listened sympathetically. When I walked home with her, helping to carry the packages, she said, "Why don't you come with me this afternoon? There's a bingo game at St. Anthony's Church."

10   "Bingo?" I echoed.

11   She laughed. "Yes, bingo. I go all the time. Last night I won fifteen dollars. That's how come the extra money for these." She shifted the sack on her arm.

12   "I don't know. Gambling. . . ." I protested.

13   "Oh, come on. It's for the benefit of charity, isn't it? And it'll give you some excitement, dear, I promise you. Maybe you'll win something too."

14   I debated with myself, but not for very long. I thought it was nice of her to invite me. And it would be heaven to have some place to go, as well as a friend to go with. That was most important; I didn't even consider that I might win any money. She explained that I couldn't really lose very much, not if I didn't buy too many cards, whatever that meant. I did have some money in my purse; Roger was never stingy with me. So I said yes.

15   I don't know what I expected, but what I found when we got to the church was a huge room crammed with long tables, folding chairs, and women of all ages. There were some men too, but most wore small denim half-aprons, and I guessed they worked there. Amelie found us places at a table facing the front where we could see the bingo cage and the board that would light up, she told me, as the numbers were called. With our dollar admission we'd received what she called a lap board, a book of colored paper cards, and a white jackpot card. In addition she bought ten more lap boards, at five for a dollar. At the table she brought out a thick red crayon and a box of tiny, round red chips and said I could use them instead of the paper ones the house provided. The paper ones, she told me, were likely to stick to your fingers.

16   I looked at my equipment. The lap board had two games on it. I thought that would be quite enough for me until I understood more of what I was doing. Then the feverish talk died down as the first game began. "B-12," the caller announced over the loudspeaker.

17   I had the number on both cards and covered it with the red chips. With her eleven boards and twenty-two games, Amelie had to be swift in locating the numbers and clicking down her chips. In fact, the whole room was clicking. I marveled. I had but one to go to fill a diagonal line when someone screamed, "Bingo!"

18   "Oh-h-h-h!" My disappointment was echoed all over the room. Amelie shrugged and began emptying her cards. One of the men read the winning card aloud to be checked against the lighted numbers on the board.

19   "You're not supposed to clear your cards until they finish checking the numbers," Amelie told me. "But nobody's ever made a mistake since I've been playing."

20   I was completely absorbed. The ushers were walking around hawking "hot cards." There were women, too, selling coffee, Cokes, cake, cookies and even hot dogs with sauerkraut. I hadn't enjoyed myself so much in months. I could hardly wait for the next game to start. Amelie said it was beginner's luck, but on the third game I had my chance to cry "Bingo!" I was so thrilled, I jumped up and down. I promptly spent a dollar for five more blue sheets for the "Blue Special" that was coming

up. This game, I learned, was marked with a red crayon, and we had three chances to win. One straight bingo, then one for numbers shaping the letter X, then one for a full card.

21   Well, I didn't win on that one, but I did win once more before the afternoon was over. When I counted up and deducted what I'd spent for extra cards, I was ahead by seventeen dollars and fifty cents. "Wait till Roger hears," I babbled to Amelie on the way out. "Will he be surprised. Seventeen fifty! We'll have to celebrate."

22   She grinned at me. "Sure, you'll have to celebrate." Then she cautioned, "But don't be disappointed if he's not as thrilled as you are, dear. Men are kind of stuffy about these things sometimes. They think of what you might have lost, instead of what you won."

23   I shook my head vigorously. "Roger's not like that. He'll be glad. Oh, Amelie, I'm so happy you asked me to go!"

24   And Roger was pleased. He didn't bubble the way I did, but he got a kick out of my excitement. "Haven't seen you so gay since we moved. Don't tell me bingo gives you more of a thrill than I do?"

25   "Oh, Roger!" I insisted we go out to celebrate. Across the restaurant table I told him, "Darling, I could never love anything or anyone more than I do you. You know that."

26   "Just keep it that way," he said. It had truly been a wonderful afternoon and evening. Even before I fell asleep that night I was wondering when I could play bingo again with Amelie. I decided to look for her the next morning and find out. And all night long, numbers tumbled around in my head.

27   I did find Amelie in the morning. I went to her apartment, which was nicely furnished and very neat. She'd told me her two daughters were married, so only her husband lived with her now, but naturally he wasn't home. Funny, she was old enough to be my mother but I couldn't think of her that way. She seemed younger than my own mother, maybe because I couldn't picture Mom at a bingo game in a million years. Anyway, Amelie chuckled when she saw me. "Ready for more, eh?" she asked. "I take it your husband doesn't object to you playing bingo."

28   "Why should he?" I demanded. "We had a wonderful time last night—my treat!"

29   She shrugged. "It won't always be that way, you know.

Sometimes you don't win for weeks. Many's the time Charlie and I have had words about it. But I tell him it's my own entertainment, and for charity too. As long as we're still eating, who does it harm?"

30   Oh, I agreed completely. I was still buoyed up from the day before, and eager to try again. I thought I'd budget myself—so much to be risked at each session and no more. That way, Roger would never have any reason to complain. I stuck to my resolve, too. I didn't win anything that day, but I wasn't too unhappy. Counting the night before I was still ahead. And it had been fun seeing the other women. Amelie told me you often saw the same faces at every game. She knew the woman across the table from us, for instance. She was there with her tiny, white-haired mother. The two of them played bingo every day, either in the afternoon or evening. Then there was the skinny stick of a woman down the table from us who talked to herself constantly. She had a full twenty cards spread out in front of her and exchanged them exactly three times during the afternoon for others that might be luckier. Once, she got so mad when someone else won a game, she threw all the cards to the floor. "They get like that sometimes," Amelie said later. "You see all kinds. At least I've never been that wrapped up in it. But bingo gets in your blood, dear. You better watch out!"

31   I didn't take her warning too seriously. I was still new at the game, and I felt very virtuous because I refused to accept Amelie's invitation to go with her again the next day. "Twice a week, that'll be my limit, Amelie," I told her.

32   Now the thought of being alone again for a few days didn't bother me. I had something to look forward to. There'd always be a place for me with people with interests in common.

33   Roger sensed the difference in me. Over the week end I was especially gay and good-humored. "You know," he mused, "I'm sure glad you've perked up—I mean, I was starting to think it was a mistake that we moved."

34   "Mistake?" I kissed him. "It was a good chance for you, wasn't it, darling?"

35   "Yes, but you're my wife, Marge. If you're not happy, what good is it?"

36   "I'm happy," I said firmly. "I just had to get used to it, that's all."

37   We were very close that night. I told myself I was only be-

ginning to see how wonderful marriage could be. I kept on feeling that way, right through that week and the next and the next. I went to bingo twice each week with Amelie, and though in all that time I won only two dollars, I didn't lose my zest. There was something compelling just about the chance of winning at each new game. Somebody had to win. I heard again and again that all you needed was one card, the right card, and I had to keep myself from buying more than five at a time. But twenty-five cents didn't seem a lot against the possibility that that extra card might be the right one. Gradually I was buying one, then two, and then a whole five extra. I had chips and red crayons of my own now, and I was as swift as Amelie in locating the numbers. True, I was starting to feel a little guilty about the money that was disappearing, but I thought that when I won I'd make up for it. Soon I'd hit a winning streak like some of the other women. Maybe I'd win the jackpot! So hope kept me going. The two days a week I was committed to accompanying Amelie began to stand out in my mind as bingo days. The fever that seized me as soon as I woke up on those mornings would grow and grow until the afternoons when I'd walk into whatever place the game was being held at. With all my equipment spread out in front of me I'd find my breath coming fast. Oh, I'd laugh and joke the same as the other women did, but behind it I was willing the game to begin. And when it did, I'd be wishing for the numbers I wanted, the ones that would make me a winner. Those times when I had only one number to go, my heart was so high up in my throat I could hardly hear. The triumphant cry would already be on my lips. Then, mostly, the number called wouldn't be mine but someone else's, and I'd feel like I'd plunged right off a cliff. But I'd remember there were more games to come, more chances, the jackpot was still ahead and wouldn't I rather win that one, anyway?

38   Then one day I did. I won the one-hundred-fifty-dollar jackpot with another woman, so we each came out with seventy-five dollars. I tell you, I'd never been so thrilled in all my life. And yet, in a way, it was the worst thing that could have happened to me. With all that extra money I felt I could afford to go once in a while to an evening game too, the nights when Roger was tired and went to bed early. I'd just save the money toward that, so he wouldn't be losing anything. That's how I broke my rule about going only twice a week.

39   After that I was lost. I was a bingo addict. In the long run the money I won did not add up to what I was putting in. Instead of calling a halt, I started economizing on my food-buying, getting cheaper cuts of meat. Luckily, I was a good cook and Roger didn't complain. Not for a long time, until even my skill at preparing a meal couldn't hide the fact my casseroles were mostly starch.

40   "What kind of junk is this, Marge?" Roger demanded at last. "It's not fit for somebody starving in China!"

41   I smiled at him weakly. "I'm sorry, darling. The magazine recipe looked good."

42   He pushed his plate away. "Seems to me you've been trying too many magazine recipes lately. What's the matter with a good old-fashioned steak?"

43   I couldn't tell him that a steak cost too much, that I only had two dollars and fifty cents to last until payday, three days away. I'd lost the rest the night before, while Amelie had won twenty. So I said, "I'll get a steak for the week end, Roger."

44   "Never mind the week end! I want one tomorrow night!"

45   When he got that look in his eyes, I knew better than to argue with him. "Of course, honey, if that's what you want. Tomorrow night." Where I'd get the money for steak, I didn't know. But if I played bingo that night, I might win it. Roger was already yawning and I could tell he'd be going to bed soon. So after I did the dishes I went over and hugged him. "Mind if I go down to Amelie's for a while?" I asked.

46   He grunted. "Shouldn't you be seeing girls more your own age?"

47   "But I like Amelie," I laughed. "She doesn't talk about babies and diapers all the time."

48   He didn't answer that one. We hadn't discussed having a baby for months now, but I guess he figured I still wanted one badly. I went down to Amelie's and then off to the game with her. The evening ended, leaving me absolutely broke. I walked out with Amelie, not listening to her chatter. She had won five dollars—that was fate for you. If only I had bought her card instead!

49   "What's the matter, dear?" she asked.

50   "Nothing." I was brooding about my promise to buy Roger a steak the next day. How was I going to manage that now? "It's just that I'm broke."

51   "Too bad," she said. "Happens to the best of us."

52 "Amelie," I burst out, "Amelie, could you lend me some money? Just two or three dollars?"

53 At first she was silent. Then she said, "I'm sorry, dear. But my motto is: 'Neither a borrower nor a lender be.' "

54 My face burned. Maybe she was right, but I wouldn't ask if I weren't desperate. And after all, she had won five dollars; she could spare it. But no, this was the kind of a friend she was.

55 I didn't stop to think that our relationship had never really been friendship. We'd been companions, that's all, conveniently attending the games together. I had no right to expect anything else from her. But we rode home on the bus in chilled silence and I didn't bother to say good night. Roger was sound asleep when I came in; for a moment I stood over him, looking at his strong relaxed form. He was going to be very angry. Suddenly I felt guilty and mad and ashamed. Roger worked hard for our money, but thanks to me we didn't have a dime for dinner the next day. I was a failure as a wife. Throwing money away on a silly game! When he found out—how I dreaded the scowl on his face and the disappointment. What if he were sorry he'd married me?

56 My problem seemed pretty big to me that night. But I resolved that when I had to ask Roger for money in the morning, I'd swear that I wouldn't gamble it away on bingo. In fact, I'd give up bingo. It was causing me more trouble than it was worth. I'd miss it, but I'd be happier just not feeling guilty any more.

57 That decided, I finally fell asleep. But my mind must have been working all through the night because, when I woke up in the morning, I decided not to confess to Roger after all. I'd open a charge account at the grocery store two blocks away. I didn't usually shop there because the prices were higher than the supermarket's. But this was a case of necessity, wasn't it? And they carried meats too—I could give Roger his steak that night without risking his displeasure. And in a few days' time, I'd have the money to pay for it.

58 I was in such good spirits that Roger gave me an extra hug and kiss before he left and whispered how much he loved me. I pinched his cheek teasingly. "You'll love me even more after dinner tonight. Only the best for a husband of mine."

59 I thought how foolish I'd been to worry so the night before.

There was always a way out of problems if you looked hard enough. As for giving up bingo, that wouldn't be necessary now. I'd simply be more careful in the future—go back to my resolution never to risk more than I could afford. I was still angry at Amelie, but I didn't really need her any more. There were lots of women I knew now at the games. I could do without company on the bus. So I continued playing. Sometimes I won and sometimes I didn't, but there was always the hope that next time would be the big one. I'd stopped telling Roger about any of it unless he asked, but I thought about it all the time—the numbers that had almost been called, the cards I might have exchanged too soon that were lucky for someone else. I didn't realize it, but somehow bingo had become a disease with me. The days when I didn't go were days to be endured somehow until the time when I could go. Gradually, I began going more often again, risking more. Sometimes I almost resented it when Roger didn't go to bed early so I could get away. I'd watch TV and wonder if maybe this would have been my lucky night, if only I'd been playing.

60   "Say, what's wrong with you lately?" he demanded once. "I talk to you and get the feeling you're not even listening!"

61   I blinked at him, startled. He was right; I hadn't been listening. I'd been wondering if they were up to the jackpot yet at the game. I lied, "Roger, I'm sorry, I—I have a headache, that's all."

62   It bothered me that he was concerned, but I knew I couldn't explain to him about bingo. How could I tell him that it fascinated me more than anything he might be saying? I'd make up my mind I'd forget about that game and concentrate only on him. Yet somehow my love didn't have much effect on my will-power, and my thoughts kept straying time after time. It got so that we snapped at each other frequently. Once Roger lost his temper and yelled at me for something silly, and I burst into tears. Instantly, he pulled me into his arms. "Honey, honey, what's happened to us? We're not close any more like we used to be. What is it—aren't you happy? Should we give it all up and go back home?"

63   I shook my head. "No, no, I'm just a little on edge, darling. I like it fine here." I didn't want to go home. There wasn't any bingo there.

293

64   After that, Roger's attitude seemed to change. He was very patient with me. I felt twice as guilty as before, knowing it was all my fault to begin with, and still not being able to stop. The game maintained its utter fascination for me, but I'd long ago stopped being light-hearted about it. I went into each session as if it were a matter of life and death. In a way I was miserable, aware that no mere game should ever be that important. Yet quarter after quarter, dollar after dollar went. I was charging more and more at the grocery store, gambling on being a winner, hoping to pay the bills before Roger could find out about them. I even neglected to spend money on personal things like underwear and stockings. I told myself nobody cared how I looked; if I wore a stocking with a run in it, no one would notice. With the first jackpot I won, I'd treat myself to everything, all at once.

65   Then came a night when Roger went to bed early but I couldn't go out because I didn't have any money left. I wouldn't have any for two days, until payday when Roger gave me my household allowance. I prowled the apartment, restless. Nothing on TV was any good. I had nothing to read. I felt as if I were going to jump clean out of my skin. I wanted to play bingo. I knew—I just knew—this would be my lucky night. Otherwise, why would I feel this way, as if something were telling me to go?

66   But I didn't have any money. Still, Roger had money. He was dead to the world, and his trousers were on a chair just inside the bedroom door. A dollar—surely he wouldn't begrudge me a dollar. Just enough for the basic cards. If he were awake I could have asked him for it, but naturally it wouldn't do to disturb him. That wouldn't be considerate, I told myself. A dollar, just a dollar.

67   I took it from his pocket, trying not to feel like a thief. If this were my lucky night, I could replace it later and he'd never know. So I calmed my conscience and left. And I did win! Only five dollars, but four more than I'd started out with. When I came back, I put a dollar in Roger's pocket and he was never the wiser. I swore to myself that I'd never do it again. Somehow, though, it became easier and easier to take from Roger's trousers, never more than two dollars, but money

I couldn't always put back. Still, he didn't seem to notice. He didn't keep his cash in a wallet, just loose, so I thought maybe if he missed any he probably assumed he'd lost it. Still, somewhere underneath all my reasoning, a part of me was saying, MARGE, YOU'RE A THIEF! I closed my ears to it. I had to, to go on living with myself.

68   Finally, Roger caught me. There came a night when he switched on the bedside lamp just when I put my hand into his pocket. I felt as if I were tingling crimson all over. For a second we just stared at each other. Then he said quietly, "How much do you want this time, Marge?"

69   I didn't even think of trying to brazen it out. My husband's face was hard and cold like a stranger's. I mumbled, "Just a dollar or two."

70   "A dollar or two. And how much last time?"

71   "I. . . ." My voice didn't seem to be coming out right. "Roger, I didn't mean to. I didn't think you'd mind. . . ."

72   "Why didn't you ask me for what you needed, Marge? Do you think I'd ever deny you?" When I was unable to answer him, he said, "I couldn't bring myself to believe it was you taking the money. But last night the phone rang, waking me up. You weren't here. It was a wrong number but I stayed awake wondering. I thought about you, that maybe you'd gone to a movie. I was awake when you came in. I heard the change in my pocket jingle when you went to it."

73   I'd been putting some money back. I'd come out even last night and thought it would be easier to replace what I'd taken, then take more tonight if I had to. Roger asked, "What goes on, Marge? Why the petty thievery?"

74   The words cut through me like a dagger of ice. I gave a little cry and sank down onto the chair to cover my face with my hands. It was hard telling him the whole story. I was so wretchedly ashamed. He kept saying, "You mean that—that game? I thought you'd stopped going long ago. When you got tired of Amelie! For Pete's sake, how much have you lost?"

75   I couldn't tell him that. I'd given up keeping track of what I lost. I only remembered what I won. I waited for his anger, for all the harsh words I deserved. But they didn't come. Instead, he said something much, much worse. He said with

bitterness in his voice, "Do you know what I was thinking? About why you were acting so strange? I got it into my stupid skull that you were pregnant. Yeah, dumb me, I thought you just didn't want to tell me yet. How do you like that for a laugh?"

76   "Oh Roger!" I wanted to go on my knees and beg for forgiveness, but all I could say was, "Oh, Roger!"

77   "I guess I don't know you very well, Marge," he said. Coming from my own husband, those words hurt. I had gambled, stolen, cheated. Was there a single thing I could say in my own defense? I wept, drearily and without hope. Then Roger showed me that I didn't know him very well, either. The next thing I knew, he had his arms around me, trying to comfort me. I lifted my head to stare at him, uncomprehending. He was somber-faced but gentle. "I won't pretend this hasn't been a blow. But I still love you, Marge. So how about starting all over?"

78   "Roger, do you mean it?" My voice cracked. "Oh, Roger, I'll never gamble again. I promise. It's like a sickness but I'm through with it. I don't care if I never have anything else to do."

79   "Maybe you will have something else," he said. "It's all been partly my fault, anyway. I knew you wanted a baby. I should have seen how important it was. But it's not too late. What do you say, Marge?"

80   What did I say? I said he was wonderful, the most marvelous, patient, unselfish man in the world. And yes, I wanted a baby. With a family, I'd never have to worry about gambling again. I really thought that. I guess we both did. And maybe, if I'd become pregnant soon, I would have been all right. But life doesn't always work out like that. Two months, then three went by and I still hadn't conceived. I was back to sitting on park benches, watching mothers and children. I even got to know some of the women, listening to their talk for future pointers. I saw Amelie once in a while and was friendly. She didn't carry a grudge. When she heard I'd quit bingo, her face was skeptical but she nodded. "A good idea. You were in pretty deep, dear. If you can't take it or leave it alone, it's not worth it."

81   That irritated me. She was right, but wasn't she just as much

of an addict as I'd been? Maybe she didn't risk as much, but she still went regularly. What business did she have sounding so smug?

82   When winter came I was stuck in the apartment more than I liked, wondering why I wasn't pregnant yet. Could God be punishing me? I began to get as restless as I'd ever been. When I went to see a doctor, he told me there was nothing wrong with me. If I still wasn't pregnant in a few more months, I should come back for further tests.

83   A few more months! Time seemed to stretch ahead of me endlessly. I thought about getting a job even though Roger had made it clear that he didn't want me to work. But it would help pass the empty days, give me something to do. Anything so I shouldn't succumb to the temptation that was haunting me again. When I put it to him that way, he looked unhappy but not unfavorable. "Where could you work?" he asked.

84   "The supermarket," I said. "I saw a sign in the window. They need checkers. And I'd be right near home. And I did work in a supermarket back home so I know something about it. Darling, we could save the money for the baby."

85   Finally he agreed. I got the job and for a week I was so tired at night that I went to bed when Roger did. And then Amelie came in one day and paused to chat. Putting her change in her purse, she gazed at me. "There's a new game's just opened up that everyone's talking about. The jackpot is seven hundred dollars!"

86   I gasped. The biggest jackpot in any of the usual places was two hundred and fifty dollars. She went on, "Not only that, but they play five nights a week."

87   "Wow!" I said. "They must be packing them in."

88   She nodded. "I was there last night. Had no luck but I'm going back tonight. Want to go?"

89   I laughed. "Not me. You know I don't play any more." I wondered if she could tell how hard my heart was pounding. Seven hundred dollars—what a haul that would be! Why it would pay for a baby and a vacation and lots of other things besides. Not that we really needed the money, but still. . . . Firmly I put the thought out of my mind. No more bingo, no matter what. I'd made a promise and I was going to keep it.

90   But, I thought suddenly, if I went I wouldn't be risking

Roger's money. I was working now—I had money of my own. That made a difference. With eyes narrowed, I watched Amelie go out. Just one night or so, how could that hurt? All the rest of the day I thought about it. When I got home, I received a call from Roger. "Honey, one of the guys here is having a smoker tonight. I'd told him I couldn't go—didn't want to leave you alone—but they're giving me a hard time about it."

91   "Go," I said. "I'll be all right."

92   "You're sure?"

93   I could tell he really wanted to join the men. It seemed like fate. If he weren't going to be home, there wouldn't be much standing in the way of my playing bingo with Amelie. The excitement inside me was bubbling. This was different. I could control the fever now. Actually it didn't take long for me to prove I was as bad as I'd ever been. I bought extra lap boards, all the specials and fifteen of the jackpot cards. It was as if all the thrill I'd ever had from this game was concentrated right here in this enormous hall tonight. Everyone was excited; I wasn't the only one. And I saw many women I'd seen before; it was just like I'd never been away. At least I was here now, tense, eager, determined. Who knew what the night would bring?

94   Well, I won. Not the jackpot, but two separate twenty-dollar games. Oh, the thrill, the joy of it! While one of the ushers read out my winning numbers Amelie told me, "You're lit up like the Fourth of July!" It was only on the way home that I began to sober up. Forty dollars wasn't like seven hundred. I mean, I could spread seven hundred whole dollars out in front of Roger and know he'd be impressed, but forty wasn't enough to justify breaking my promise. So I'd have to keep it a secret again. But I'd save it and spend it all on him, on his birthday in April.

95   Of course, that was weeks away. In the meantime, I was back to bingo. Sure, I'd stopped for a while; I'd tried to have a baby—but nothing had happened. What if I weren't meant to have children, I asked myself. Could Roger expect me to keep that silly promise all my life? It wasn't as if I couldn't pay for my hobby now myself. That was what bingo was, my hobby, the one thing I enjoyed. I had a right to play.

96   My reasoning sounded all right, except for one thing. I

298

couldn't tell Roger about it. I tried to, but the words wouldn't come. These nights, because I made sure he was asleep before I left, I had to buy more cards than before to make up for what I might have lost by being so late. My recent winnings went; so did the money I was earning at the market. Night after night I heard some other woman win seven hundred dollars. Surely the time was coming when I would win.

97   One evening I heard a woman at the next table say, "My husband thinks I'm at the movies tonight." The women around her laughed understandingly. So I'm not alone, I thought, in more ways than one. Looking up, I happened to meet the eyes of an usher standing nearby. He too had heard her, and he winked at me. I knew he'd read the expression on my face, and I looked away quickly. I felt him watching me after that. I'd seen him ushering before. In a while he came over and asked if I wanted some more specials.

98   "No," I said. "I'm broke."

99   "Too bad," he sympathized. "But you can exchange the boards you have."

100   I did, but I wasn't any luckier. I forgot about him until the next time I went. Then he sort of hovered around me the whole evening. I was puzzled. Amelie hadn't come; she'd been fighting the flu for a week. So there wasn't anyone I could really talk it over with. It didn't seem to me that he was interested in me as a woman. Yet every time I looked up I seemed to meet his gaze. When I won a straight game he leaped forward to read my numbers. Returning with the cash, he grinned. "Maybe you'll do better now, Mrs. Stark."

101   He knew my name. Of course, a lot of women there did; he could have found it out easily enough. At the moment it didn't seem important. I told him: "I hope so. You can just keep some of that money. I'll take ten jackpot cards. Then we'll see!"

102   I was so sure I'd started a winning streak. I felt it in my blood. That seven hundred—it was going to be mine tonight, to make up for the sneaking I'd done, the cheating, the long struggles with my conscience. Seven hundred dollars and I'd quit bingo forever. And right up to the last moment, I was positive this would be it. I had just one number to go when someone else shrieked, "Bingo!"

103   It didn't seem fair. The sick disappointment in the pit of my stomach spread. I hardly felt the man's consoling pat on my shoulder. Over the hubbub he whispered, "Tomorrow night you're going to win, Mrs. Stark." Empty words were no use to me. But he was whispering again. "I mean it. Stick around after this is over. Someone wants to talk to you."

104   I didn't understand him. What did he mean? And who wanted to talk to me? He moved away before I could ask questions. When the last game ended, I just sat there. I saw him over by the exit, so I gathered my equipment slowly together and rose. As I reached the door, he turned and walked down the hall and I followed. After all there were still people around—it couldn't be dangerous. He led me into a small room where a man was seated behind a desk. "This is Mrs. Stark, boss," he said. Then he went out.

105   I looked at the man behind the desk, bewildered. He had a bony, unsmiling face. "You're a regular here, aren't you, Mrs. Stark?" he asked very businesslike.

106   "Yes, I guess so, Mr.—" I stammered.

107   "Johnson," he said. "We know you're married, no children, and you've been losing a lot lately. More than you can afford, maybe?"

108   I didn't know what to say to him. But I didn't think my affairs were any of his business. I asked stiffly, "Who are you?"

109   He leaned back in his chair. "I run the game here. It's for a very good cause. We help crippled children, you know." I hadn't known, but he went right on. "We take in a lot of money because of the crowd we're able to attract. And how do we attract them? With a seven hundred dollar jackpot. Now, Mrs. Stark, you can see that if we didn't have to give out seven hundred dollars, we'd have a lot more to help those kids. But without the jackpot we couldn't get the crowds." He took out a cigarette. "Mrs. Stark, how would you like to play every night for free?"

110   I just stared at him. "I don't follow you."

111   He explained. I could play as many games as I wanted to, and my money for the cards would be refunded whether I won or not. All I had to do was pretend to win the jackpot every so often. "Oh, not here all the time," he said. "We're opening up other games too."

112   "But—but that's dishonest!" I cried. "That would be cheating!"

113   "Cheating who, Mrs. Stark? Some women who have all evening to win on the other games? Or the crippled children? We're building a fine clinic. You can go over and see for yourself."

114   My lips were suddenly very dry. "It . . . it doesn't sound right to me."

115   "Mrs. Stark, we're not offering to pay you. You take the same chances as everyone else on the other games. Remember this is for charity. You'd be volunteer help in a worthy cause."

116   I swallowed. "But what if the police should find out? Isn't it against the law?"

117   "As I said, it's for charity. The police—ah—understand that, too." He paused. "Well, Mrs. Stark. You'd be helping yourself, wouldn't you? Your husband—he'd have no more reason to complain about money being lost. You could play as much as you wanted to, and all your winnings on the other games would be clear."

118   My head was spinning. Mr. Johnson sounded so sure of himself. And why shouldn't he be? He'd hinted that the police were taken care of. I thought about playing as much as I wanted, without risking a penny. Oh the temptation! But Roger —in a million years he wouldn't approve of this kind of arrangement. It wasn't honest. They pretended to give away a jackpot prize that no one ever won. Yet who was I to worry about honesty? The way I'd been acting, would it make any difference if I went one step further? Who would I hurt? If I didn't tell him, Roger wouldn't find out. Even if he discovered I was playing bingo again, I could explain that I wasn't losing money. I could have my cake and eat it, too.

119   The man was waiting for an answer. I still hadn't decided when he said, "I'll have to know now, Mrs. Stark."

120   I hesitated a moment. Then I said, "All right, Mr. Johnson."

121   This is how it worked. For the jackpot, one had to fill out a whole card. When enough calls were made, all I had to do was yell. The usher would come and read the numbers aloud, just as usual. Only, he'd be sure to repeat the numbers that had been called, whether they were on my card or not. So simple. And no one would know the difference. I could play

as many nights as I wished, whether or not I was going to fake the jackpot that night.

122   So I went into the next stage of my life. I found out later that the word for my new role was "shill." I was the come-on girl for all the others who would think that the next time they might win, if only they kept trying. Funny thing, the first few times I was almost as excited as if I'd really won, that's how much the game was in my blood. And when they put those crisp hundred-dollar bills in my hand, I absolutely shook. Giving them back afterward was hard, but I found myself on a winning streak in the other games, so I told myself not to be selfish. Of course, I had to make sure I wasn't going to be at a game where Amelie was. She lived too close. But the other women didn't know that much about me. Let them think I was getting rich!

123   It was only late at night that I felt little pangs of regret pricking me. When I was in Roger's arms, I'd find myself sighing. Down deep where I'd buried my conscience something was still alive, something I tried to crush. If Roger asked what was wrong I'd say I was worried about not conceiving.

124   One evening he kept staring at me over dinner. He'd hardly touched a bite on his plate, and it was my turn to ask him what the matter was. He said, "Nothing. Well, I mean—Marge, is anything new? Anything you haven't told me?"

125   I frowned. "I'm not pregnant, if that's what you mean."

126   "No, Marge. A girl at my office plays bingo. She said a Mrs. Stark won seven hundred dollars the other night, and she thought it was my wife. She described you, Marge."

127   I tried to smile. "How could it be me, darling? If—if I won seven hundred dollars, I'd be shouting it from the rooftops."

128   "You're sure? You don't play any more, do you?"

129   I should have confessed, but somehow it was too complicated now. How could I tell him about the arrangement I had with Mr. Johnson? "No, darling. No, I don't," I lied.

130   Two nights later I told Roger I was going to visit Amelie, an excuse I used frequently. The jackpot had just been played and I'd screamed "Bingo!" when something made me look up at the door. There was Roger, his face a mixture of shock and disbelief. The usher seized the card from me and began "reading" it, actually repeating numbers which had been called,

as if they were really on my card. Suddenly a woman came up and snatched the card out of his hand. "Let me see that!" she yelled. She jumped right up on a table and began to read off the numbers which were really on my card. The second number created a stir. As anyone could see from the big board showing all the numbers that had been called—my number wasn't a winner. Then as she read another uncalled number, there was pandemonium.

131   The caller tried to restore order, saying it was just a mistake. "How could it be a mistake?" some woman shrieked, pointing at me. "She called bingo and he confirmed it! A fake, it's all a fake!"

132   Before I knew what was happening, fingernails were clawing at me, chairs were overturned, and women were screaming. Somewhere a whistle blew while I was trying to protect myself. Then someone—Roger—grabbed me, his bulk fending off my attackers. My hair was still being yanked, when the police swarmed through the doorway and Roger and I were taken into custody. The "Bingo Riot," that's what the papers called it the next morning.

133   They let Roger stay while I was questioned and booked. Now when it was too late, I didn't hold anything back. When I told about Mr. Johnson's proposition, my husband swore aloud. "I could kill him!"

134   The lieutenant we talked to shook his head. "We've got him too, Mr. Stark. He'll get what's coming to him. So will the ones he bribed."

135   It turned out that there was a clinic for crippled children, all right, but most of the money was going into the racketeers' pockets. The woman who grabbed my card had been a detective. They'd been watching the operation for a while. That's why the police had been so handy. Roger told me he'd been looking for me the whole evening. After finding Amelie at home and realizing I had lied, he'd made her give him a list of places where I might be, and he'd driven around until he found me.

136   I had to spend the night in jail. Finally I had to face myself. I and nobody else had degraded myself. Most people could control the gambling urge but I couldn't. Why hadn't I seen what was happening and stopped before it was too late? Roger,

in his goodness, had given me a second chance; this was how I'd repaid him! I knew that no matter what happened now, I'd never again be a gambler.

137   Well, there isn't much more to tell. The trial hasn't come up yet, and I don't know what my future holds. Roger is standing by me. My husband's an old-fashioned man who believes the words in our wedding ceremony, ". . . for better or worse . . ." So we're together, like strangers, but together. That I think is my real punishment to have to live with the man I love and know he may never trust me again. To see in his eyes the dreadful scope of his disillusion. To go on trying for as long as I live to heal the scars that my heedless fever for a game has left on our hearts.

COMMENTARY ON "WINNER AT BINGO —LOSER AT MARRIAGE"

We would like to preface this commentary by pointing out that many confession stories are published that violate the plot structure of the chronological or formula story. The reason for this is that confession magazines do publish stories written by amateurs, some of which are the first stories the authors have ever sold. However, the best stories appearing in confession magazines are written by professionals and faithfully follow the plot structure of the chronological or formula story.

BASIC PLOT

The plot of this confession story is conflict to overcome an obstacle and reach a worthwhile goal. The obstacle Marge Stark must overcome is her weakness for gambling. Only in this way may she solve her complication and reach the worthwhile goal of preserving her marriage and regaining her social position as an inherently decent and honest person.

THEME

The lesson the author wanted to teach was that gambling can corrupt the character of an inherently decent person to such a point that it makes one a liar, deceiver, and cheat, and can wreck a marriage.

This theme of the corruption of character makes a regular appearance in confession magazines. In one magazine, the theme appears in a story where drinking corrupts the character of a husband and almost wrecks a marriage. In another, excessive mother love corrupts the character of her only child and almost ruins the daughter's life. The exploitation of a weakness of any kind that corrupts character is a common theme, particularly in confession stories, where the protagonist must have something to confess.

COMPLICATION

This adult pulp story presents a complication and the solution to it in the life of Marge Stark, which is more interesting than it would seem in real life and, at the same time, believable to the reader. In real life it is extremely unlikely that an inherently decent person like Marge would stoop so low as to cheat, lie, and even steal from the man she loved. The author develops the complication by the following series of exaggerations:

1. Marge Stark is bored and lonely after moving to a strange city with her husband Roger.
2. Her boredom and loneliness are made worse by the hours her husband works, by his going to bed so early, by his decision they won't have a baby for a year, and by Marge's being a small-town girl who can't make friends easily in a big city.
3. Marge meets Amelie Price and, to escape from her boredom and loneliness, starts playing bingo.
4. Marge loses so much money at bingo she cheats on her food budget until Roger demands she serve him a steak. She lies to him, telling him the recipe sounded as though it would taste good when she read it in a magazine. She deceives him by opening a charge account at the corner grocery store without his knowledge.
5. Marge's mania for gambling at bingo corrupts her character to the point that she begins stealing money from Roger's pockets while he is asleep.
6. Roger catches her stealing money from him. He takes part of the blame and tells her they needn't wait a year to have a baby. The complication appears to be solved as three months pass and Marge abstains from playing bingo.
7. The author uses the technique of discovery and change to make the complication deeper. Marge, failing to become pregnant, takes a job in a supermarket to escape from her boredom, which makes her return to playing bingo again after Amelie Price tells her about the jackpot game. Marge justifies her action by telling herself it is her own money she is using.

8. Marge is now an apparently hopeless bingo addict. The author again uses the technique of discovery and change to make the complication so serious that something of importance is at stake. When Marge discovers from Mr. Johnson that the seven-hundred-dollar jackpot is not on the level, she is shocked at first and refuses to pretend to win it, but changes her mind and agrees to the proposition. The important things at stake if the complication isn't solved are Marge Stark's marriage and her integrity as an inherently decent person.

9. The agonizing decision made by the protagonist in the pulp or slick story must point to the solution. Marge's agonizing decision to accept Mr. Johnson's proposition points to the solution. As a result of this decision, Marge is arrested as she pretends to win the seven-hundred-dollar jackpot.

10. Marge's arrest and her being forced to spend the night in jail bring her to the moment of truth, in the next to the last paragraph of the story, leaving the reader convinced she has learned her lesson and will never gamble again.

The story emphasizes the pulp appeal of basic narrative excitement, without a full dramatic working out of the complication. The complication is something unpleasant that happens to Marge Stark. Had she freedom of choice she would not have chosen to become a bingo addict. Emotion is communicated to the reader by dropping a monkey wrench into Marge Stark's peaceful scheme of things, and making her discover the lure of bingo. The reader vicariously experiences all the emotions Marge does as she tries to solve her complication. Conflict is produced by Marge's struggle to solve her complication. The story is made believable to the reader through Marge's character trait of having a mania for gambling, which makes it believable that such a person would stoop to cheating, lying, and even stealing in order to satisfy her craving.

PLOT STRUCTURE

"Winner at Bingo—Loser at Marriage" faithfully follows the plot structure of the chronological story.

BEGINNING (Paragraphs 1 through 38)

1. The scene is set, paragraph 1, in a large city. The reader knows that Marge and Roger live in a large apartment house from reading paragraph 6.

2. The principal characters are introduced, Marge Stark, her husband Roger, and Amelie Price, with an indication of their approximate ages. The point of view is established: this is Marge Stark's story.

306

3. The reader knows from the tone of the prose that he is reading an adult pulp story.
4. The background of circumstances that eventually lead to the complication is presented as the reader learns how Marge's boredom and loneliness lead her to playing bingo.
5. The reader is trapped into reading the rest of the story as he senses that Marge's minor problem of being bored and lonely, which started her playing bingo, is nothing to what might happen to her if she doesn't learn to control her love of gambling. He reads on to find out what will happen.

MIDDLE (Paragraphs 39 through 132)

1. Paragraph 39 presents the complication: Marge has become a bingo addict.
2. Marge attempts to give up playing bingo when she resolves in paragraph 56 never to gamble again, only to meet with failure. In paragraph 59 she starts playing bingo again. Again she attempts to solve her complication by having a baby, only to meet with failure when she fails to become pregnant.
3. Paragraphs 83 through 95 present a situation of ante-climax in which it appears Marge will finally solve her complication. When she fails to become pregnant and goes to work in the supermarket, Marge has not played bingo for three months, and her complication appears to be solved. Then when she learns about the seven-hundred-dollar jackpot game from Amelie Price and yields to temptation, the reader is convinced that the complication is beyond satisfactory solution.
4. Therefore in paragraphs 118 through 120, Marge is forced to make an agonizing decision that points to the solution. In paragraph 118, Marge mentally starts to make the agonizing decision to accept Mr. Johnson's proposition. As a result of this decision she is arrested later and is forced to spend the night in jail.

END (Paragraphs 133 through 137)

1. The solution of Marge's complication is satisfactory and believable to the reader. The disgrace of being arrested and the degradation of being forced to spend a night in jail make it believable that Marge, during her moment of truth, in paragraph 136, is sincere and will never gamble again. The ending is satisfactory to the reader who believes that Marge will never gamble again and that she and Roger will eventually find happiness. Time will heal the scars left on their hearts.

Isn't It a Perfect Crime?

by JAMES GILMORE

1   The thirty-three years Ira had spent as a Certified Public
Accountant had taught him the importance of details. Details
and figures were his life, the only things he really trusted or
understood. And now, as his train slowly pulled out of the
Minneapolis Depot and snaked its way across the old stone
bridge over the Mississippi, he sat back in the privacy and
comfort of his compartment, put on his steel-rimmed bifocals
and studied the details of his master plan for the last time.

2   As he did, a self-satisfied smile crept across his lips. He
looked upon the plan as his work of art, his masterpiece. It
was Ira Hovel's blueprint of the perfect crime. Oh, he knew
others had tried it before and failed; but, then, they didn't
have his training or passion for detail.

3   He took out a pencil, wet the lead with the tip of his tongue,
and crossed out item number one. It had already been accomplished. Ira's wife, Emily, and his mother-in-law, Bertha,
had driven him to the depot and seen him board the 11 P.M.
train to Chicago. During the past seven years it had become
a regular Sunday night ritual. He smiled again as he thought
how fortunate he was to have a client with a branch in Chicago.
The weekly trip to check their books had been the inspiration
for his plan. Without it, he would have given up hope long ago.
And at fifty-seven a man needs hope.

4   Ira crossed out the second item on the list. It, too, was a
simple detail. All he had to do was tell the porter he didn't
want to be disturbed—no matter what—until the train reached
Chicago. To make sure the man followed his orders, he had
tipped him five dollars. He knew he wouldn't be disturbed.

5   The third item was hardly more difficult. Ira merely had to slip off the train when it reached St. Paul, without being seen. To accomplish it, he'd just walk to the last car, where the porter didn't know him, and get off. He knew from years of experience that porters and conductors are too busy with boarding passengers in St. Paul to pay any attention to one getting off, especially one as inconspicuous as himself.

6   In a way, item four had proved to be the most challenging. Ira needed a car for the forty-five minute drive from the St. Paul Union Station to his home in the Minneapolis suburb of Ednina. At first he planned to rent one, but he finally gave up the idea as too dangerous. The rental agencies required positive identification; he would have had to sign for the car and show his driver's license. He just couldn't afford to take chances like that. He finally solved the problem by buying an old, but perfectly serviceable, 1951 Ford. It cost him exactly two hundred and fifty dollars, a lot of money for one night's work, but with so much at stake it was worth every penny. Ira had driven the car to the station parking lot the morning before. It was there now, waiting for him.

7   The fifth item was the most important of all, and by far the most difficult. It would be difficult because, basically, Ira was a very proper man; violence and crime repelled him. And since murder was the most violent of all crimes, it held a particularly repugnant position in Ira's mind. But what was he to do? Even at the age of eighty-three, his mother-in-law, Bertha, was much too healthy, and much too stubborn to die all by herself. And Bertha had to die; it was the only way Ira could live.

8   The method of the murder had also posed somewhat of a problem. Ira had absolutely no working knowledge of firearms; besides, they were noisy and, he imagined, quite messy. He finally settled on strangulation—it was quick, clean, and quiet. And, since Bertha, in spite of her monstrous personality, was not a large woman, he couldn't imagine that it would be any trouble at all. Getting into her bedroom would not be difficult —her room was on the ground floor in the back of the house —he had even unhooked her screen window that very morning just before church. And he knew Emily wouldn't hear a thing, even if Bertha managed to scream before she lost conscious-

ness, because she always took a sleeping pill when he was out of town.

9   After it was over, he planned to take a few of the knick-knacks Bertha had scattered about her room, something that easily could be disposed of later, to make it look like a simple case of robbery and murder. And, of course, he would wear gloves so there wouldn't be any fingerprints left behind.

10   Yes, Ira thought, item five would be easy enough, so long as he didn't get squeamish at the last moment. And he didn't see how that would be possible.

11   Everything would be downhill after that. Item six consisted of nothing more than driving the car to the airport. He allowed himself a full hour for that, even though he knew it would take only twenty minutes. He'd leave the car in the free parking lot, where passengers were allowed to park their cars for long periods of time without any charge. In about a week's time, he'd pick it up and sell it to a junk yard. There would be nothing to tie the car to the crime.

12   At 2:10 A.M. he would proceed with item seven, boarding Flight 412 to Milwaukee. He had made the reservation under the name of William Hill three weeks before and had reconfirmed it that afternoon. He wasn't worried about bumping into any of his friends on the flight. It was a night coach. Ira's friends were either quite well off, or else they traveled on expense acounts. They'd never dream of taking a coach—especially one leaving at 2:10 A.M.

13   The flight to Milwaukee would take one hour. Even if the plane were delayed, a remote possibility because the weather was perfect and the flight originated in Minneapolis, he would have plenty of time to complete item eight: reboarding his train when it arrived in Milwaukee at 6:00 A.M. This would be simple, too. For the past year he had left the train every Monday morning when it reached Milwaukee, to buy a paper. It was an eccentric habit, and one the porter was well aware of. He knew no one would question him when he got back on the train. Once he was on the train it would be over. He'd have a perfect alibi and his masterpiece would be complete.

14   "St. Paul!" the conductor yelled as he walked by Ira's compartment. Ira looked out the window. They were backing into the St. Paul Depot. There was just time for one more little

detail. He held up his master plan and lit a corner of the paper with his cigarette lighter. Just before the flames reached his fingertips, he put it in the ash tray. He waited patiently until it was completely consumed, then carefully broke up the pieces of ash with his pencil. When the train stopped, he removed his bifocals, put them in their case, tucked it into his inside coat pocket. He pulled out his watch and checked the time. It was exactly 11:27. The train was right on schedule.

15   As Ira climbed the long flight of stairs to the St. Paul Union Station waiting room, he mentally crossed item three off his list. He had left the train exactly as planned and, just as he had expected, no one paid him the slightest attention.

16   He walked quickly through the waiting room and out the front entrance. The car was right where he left it. He slid in behind the steering wheel, turned the key in the ignition and pressed the starter button. The motor turned over, but refused to start. The choke, Ira said to himself, how could you forget a simple detail like that? The used-car salesman had explained the car didn't have an automatic choke. He reached over and pulled it out about half way. The car started at once.

17   Ira paid the parking lot attendant and started the forty-five minute drive home. He felt a strange sensation in his chest and his hands felt clammy on the steering wheel. Don't panic now, he told himself, you've planned this too long. He stopped for a red light at Kellogg and Wabash. While he was waiting for it to change, he looked about the car. It wasn't what he was used to driving; the upholstery was faded and worn, and it had a slightly musty smell. But the motor ran smoothly, and the clutch, transmission, and brakes were good. It would do very nicely.

18   As the light changed he noticed the radio on the dashboard. The salesman had said it worked, and Ira wondered if it actually did. He turned it on. The tuning dial lit up and the vibrator tube began to buzz. Within a block the car was filled with music.

19   Ira was glad the radio did work. The music would soothe him on the long drive. Ira had never been one to keep up with popular music—the classics were more to his liking—but he did recognize the tune that was playing: "Thanks for the Memory." It had been quite popular that damp, miserable fall

in 1938 when Bertha had come to live with Emily and him.

20 His mind couldn't help drifting back to that black day. Bertha had just been widowed. Since Emily was her only child, it was natural that she should stay with them during her period of grief, a grief that even then Ira suspected didn't exist. At first Bertha talked of moving out to the Coast to live with an unmarried younger sister. But the weeks dragged on to months, and the months dragged on to years and now, twenty-two years later, she was still with them. Once in a while, usually at the end of January, when the Minnesota winter was at its worst, she talked of moving out to the Coast to live with her sister. But Ira was almost certain she never would. She enjoyed tormenting him too much; it was the only pleasure she had left in her life.

21 Ira probably could have put up with Bertha if she had withdrawn and kept to herself, but she didn't. Quite the contrary, she took over the household and ran it with an iron hand. And Emily, poor Emily, was completely incapable of standing up to her mother.

22 Somehow it seemed to be the little things that hurt the most. Ira had always wanted a dog to take the place of the children he and Emily had never been fortunate enough to have. But Bertha didn't like dogs.

23 Ira had always wanted to see the world, but Bertha was too old to travel and they couldn't leave her home alone. Consequently, the only traveling Ira ever did was his weekly trip to Chicago and the monthly flight of fancy he took when the *National Geographic* came.

24 But the crowning blow, the event that finally spurred Ira into putting his plan into action, had taken place just a little over three weeks ago. Bertha had just received a letter from her sister on the Coast. The sister was lonely, she needed companionship during her last years, and she pleaded with Bertha to come and live with her. Bertha was still in the process of making up her mind when Ira came home to dinner that night. He believed she might have gone if it hadn't been for Emily.

25 "Oh, Mother, you can't go," Emily said tearfully when Bertha read the letter to Ira.

26 Ira was dumbfounded. "But your Aunt Kate needs her," he said.

27 "So do we," Emily said. "I don't know what I'd do without Mother."

28 It was the first time Ira realized Emily no longer felt the same way about Bertha that he did. Bertha's domination had become so complete during the past twenty-two years that Emily had given up her yearning for freedom. She was content to have Bertha run her forever.

29 "But, Emily," Ira said desperately, "think of your poor Aunt Kate."

30 But it was too late.

31 "Emily's right," Bertha said. "She needs me more than Kate does. Besides, California is so far away—and it's such a strange place—I don't think I'd ever feel secure out there. No, I'll stay here in Minneapolis with you till the day I die."

32 And Ira was sure she would. His plan was the only escape left now. And much as he hated to do it, he had to kill her. He owed it to himself and to Emily, whom, in spite of her mother, he dearly loved. After all, the twenty-two years of hell he had had to endure gave him the right to enjoy the few good years he had left.

33 Ira parked the car a block from the home and walked down the alley to his garage. The house was completely dark, just as he expected. He took out his pocket watch and held it up so he could read the face by the feeble light that came from the street light in front of the house. It was 12:15 A.M. He still had plenty of time, and he wanted to make sure that Bertha and Emily were asleep, so he took out a cigarette. When he was finished, he stamped out the cigarette and pulled on his leather gloves. Then he made his way to the back of the house, being careful to keep in the shade of the lilac bushes.

34 Ira stood outside Bertha's window and listened. He could hear her snoring peacefully in her bed. This is it, he said to himself. He carefully opened the screen and climbed in the window. The inside of the bedroom was black as India ink, but he had memorized the exact position of every piece of furniture in the room. He started for Bertha.

35 As he reached her bedside, his knees suddenly felt weak, and

313

he could feel the fear and excitement welling up inside of him. He pulled the gloves on tighter and reached for her throat. As he did he heard a strange, panting noise and realized it was his own breathing. His arms felt leaden and he pulled them back, letting them hang at his sides. He flexed his almost paralyzed fingers to loosen them. He tried to reach for her throat again, but his arms refused to move. For some strange reason he just couldn't do it. Drops of perspiration began to run down his face. The room started to spin. His whole careful plan seemed to explode in his mind. A long sob came involuntarily out of his choked throat. He reeled backward, stumbling over Bertha's old maple rocker. At the sound of his fall, Bertha snorted and sat up in bed.

36   Ira picked himself up and lunged toward the window, upsetting a table and knocking a lamp to the floor in another series of crashes. Bertha screamed, a horrible, piercing scream. He half jumped, half fell out the window, tearing the screen off along the way. "Murder! Murder! Murder!" Bertha shouted. He rolled over and somehow managed to get to his feet. The light went on in Bertha's room. He crashed through the lilac bushes and ran across his neighbor's backyard. A yapping dog came out of nowhere and started snapping at his heels. He was sure he'd have a heart attack any second and the whole, terrible nightmare would be over.

37   When Ira reached the car, he tore the door open and jumped into the driver's seat. His hands were shaking so he barely got the key into the ignition. Don't forget the choke, he told himself. He pulled it out and pressed the starter button. The motor turned over about ten times but refused to start. He pulled the choke out further. It still wouldn't start. Then he smelled gasoline fumes and realized he had flooded the motor by choking it when it was still warm.

38   Ira sat back and tried to remember all the things one is supposed to do to start a flooded motor. He pushed the choke in and held the gas pedal all the way down to the floor boards as long as he dared. Then he tried again. The motor groaned, sputtered, and finally caught. He put the car in low and drove down the street with the lights off for two blocks.

39   As he turned east on Fiftieth Street he saw the flashing lights and heard the siren of an approaching police car. He pulled

over to the curb and watched it go by, knowing only too well where it was going. Bertha or Emily hadn't wasted any time in calling the police.

40   Ira tried his best to keep under the thirty-mile-an-hour speed limit as he headed down Fiftieth Street toward the airport. At Upton Avenue he had to stop for a red light. As he sat there, wondering what could go wrong next, he heard a sudden screech of brakes behind him. He just had time to look up at his rear-vision mirror. He was horrified by what he saw. The headlights reflected in the mirror weren't going to stop.

41   The impact of the crash knocked Ira's car half-way across the intersection. His first impulse was to step on the gas and get out of there, but the jar had knocked his foot off the clutch and the motor had killed. By the time he got it started, the other driver was at his door.

42   "Say, what'sa matter with you, buddy? Don't you know there's a law against parking in the middle of the street?" the man said, opening Ira's door.

43   "I wasn't parking," Ira said as he got out of his car. "I was waiting for the light to change."

44   The other man pushed Ira. "Don't get wise with me, buddy," he said, slurring the words together. For the first time Ira realized the man had been drinking.

45   "But I assure you, I was just waiting for the light to change."

46   "Oh, you were, were you," the man said, following Ira as he walked to the back of the car to inspect the damage. "For your information, buddy, the light was green."

47   "It was red," Ira said as firmly as his courage would allow. He was somewhat relieved when he saw there were no visible signs of damage to his car, although the other car had a broken bumper guard.

48   "It was green," the other driver said, pushing Ira again. Then he noticed a small crowd beginning to gather. "Somebody call a cop. I demand my rights!"

49   "Oh, I wouldn't call the police," Ira said, trying to soothe the man. "Very little damage has been done."

50   "You afraid of cops?" the man asked.

51   "No," Ira lied, "but after all, man, you've been drinking."

52   The man swung wildly at Ira, missing him by a good two

315

feet. "All I had was one beer," he said, "and you're trying to hang a drunk charge on me."

53   "I'm not trying to hang anything on you. I just want to settle this without any fuss," Ira said.

54   "Well, it's going to cost you plenty," the man said, staggering back to inspect the front end of his car.

55   Ira took out his billfold. "Would fifty dollars do?" he asked.

56   The man looked up at Ira, trying to focus his eyes. "A hundred and fifty would be more like it," he said loudly.

57   "But your car is hardly scratched," Ira protested.

58   A young man about nineteen stepped forward and sided with Ira. "If you ask me, fifty dollars is plenty," he volunteered.

59   "Who asked you?" the man said, swinging at the boy. The boy gave him a little push and he sat down on the pavement. "Well, I guess you're right," he said, making no effort to get up. "I'll take the fifty."

60   "I wouldn't give him a cent," the boy said, looking down at the drunk with disgust.

61   "Who asked you?" the man snapped again.

62   "Here," Ira said, "take the fifty dollars and buy a cup of coffee."

63   "Don't want any coffee," the man said as he took the money and got to his feet. "But I'll buy you a drink." He tried to put his arm around Ira.

64   "No, thank you," Ira said, fending him off.

65   He made his way through the laughing crowd to his car. About six blocks later he noticed a clock in a drug store window. The hands pointed to 1:50. That can't be right, Ira thought. He pulled out his pocket watch and found that it was the correct time. If he didn't hurry, he'd miss his plane. He stepped on the gas, but instead of accelerating, the engine coughed and died. He put in the clutch and coasted over to the curb.

66   Ira pushed the starter button again and again until the battery completely died. "What now?" he said out loud. Then he noticed the gas gauge. It was on empty. But that's impossible, he thought, I filled the tank before I took the car to the parking lot yesterday. Then it dawned on him; the crash had apparently caused a small rip in the gas tank.

67   Now Ira really began to panic. His plane left in just fifteen

316

minutes. How was he going to get to the airport without a car? He decided he'd have to hitchhike and got out of the car. Then, for the first time that night, Ira had a bit of luck. He saw a cab coming down Fiftieth Street toward him. He stood in the middle of the street and flagged it down.

68   "Where to?" the cabbie asked.

69   "The airport," Ira said, his voice quivering with emotion. "And please hurry. I've got to catch a 2:10 plane."

70   "We'll never make it," the cabbie said as he pushed his flag down.

71   "Well, you can try," Ira pleaded. "It's a matter of life and death."

72   Ira's disheveled, frantic appearance must have convinced the cabbie that it was because he really tried. At times the cab's speedometer hit forty-five miles an hour and they ran through two stop signs on Thirty-fourth Avenue.

73   It was exactly 2:10 A.M. when the cab screeched to a stop in front of the terminal building at Wold-Chamberlain Field. "Here," Ira said, throwing a ten dollar bill at the cabbie, "keep the change." He ran into the terminal and across the drab waiting room to the ticket counter. "Am I too late for Flight 412?" he asked the ticket agent, who was posting arrival times on the flight schedule board.

74   "It's just pulling away from the ramp now," the agent said, turning around.

75   "Well, stop it," Ira shouted.

76   "Can't," the agent said. "Once they leave the ramp we can't call them back."

77   Ira felt faint. "When's the next flight to Milwaukee?"

78   "Seven A.M.," the agent answered.

79   "But that's too late," Ira protested, "much too late."

80   "Sorry, sir," the agent said, a little irritated. "It's the best I can do."

81   Ira walked away from the ticket counter in a daze and collapsed in a heap on one of the hard, wooden waiting-room seats. It was at least five minutes before his mind began to function again. Then he tried to work out the details of another plan. But the complete collapse of his masterpiece had so shattered his faith in details that he found it impossible to concentrate.

82   Strange as it may seem, Ira wasn't afraid of going to jail. That would be a pleasure compared to living with Bertha for the rest of his life. The thing that bothered him most was that there was no hope of escaping her now, no hope at all.

83   But he still had to try to keep Bertha from finding out about the horrible thing he had tried to do to her. His failure, and the fact that he would resort to such a terrible thing, would be just one more thing for her to lord over Emily. No, if only for Emily's sake, he had to try to cover up his tracks. How? How? He couldn't reboard the train in Milwaukee; the on-time departure of Flight 412 had seen to that. What about Chicago? If there was a flight to Chicago maybe he could get back on the train there and somehow save his alibi.

84   Ira got up and went back to the ticket counter.

85   "When's the next flight to Chicago?" he asked.

86   "Three-thirty A.M.," said the agent.

87   "And what time does it arrive?" Ira asked.

88   "Four fifty-five," the agent answered.

89   "I'd like to buy a ticket," Ira said with renewed hope.

90   While Ira waited for the flight to leave, he called an all-night garage and asked them to pick up the car. He couldn't afford to have the police spot it as an abandoned car. They might call Emily and ask her about it.

91   Ira had always been fearful of flying, but as he boarded the plane to Chicago he wasn't the least bit afraid. If it crashed, everything would be solved.

92   But the flight to Chicago was uneventful. The steady drone of the engines, and Ira's mental and physical exhaustion, combined to put him to sleep right after take-off. And he didn't wake up until the plane had taxied to a stop in front of the terminal at Midway Airport.

93   Ira was waiting at Track 18 when the Minneapolis train pulled into Union Station at 8:00 A.M. He told the man at the gate that his invalid mother was arriving and he was allowed to go down to the platform. He boarded the front car of the train and walked through the diner to his car. He took his overnight bag and briefcase out of his compartment and walked to the end of the car.

94   "You sure look like you had a bad night, Mistah Hovel," the porter said as he helped him off.

318

95   "Terrible," Ira said.

96   When Ira reached his client's Chicago office, he went right to the Accounting Department. He knew there would be a message from Emily waiting for him there and he steeled himself against making any kind of reaction that would give himself away. Mr. Ashley, the head accountant, met him at the door of the department, looking very grave.

97   "Good morning, Ashley," Ira said in his usual brisk manner. "Let's get right at the books, shall we?"

98   "Better call your wife first," Ashley said. "She's been trying to get you ever since we opened."

99   "Oh? I wonder why," Ira said. "I do hope nothing has gone wrong at home."

100   "Use the phone in my office," Ashley said. "It'll be more private."

101   "Why, thank you, Ashley," Ira said. He placed a collect call to Emily. It took about thirty seconds to complete.

102   "Ira?" Emily asked.

103   "Yes, dear," Ira said. "Anything wrong?"

104   "Oh, Ira, something terrible happened last night. . . ."

105   "Terrible?"

106   "A burglar broke into Mother's room—scared her half to death. She's leaving."

107   "Leaving?"

108   "Going to Aunt Kate's in California. . . ."

109   "But I don't understand," Ira interrupted.

110   "She's afraid of being murdered. Says she won't stay in this house another night. She's already made her reservations. Isn't it awful?"

111   Ira sighed. "Well, I think we'll be able to manage somehow."

112   "I know, Ira," Emily said. "But Mother was frightened half to death. It's a perfect crime. . . ."

113   "Yes," Ira said, "a perfect crime."

COMMENTARY ON THE MYSTERY AND SUSPENSE STORY

Mystery and suspense stories generally fall into two categories:

1. Stories that begin with a crime or the threat of a crime and have a sympathetic protagonist

2. Stories that begin with a crime or the threat of a crime and have an unsympathetic protagonist

The plot structure of either the chronological or formula story is designed for stories with sympathetic protagonists because, no matter how serious the complication, the protagonist always solves it to the reader's satisfaction. Any story, therefore, with an unsympathetic protagonist must violate the plot structure of the chronological or formula story because the reader does not want the unsympathetic protagonist to win.

We did not include a chapter on the mystery and suspense story in this book because we could not do justice to it in a single chapter. To the student or reader who wants to specialize in mystery writing, we recommend the following books: Gilbert's *Crime in Good Company,* Soderman and O'Connell's *Modern Criminal Investigation,* Brean's *Mystery Writer's Handbook,* and Burack's *Writing Detective and Mystery Fiction.*[1]

We believe the apprentice writer should confine himself to writing mystery stories with sympathetic protagonists; i.e., those that can be built using the plot of the chronological or formula story, until he has gained the experience necessary to write stories with unsympathetic protagonists. While it is true that the plot structure of the mystery story was originally based on the formula or chronological plot, the trend in today's mystery fiction appears to be toward the off-beat suspense story in which an unsympathetic protagonist tries to commit the perfect crime. Let us now look at three of the most frequently used plot structures for those mystery and suspense stories that are *not* off-beat.

I. CHRONOLOGICAL MYSTERY AND SUSPENSE STORIES THAT BEGIN WITH THE THREAT OF A CRIME

BEGINNING

1. The scene is set.
2. The principal characters are introduced—the sympathetic protagonist and the person or persons who have been threatened. The point of view is established.

[1] These books may be purchased directly from the *Writer's Digest,* 22 East 12 Street, Cincinnati 10, Ohio, or ordered through your local bookseller.

3. The reader knows from the tone of the prose that he is reading a suspense story.
4. The circumstances that eventually lead to the complication are presented.
5. The reader is trapped into reading the rest of the story to discover if the protagonist can prevent the crime.

MIDDLE

1. The complication is presented: a crime has been threatened, and the protagonist must prevent it.
2. A series of attempts by the protagonist to prevent the crime are presented. He runs down false leads and clues, only to meet with failure.
3. A situation of ante-climax is presented in which it appears that the protagonist will finally solve his complication (the prevention of the crime), only to meet with such disastrous failure that the reader is convinced that there is no way for the protagonist to prevent the crime. The most frequently used technique is to have the prime suspect proved innocent.
4. Thus, the protagonist is forced to make the agonizing decision that he must start all over again, and it is this that will point to the solution. The most frequently used technique is for the protagonist to go back over the case—either in terms of his thought about it, or in conversation with a foil—in an attempt to discover where he got off the track. Thus, usually he discovers that a clue that seemed unimportant at the time—since all evidence pointed toward the prime suspect—now becomes very important and points toward the guilty person.

END

1. The solution is satisfactory and believable to the reader.

Let us now look at the two most commonly used plot structures of mystery stories that have an unsympathetic protagonist. The reader will recall that a story with an unsympathetic protagonist requires a change of structure in terms of the formula plot. That this structural shift does occur, however, does not make such mystery stories off-beat, for the unsympathetic protagonist must always be punished for his crime. Mystery stories with unsympathetic protagonists may, thus, undergo some changes within their internal structure, but if they end by returning to the triumph of law (which is generally acknowledged to be the most satisfactory ending for the reader), they are not classed as off-beat stories.

II. MYSTERY STORIES WITH AN UNSYMPATHETIC PROTAGONIST THAT BEGIN WITH THE THREAT OF A CRIME (We will make the crime murder.)

BEGINNING

1. The scene is set.
2. The principal character, the unsympathetic protagonist, is presented to the reader. His intended victim usually is presented in the protagonist's thoughts. The point of view is established: this is the unsympathetic protagonist's story.
3. The reader knows from the tone of the prose that he is reading a mystery story.
4. The complication is presented: the protagonist is going to commit a perfect crime.
5. The beginning is placed in time as close to the ending as possible, with the protagonist planning how he will commit the murder.
6. The beginning implies what ending is desired. The reader hopes the protagonist will fail to commit the perfect crime.
7. The reader is trapped into reading the rest of the story to find out what happens and what little slip the protagonist will make to cause his downfall.

MIDDLE

1. The circumstances that produced the complication are presented as the reader is transported into the past and learns why the protagonist wants to commit murder.
2. A series of attempts to commit the murder are presented only for him to meet with failure. (Note: Up to this point in the plot the steps are identical to those in the formula story. From this point on the plot of the formula story is violated.)
3. A situation of ante-climax is, therefore, presented in which it appears that the protagonist has succeeded, or will succeed, in committing the perfect crime. The reader is convinced that the protagonist will never be caught or punished.
4. The protagonist is forced to make the agonizing decision that he has overlooked one little detail or clue that will betray him. This detail he will either discover by himself, or his antagonist (the character representing law and order) will discover it.

322

1. The story ends with the reader convinced that the protagonist will be punished for his crime.

III. MYSTERY AND SUSPENSE STORIES WITH AN UNSYMPATHETIC PROTAGONIST WHICH BEGIN WITH A CRIME (Again let us make the crime murder.)

BEGINNING

1. The scene is set.
2. The principal character is introduced with his victim. The viewpoint is established: this is the unsympathetic protagonist's story.
3. The reader knows from the tone of the prose that he is reading a suspense story.
4. The complication is presented: the protagonist is going to commit a perfect crime.
5. The beginning is placed in time as close to the ending as possible: the murder is being, or has been, committed.
6. The beginning implies what ending is desired. The reader hopes the protagonist will pay for his crime.
7. The reader is trapped into reading the rest of the story to find out what little slip the protagonist makes that betrays him as the murderer.

MIDDLE

1. The background of circumstances that produce the complication are given. The reader is transported into the past in the memory of the protagonist and learns why he committed the murder.
2. A series of attempts by the protagonist to cover up his tracks are presented, so that the murder cannot be traced to him; he is successful in these attempts.
3. A situation of ante-climax is presented, therefore, in which it appears that the protagonist has succeeded in committing the perfect crime. The reader is convinced that the protagonist will never be caught or punished.
4. The protagonist is forced to make the agonizing decision that he has overlooked one little detail or clue that will betray him; either this is discovered by himself or by the character representing law and order.

END

1. The story ends with the reader convinced that the protagonist will be punished for his crime.

The plot structures described above may make it appear that plotting a mystery or suspense story is as easy as plotting a chronological or formula confession story. Nothing could be further from the truth. Of twenty-nine stories in three issues of current pulp mystery magazines, only seventeen of them employed one of these three plot structures—the rest were off-beat. The difficulty for the inexperienced writer in this field lies in his adapting his story to current knowledge.

The popularity of the off-beat mystery story, which violates the plot structure of the formula and chronological story, is due to the emergence of the study of psychology to such a point that even a layman has a working knowledge of it. This has enabled the mystery writer to explore the abnormality of the psychopathic and psychotic mind. In Chapter One we pointed out that a character never alters his nature in a story without a reason being fully suggested or given. If the character acts in a way beyond what we know of him, we feel cheated. But we were speaking of sane people. In a mystery story with a psychopathic or psychotic unsympathetic protagonist, no such restraint is placed upon the writer because he is dealing with an abnormal personality. The abnormal protagonist or villain may kill a perfect stranger for no other reason than the fact that the protagonist is abnormal. An entirely new field of crime detection opens up and consequently a new field of mystery fiction.

The mystery story is the most difficult form of commercial story to write. The mystery field is the most competitive market there is in commercial fiction, for the new writer must compete against well-known and established professionals. His chances of selling a confession story, for example, are a hundred times better than for his selling a mystery story.

Let us soften this for the would-be writer of mystery stories by pointing out that even so, if he has a good original story, he can find a market for it. "Isn't It a Perfect Crime?" by James Gilmore was published in *Alfred Hitchcock's Mystery Magazine*. In the same issue were stories written by well-known established writers; Mr. Gilmore is not a member of this group.

We wanted to include in the Appendix one pulp story written by a writer still learning his craft. We felt we could use such a story as a model to show how to locate and correct weaknesses in the plot structure of pulp or slick formula and chronological stories. This in no way detracts from Mr. Gilmore's story. He wrote a mystery story that was accepted and published. This is quite a feat for a writer still learning his craft. The agent who selected the story for us wrote: "Although this story is lacking in craftsmanship . . . in the final analysis, a mystery story shows the author pitting his wits against the reader. I'm certain you'll agree with me that Mr. Gilmore convinced the reader there was no possible way for Ira Hovel to solve his complication until the author sprang the totally unexpected and yet satisfactory ending upon the reader."

We do not know James Gilmore. We assume that he is a serious young writer, that he holds down a full-time job, that he writes in his spare time and is learning his craft through trial and error, and that he has several published short stories to his credit. We do know that Mr. Gilmore has the ability to become a successful short-story writer from the originality he displays in "Isn't It a Perfect Crime?"

COMMENTARY ON "ISN'T IT A PERFECT CRIME?"

Let us now take a critical look at the story and see if we can discover weaknesses in its structure that we can correct, in order to turn it into a story that could be sold to a slick magazine.

BASIC PLOT

The basic plot used in this story is conflict to overcome an opponent in order to solve the protagonist's complication and reach a worthwhile goal. The opponent Ira must overcome is his mother-in-law in order to solve his complication and reach what to him is the worthwhile goal of living out his remaining years in peace.

THEME

This story does not have the usual theme that crime does not pay. Rather the time-tested truth the author wanted to prove was that an inherently decent and sane person cannot bring himself to commit murder, no matter what the provocation.

COMPLICATION

The complication is certainly something unpleasant that happens to Ira. Had he freedom of choice, he certainly would not choose for his mother-in-law to live with him.

The story has the pulp appeal of basic narrative excitement. The reader shares Ira's emotions as Ira attempts to solve his complication. The author employs the technique of selecting a minor complication and exaggerating it sufficiently to make it seem more interesting than it would be in real life and serious enough to become a salable short story.

Yet, as we noted, the story exhibits certain weaknesses in structure. These weaknesses will become apparent if we unravel the story by outlining the complication. Let us, then, look at each step in the outline to see whether or not we can improve upon the exaggerations that the author has made. Having done this, let us next see whether or not the author has used all the steps in the formula plot, and if he has not, we can then insert the revisions we have made so as to improve the story.

Ira Hovel's life is complicated when his recently widowed mother-in-law comes to live with him and his wife, Emily.

1. Ira thinks Bertha is only going to live with them during the short period of her grief, but she stays on and on.
2. The complication becomes more serious because Ira, who has always wanted a dog, cannot have one; Bertha does not like dogs.
   Comment: The weakness is apparent. This is much too familiar; the author does not use enough of an exaggeration.
2 revised: After a short period of mourning, Bertha, a forceful and domineering woman, begins to assert herself. Let us make her a vegetarian who takes over the supervision of the meals. She insists that Ira and Emily both become vegetarians. This makes the complication more serious since Ira, in the absence of other joys, has always managed to find one of his greatest pleasures in eating steak.
3. Ira's complication becomes deeper because he has always wanted to travel and see the world with Emily. Now he cannot do that because Bertha is too old to travel.
   Comment: Here again, there is a weakness. The exaggeration should be more pronounced to give us a sense of sympathy for Ira.
3 revised: Bertha has no trouble in completely dominating Emily. As a result, Bertha takes charge of Ira's paycheck. She keeps the budget, doles out to Ira his weekly carfare, forces him to have watercress sandwiches for lunch, selects his clothes for him. Perhaps we could use a scene in which she accompanies him to the store to buy him a suit of clothes, thus humiliating him in front of the salesman.
4. The complication is made more serious when Bertha takes over as head of the household, bossing Ira around, completely dominating Emily, and making Ira's life a "living hell."
   Comment: The weakness here is in employing narrative instead of ac-

tion to convey this information to the reader. As a result the reader does not feel what Ira is undergoing because he cannot experience it vicariously; he is simply told. This weakens Ira's motivation for wanting to kill Bertha.

4 revised: Show in action a typical day in the life of Ira so that the reader will experience and feel what Ira is undergoing. Begin the day with Ira's coming to breakfast only to be told by Bertha that the necktie he is wearing does not go with his suit. He is forced to go and change it. Show him sitting down to a breakfast of vegetable juice and Melba toast, mentally yearning for the big breakfasts of ham and eggs, hot cakes, etc., he used to eat before Bertha arrived. Show Bertha giving him his weekly carfare and his lunch of watercress sandwiches. Show him coming home from work, hating to enter his own home, and finally entering it, only to find that Bertha has bought new furniture and thrown out his favorite old chair. End the day with Bertha's selecting the TV programs they will watch instead of letting him select the fights or wrestling matches he prefers. (By now we have made the reader feel real sympathy for Ira. He hates Bertha, and thinks about murder just as Ira does when he goes to bed that night.)

5. The author uses the technique of discovery and change to make the complication deeper. When Bertha discovers her sister wants her to go to California and live with her she almost decides to do so, but changes her mind when Emily pleads with her to stay.

Comment: This step in the outline of the complication belongs in step 3 of the middle of the chronological or formula story. The weakness in structure here is that in this important step in the middle the protagonist must make one final attempt to solve his complication. Ira had no part in the sister's writing to Bertha.

5 revised: In a desperate attempt to solve his complication, Ira secretly writes to Bertha's sister telling her how lonesome Bertha is for her and suggesting she ask Bertha to come and spend her remaining years with her. Upon receiving the letter from her sister, Bertha decides to join her sister immediately, only to change her mind when Emily cries and pleads with her to stay, leaving the reader convinced that the complication is beyond solution.

Comment: At this point in the story, nothing of importance is yet at stake if the complication is not solved. Ira, who has lived with Bertha for twenty-two years, faces the prospect of going on living with her until she dies. The author uses the technique of discovery and change to make certain something of importance is at stake.

6. When Ira discovers that Bertha isn't going to join her sister in California, he changes his mind about putting up with her for the rest of her life and decides to murder her. The important things at stake, if the complication is not solved some other way, are a human life and

the fact that Ira, for whom the reader is by now sympathetic, will be a murderer.

7. The agonizing decision Ira makes to murder Bertha must point to the solution, which it does (paragraph 35, moment of truth). As a result of Ira's attempt at murder, Bertha is so frightened that she leaves at once for California.

We have now taken care of the weaknesses in constructing the complication. Let us now examine the story for weaknesses in plot structure and correct them as we go along. The story is built upon the plot structure of the formula story, but the author has failed to utilize fully all the steps in the plot structure.

BEGINNING (Paragraphs 1 through 19)

1. The beginning is placed in time as close to the ending as possible: Ira mentally checks over his plans to murder Bertha and commit the perfect crime.
2. The complication is presented: Bertha has made Ira's life such a "living hell" he has decided to solve his complication by murder.
3. The scene is set on a train pulling out of the Minneapolis Depot.
4. The principal characters are introduced with an indication of their approximate ages, Ira on the scene, Bertha and Emily in his thoughts. The point of view is established: this is Ira's story.
5. The reader knows from the tone of the prose that he is reading a suspense story.
6. The beginning implies what ending is desired: the reader hopes that Ira will fail to commit the murder.
7. The reader is trapped into reading the story by the use of a narrative hook: will Ira commit the murder as planned? If so, what little mistake will he make that will betray him? If he does not succeed in committing the murder, why not? The reader reads on to find the answer.

The author has used all seven steps in the beginning of the plot structure of the formula story. But let us now take a look at the rest of the plot structure and find the places where the author failed to utilize each step.

MIDDLE (Paragraphs 20 through 95)

1. The author has presented the background of circumstances that produced the complication. (Paragraphs 20 and 21)
   Comment: As we can see in the outline of the complication, the author has failed to build up sufficient sympathy in the background of circumstances that formed Ira's decision to murder Bertha.

328

1 revised: To correct this weakness, delete paragraphs 20 and 21, and use 1, 2 revised, 3 revised, and 4 revised of the complication outline.

2. This step in the middle of the formula story presents a series of attempts by the protagonist to solve his complication, only to meet with failure. This step is so muted in paragraphs 22 and 23 as to be practically nonexistent.

   Comment: Ira wants a dog but cannot have one because Bertha does not like dogs. Ira wants to travel, but cannot because Bertha is too old to travel. To correct the weakness in this step of the middle, it will be necessary to create some real attempts by Ira to solve his complication, only to have him meet with failure. For Ira to suddenly decide to murder Bertha, particularly after so great a time and without his having tried to solve his complication in other ways, will lose sympathy for him and weaken his motivation for trying to kill her.

   2 revised: Ira attempts to solve his complication by trying to get Bertha to join a Senior Citizens Club, hoping it will take up some of her evenings so he can get a little peace, only to meet with failure when she refuses. Ira tries to get Bertha interested in adult education and is overjoyed when she joins a class in basket-weaving that will take her out of the house at least one night a week, so he can watch the fights on TV, only to meet with failure when Bertha—after attending just a single class—stops going because the teacher dared to criticize her efforts. We could make Bertha younger, around sixty, and have Ira bring home an eligible widower from work who is a vegetarian, hoping this mutual interest might lead to romance, only to meet with failure.

3. This step in the formula story presents a situation of ante-climax in which it appears the protagonist will finally solve his complication only to meet with such disastrous failure that the reader is convinced that there is no hope of a satisfactory solution.

   Comment: The author does present such a situation when Bertha receives the letter from her sister. The weakness in this step is that Ira had nothing to do with it. In the formula or chronological story it must be the protagonist who makes the one final effort to solve his complication in step 3 of the middle.

   3 revised: To correct this weakness we would use 5 revised of the outlined complication.

4. In this step in the middle of the formula story the protagonist is forced to make an agonizing decision that will point to the solution.

   Comment: The author does have Ira make the agonizing decision in this step of the middle when he decides to murder Bertha; but in its published form, he failed to build up enough sympathy for Ira and to provide enough motivation. By correcting the weaknesses in the complication outline and the plot structure we have prepared the

329

reader to believe, along with Ira, that murder is the only way left for Ira to solve his complication. Once Ira has made this decision, the reader must be transported out of the past, where he has vicariously lived during the four steps in the middle in the memory of the protagonist. A transition must be made to paragraph 33.

4 revised: When Bertha decides to remain, Ira is forced to make the agonizing decision that the only way he can get rid of Bertha is to murder her. After he has made this decision, a transition is employed to take the reader out of the past and back into the present in paragraph 33. This step would also include parargaph 34 through 39 (paragraph 35 gives the moment of truth).

Comment: Paragraphs 40 through 90 should be deleted and the suggested revision used instead. These paragraphs, which the author used to build up suspense, are not needed in a slick story. A transition from paragraph 39 to paragraph 91 would prepare the reader for the unexpected ending. We see Ira aboard the plane and commiserate with him as he thinks that going to jail would be a pleasure compared to living with Bertha the rest of her life, and as he wryly meditates that the only way now to solve his complication would be for the plane to crash.

END (Paragraphs 96 through 112)

1. The single step in the end of the formula story must provide a solution that is believable and satisfactory to the reader. That Bertha would be so terrified and leave for California at once is believable to the reader. The solution is certainly satisfactory to the reader, who cannot help sharing Ira's joy upon learning that Bertha has gone.

We have confined ourselves solely to locating and correcting weaknesses in the structure of the story, although there is no question that there are places where the writing must also be improved to turn this into a slick story. For example, paragraphs 25 through 31 are written in the present tense although the action takes place in the past in the memory of the protagonist, and the repetitious use of the name "Ira" instead of varying it by the pronoun "he" is very jarring.

But for all its faults, the author has written an entertaining story that merited publication and we predict that he will have a successful writing career.

No Margin for Error

by W. L. HEATH

1   I discovered my mistake at a quarter to five on Friday afternoon—in other words, just fifteen minutes before the office closed for the week end. I can pinpoint the time for you because it was one of those "unforgettable moments" they talk about—the moment when an ambitious junior executive stares at a column of figures and realizes he has made an error that is going to cost his company thousands of dollars, and very likely cost him his job.

2   My first reaction was a sort of numb dismay mixed with disbelief. That was followed by some frantic slide-rule work which only served to confirm the worst. I had made a gross error in computing the production cost of a new nylon rug the Fairchild Chenille Company was preparing to manufacture in considerable volume. A mistake discovered soon enough usually can be rectified; but this was an old mistake, weeks old.

3   When I finally looked up from my desk and wiped the sweat from my face it was well past quitting time and one of the office girls was waiting, pocketbook in hand, to ask if I'd turn off the air conditioner when I left. I guess I answered, but don't remember. I do remember that I saw Stanley Gibbs waiting for me out there in the hall, and the sight of him seemed to compound my anguish. Stanley was the man I had passed on my way up to the $12,000-a-year position I was now holding with Fairchild Chenille. You know Stanley yourself, because he is not so much a man as a prototype. At forty-eight, lodged permanently at $5,000.00 a year, he is a bald, mousy little man with a big brood of children, all of whom are girls. He lives in a modest suburban home where he supports his wife's widowed

mother, drinks an occasional Saturday night beer, and helps with the dishes. Stanley is not a winner, and yet he is an almost indispensable adjunct to every office. He takes up the money for the football pool and works steadfastly for forty years at whatever job you give him.

4   These are unkind remarks. I find it hard to explain why I have always felt the way I do toward the Stanley Gibbses of this world, unless it's because, deep down somewhere, I see in him a disturbing facet of myself—a subconscious urge to give in to security and domesticity. We all have an enemy within us, and I guess Stanley Gibbs is mine.

5   I sat there looking through the glass at Stanley and thought to myself, Brother, what you wouldn't give to know what I know now. The wonder boy has finally stubbed his toe.

6   I gathered up my things, turned off the lights and the air conditioner, and went out to where Stanley was waiting.

7   "Well," he said, "The Phillies got beat again today."

8   It was like Stanley to pick a cellar team for his favorite baseball club. He would go through life backing the wrong horse, the lost cause.

9   We rode home. That's about all I can say with any certainty. Stanley talked all the way in his weak, reedy voice, but I still wasn't listening; I was still numb, still staggered by that incredible mistake.

10   When I dropped Stanley off at his house in Alton Park, he asked me if I'd come in for a cup of coffee. He always asked me that, and I always turned him down. It was one of those things. Even on a good day the prospect of all those kids in that tiny living room was just too formidable.

11   I told him no thanks, and he muttered something about a raincheck—that was standard, too—and I turned the corner and headed for home.

12   By this time I had stopped cursing myself and was mentally rehearsing the little speeches I would have to make. One to my wife, Peggy, who was hopefully laying plans for a new home in East Ridge; and one to my boss, Ben Haralson, when I went in Monday morning to break the news. This latter speech was going to be the tough one. I tried to visualize a scene in which Ben got up from behind his desk, praised my honesty and forth-

rightness, and assured me that the job was still mine. But somehow it wasn't convincing. This was a real boo-boo, the kind that went all the way down the hall to Mr. Fairchild himself, and I doubted very much that Ben could save me.

13   Just about this time, too, some of the ramifications began to reach me. The particular rug on which I had made my mistake was one that Mr. Fairchild had opposed putting into our line because it involved the purchase of some new equipment. It was what we call a sculptured rug in this trade—a rug with the design carved into the tufted pile with a special machine. Ben had pressed the decision on Mr. Fairchild with my assistance, using the cost figures I had computed. In other words I had my boss in a real jam, too.

14   When I reached the apartment I found Peggy, dressed in shorts and a halter, sitting in the middle of the living-room floor with blueprints of her dream house spread out all around her. It was like a movie scene which is deliberately staged for the effect of irony.

15   "Jack," she said, even before I had time to say hello, "do you really think we'll need a second bathroom?"

16   I said I thought we could decide later.

17   "It would save money to leave it out," she said. "On the other hand, in a year or two we'll be having children, and we'll probably need it then."

18   I looked at her, blonde and blue-eyed, and I thought, "In a year or two we may be lucky even to have this apartment." Now was the time to tell her, but somehow I couldn't get my nerve up.

19   I went to the kitchen, made us each a strong highball and came back.

20   "I guess the thing to do would be just to rough it in for the time being," she said. "Then we could have the fixtures installed later, when we can afford it."

21   "Peg," I said, "I don't know if we're going to be able to build that house."

22   There was a long moment of total silence. She looked shocked. "But you said when your last raise. . . ."

23   "I know, honey, I gave you the go-ahead, but something has happened. I discovered something today that . . . well, changes the picture. Can you take some bad news?"

24   She was looking at me intently now, and I found it mighty hard to look back.

25   "I made a mistake, Peg. A big mistake, at the office. I may lose my job."

26   Her face drained and she just sat there for a minute staring at me. "What sort of a mistake, Jack?"

27   "I miscalculated on a new rug we're putting in. Figured the cost a lot lower than it actually will be."

28   "What can you do?"

29   "Nothing. It's too late. I'll just have to go in and tell them and take the lumps, that's all."

30   There was another long moment of silence.

31   She got up and kissed me.

32   "Just don't let it worry you," she said. "One bad break never ruined anybody."

33   "About the house. . . ."

34   "The house will be delayed a little, that's all. The house is not important. Your confidence and self-respect are what matter."

35   She gathered up all her blueprints then, rolled them up, and stored them away in the bookcase. I sat there watching her, and I think that's what did it. I think that's when the idea first occurred to me that maybe I could cover up my mistake and get away with it. I just couldn't stand to see her putting those blueprints away.

36   Naturally Peg wanted to know all about the thing, so I made us a second drink and sat down to explain it to her in detail.

37   "What happened was this," I said. "In figuring the total production cost of these rugs, I underestimated the yarn content. I figured each rug would have one pound of fours-two nylon yarn in it. But actually it comes nearer a pound and a half. Fours-two nylon costs us a dollar and twenty cents a pound; so you see, that extra half-pound is going to add sixty cents to the cost of each rug. Figuring a ten percent mark-up, I priced the rugs at two-thirty, giving us a profit of roughly twenty-five cents each. But when you add sixty cents to the cost, instead of making twenty-five, we'll be losing thirty-five cents on every one we sell."

38   She was listening worriedly. "But how did you arrive at the wrong figure in the first place?"

39   "That's what I've been asking myself," I said.

40   "Isn't it possible that someone else made a mistake and fouled up your figures?"

41   I admit the idea appealed to me, but I had to shake my head. "I do all the figuring myself," I said. "That's my job. There's a sheet called the Sample Sheet which gives the weight of the duck back before and after the yarn is sewn into it. It's signed and dated and pinned right on the cost sheet where I did my figuring. I either read it wrong or made a mistake in setting up my slide rule."

42   "Well, how did you happen to discover your mistake today?"

43   "Just an accident. Ben gave me a list of prices to check, and when I brought this one out of the file, there it was as plain as the nose on my face."

44   She blew out a long, discouraged sigh. "You estimate the company would lose thirty-five cents on each rug. How much money would that run to?"

45   I shrugged. "If the rug doesn't sell too well—say we make only twenty-five thousand of them this year—a little under nine thousand dollars."

46   "That's not so terribly much, is it?"

47   "Frankly, I doubt if it would ever be noticed. On the other hand, if it turned out to be a pretty good seller and we made two hundred thousand of them, you've got a loss of something like seventy thousand dollars. That's a direct loss. It would be well over a hundred thousand if you consider the reduction in expected net profit as a loss too."

48   "And that would be noticed."

49   "Undoubtedly. They'd hunt for it in the records."

50   "Oh, Jack, I think it's the worst luck anyone ever had."

51   I thought so too, but that other idea was now nibbling away at the corner of my mind. Maybe before I rushed in and started making heroic confessions it would pay me to look into the thing a little further and try to determine just what the risk was.

52   Well, it was a miserable week end for both of us. We went to a show Saturday night and I couldn't tell you to save myself what it was or who was in it. On Sunday I broke a golf date to spend the afternoon pacing the living room floor. I wasn't just worried now; I was scared—scared by what I was thinking. The temptation, every time it hit me, made my pulse thud in

335

my ears. Could I swing it? The more I thought of it, the more possible it seemed. And here's how my reasoning went:

53   The rug I'd made my mistake on had been put into our line of products specifically to replace an old style, one we'd been manufacturing for years. That gave me a basis for comparison. By looking up the sales record of the old one I'd be able to get a fair idea what volume we could expect in the new one. Now, if the sales on that old style were pretty low—and I thought they were—then that would reduce the magnitude of my mistake automatically. Then wouldn't it be possible for me to cover the mistake further by padding my other figures a little? I had two more rugs to set prices on within the next week. Why not add a little to those to make up some of the slack in the nylon?

54   Riding along with all this was the fact of my loyalty to Ben Haralson. I owed Ben a lot. Wouldn't this be a way of paying him back? Shouldn't I cover up for his sake?

55   This was rationalizing pure and simple and I can see it now, but then I couldn't. Only one thing was really left hanging in my mind by this time, and that was this: would anyone else be likely to catch my mistake? Ben Haralson could do it any time he decided to go into my file. But even on this I had the guilty assurance of Ben's confidence in me. Ben trusted me so completely that he never checked my work at all—hadn't done so in over a year.

56   So the door was open to a way out, and I was looking through that door already. Monday morning after a glance at the sales figures, I would make up my mind whether to step through that door or slam it shut on my career.

57   "Well, the Phillies finally won one," Stanley Gibbs said when I picked him up the next morning.

58   "Did they, Stanley?"

59   "Sure did. Took a double-header from St. Louis, six-two and five-three."

60   "Wonder how the Yankees came out."

61   "They got beat," Stanley said. "The Yankees have really hit the skids this year. I don't understand it. Say, Jack, would you mind stopping by the drugstore? One of my kids caught a cold over the week end and I have to pick up some medicine."

62   Five thousand a year, kids with colds, mothers-in-law to sup-

port—Lord, save me, I thought, from ever becoming a Stanley Gibbs. I had another momentary glimpse of Peggy putting those blueprints away and I gripped the steering wheel a little tighter.

63   When we got to the office, the first thing I did was dig out last year's sales records. And when I looked at them I could have shouted for joy. The old-style rug for which we were substituting the new nylon one had never been accepted by a major account, and showed a piddling sale for the previous year of only 8,000 pieces. Practically dead stock. They expected the new one to sell better, of course, because it was a more attractive pattern; but even if it tripled the sale of its predecessor, I wasn't so bad off. I had been premature in my forecast of the disaster. I sat back and relaxed for the first time in about sixty hours. There was no point in telling anybody about my mistake. After all, a confession couldn't really change anything; it would only make me look like a fool.

64   Just then the squawk-box on my desk came to life and I heard Stanley Gibbs' voice saying, "Jack, Mr. Haralson wants you in his office."

65   "Right, Stanley."

66   "He wants you to bring your cost sheet on that new nylon sculptured rug."

67   If you've ever topped a blind hill and met a truck coming on the wrong side of the road you have a pretty good idea of how I felt when I heard that last sentence. It only lasted a minute, though. Okay, so I was caught. The man surely wouldn't fire me when I showed him the comparison figures.

68   Pulling the cost sheet out of the file, I took a deep breath, and went into his office. To my surprise, he smiled as friendly as ever. Ben is a big man, a former college athlete, and I guess about the best way to describe him is to say he looks like a newspaper editor—the sort you see in the movies, particularly.

69   "How was the golf this week end?" he asked.

70   "Fine," I said, forgetting in my confusion that I hadn't played golf that week end.

71   "I'm not hitting the ball lately," he said. "You got that cost sheet on the new nylon?"

72   "Yes."

73   "We quoted them two dollars and thirty cents, didn't we?"

74 "That's right."

75 "You sure of your figures?"

76 "Here it is, Ben." I held the sheet out to him.

77 "Hell, I don't want to see it. I just wanted to make sure I hadn't made a mistake in quoting it to New York. Mr. Fairchild thought it looked a little low, but the old guy is out of touch nowadays; you can't pay much attention to him."

78 There was a pause and I had a chance right then to say it.

79 But I didn't.

80 Ben launched into a dozen other things he wanted to talk about, and the next thing I knew I was back at my desk and the die was cast. Well, it was all right. Even if we sold 25,000 of them it was still all right; nobody would ever know the difference. I did stop to reflect, though, how sometimes a man can tell a lie, just by keeping his mouth shut.

81 When I got home that afternoon Peggy was waiting for me at the door. She took one look at my face and said, "Jack, you didn't tell them."

82 "No, I didn't, Peg."

83 "Why?"

84 "Well, I did some more figuring and some more thinking, and it doesn't look as serious as I thought."

85 "That should have made it easier to tell them."

86 She was right, of course, but I had committed myself to deception now, and I had to try to justify it. I went into all that business about protecting Ben and tried very hard to minimize the whole thing by quoting her the comparison figures. "I doubt if we sell ten thousand of those rugs in a year," I said rashly. "A loss as small as that will be swallowed a dozen times over in the year's net profits."

87 But Peg was not convinced. "Jack," she said, "I think you've made another mistake—this one bigger than the first."

88 For three days everything was fine. I carefully padded the costs on the next two rugs I figured and sat back to see how the nylon was running. We'd had only four orders for it so far, and the largest of those was a hundred and fifty rugs. We weren't getting hurt; it was selling very slowly. But then on Thursday afternoon Ben came out and laid a letter on my desk. He was smiling broadly.

89 "Here's something we'll be glad to show Mr. Fairchild," he

said. "Remember how he opposed putting in the nylon sculptured rug?"

90   I read the letter and went sick inside. J. C. Penney, our biggest account, had decided to take it. J. C. Penney with over 1,700 stores. They anticipated a volume of a hundred to a hundred and fifty thousand.

91   So there it was. The worst had happened.

92   On the way home that afternoon I was so sunk in my own imbroglio it didn't dawn on me until I stopped the car in Alton Park that Stanley Gibbs had not said a single word all the way —not even about the Phillies.

93   "Stanley, you feeling bad, too?" I asked listlessly.

94   "Just worried, Jack," Stanley answered.

95   "Worried about what?"

96   "That kid of mine."

97   "The one with the cold?"

98   "Yeah. She developed pneumonia yesterday. We've got her in the hospital under an oxygen tent."

99   "I'm sorry, Stanley," I said. "That's really tough. I hope she does all right."

100   I was sorry too—in a very remote corner of my preoccupied mind. Stanley had his troubles; I had mine.

101   Now here's something I haven't mentioned before, but if I'm going to tell the whole story I may as well say it. Since Monday afternoon when Peggy found out that I hadn't revealed my mistake, there had been a slight but perceptible change in the structure of our marriage. It was as if there had been a shift in our footings—a crack somewhere in the foundation. I fought against admitting it to myself, and I think she did, too; but it was there all right. Some vital support had slipped a little. I was irritable; she was exasperatingly patient. We began to be formal, like strangers. Every afternoon when I got home she would look at me—just one quick, searching look—and with that look, she asked a question, "Have you told them yet?" And I guess the expression on my face answered it for her. We never actually said a word about it. In fact, it was getting so we talked very little about anything.

102   "Stanley Gibbs' little girl is in the hospital," I told her that night at the supper table.

103   "That's too bad."

104 "Yes. If you think of it, I wish you'd send some flowers."

105 "All right."

106 And so it went.

107 The next morning Stanley was not waiting for me in front of his house. Instead, his mother-in-law came out, wearing a horrible-looking housecoat, her hair up in curlers.

108 "Stanley's at the hospital," she said. "He said to tell you he'd get a bus on to the office from there."

109 "Is the little girl worse?"

110 "She had a bad night."

111 "Well, I'm sorry to hear it."

112 "He said to tell you he'd be on to work, though, even if he's a little late."

113 Sure, I thought. The poor devil can't afford to miss a day. He's got hospital bills to pay now.

114 When I reached the office there were two notes on my desk. One said that Ben Haralson wanted me in his office; the other told me to phone Stanley Gibbs at a certain number. I took them in order of importance and went in to see Ben first.

115 "Jack," he said, "this nylon rug is looking better every minute. We got word this morning that Montgomery Ward is interested, too."

116 I groaned inwardly and tried to control my voice. "Ben, we can't sell that rug to Ward."

117 "I know we can't," he said. "Not the same rug—Penny's wouldn't like it. But I've sent word to the designing department to work up another pattern on the same back. Something we could let them have at the same price, you see?"

118 I don't know why, but I couldn't say anything. I do know why, too. I was like a man drowning—drowning in wave after wave of incredible circumstance. J. C. Penney and now Montgomery Ward—the sales might run to half a million, financial disaster for the whole company. I was watching a nightmare come to reality.

119 "What's the matter?" he said sharply.

120 "Ben. . . ."

121 I was rescued at that moment by one of the office girls, who stuck her head in and said that Stanley Gibbs wanted to speak to me on the telephone. "It's urgent," she said.

122 "Urgent?"

123   I went back to my desk like a sleepwalker and picked up the phone.

124   "Jack," he said, "I've got to talk to you."

125   "What is it, Stanley, your little girl. . . . ?"

126   "No, this is business, Jack. Can you meet me at the corner drugstore in five minutes?"

127   "Golly, I don't know, Stanley, I'm up to my ears. . . ."

128   "This is urgent, Jack. It's about that nylon rug we just put into the line. There's something I've got to tell you about it before it goes any further. I made a mistake."

129   My brain felt waterlogged. I couldn't absorb it. "What on earth are you talking about?"

130   "Meet me, Jack. Five minutes."

131   I met him all right. That "I made a mistake" was what turned the trick. When I got to the drugstore he was sitting in a booth, way back, with an untouched cup of coffee in front of him, looking as though he hadn't slept for a week.

132   "Jack," he said, "this is the hardest thing I ever tried to do in my life, but I gotta tell you. I know it means my job, but I just can't stand it any longer. You remember the Sample Sheet you figured the nylon rug from?"

133   "Yes."

134   "It was wrong. I made a mistake putting the weights down. There's half a pound more yarn in that rug than you figured."

135   I just sat there looking at him.

136   "But that's not the worst of it, Jack. After you figured your cost, I went back in the file and changed it."

137   "You mean the one that's pinned to the cost sheet. . . . ?"

138   "It's counterfeit. I forged the date and signature and tore up the original."

139   "Why, Stanley?"

140   His pale little face was twisted with agony. "I don't know," he said. "It was too late when I discovered the mistake and it didn't look like it would amount to much, so I tried to cover it up."

141   I sat there and I studied him. I wanted to see what it did to a man to cut loose the last rope. At his age and with that on his record he wouldn't find another job in a million years. He was giving up everything he had, because of a guilty conscience.

142   "What made you decide to tell me, Stanley? That could have

gone down as my error and no one would ever have known the difference, not even I."

143 He shook his head. "I just couldn't go through with it, Jack, not after I saw the flowers."

144 "The flowers?"

145 His eyes filled suddenly with tears. "The flowers you sent my little girl at the hospital. I've always looked up to you, thought you were a helluva nice guy, and I don't know, somehow that just did it. I couldn't stand by and see you thrown to the wolves for something I did."

146 "Stanley," I said, "how is your little girl?"

147 He looked mildly startled. "She's better, thanks."

148 When I got back to the office I sat down at my desk, smoked two cigarettes in a row, then got up, went into Ben's office, and shut the door.

149 "Ben," I said, "I've made a very serious mistake on the nylon carved rug. I figured wrong on the yarn. We're going to lose a lot of money."

150 He took the cigar out of his mouth and looked at me with amazement. *"You* made a mistake, Jack?"

151 "A real bad one, Ben. So bad I'm afraid I've got you in trouble too. What's more, I've known about it since last Friday. I've been trying to cover it up."

152 He leaned back and looked up at the clock. "Well," he said, "you just barely made it."

153 "Made what?"

154 "You had exactly four minutes to get in here with that, and you made it."

155 "Then you knew already?"

156 He nodded. "Stanley phoned me as soon as you left him. Why did you try to protect him, Jack?"

157 "I'm as guilty as he is, Ben. I was covering when I thought it was my mistake. Morally, I'm just as guilty as he is."

158 "Yeah, I guess you're right."

159 "And I thought maybe I could save him his job, Ben. He needs it worse than I do. For that matter, he's a better man than I am. He did what I couldn't do. If one of us goes, it ought to be me."

160 "It ought to be both of you," he said. "The trouble is, I can't very well get along without either of you."

342

161   I started to protest, but he went on ahead of me.

162   "Okay, so you made a mistake and it's going to cost us. But we can still pull most of it out of the fire."

163   "Ben, I'm not here to beg for my job. I did a lousy thing and I'm ashamed of it. I really think I'd feel better if you did fire me."

164   "Stop telling me my job," he said. "No, I'm going to keep you. You helped me make this mess, you can help clean it up."

165   "What I'm worried about now is you," I said. "You've got to take this to Mr. Fairchild."

166   "That's right."

167   "What will you say?"

168   "Just shell the corn, that's all. Just tell him I made a mistake."

169   "*You* made a mistake?"

170   "Sure. I'm the guy who's supposed to check your work. Remember?"

171   I swallowed hard. "He'll raise hell."

172   "You're darn right he will. That's his job and he has an uncommon talent for it."

173   "You think he'll . . . I mean is there really a chance . . . ?"

174   "He'll fire me? I'd say about a fifty-fifty chance. He's fired me four times in the twenty years I've worked for him."

175   He looked at me and then gave me a wink that restored my world to order.

176   "Take my advice," he said. "You've made a good-sized mistake, but don't let it worry you too much. Let it worry you some, but not too much. Anybody can make a mistake. I've made a few myself." He grinned suddenly. "As a matter of fact, so has Mr. Fairchild. You ought to ask him sometime about the year we tried to break into the bedspread business. No, on second thought, don't ask him. He's still trying to cover that one up."

177   He gathered up the papers on his desk then and started the long walk down the hall to Mr. Fairchild's office. Suddenly I wanted to go in there with him—really wanted to. And you can believe me, that's as strong a feeling as one man can have for another man.

178   Just before quitting time that afternoon I phoned Stanley

Gibbs' house. "Stanley," I said, "How's if I stop by this afternoon for that cup of coffee you're always offering me?"

179   "You mean it, Jack?"

180   "Of course I do. Matter of fact, I'd like to bring my wife along so she can meet your wife and kids and mother-in-law. She's a nice girl and I think you'll like her."

COMMENTARY ON "NO MARGIN FOR ERROR"

The career story has always been popular with editors and readers of slick magazines. This story was written by a very well-known professional author and shows in its concern for structural details the writer's desire to build a good story.

BASIC PLOT

The commercial plot used is conflict to overcome an obstacle so that the protagonist may solve his complication and reach a worthwhile goal. The obstacle Jack must overcome is his own selfishness. If he does this, he may solve his complication satisfactorily and therefore preserve his integrity and self-respect as a decent person.

THEME

It would be fairly easy to state a moral to the story. Perhaps one could use some such proverb as "What a tangled web we weave when first we practice to deceive." But we do not think that the author was attempting to establish a moral. What seems to have attracted his interest was the world of organized business and the dilemmas—whether moral or not—that face people in that world. Certainly, the author demonstrates that an inherently decent person cannot bring himself to let another person—however hateful to himself—take the blame for some error he has made. And the author has very clearly shown that the mistake, which the protagonist is responsible for, is a moral mistake that has its repercussions in a completely practical world: the protagonist endangers his own job; he endangers the job of his boss; he stands to lose the respect and love of his wife; and finally, he tends to lose his own sense of integrity. The moral and the practical considerations of any act, one seems to realize in the story, are not easily to be disentangled. And perhaps this is as good a way to put the theme of the story as any other.

The story presents a complication in the life of the protagonist that is more interesting than it would seem in real life, and yet at the same time it is believable to the reader. The complication is something unpleasant that happens to Jack. Had he freedom of choice, he certainly would not choose for it to occur. Thus, the principle of conflict in the story resides in his attempts to solve the complication. It would be instructive for the reader to follow Jack's emotional reactions throughout the story, for then he would discover that Jack feels dismay, anguish, fear, disappointment, joy, apprehension, despair, hopelessness, surprise, compassion, and eventually contentment. This development of emotions serves as an analogy, as we have previously pointed out, to the attack made upon the protagonist's basic character by the complication, his movement away from his general traits, and his eventual return to them.

The complication is made more interesting than it would seem in real life through exaggeration. In actuality, a person in Jack's position would simply have told Ben Haralson and Mr. Fairchild of the error and asked them to take the rug out of the production schedule and off sale.

1. The consequences facing Jack if he does confess his mistake are presented: he'll lose his job, his wife Peggy won't get the house they've been planning to build, and his superior, Ben Haralson, will be in a jam.
2. Discovery and change are used to make the complication more serious. When Peggy discovers Jack hasn't confessed, a rift comes between them.
3. Again discovery and change are used to make the complication so deep that it appears to be beyond solution. When Jack discovers that first J. C. Penney and then Montgomery Ward are interested in the rug and will place orders that could bankrupt the company, he changes his mind in thinking he can get away with covering up the error.
4. The complication is so serious that something of importance is at stake when Jack discovers Stanley Gibbs is primarily responsible for the error. The important thing at stake, if the complication isn't satisfactorily solved, is Jack's integrity and self-respect as a decent person. If he lets Stanley Gibbs take all the blame for the error, he will not be able to endure himself.

Note: At this point in the story, there just does not appear to be any way to resolve the complication to the satisfaction of the reader. Again the technique of discovery and change is used to find a satisfactory ending.

345

5. Jack's moment of truth is not stated but is implied in paragraph 148, when he discovers that he is not the sort of person who can stand by and let Stanley Gibbs take all the blame—which makes him change his mind about concealing his part in the error.
6. Jack's agonizing decision to confess and to save Stanley Gibbs from losing his job points to the solution.

The complication and solution are made believable because they are based on the dominant character traits of Stanley Gibbs and Jack. The characterization in paragraphs 3 through 8 makes it believable that a man in Stanley Gibbs' circumstances would cover up his mistake for the security of his family. But this same characterization also makes it believable that such a man would not stand by and see someone he liked thrown to the wolves for his mistake. The fact that Jack's general character is that of an ambitious junior executive makes it believable that he would selfishly try to cover up a mistake he thought would lose him his job and ruin his ambitious plans for the future. And yet, his characterization is such that the reader senses upon reading paragraph 141 that Jack will not let Stanley Gibbs take all the blame.

PLOT STRUCTURE

Although "No Margin for Error" is told in the first person, it follows the plot structure of the formula story.

BEGINNING (Paragraphs 1 through 36)

1. The beginning is placed in time as close to the ending as possible, with Jack discovering he has made an error that will cost his company thousands of dollars.
2. The scene is set in the offices of the Fairchild Chenille Company with a transition to the scene in the apartment where Jack lives with his wife, Peggy. (Note: In the pulp story the scene in the beginning is usually confined to a single scene. In the slick story the writer can use as many scenes in the beginning as he deems necessary. Sometimes a writer may use a setting in the beginning and break it up into several scenes. See the commentary on the slick story "The Next to the Last Word" on page 366.)
3. The principal characters are introduced with an indication of their approximate ages—Jack, Stanley Gibbs, and Jack's wife, Peggy. The point of view is established: this is Jack's story.
4. The complication is presented: Jack has made an error that can cost his company thousands of dollars and may cost him his job.

346

5. The reader knows from the tone of the prose that he is reading a dramatic slick story.
6. The beginning implies what ending is desired. The reader is aware that this story is optimistic and that Jack will somehow solve his complication.
7. A narrative hook is used in paragraph 35 to make the reader read on to find out if Jack does try to cover up his mistake.

MIDDLE (Paragraphs 37 through 159)

1. Paragraphs 37 through 50 give the background of circumstances that produced the complication. (Note how this professional author avoided using a flash back by keeping this dullest part of the story in the past, rather than past perfect tense.)
2. Paragraphs 51 through 118 present a series of attempts by Jack to cover up his error, only to meet with failure.
3. Paragraphs 121 through 147 present a situation of ante-climax, in which it appears the complication will finally be solved, when Jack learns Stanley Gibbs is responsible for the error. Yet the reader is convinced the complication is beyond a satisfactory solution. It must be remembered that the formula story must have an ending that is satisfactory and believable to the reader. At this point in the story to let Stanley Gibbs take all the blame would certainly solve Jack's complication, but it would be very unsatisfactory to the reader, who wants, like Jack's wife Peggy, for him to do what is right, no matter what the cost.
4. Jack makes the agonizing decision in paragraph 148, to take all the blame so that Stanley Gibbs will not lose his job. He tries to save Gibbs in paragraphs 149 through 159.

END (Paragraphs 160 through 180)

1. The solution is satisfactory and believable to the reader. The reader leaves the story knowing that neither Jack nor Stanley Gibbs will lose his job and that both have learned their lesson; they will never try to cover up another error. The ending is made believable to the reader by what Ben Haralson says to Jack.

Interestingly enough, we again have a story in which the moment of truth is implied, and not explicitly stated. (See "Maggie Mix-up.") In the pulp story the moment of truth, conventionally, consists of an open recognition on the part of the protagonist of what is involved in the conflict, when he finally comes face to face with himself. In this well-formed slick story, Jack goes back to his office, smokes two cigarettes in a row, and then goes to make his confession. The author uses the smoking of two cigarettes as a symbolic act signifying the soul-searching that Jack is undergoing. That the author uses this indirect means of presenting the moment of truth contributes to our sense of suspense without at the same time making it impossible to realize what the character is really doing.

The Next to
the Last Word

by MAX HAMPTON

1   Mike Elliott lounged in the doorway of Joe Douglas' bedroom. "So you're that serious about her?"

2   "As serious as you can get." Joe was picking a tie.

3   "Strange. You prowl New York for six years and then get yourself snared in some hamlet in Missouri. It was Missouri, wasn't it?" in the tone of voice he might have used if it had been the Australian bush.

4   "It was Missouri." Joe looked up. "That's just the point. Sally isn't like the women here. She's scrubbed and fresh and. . . ."

5   "You make her sound like someone's laundry."

6   Joe took ties from the rack. He glanced complacently at Elliott. "You may not believe it, old boy, but Sally is different. She's sweet and unspoiled. There isn't a vain bone in her body. To her, glamour is so much tapioca. She is a down-to-earth, straightforward, blessedly unspoiled female. Probably the last of her species," he ended wisely. "And she is just what I always wanted."

7   Mike lifted an eyebrow. "Correction. There is no such creature as a different woman. They're all alike. I've known thousands of them. It just takes you a little longer to find out about them."

8   "You've been with that agency so long, you're a jaded cynic. You haven't seen anything like my Sally in years. She wouldn't give that"—his fingers snapped contemptuously—"for all your

349

models and contracts tied up in cellophane and a big plaid bow! She is as different from those gaunt clotheshorses you beau around as—as night from day," he concluded lamely.

9   "If you're referring to Elaine, she is one of the highest-paid fashion models in New York. Anyway, I think I'll probably marry her."

10   "You've said that before."

11   "So Elaine keeps pointing out," he said cheerfully. He glanced around the cluttered bachelor apartment. "Going to live here when you two become one?"

12   "We are not," Joe snorted. "I'm through with these badger burrows. We're going to take a place on the Island or in Connecticut. A house with a lawn, and sunlight pouring in the windows." He smiled musingly as he envisioned the ruffled curtains in the kitchen, the smell of pot roast drifting through an immaculate house, Sally at the front door to greet him at night. "We're going to live like people were meant to live," he said firmly.

13   Elliott winced. "Isn't all this a touch . . . well, sudden? I've known you a long time, and. . . ."

14   "It isn't sudden at all. It is just exactly like I want to live. I have it all planned," he replied emphatically.

15   Mike raised his eyes to the ceiling. "Everything but the patter of little feet!"

16   "And there'll be that, too," Joe said stoutly. "Unless you come out and visit, you'll be lucky to see us once a month. I'm through with this neon circuit. We're going to live quiet, comfortable, sane lives."

17   "The new you, huh?" Mike asked wryly. "And this is all just dandy with Sally?"

18   "The new me and, yes, it is dandy with Sally."

19   "Besides looking at you with adoring eyes, what is this lovable bundle of wet wash going to do in New York?"

20   "She is finishing the research for her master's thesis. Fine arts."

21   "Why does she want a master's degree just to marry you?"

22   Joe shrugged. "That's the kind of a girl she is. I told you. She started on it before we met and she believes in seeing things through. Anyway, she's never seen New York. Aunt Lucy

finally gave permission when I promised to guard Sally's every waking hour, and to be the perfect little gent myself."

23 "And who might this Aunt Lucy be?"

24 "Sally's guardian. A sort of a female gladiator."

25 "You certainly unearthed a fascinating family," Elliott murmured.

26 "Which of these ties?" Joe held up four.

27 "The stripe. This little prairie flower really has you unglued, hasn't she? Well, time for me to pick up my gaunt clotheshorse. We'll see you at dinner."

28 Joe was working on his pocket handkerchief. He had never, he thought unhappily, been able to flick a handkerchief, poke it in, and walk jauntily away. With him it looked poked. "Hey, keep the conversation clean tonight. And no cracks about Missouri."

29 "Except for the river and Mr. Truman, I'd never have heard the word. So how can I make cracks?" The door closed.

30 On the way out of the apartment, Joe looked about, grimacing. Thank heavens there would soon be order and harmony in his life, a master plan instead of hurried, hectic little forays against life's daily problems. He kicked a dirty shirt under a chair. So far as he could tell, the maid's idea of cleaning was just to rearrange the debris. But as he ran down the stairs, he began to smile. It was hard to believe Sally was only a ten-minute taxi drive away!

31 Sally's plane had arrived that afternoon. She was settled in the Chester, a hotel of such quiet worth you'd feel nary a qualm about leaving your life savings in the middle of the lobby overnight. The desk clerk, who looked like a retired diplomat, peered with polite suspicion when Joe told him he wished to see Sally.

32 She was waiting, the door opened, when Joe arrived. "Golly, you're prompt!"

33 He held her very tightly for over a minute, assuring himself that she was really there at last, that she was actually going to marry him. "By the way," he murmured, "the odds are going way down that a certain party will wait for a Christmas wedding. Meaning me."

34 "My plans are so set they can't be changed a bit," she

whispered. She pushed away. "I'll get all mussed. How do I look?"

35   "Simply fabulous," he told her, trying to put his arms around her again.

36   "Joe!"

37   Dutifully, he stepped back, frowning with exaggerated criticalness. She was, he decided, the loveliest woman on earth. Her soft, fair hair curled about her ears. Her eyes, watching him anxiously, were fine cobalt blue. Her skin glowing from soap, water, and health, was flawless. In that plain black dress she was like a little girl all dressed up for a party. Not so much of a little girl, either, when you stopped to. . . . "You're going to look teddibly fancy in a wedding dress," he said softly.

38   "Then it's all right?" She whirled. "I was afraid it wouldn't be," she said. "The girls at home said it was what they were wearing in New York, but you can never be sure."

39   "To heck with what they're wearing in New York. There isn't a woman here who can touch you with the help of radar."

40   She stood on tiptoe and kissed him very lightly. She wouldn't let him put his arms around her. "All you want to do is neck," she chided. She walked across the room. "I talked to Doctor Bailey today. He was awfully kind. He's going to let me use his library. You know," she said seriously, "he's a leading authority on Renaissance art."

41   "You stay out of other men's libraries," Joe grinned, reaching for her.

42   She side-stepped him gracefully. "And remember, you promised to start showing me the Metropolitan Museum Sunday. Three hours a trip until we've done it all."

43   He moaned. "I remember." He would have promised to swim with the sea lions in the Bronx Zoo to have gotten her to New York.

44   She picked up her gloves. "All set?"

45   "At this moment, I wish Mike and his gaunt clotheshorse were in Siam."

46   "Mike and his what?"

47   "His girl. She's a model. Looks like she lives on artichokes. All joints and angles."

48   Sally stopped in the corridor. "Is she really?"

49   "Joints and angles? Mostly."

50   "A model, I mean." She frowned throughfully. "Do you think this dress will be all right? I have another one—navy blue. . . ."

51   He took her arm. "She can't hold a candle to you. She's shaped like a bent bobby pin."

52   She smiled, reassured, and tucked her arm in his. "That's a dreadful thing to say about a woman. The poor thing can't help it!"

53   Joe smirked at the Anthony Eden behind the desk and asked the doorman to get a cab. The lights of the city were on. There was still some fading light of day over Triboro Bridge and the red light on the Empire State TV antenna gleamed reassuringly in the paleness of the new twilight.

54   Sally drew a deep breath and sank back against the seat of the cab. "Oh, it's so wonderful finally being here. Being with you." She leaned against him for a moment and then said earnestly, "I think you look awfully elegant, Joe. I really do."

55   No one had told him he looked elegant in his entire life. That, combined with the glory of finally having Sally with him, gave him a distinct ringing in his ears.

56   Mike and Elaine were at L'Aiglon when they arrived. Mike waved. "Wonderful timing," he said, rising. "Elaine was bullying me into naming the date."

57   "I'm sick to death of dieting. Hello, Joe."

58   "And this would be Sally," Mike crooned. "My, aren't you a pretty little fixing! This elderly party is Elaine Farrell."

59   The women smiled and spoke. Sally wasn't exactly staring, but it was close. "What a stunning hat!" she breathed at last.

60   Elaine touched the sleek black feathers. "I chopped me an awful lot of cotton for it. But, child, where did you get that skin! Is that what happens to girls in Missouri?"

61   "Don't be putting on airs," Mike beckoned for the waiter. "The folks of Georgia voted her Miss Hush Puppy of 1923," he confided to Sally, "and she immediately packed her Southern accent into an old carpetbag and hit the road for the Big City."

62   "Actually, it was Miss Boll Weevil," Elaine said coldly.

63   Sally was looking at first one of them and then the other. Her smile was uncertain. Joe put his hand over hers. She was,

he decided, by far the prettiest girl in the room. Elaine, he thought, was wearing too much make-up. And she was too skinny. He didn't care how chic it was. But Sally was just right. In all departments.

64   "You know, pigeon," Mike said slowly, "you'd photograph like ten thousand dollars. Did you ever think of modeling?"

65   Sally flushed. "Me! Good heavens, no!"

66   "I told you she couldn't possibly care less about that sort of thing," Joe said firmly. "She's going to write that thesis and then we're going to Missouri and be married."

67   "Why not get married here? Elaine and I will go all out. She'll sob quietly and afterward I'll pelt you with old shoes."

68   "Because of Aunt Lucy," Joe explained. "She wants us to be married in Missouri."

69   "Suggest to Aunt Lucy—in a nice way, of course—that she go roll her hoop."

70   Both Sally and Joe laughed. Mike looked up. "What's so funny?"

71   "You just don't tell Aunt Lucy to roll hoops," Sally said.

72   "If Aunt Lucy wants us to be married in a punch bowl shooting Niagara Falls, then we will," Joe added.

73   Mike pursed his lips. "She sounds dreamy. I'd like to meet her."

74   "You will. She's coming East as soon as she recovers."

75   "Recovers?" Elaine asked politely.

76   "She fell off a tractor," Sally said gravely.

77   "What was she doing on a tractor?" Mike asked.

78   "Singing *Stardust*," Joe said crossly. "She was driving it, of course."

79   "Oh, of course," Mike said softly. "What else would a middle-aged lady be doing these fine summer evenings but bounding over hill and dale on a tractor."

80   "We have a farm a few miles out of town," Sally explained. "Aunt Lucy loves it. She was helping with the plowing."

81   Mike nodded understandingly. "I see what you mean about the hoop. Best you get married in Missouri." He opened the menu. "And what hearty meal will you have, my dieting friend?" he asked Elaine. "How about a sautéed carrot?"

82   The party ended after dinner. Elaine had an early booking and Joe wanted Sally to get some sleep. She had had a big

day. He stayed only long enough for a cigarette. She lighted it for him. "Wasn't that Elaine simply incredible?"

83 Joe shook his head. "Great gal, but she looks emaciated."

84 "I recognized her at once. I've seen her pictures hundreds of times. She's gorgeous!" She curled up on the other end of the divan. "What does Mike do?"

85 "Deals in flesh, roughly speaking."

86 "Joe!"

87 "He has to do with models. With models, many are called but few are chosen. Mike is the lad at the agency who does the choosing."

88 She sighed. "Do you suppose he could possibly have been serious about my being a model?"

89 Joe kissed her. "Heavens, no. Just part of his line. There must be seven hundred women from Sicily to Berlin, left from the war, waiting for Mike to come back and put them on the cover of a magazine. Anyway, even if he had been, you want no part of that rat race, baby. Believe me. You'd loathe it." He rose. "I'll shove so you can hit the pad."

90 "Good night, dear." She patted his cheek absently after his kiss. "He was probably just being nice," she said wistfully.

91 Joe called her at ten sharp the next morning. "Top of what's left of the morning. What's with you?"

92 "I've been for a walk."

93 "You were supposed to rest," he reminded her.

94 "I can do that at home. And you know what, Joe?"

95 He could tell she was excited. Something about the thesis, he assumed fondly. "What?"

96 "Mike called. He wants me to come to his office."

97 "What for?" instantly suspicious.

98 "It's crazy, I know, but he wants me to take a test. He was serious last night. He thinks I may be just the girl they're looking for."

99 "Well, he can go right on looking."

100 "Darling, wouldn't it be fun!"

101 "Fun!" Joe cried. "You mean you think you'd actually enjoy that inane nonsense."

102 "I know I would," she said flatly. "I'm so thrilled right this instant I can hardly stand it."

103 "Now, look, Sally," Joe began sternly. "You just don't know

355

what you are doing. Believe me, I know best about this. I will not have you getting involved with. . . ."

104   "I'm not getting involved with anything. I'm simply going to see him."

105   "What about your thesis? I thought you were going to see Doctor What's-his-name. All his stuff on art."

106   "I wish I'd had my hair done. It looks like seaweed."

107   "Sally, how about lunch?" By then he would have thought of something.

108   "Love to."

109   "Twenty-one?"

110   "Oh, yes! I've always wanted to go there. Can you afford it?" suddenly concerned.

111   "No, but I'll meet you there at one-thirty."

112   "All right, dear. Now I've got to go. I'm late."

113   In from Missouri less than twenty-four hours and already she had to rush. She had appointments yet! He slumped down in his chair. Then he buzzed his secretary. "I want to speak to Mike Elliott. It's urgent."

114   In a few seconds Mike was on the telephone. "I wondered what was holding you up," he said brightly.

115   "Mike," Joe began, "what in the name of. . . ."

116   "Temper, Joseph." He was laughing.

117   "Sally couldn't have made it any clearer last night that she wasn't remotely interested in being a model. Yet you roust her out at dawn and get her all confused and upset about. . . ."

118   "You know, Joe, I was thinking about that," Mike was almost crooning. "I don't recall Sally saying a word about not wanting to be a model. You've made a few resounding statements, but she hasn't. She sounded quite thrilled, actually."

119   "Now, you look, Mike. . . ."

120   "Now, you look, Joe," he interrupted crisply. "Of course, she's thrilled. What woman wouldn't be? She's suddenly aware that maybe she's even pretty enough to have people pay to look at her. That is a wonderful thing for any gal's ego. What possible harm can it do? It is something she'll remember all of her life."

121   "O.K.," Joe said grudgingly. "Just this once, Mike. She's going to write a thesis and then she's going to marry me."

356

122   "I know. In Missouri with Aunt Lucy riding herd. Just keep one thing in mind, Joe."

123   "Hum?"

124   "All Sally has to do to bring this to a screaming halt is to just say, 'No.' Believe me, that'll do the trick. See you, Joe."

125   Joe hung up. Well, he'd see. It'd take a girl like Sally about fifteen minutes to decide she wanted no part of it. He knew his Sally. And then there was Aunt Lucy. She would do backflips all over the east-forty if she knew. He flung down his pencil and looked impatiently at his watch.

126   Sally was twenty minutes late for lunch. He could tell the instant he saw her that they had accepted her. Seeing her so happy, he felt guilty at having hoped they'd give her the old, "Thank you very much. We'll let you know."

127   She chattered through lunch, scarcely touching her food. "I have good bones, you know," she said gravely.

128   "You have what?"

129   "Very good bones. Mike said so. They're terribly important."

130   "I've always found them most convenient to have around."

131   "Oh, be serious. I mean for photography. You would be amazed at the girls who don't make the grade on that very account."

132   "Bad bones, huh?"

133   "Yes. You see. . . ." She paused. "Joe, you're making fun of me."

134   "Well, you have to admit it's sort of peculiar table talk. Your bones." Then he was sorry. He took her hand. "I'm sorry, darling. Really," he said contritely.

135   "You know what account I'm doing?"

136   "What?"

137   She giggled. "Cottage cheese! Mike says it is an important one."

138   "What else did Mike say? That he would have you Miss Curdled Milk in six months?" She had mentioned Mike's name at least a dozen times since they had started lunch. Then he was sorry again. "Forgive me, Sally. I'm behaving like a dolt. It is just that I do not want you to get up in one of the hassles every other woman in New York seems to be having."

139   "You certainly are being wonderful about it," she said stiffly. "I thought you would be pleased."

140   "I am, dear, really," he lied. "I know you're getting a huge charge out of it and you know I'm for anything that makes you happy. After all"—with forced cheerfulness—"once can't hurt you, can it? Once," he repeated, looking sharply at her.

141   She nibbled reflectively on a piece of Melba toast. "I have to have pictures taken this afternoon. A whole slew of them."

142   "What on earth for?"

143   "Mike says they are absolutely vital. He made an appointment for me. This guy is supposed to be fabulous with a camera."

144   "Be sure you warn him about your bones. I wouldn't want him slighting them."

145   Sally smiled sweetly. "You know, if you weren't such a grown man and if I weren't engaged to you, I think I'd believe you were behaving like a sulky child. Now I have to run."

146   He put her in a cab. "Can you squeeze me in for dinner?"

147   She blew him a kiss. "Come by the hotel."

148   He walked glumly back to the office. She was right. He was behaving badly. A fuss over nothing. So she posed for a few pictures. So she was Miss Sour Cream or whatever it was Mike had in mind. So what? One time wouldn't hurt. He had almost talked his blood pressure back to normal by the time he reached his desk.

149   After he met Sally that night it took approximately six and one-fourth minutes to have that blood pressure right back to its all-time high at luncheon. It seemed to him she had changed already. She was full of herself. She had been in New York a little over twenty-four hours and she was spouting names he had never heard and addresses he didn't recognize. She had also begun to use the word "divine." She was due back at the photographer's at nine the following morning, so they could not stay out late.

150   "It shows, you know," she said, glancing in the mirror and running the tip of one finger under her eye. Her skin was as smooth and unlined as alabaster.

151   "What shows?"

152   "Late hours. And you can't bluff a camera. He doesn't like my nose," she said thoughtfully, turning her head first to the left and then to the right.

153   "Who doesn't?" indignantly.

154   "André. The photographer."

155   "He's got a nerve not liking your nose. Who does he think he is? What's wrong with it?"

156   "It sort of tilts," she said soberly.

157   He strode across the room and put his arms around her. "You've got the cutest nose in the country. If he says one more word—just one word—about your nose, your hair or your bones, I'll smash him! I'll hit him so hard with that camera of his he won't know whether he's taking pictures or having a gall-bladder attack!"

158   Sally's arms slid about his neck. "Would you, sweetie?" She kissed his cheek. "You're cute, Joe. You really are."

159   She *sounded* different even, Joe thought tragically. She sounded just like Elaine.

160   In the next ten days he saw Sally for lunch twice. They dined together each night, but the evenings ended before he really felt out of the house and on the town. You would have thought she was fifty years old and had been in burlesque for forty of them, the way she worried about fatigue lines, puffy eyes and crow's-feet, he thought miserably. She knew perfectly well she would awaken in the morning looking as fresh and shining as rain, but Joe was sure it was just part of what she thought she ought to do to stay in the league. Some of the girls worried about it so, by gosh, she did too. Enough fuss was being made about her by enough people that she was kept just two feet off the ground. She had started on her thesis; she had at least half a page of notes. Joe fought it every inch of the way. He began to feel as if he were fighting brush fires. The second he thought he had one extinguished, another broke out. Sally, by that time, was posing for a peanut-butter advertisement.

161   They were finishing dinner one night. He was on his fourth cup of coffee, listening to her. "Twelve is really a small size, but not for modeling. You almost have to be a ten."

162   "Um." That was about the extent of his conversation by that time.

163   "So I was really lucky. I always assumed they were really tall girls, didn't you?"

164   "Um."

165   "You know what André wants me to do?"

166   "I have a rather rough idea," Joe said grimly. How he had come to loathe that man!

167   She reached across and patted his hand. "He says I could be really fabulous if I had a crew cut."

168   "A crew cut!" he bellowed, clattering his cup onto the saucer.

169   "Sh-h-h, darling." He glanced about. Everyone in L'Aiglon had turned to stare. "Not a real one, of course. But terribly short and done sort of. . . ." She made motions about her head with her hands. "What do you think?" she asked anxiously.

170   "That it would be like dating Mickey Rooney!"

171   She sighed. "Come on, Joe. Let's go."

172   They rode to her hotel in silence.

173   "Don't come up. It's late." She kissed his cheek. "Good night, dear. And won't you try to. . . ."

174   "To what?"

175   "Oh, nothing. Good night."

176   Back on the street, he glanced at his watch. It was ten-thirty. Joe felt an ungovernable urge to speak to the root of all this recent evil. Laden with dimes, he shut himself in a telephone booth. He called twelve places before he tried the apartment. "May I speak to Mr. Elliott, please?" he asked gruffly in reply to a woman's casual, "Hello?"

177   "He has his mouth full of pastrami, but he'll be along. Who is this?"

178   "The vice squad. Tell him to chew faster."

179   "Oh, Joe, angel. Elaine."

180   "I guessed."

181   "My, you sound cheery. Been picking the wings off flies?"

182   "You're getting warm. I've been thinking about an insect."

183   Then Mike was on the telephone.

184   "I want to talk to you," Joe said belligerently.

185   "I guessed that was why you called. What's on your mind, Joseph?"

186   "Can you have lunch with me tomorrow?"

187   "I guess so."

188   "How about the King Cole Room at one? Women aren't

allowed that early. Think you can bear up without 'em for an hour or so?"

189 "I have pictures in my billfold I can spread on the table."

190 "See you at one."

191 "Fine. Oh, one thing, Joseph. I'd suggest a cold shower before you turn in. You sound a touch feverish to me."

192 Joe hung up on Mike's laughter.

193 He was there before Mike the next day. He watched him walk through the maze of tables in the large room. Mike grinned. "What's bothering you, as if I didn't know?"

194 "Sally."

195 "I knew. You'd be unnatural if she didn't. Lovely child, that Sally."

196 "I don't like this stuff she's doing, Mike."

197 "She's a pretty hot item right now."

198 "Please do not refer to my fiancée as a pretty hot item," Joe said coldly.

199 "She's a new face. Everyone is always after new faces. She has a sweetness and a charm which show right through. And, by the way, she's having herself a time."

200 "How can I stop it, Mike?"

201 "Why do you want to?"

202 "I do not want Sally working. I do not want her turning into a lovely carbon of a thousand other lovely women. I want her just like she used to be; I want that same sweet girl. I do not want her with a crew cut!" His voice was nearing a shout.

203 "You just caused that nice old man to drop french fries in his lap," Mike said reproachfully.

204 "I'm lucky if I see her for dinner. She turns in so early you'd think she was tubercular. She does exercises and keeps her feet in the air for thirty minutes a day. She calls me 'sweetie.' She talks different. She looks different. She is different."

205 Mike made small circles on the table top with his glass. "You know, I'd never have believed you could act like such an ass."

206 Joe's eyes widened. "Me!"

207 "Yes, you. You've behaved like the worst sort of stiff-necked,

361

mid-Victorian squire. Instead of being giddy with pride that your girl is so special, you've pouted. She still loves you. She is still going to marry you. She's still going to wear dimity aprons in that Long Island bungalow. Where you got these idiotic notions that this is changing Sally, I cannot imagine. It'll do her good, man! For the rest of her days—while she's poaching your breakfast egg and tending your brood of progeny —she can think, 'I was special!' " Mike smiled thinly. "You know, you don't act like a guy in love. You sound like someone who bought a car and is mad because it doesn't get the exact gas mileage he'd hoped for. If I were Sally, I'd tell you to go fly a kite."

208   Joe blinked. He sat silent while the waiter served the lunch. Finally he muttered, "But I didn't think she'd want all this. I thought Sally was different."

209   "I told you once there is no such thing as a different woman. Remember the line from the fairy tale: 'Mirror, mirror, on the wall, who's the fairest one of all?' "

210   Joe nodded impatiently.

211   "Well," Mike said easily, "there isn't a woman living who wouldn't like to make that speech to a mirror and get some kind of a favorable reply. I don't care if she's eighteen or eighty-eight. In effect, Sally spoke to a mirror—me, André, and the like—and she got a rousing vote of confidence. I say bully for her," Mike said emphatically.

212   Joe put money on the check. "Well, I don't. She can take her pick: me, or . . . or the lot of you."

213   "Hammiest speech I ever heard," Mike said mildly.

214   "Anyway," Joe concluded loftily, "it is actually a matter which concerns only Sally and me."

215   "Then why did you ask me to lunch and cry into my vichyssoise?" Mike asked gently, rising. "See you. Thanks."

216   Joe was finishing dressing that night and putting the last touches to the speech he was going to make to Sally, when his telephone rang. He picked it up. "Hello?"

217   "Joe?"

218   It was Sally. "What's wrong?" he asked in concern.

219   "Aunt Lucy," she wailed.

220   "What about her?"

221 "She's arriving tonight on the nine o'clock plane!"

222 "Here? What about her sprained ankle?"

223 "She may be carrying it in her overnight bag for all I know. The telegram was here when I got back."

224 "Have you been working this late?"

225 "There's a man who thinks I might be what they want for a television thing. Joe, what are we going to do?"

226 "Television!"

227 "Just a commercial. I blow smoke at the camera and sort of purr happily. I'll tell you about it later," she said impatiently. "What about Aunt Lucy?"

228 Suddenly Joe heard violins. Jasmine floated in his window and there was the tinkle of temple bells. Aunt Lucy! He grinned gleefully. The perfect answer. Wait until she got a good briefing on these carryings-on!

229 "Sally, darling," he said gently, "what do you mean 'What about Aunt Lucy?' We'll meet her plane, of course. We'll buy her some dinner and then I will leave you two girls alone to talk about old times."

230 "You don't seem too upset," she said suspiciously. "The last time you referred to her it was as a female John L. Lewis."

231 "She's going to be my aunt-in-law," he said righteously. "If that's the right phrase."

232 "All right. Give me thirty minutes."

233 On the way to the airport, Sally leaned her head on his shoulder. "You're terribly sweet to be so nice. I know she's a problem, but"—she kissed his cheek—"maybe she'll only stay a little while. She hates being away from the farm."

234 He held her tightly and sighed contentedly. It would, he figured, take Aunt Lucy about thirty minutes. That, added to his own speech, would do it. The vision of the cottage became vivid again.

235 They were late. Aunt Lucy's plane had landed. She was shouting at a cowering attendant in the luggage room. Her ankle appeared to be completely healed. She probably, Joe decided, gave it a good talking to, said enough was enough, and that was that.

236 "The pilot was incompetent," she said in the cab. "The stewardess was flip. They lied to me in Kansas City. They promised—gave their word, mark you—that it would be a

smooth trip. There were three distinct bumps. The worst one was over Cleveland during dinner. I spilled my prunes. You're looking peaked, Sally." She took Sally's face in one large hand, and turned it first this way and that. "You look downright liverish."

237 "I feed her regularly," Joe said hastily. "She's been home before midnight every night."

238 Aunt Lucy looked at him. "Likely," she said. She settled back in the cab and gave her attention to the driving and meter.

239 At dinner she ate a steak roughly the size of a coffee table and declared it wholly unpalatable. She raked Joe with a glance of withering scorn because he refused to fight with the management over the size of the bill. At the hotel she said briskly, "I'll go on up. You two will want to say good night." She glanced up and down the brightly lighted street. "Crazy place for sparking, I must say!" She strode through the revolving door.

240 Sally and Joe walked to a small place down the street. At a cozy table Joe made his speech. He remembered all of it. "That's my last word, Sally," he said gravely. "And you'll see. Aunt Lucy will agree with me."

241 Sally twirled a glass slowly about on the paper napkin. "Number one, I'm of age. If Aunt Lucy doesn't like what I'm doing, she'll just have to be sad. Number two, I'm not a rosebush you happened to fancy in Missouri which you can tote out to Long Island and just plant. Number three, I will not be given ridiculous ultimatums by someone who behaves as idiotically as you. I love you, Joe. I was very much looking forward to marrying you. Notice I said 'was,' Joe. And that is *my* last word."

242 She walked out on him, her head held high, causing every male to turn and watch that exit. Joe went home to face the impossible task of trying to sleep. Had he been drowning, his past could not have passed before his eyes more effectively.

243 By three A.M. it was shatteringly apparent to him that he had to have Sally if she worked for the rest of her days as a professional yodeler. He risked Aunt Lucy's wrath and called the hotel. Sally had directed that a "Do Not Disturb" sign be placed on her telephone. It was there at eight-thirty. At nine the sign had been removed, but no one answered the telephone.

Nor did anyone any of the times it rang every fifteen minutes after that.

244   By four-thirty the hotel had graciously accepted, and would deliver to Sally upon her return, five telegrams, one forty-seven words long in which the words "sorry" and "love" appeared eight times each.

245   At five-twenty Aunt Lucy answered the telephone. "Don't go away!" Joe shouted, hung up, and began to run. He was out of breath when he reached the hotel. The retired diplomat at the desk looked upon him with freezing disapproval when he rang up to say that a Mr. Douglas was downstairs. It was apparent he fought with his conscience as to whether or not he should warn the elderly lady that Mr. Douglas appeared to have taken complete leave of his senses.

246   "Where's Sally?" Joe demanded when Aunt Lucy opened the door.

247   "With some people named Mike and Elaine. You look very odd to me, your face all flushed that way," she said, returning to the studio couch and lying down.

248   "Aunt Lucy," he said desperately, "we've got to go back to Missouri right away."

249   She opened one eye. "Don't be absurd. I just got here. They scratched my luggage, too. In three places."

250   "I'm in love with Sally!" he cried.

251   "I know. Hand me that dab of wet cotton." She placed it carefully over her eyes. "Sally says witch hazel is good for the eyes," she explained, lying back down.

252   "I want to get married right now, before there are any more fights or misunderstandings. I don't care what you say. I don't care if Sally models until she can pose as Whistler's Mother!"

253   "Don't be foolish. A few months will be plenty for her. You should have known that. You should also have known better than to hand ultimatums to a girl like Sally." She lifted one cotton pad and glared balefully at him. "After all, she is *my* niece."

254   "You don't mind her being a model?" Joe asked incredulously.

255   "Heavens, no. Have you any idea how many bushels of wheat it would take me to make what Sally did last week? Nice crowd of people she knows, too."

256   "But you'd rather she'd be married to me, wouldn't you?"
Joe asked anxiously.

257   "Not necessarily. Anyone's niece can get married. Darned
few can get on the cover of a magazine. You're a nice enough
boy, Joe, but I'm beginning to think you're not overly bright."
She lifted the other witch-hazel pad. "If you want to get
married, you'll have to do it right here in New York. I'm not
going back to Missouri just yet."

258   "Will Sally still marry me, do you think?"

259   "As soon as she sees you've found some sense," Aunt Lucy
sat upright. "You know, Joe, the craziest thing. . . ." For the
first time in his life Joe saw her look ill at ease. "That fool
Mike thinks I'm a good type. I'm being tested tomorrow. A
baking-powder account, I think he said." He stared open-
mouthed at her. She lay back down. "He said I was a distinct
type," she said serenely. "I have very good bones."

260   Slowly Joe walked to the telephone. He called Twenty-one
and asked for Mike. "Do you want to be best man right away,"
he asked hollowly, "if I can talk Sally into it?"

261   "Old shoes and all?"

262   "Old shoes and all."

263   "Elaine promises to weep buckets."

264   "I want to speak to Sally, Mike, but first I admit defeat.
You were right." He glanced at Aunt Lucy's prostrate form
and drew a deep breath. "About that 'mirror, mirror, on the
wall' I mean."

265   Mike laughed. "You mean Aunt Lucy? Grand old gal. I'll
get Sally for you. I've been trying to talk some sense into her.
She flatly refuses to agree to that television deal until she gets
your okay. She seems sort of upset, but try and talk her into
it, huh, Joe?"

266   "That will be between Sally and me," Joe said calmly.
"We'll let you know what we decide. Now, about letting me
speak to my fiancée. . . ."

COMMENTARY ON "THE NEXT TO
THE LAST WORD"

This slick young love story is an excellent example of an author's
taking the oldest love story plot in fiction—boy meets girl, boy loses

366

girl, boy gets girl—and through fresh and original situations, making it into a very entertaining story. The writing is sophisticated and witty, the sort so dear to the hearts of editors and readers of slick magazines.

BASIC PLOT

Once more we find an author using the basic plot of conflict to overcome an obstacle and reach a worthwhile goal. The obstacle Joe Douglas must overcome is his own selfish dislike of his environment, which hinders his reaching the worthwhile goal of marrying the girl he loves.

THEME

Although the title indicates that a woman always has the last word, what the author was actually trying to prove is summed up in the first sentence of paragraph 243. If a man really loves a girl, he must not selfishly try to live her life for her.

Now we use the word "actually" with some reservations. As we have pointed out several times, it is not necessary for a writer to be so aware of his theme in the development of a slick story as to be able to state it explicitly. Yet the author of "The Next to the Last Word" may, indeed, have worked with the bald statement of this suggested theme as the handiest way of expressing his view of the story he is telling. Certainly, in doing so he would be enabled to keep constantly in mind the nature of the conflict, which he wishes to demonstrate. Yet though the theme the writer works with may be used only as a means in writing the story, this does not prevent the implications of his own summary statement from spreading outward and becoming more significant.

Some such statement seems necessary, for this is the sort of story against which the charge of flippancy and lack of seriousness is so often hurled; i.e., the story presents a glib view of the world in which a glow of facile optimism shuts out deeper values. To entertain such criticism is to overlook and mistake the nature of comedy. Without defending the story in terms of the great comic masterpieces of literature, such as those written by Ben Jonson or Molière, let us admit, nonetheless, that it does belong to the realm of comedy, and see below the surface sufficiently to recognize the hidden threats that Joe imagines might engulf his Sally.

These threats lurk within the complacent and somewhat cynical attitude of Mike Elliott, in the blasé and overly self-conscious world of Elaine, and in the mechanized glamor of the complex city. In a real sense, Joe is acquainted with two worlds, both of which he sentimentalizes. To him the rural world from which Sally has come is good, and the urban civilization, of which he is apparently a reluctant member, is bad. As a consequence, he exaggerates the corruption that Sally will encounter when she comes to the city, not having faith in her incorruptibility. And his desire to be protective leads him into overprotectiveness. He has cause. It is obvious that Sally is flattered by becoming a model, and there is a chance—more than hinted at—that the neurotic world of the clotheshorse will engulf her. If Joe acts the part of a fool, there is some ground for his folly. That he should be a comic figure is, in fact, an interesting commentary upon the subtle and pervasive shift of values that still have not wholly brought the United States from an agricultural orientation to a more realistic urban one.

The values that make comedy a serious affair must always be treated with a tone ranging from teasing laughter to downright flippancy. It is the method of comedy to take serious things lightly —without in the least negating their seriousness. For it is part of the comic view to believe that man has sufficient power over his own affairs to be able to recognize—after making several mistakes, to be sure—what is essentially worthwhile. In short, in the absence of a body of comic literature today, it may be of some interest to a writer, to try his hand at the one market that keeps the comic spirit alive.

COMPLICATION

The story presents a complication in the life of Joe Douglas that is made more interesting than it would seem in real life because of certain exaggerations. And, as in all complications in slick stories, the complication is unpleasant for the protagonist. Had Joe freedom of choice, he would not have chosen for Sally to accept Mike's offer to test her as a model. Certainly, Joe, very much in love with Sally and smugly dreaming of escaping from the "badger burrows" and "neon circuit" of New York, suddenly discovers a monkey wrench clogging up the gears in his scheme of things. Gone is the dream cottage on the Island or in Connecticut with Sally to greet him at the front door each night. And though Joe's emotions are never so seriously phrased that we feel compassion for him—certainly compassion as an emotion is somewhat foreign to comic literature—nevertheless, they range the gamut.

In real life it is extremely unlikely that Mike Elliott would choose an inexperienced girl like Sally to be a model, when there are thousands of professional ones available in New York City. By invoking the Cinderella myth, the author makes the complication more interesting than it would seem in real life, and after this first exaggeration continues to make it progressively deeper until it becomes major enough to turn into a salable short story.

Let us consider the series of exaggerations that are based upon the minor complication:

1. Sally passes the test and lands the job as model for the Cottage Cheese Account.
2. Sally begins to change from the "sweet and unspoiled" girl Joe knew into a typical New York model like Elaine, rushing around, making appointments, neglecting Joe.
3. Joe's friend, Mike Elliott, refuses to help him persuade Sally to give up her modeling career.
4. Even when she is not working, Joe cannot spend much time with Sally because, now that she is a model, she has to go to bed early.
5. Sally's career makes her and Joe drift further and further apart.
6. It appears Sally will never give up modeling when she is offered a test for a TV commercial.
7. The author uses the technique of discovery and change to make the complication so deep that something of importance is at stake. With the arrival of Aunt Lucy in New York, Joe musters his courage and gives Sally an ultimatum. When Sally discovers that Joe is issuing her an ultimatum, she changes her mind about marrying him (paragraph 241). The important thing at stake, if the complication is not solved, is the happiness of two people who really love each other.
8. The author uses the same technique to solve the complication in paragraphs 242-243, when Joe discovers that Sally refuses to accept his ultimatum. He, therefore, changes his mind about her modeling career.
9. The agonizing decision made in the situation of ante-climax in the pulp or slick story must point to the solution. When Joe decides "he had to have Sally if she worked for the rest of her days as a professional yodeler," this decision points to the solution.

The complication seems believable because of the emphasis placed on Joe's selfishness in wanting Sally. But his selfishness is based upon his deep love for Sally, and this makes it credible that his love would overcome his personal desires when he is faced with the prospect of losing Sally forever.

Incidentally, the characterizations of Mike Elliott and Aunt Lucy are excellent examples for studying how to establish very real and forceful minor characters. The reader should note how much their characters are established through dialogue.

PLOT STRUCTURE

The story is told in chronological form.

BEGINNING (Paragraphs 1 through 90)

1. The scene is set in New York City. There are three scenes in this long beginning: Joe Douglas' apartment, the Chester Hotel, and L'Aiglon Restaurant. (Note: Three scenes were needed in this beginning to accomplish all five steps of the opening of the chronological story.)
2. The characters are introduced with an indication of their approximate ages. Joe, Mike, Sally, and Elaine are viewed by the reader; Aunt Lucy is introduced by dialogue. (Incidentally, a delayed view of a character always tends to give dramatic value. The reader should study how much Aunt Lucy tends to support or refute the statements made about her by Sally and Joe. The writer can gain a good deal of characterization by the use of this technique, since it may happen that those who speak about a character to be introduced later will reveal their own blindnesses, biases, and controlling emotions.)
3. The reader knows from the tone of the prose that he is reading a witty, sophisticated slick story.
4. The circumstances that produced the complication are presented. Joe has met and fallen in love with Sally, who lives in Missouri. She comes to New York to study for her master's thesis in Fine Arts.
5. The reader is trapped into reading the rest of the story by a subtle narrative hook: the hint that Sally might like to become a model, which would upset all of Joe's plans for their future.

MIDDLE (Paragraphs 91 through 243)

1. The complication is presented: Sally is offered a job as model for the Cottage Cheese Account, which upsets all of Joe's cozy plans for their future.
2. Joe attempts to solve his complication by trying to talk Sally out of a modeling career. He tries to get Mike Elliott to intercede for him with Sally to give up her modeling. He meets with failure.
3. A situation of ante-climax is presented with the arrival of Aunt Lucy in New York. It now appears that Joe will finally solve his complication

370

with Aunt Lucy's help, and Sally will have to give up her career when he issues her an ultimatum. However, he meets with such disastrous failure that the reader is convinced that there is no hope of any satisfactory solution.

4. During his moment of truth, in paragraphs 242 and 243, Joe is forced to make the agonizing decision that he loves Sally so much he would marry her if she spent the rest of her days as a professional yodeler. This decision points to the solution.

END (Paragraphs 244 through 266)

1. The solution is satisfactory and believable to the reader. He leaves the story knowing that Joe and Sally will find happiness. He believes along with Aunt Lucy that Sally will finally give up her modeling career, and that Joe's dream of a cottage on the Island or in Connecticut will come true.

If the ending of this story seems too euphoric, then the reader will have to examine his own beliefs about human nature. For the ending comes out of the way in which characters operate who are given the power to alter their lives in terms of the conditions in which they live.

Precious Moment

1   Dave Lommax' town hadn't a hospital. The nearest one was in Dallas, a good forty minutes away—which would have been okay for some women; but Dave's wife, Kitts, had had the other two children in a big hurry. Doctor Prentiss said there wasn't any point taking chances. So Dave drove Kitts to Dallas a few days before time and installed her in a cheerful hospital room with a telephone, a radio, and a bale of paperback whodunits.

2   Kitts' mother, Mrs. Billingsley, left Mr. Billingsley to fend for himself and came up from Houston to keep house and take care of her grandchildren. She wasn't bossy or nosy or fussy, the way Dave had heard mothers-in-law are. She cooked his favorite chicken stew almost as well as Kitts did. She left the furniture where it was, even the small, easily moved pieces. In the evenings, when he came home from the hospital, she didn't rush at him, but waited calmly for the latest news. She didn't carry on, even when Dave forgot to call the plumber to fix the hot-water tank.

3   Of course, she didn't play with the children in the gay young way Kitts played with them. But she tried to. Whenever little David or Susan popped out at her from under a table or behind a door, she would stop whatever she was doing and say, "Boo," lovingly and earnestly. It brought a lump to Dave's throat. Mrs. Billingsley was such a large, dignified and stately woman to be saying "Boo."

4   Dave liked her fine. She made it easy for him to go off to the plant in the mornings and not have to worry about a thing except Kitts. It was just that having her in the house in the

circumstances put Dave in a peculiar position. He realized that he had never been around Kitts' mother without Kitts.

5   On the third morning of Mrs. Billingsley's stay, he asked Herb Dawson at the plant, "What do you call your mother-in-law?"

6   "What do you mean, what do I call her?" Herb demanded. "Look here, Dave, I *like* my mother-in-law! Why, she lent me money to make the down payment on my house . . ."

7   "I meant," Dave said hastily, "what *name* do you call her by?"

8   Herb relaxed. "Peggy," he said comfortably. "She's a good egg."

9   Mrs. Billingsley was a fine, responsible woman, but she was not the good-egg type. Her first name was Letitia. The mere thought of saying "Letitia" or, worse, "Letty" aloud gave Dave the feeling that somebody was running an elevator up and down inside him. He knew he couldn't possibly bring himself to do it.

10   At lunch, he asked Dub Forrester from Sales what he called his mother-in-law. Dub said his mother-in-law lived in Alaska. "We don't get up that way. If we did, I guess I'd call her Mrs. Porter."

11   "You wouldn't," Dave said earnestly, "if she was doing your cooking and taking care of your children in your own home. It would sound so impersonal, as if you didn't appreciate her."

12   Arthur Landy was no help, either. He said that he called his mother-in-law, "Mother Longmire"!

13   "Mother Billingsley." Dave tested it and shook his head in despair. "It's too long. Anyway, she might not like my calling her 'Mother'. There's just ten, twelve years' difference in our ages."

14   "That's what you get for taking a child bride," Arthur said.

15   Henry Littleton called his wife's mother "Gran," just as his kids did. "What do your kids call your mother-in-law?" he asked Dave.

16   "Momma-ny," Dave said faintly.

17   "Oh, lord," said Henry. "I see your point."

18   When Dave asked Marvin Peters, who rode with him to and from work and who should have been the most helpful, because his mother-in-law lived at his house, he drew a blank. Marvin

scratched his bald head and looked thoughtful, then sheepish. "Darned if I know," he answered. "I don't guess I call her anything."

19   "But you must call her *something!*"

20   "Well, I don't," said Marvin. "I like her, I talk to her all the time, but I don't call her anything. I pass through Lucy, that's what I do. You want to say something to your mother-in-law, you make the pitch. Kitts catches on and passes it. 'Mama,' she says. . . ."

21   "Kitts is in the hospital," Dave said coldly. He looked at his friend. "If Lucy ever has to go to the hospital, you're in trouble."

22   He drove off and left Marvin among the lengthening autumn shadows, staring at his house as though he were afraid to go in.

23   Dave found his home tidy, but not oppressively so. The air was fragrant with essence of pork chops, apple rings and chocolate pie. The children were under control. Even when little David decided to play hide-and-seek instead of coming to dinner, Mrs. Billingsley was not daunted. She went around to all the downstairs closets, saying "Boo," until little David popped out of the guest closet. Then she brought him to the table.

24   This wonderful woman, Dave thought miserably. Why can't I think of something warm and appropriate to call her? He was so ashamed that he couldn't look directly at Mrs. Billingsley, which meant all his remarks floated off to her left or to her right. Finally, even Mrs. Billingsley seemed confused. The next thing, she'd be getting hurt feelings. Good heavens, he thought, I'll have to call her *something!*

25   He was about to take the situation by the horns and say, "Please pass the salt, Mother Billingsley," or "Letitia," or whatever came first to his mind, when the phone rang.

26   It was Doctor Prentiss. "I'm going to the hospital on some pretty important business. Thought you would like to join me there, Dave," he said casually. "Take your time, though. Finish your dinner. No sense getting there before I do."

27   Dave didn't finish his dinner. He shouted to Mrs. Billingsley and ran out to the garage in his shirt sleeves, forgetting the bale of fresh whodunits he'd intended taking Kitts, and he drove as swiftly as a jet-propelled arrow toward Dallas.

28   Two miles out of town, his car's fine expensive motor quit. One minute it was purring; the next minute there was only the wind's diminishing whistle past his left ear. He coasted onto the gravel apron of an abandoned filling station. He was out of gas.

29   He dogtrotted some distance toward town before he realized he'd left the keys in the ignition. He sprinted back, against an occasional glare of headlights, but nobody stopped to find out why he was running along the highway in his shirt sleeves on this chill October evening.

30   He had pocketed the keys and was resting against the gleaming, useless hulk of his car, getting his wind back, when a car, headed for Dallas, slowed and stopped.

31   Marvin Peters' voice came out of it. "That you, Dave? What's your trouble?"

32   Dave told him. Marvin said, heck, he and his brother-in-law Sam could bowl any night in the week. That's where they were going—to a Dallas bowling alley. Instead, they took Dave straight to the hospital and stayed with him.

33   Kitts was already in the delivery room, and Dave didn't know what he'd have done if Marvin and Sam hadn't been there. Especially when the doctor said it was twins. Two boys, identical as peas. The doctor admitted that he and Kitts had known for some time; that was why he'd had her come early.

34   "Darling, I didn't like holding out on you," whispered Kitts, when Dave tottered up to see her, "but you take things so big. I knew you'd buy two of every little old thing and make such a fuss."

35   Ever since he'd met her, Dave remembered, she'd held out on him. And this was always her excuse—that he took things so big. The minute he saw her, he knew she was the girl for him. Perhaps he was overenthusiastic about every date they had and "took it big" when she agreed merely to go to a movie. Kitts was always matter-of-fact, as if she were determined to keep him calm. And whenever he tried to propose, she was evasive and neatly turned the conversation.

36   Finally, in desperation, Dave took her rowing one day, swearing to himself he'd not return to shore until he had asked the question and she had answered. When he had and she had said yes, he nearly upset the boat in jubilation.

37   "Why wouldn't you let me ask you before?" he demanded. "You knew I was trying to."

38   "Because I was afraid of what you'd do," she told him. "Like drowning us now. You always take things so big."

39   Now here she was, still protecting him from his own exuberance. He was too happy to worry about that—or anything. He grinned at Kitts, then beamed at his two new sons.

40   "Oh, Dave, aren't they beautiful?" she asked.

41   They weren't exactly beautiful, but Marvin assured Dave that if they looked anything like Kitts, they were fine babies. The doctors said they were fine and so was Kitts, so why didn't Dave go on home and get some sleep and come back to the hospital in the morning?

42   At the service station where they stopped so he could get a can of gasoline, Dave realized guiltily that he hadn't called Mrs. Billingsley; he hadn't given her a thought. He started for the phone booth, but decided it would be friendlier to tell her in person and watch her face as he gave her all the details.

43   As Marvin drove back to Dave's car with the gas, they passed Sam's house. Sam said they might as well let him out now, and since it was such a big occasion and still so early, why the heck didn't Dave and Marvin come in and have a drink?

44   Dave hesitated only a moment. After all, they had been so nice to him, he couldn't decently refuse. He wasn't a drinking man, but surely one drink wouldn't be amiss on this occasion.

45   As a matter of fact, he had three drinks. After all his running up and down the highway, freezing and starving, then having twins, it was like being nudged by dynamite. Dimly he heard Marvin's sister, Sam's wife, telling Marvin to take him home and forget the car; Dave could get it in the morning.

46   Sam had a better idea. If Dave would give him the keys, he and Marvin would go out after they dropped Dave at home. Sam would put gas in Dave's car, and Sam would "bring 'er in to 'er own driveway tonight," so Dave wouldn't have to lose any time getting to Dallas in the morning.

47   So it was that Dave Lommax was assisted up his front steps at one A.M. by two steadfast friends.

48   "Do we ring the bell?" Sam asked hoarsely.

49   They didn't have to; the door wasn't locked. They were stand-

ing in the hall, supporting Dave and wondering in loud stage whispers if they ought to go the whole way and put him to bed, when a purple-robed queen-mother figure appeared on the stairs.

50   "Uh-uh," groaned Sam, as the figure floated down to them.

51   But all the queen mother said was, "How is Kitts?"

52   "Kitts is fine," Dave blurted out, giddier now with shame and remorse than with drink. "I would've called you but— Well, she had twins—boys—two. . . ." He tried to hold up two fingers, lost Sam's support on that side, and almost fell. Dimly he wished he were dead.

53   Oddly enough, the queen mother was beaming at him. "Twin boys! Isn't that something?" Then the warm voice turned practical. "Now, if you two gentlemen will assist him into the kitchen, I think several cups of strong hot coffee, don't you?"

54   No recriminations, no lectures on behavior unbecoming a father of four. I love this woman, Dave thought, his heart bursting. He was filled with a triple compulsion: to perform the amenities, to prove he thought her the most wonderful mother-in-law in the world, and at the same time to convince her he was not the world's worst son-in-law.

55   He flexed his leaden tongue. He tugged at the two who supported him. By some miracle his voice rose clear and unslurred. "I want you to meet Marvin and Sam, my good friends." He drew a deep breath. "Marvin, Sam, I want you to meet. . . ."

56   And there he stood at the golden pinnacle of his tribute, his memory gone clean and dry as a picked bone. The silence was awful. His desperate mind seized on something—a picture of little David popping out of a closet and his mother-in-law saying, "Boo!"

57   "I want you to meet Boo-Boo," he said.

58   Boo-Boo. If he had been little David, he would have burst into tears. He would have thrown himself on the floor and screamed. For the moment the terrible thing was done, his memory returned. For all it was worth, he mumbled an amendment: "My mother-in-law, Mrs. Billingsley."

59   "But Dave . . ." said her voice, incredibly pleased, for all it was a bit startled . . . "but, Dave, I like 'Boo-Boo' much better." And from the stately incomparable queen mother came Kitts' own gay giggle. "Just wait until I tell Mr. Billingsley!"

377

60   Then Sam and Marvin and Boo-Boo took Dave to the
kitchen for some of that strong hot coffee.

COMMENTARY ON "PRECIOUS MOMENT"

This slick young-married-adult story written by a well-known professional author was selected because the author employs the deviation
in step IV of the middle of the plot structure, which we discussed in
Chapter Three.

BASIC PLOT

The basic plot is conflict to overcome an obstacle in order to reach
a worthwhile goal. The obstacle Dave Lommax must overcome is his
own inadequacy in expressing the love and affection he feels for his
mother-in-law in order to reach the worthwhile goal of letting her
know how much he really likes her.

THEME

We are certain the author wasn't even thinking about theme when
she wrote this story, except as a resultant condition and not as an initial ingredient. She knew that any complication in the lives of people
and their reaction to it must have a theme because a complication
shows something about people and life. The story shows, of course,
that if one loves a person enough, he will find a way of expressing it.

COMPLICATION

The complication is made more interesting than it would seem in
real life by certain exaggerations. The author uses the technique of
taking a minor complication and making it major enough so that the
story becomes salable.

The minor complication consists of the visit of Dave Lommax's
mother-in-law, who comes to keep house for him and take care of his
two children. In real life it is extremely unlikely that a man who must
have been in his future mother-in-law's presence many times while
courting her daughter, and also must have seen her a great deal after
his marriage, would have gone all that time without once calling her
by some name. To make the complication more interesting than it
would seem in real life the author uses a series of exaggerations.

378

1. Dave has never been around his mother-in-law without his wife, Kitts, being present. He does not know what to call her. This is the complication that happens to Dave. Had he freedom of choice he would have chosen to have a name to call Mrs. Billingsley.
2. The complication is made deeper because Mrs. Billingsley's first name is Letitia, which Dave cannot bring himself to use, and to call her Letty is unthinkable.
3. The author uses the principle of discovery and change to make the complication deeper. When Dave discovers that his mother-in-law is not "bossy or nosy or fussy, the way Dave had heard mothers-in-law are," he finds himself liking Mrs. Billingsley very much, which makes his complication worse.
4. The important thing at stake if Dave does not solve his complication is that his mother-in-law's feelings will be hurt, and she will never know how much he really admires her.
5. Discovery and change are again used to make it appear that the complication will never be solved. Dave decides during dinner (paragraph 25) to call Mrs. Billingsley the first name that pops into his mind. The phone rings. Dave discovers from Dr. Prentiss that Kitts' time is near, which makes him change his mind about calling Mrs. Billingsley by the first name to pop into his mind. He dashes out of the house, leaving the reader convinced that there is no hope of a satisfactory solution.

The agonizing decision made in the situation of ante-climax in the pulp or slick story must point to the solution: Dave's agonizing decision to introduce his mother-in-law, when he calls her "Boo-Boo," points to the solution.

The complication is made believable by Dave's characterization (paragraphs 35 through 38) which portrays him as a man who "takes things big." It is, therefore, believable to the reader that such a man would make a big thing out of a simple little thing like finding a suitable name for his mother-in-law. His further characterization as a man unable to express adequately what he feels lends reality to the complication.

The solution is made believable by Dave's characterization as a man who does not drink. This makes it believable that he would get drunk on three drinks, and in his drunken, desperate condition would blurt out "Boo-Boo" in introducing his mother-in-law. Had Dave been sober he would have stood on formality and introduced her as Mrs. Billingsley.

Mrs. Billingsley's cheerful and pleased acceptance of the name is made believable by planting material earlier, which has characterized her as a person with a sense of humor, and shown her playing hide-and-seek and saying "boo" to the two children.

Although the story contains a flash back (paragraphs 35 through 38), it otherwise follows the plot structure of the chronological story, with the exception of the deviation in step 4 of the middle. (See Chapter Three.)

BEGINNING (Paragraphs 1 through 4)

1. The scene is set in the home of Dave Lommax.
2. The principal characters, Dave Lommax and Mrs. Billingsley, are introduced with an indication of their approximate ages. The point of view is established: this is Dave's story.
3. The reader knows from the tone of the prose that he is reading a slick story.
4. The circumstances that produced the complication are presented. Mrs. Billingsley has come to keep house for Dave and to take care of his two children while his wife is in the hospital, expecting a baby.
5. The minor problem that later results in the complication is presented. Having his mother-in-law around the house has placed Dave "in a peculiar position," because he has never been around Mrs. Billingsley without his wife, Kitts, being present.

MIDDLE (Paragraphs 5 through 57)

1. The complication is presented. Dave does not know what to call his mother-in-law.
2. Several attempts are made by Dave to solve his complication (paragraphs 5 through 21), only for him to meet with failure.
3. A situation of ante-climax is, therefore, presented in which it appears that Dave will finally solve his complication. One evening during dinner he decides "to take the situation by the horns" and call his mother-in-law the first name that pops into his mind. However, he fails when Dr. Prentiss phones and Dave dashes out of the house, leaving the reader convinced that there is no hope of a satisfactory solution. (Paragraphs 28 through 32 are needed to get Marvin and Sam on the scene with Dave.) The flash-back paragraphs (35 through 38) are employed to characterize Dave as a man who "takes things big," including a simple thing like finding a suitable name for his mother-in-law.
4. Deviation. The protagonist makes a minor decision that will force him to make an agonizing decision, which points to the solution. The reader

will recall that this deviation is used to make the agonizing decision that follows believable to the reader. Dave makes the minor decision to stop off with Marvin and Sam and have a drink. This minor decision leads to his getting so drunk that his two friends have to take him home. There he is forced to make the agonizing decision to call his mother-in-law by some name in order to introduce her to Marvin and Sam. The minor decision, which led to his getting drunk, makes it believable that under the influence of liquor Dave would blurt out a name like Boo-Boo. Dave's moment of truth occurs in paragraphs 54 through 56 when he knows he must somehow express the love and affection he really feels for his mother-in-law.

END (Paragraphs 58 through 60)

1. The solution is satisfactory to the reader who is sympathetic toward both Dave and Mrs. Billingsley and who wants to see the complication solved. The solution is made believable to the reader by the deviation in step 4 of the middle, and by the earlier characterization of Mrs. Billingsley.

The deviation of a minor decision in step 4 of the middle of either the chronological or formula story is an excellent technique for a writer to use when he is confronted with the fact, in plotting a story, that the agonizing decision to be made is out of character. Here is another example of the use of the technique, taken from a story in a current magazine. The author faced a situation in which it would be completely out of character for the heroine to visit a man's home alone, knowing that she would be seduced by the man if she did. The minor decision she made was to accept an invitation from the man to attend what she believed to be a party where many other guests would be present. Upon arrival at the home of the man, she discovered that she had been tricked; there was no party or other guests. The minor decision made believable to the reader the agonizing decision she then had to make as to whether or not to let the man seduce her.

I Will Not Talk

by ANDREW MEISELS

1 Arpad Arpady stood on the brightly lighted stage in the theater and directed his gaze at the pretty girl in front of him. "Just look at the ruby," he said, pointing to the cheap piece of glass imbedded in the turban he wore. "Just look at the ruby, and very soon you will find yourself beginning to sway, back and forth, back and forth." The girl, her eyes fixed on the diadem, swayed back and forth as instructed.

2 "That's it," Arpady said softly. "You're moving very gracefully now. Just like a fish through the water. In fact," he informed her, "you are a fish." The girl began making pouting movements with her lips and did look, indeed, very much like a fish. The audience burst into laughter and applause.

3 "You are conscious of nothing but my voice. You hear nothing but my voice," Arpady intoned. "We are alone in a room, and you will obey me, as a dog obeys its master. For, of course, you are a dog." The girl got down on her hands and knees and began barking, to the audience's delight. "Why are you barking like a dog?" the hypnotist demanded. "You are not a dog, but a cat." At that, the girl instantly stopped her barking and started moving down the stage with the utmost grace, licking her shoulders as she went. This brought the house down, as it did every night.

4 A few moments later Arpady awakened the girl from the trance, being careful to remind her first that she was not a fish, nor a dog nor a cat, but an attractive young woman. A brief explanation of hypnosis concluded the show.

5 Colonel August von Struckel applauded along with the rest of the audience, not so much out of appreciation as from a

sense of duty. He had seen better hypnotists in Berlin, of course, and he was not much of a theater-goer. Colonel von Struckel was here on business.

6   As the lights went on, he motioned to three SS men sitting at the rear of the large auditorium. They rose at once and proceeded to Arpady's dressing-room, where they politely but firmly invited the hypnotist to a command performance at Gestapo headquarters. Arpady knew that such an invitation was not to be scorned. With as much good grace and calm as he could muster, he removed his turban, washed off his stage make-up and went with the men.

7   The grim-looking building at 60 Andrassy Ut could hardly inspire confidence in anyone who went through its portals. The building itself, as if knowing of its own reputation, appeared cold and uncaring, efficient, official, and perhaps even a little cruel. Many Hungarians had perished in the building, Arpady knew. Many others had been carried from it physical and mental wrecks, their bodies broken, their minds squeezed dry, their spirits beaten to death.

8   The tight-lipped SS men ushered Arpady inside the building, took him up the stairs and motioned him through two huge wood-paneled doors into a plushly carpeted office. Sitting behind a desk at the far end of the office was Colonel von Struckel, bending over a sheaf of papers and working studiously.

9   Arpady glanced quickly about the large room. A single lamp on the colonel's desk provided the only illumination. The windows were barred. It occurred to the hypnotist at once that all this was psychologically quite sound, that this atmosphere and this behavior would instill fear in any man. He had to admit that he was no exception.

10   The Hungarian stood there for what seemed like hours, fears and hopes crisscrossing through his mind. He'd heard of Von Struckel, and what he'd heard had not been good. How much did the man know? Perhaps he knew nothing at all. Perhaps he was just fishing. Perhaps it was another matter altogether.

11   At long last the colonel put the papers in a neat pile, closed his pen carefully and seemed to take notice of Arpady for the first time. Wordlessly he motioned the hypnotist into a chair, while he himself stood up and began pacing, fingering a riding crop. Tossing the crop nervously from one hand to another,

Von Struckel walked back and forth across the spacious office. Suddenly he stopped. "Herr Arpady," he said, "I will come directly to the point. We know what you've been up to."

12   "Well," said the hypnotist, forcing a smile, "in that case there's no problem." He made as if to rise from the chair.

13   "Sit down," roared Von Struckel. "You're not in the theater now, giving a performance." He moved back to the desk and glared menacingly at the Hungarian. "We know that you've been collaborating with the enemy. We know also that you have used your stage tricks to wheedle information out of some of our people. We know that you have managed to transmit this information to agents of the Allies."

14   "Where did you get all this?" asked Arpady, still flashing his best stage smile of mild amusement.

15   "What you want to know," the German said, "is how we found out. Madame Letitzer remembered some of the questions you asked when you hypnotized her at the Halasz cocktail party last week."

16   "Ah," sighed Arpady, the smile vanishing, "the light subject. The bane of the stage hypnotist. But"—he looked up at the colonel—"the information she gave me was correct?"

17   "Unfortunately, yes. What we want to know is what you did with this information, how you transmitted it to the enemy, and with whose help. We want names and places. And," he added with a smile, "you will give them to us."

18   "I doubt it, colonel," said the hypnotist.

19   "I do not. You might begin by telling me your real name. Arpad Arpady is for stage purposes, I assume."

20   "My real name is David Cohen."

21   The German lashed out at Arpady with the riding crop, cutting him across the arm. The hypnotist felt a sudden shock of pain, then he concentrated on the arm for a moment, and the pain subsided. He could do that type of self-hypnosis at will. The colonel didn't know it, but pain would not be a very effective weapon against him.

22   "Now then," Von Struckel continued. "Your real name is Lawrence Meszaros. But that is not important, Herr Arpady. Other names are important."

23   "You will not get those other names from me, Colonel von Struckel," he said calmly.

24   The German officer sat down at his desk and looked at the hypnotist almost benignly for a long moment. "You are no stranger to the will, Herr Arpady," he said at last. "Well, neither am I. You might say we are in the same line of work, but from different points of view. You are an artist. I am a scientist. You play with the will for the amusement of others. I break the will for the furtherance of our cause. To you the will is a toy. To me, it is a tool. Like all true artists, you work and stand alone. I, on the other hand, stand backed by the might of the greatest nation, the purest people, and the most powerful military machine the world has ever known."

25   "I know," said Arpady dryly, looking up at the colonel. "You are all supermen."

26   "But you are not," snapped Von Struckel. He surveyed the man before him, noting how much shorter he was than he had appeared on the stage, noting that he was beginning to paunch, noting that his black hair was graying at the temples. "Your will is not going to be hard to break," he said, pressing the button on his desk to summon his aides.

27   The cell in which Arpady found himself was little more than a small hole in the ground. The same three SS men who had called for him at the theater now followed him into the hole, closing the door behind them. Arpady noticed how bored they looked.

28   One of the men stepped up to Arpady and, with that same look of dull unconcern, hit him in the mouth, hard. The hypnotist fell back into the arms of another SS man. This one hit him in the groin and then kneed his jaw as he doubled over with pain. The rest of what happened Arpady could remember only dimly, through a haze of semiconsciousness.

29   When it was over, the hypnotist took stock. There were no bones broken. Blood was spurting from his mouth, but he could stop that by deciding that it would stop. There . . . he had stopped it. His face was a battered pulp, but it would heal. Fistfuls of hair had been torn from his head, but it would grow back. And he hadn't told them what they wanted to know. The tormentors returned again and again. They tore at Arpady's flesh. They beat it. They squeezed it. They mangled it. But his will remained intact, and Von Struckel began to realize that perhaps the usual methods would not work for this man.

30   Arpady looked into the bright light, and he was mildly amused. Three days he had been looking into that light and three nights, but if there was any strain on him from lack of sleep, it didn't show. It was, however, beginning to show on the colonel. "Talk, damn you. Talk or I'll tear your guts out," he snarled at the man lying on the makeshift cot with his arms tied back and his legs bound together.

31   Arpady remained silent, staring at the light above his head. The light was a favor, but Von Struckel couldn't know that. It fixed his attention and helped him concentrate. How funny it all was, Arpady thought. They were trying to break him by depriving him of sleep, a man who had spent twenty years learning the art of concentrated relaxation, the art of doing with a minimum of sleep. Von Struckel could have him there for a week before he would tire. The hypnotist felt like smiling, but he thought better of it.

32   "Talk, you swine," screamed the colonel. "Say something, anything."

33   But Arpady said nothing. He had shut out the colonel and the cell and the war. He was thinking of Helena, of how beautiful she had been, of their years together. It was a good thing she was dead. It was horrible even to think that, but it was true. This way they couldn't get to him through her.

34   History made strange heroes, he mused. For himself, he had never wanted anything but a comfortable living and a chance to perform. He'd never cared about politics one way or the other. But what do you do when politics begins to care about you? What do you do when it begins to dictate your life? What do you do when you see the woman you love first annoyed, then harassed, and finally hounded to her death because her grandparents had belonged to a faith that was not in keeping with the present politics? You have to do something.

35   "Hit him," shrieked the colonel. An SS man stepped up to Arpady and hit him full in the face twice with his clenched fist. A piece of tooth clicked to the floor. A small stream of blood trickled down the hypnotist's chin.

36   You have to do something, Arpady thought, so he did what he knew how to do. He had used his talent, his gift, to get bits of information. It was little enough but it was something.

37   "Out, out," Von Struckel shouted. "Get out." The three SS

men moved out the door, leaving the colonel alone with Arpady. The officer paced the cell nervously. "I don't understand you," he said. "I never thought you'd hold out this long."

38   "It's a matter of will, colonel," said the hypnotist, interrupting his musings.

39   "I can break you," grated Von Struckel angrily. "I can make you scream and beg for death. But"—he paused—"why should you die? Give me the information I seek, and you can go free."

40   Arpady chuckled. "Free, colonel? Nobody ever leaves here free except the dead."

41   "All right, all right," conceded the German, waving his arms. "So you won't go free. You'll go to a camp for a while. But you'll be alive. Think it over," he said, freeing Arpady's arms and legs. "Don't give me your answer right away. I'll be back tomorrow. Think it over."

42   The hypnotist rubbed his numb wrists and looked at Von Struckel. Beads of perspiration had formed on his small brow, and his clothes were sticking to his fat body. "You look worried, colonel," he said almost solicitously. "You must learn to relax." The officer looked at him long and hard. Then he walked out.

43   Arpady was being shaken. He opened his eyes, and it took him a moment to realize where he was. Glancing up, he saw Von Struckel standing in front of him, the familiar riding crop in his hand, and he knew where he was. "You slept almost twenty-four hours," said the German with a smile. "You must have been more tired than I thought. We should have continued the questioning." Arpady looked about him. He and the colonel were alone. Von Struckel was still smiling, and the hypnotist didn't like the smile.

44   "You could have continued all year," Arpady said, "I still won't tell you what you want to know."

45   "I wouldn't be so hasty," said Von Struckel, resuming his pacing. "When I first started with you, I knew I could get what I wanted. There is a key to every man's will. I've just been using the wrong set of keys."

46   "There is no right key."

47   "Oh, yes there is." The German stopped his pacing suddenly and stood facing the hypnotist. "I have learned that you have a daughter," he said.

48   Arpady stiffened, then checked himself almost instantly. He

hoped the colonel hadn't noticed. "I have no children," he said calmly. "I had a wife, but you took care of that."

49   "Yes, your wife, most unfortunate. A heart attack, I believe. I am sorry. Still, she was not of pure blood. Nor," he added, "is your daughter."

50   "I have no daughter," the hypnotist said dumbly.

51   Now it was the colonel's turn to be solicitous. "Come now," he said. "Shall we stop fencing?" He took a piece of paper from his pocket, put on his metal-rimmed glasses carefully and began reading. "Name: Anna Meszaros. Born: July 14, 1922, in Budapest. Sent to Paris in January, 1939. Was art student at Sorbonne until liberation of France. Now living with friends in Paris under the name of Anne Monsant." He looked up from the paper. "Shall I continue?"

52   Arpady had only so much control. In one movement he lunged up from the cot and grabbed for the German's throat. But the days and nights of torture had weakened him badly, and Von Struckel had little trouble knocking the small man to the floor.

53   He lay there for a time, pretending to be unconscious. But actually he was thinking, thinking of Anna and of the "key" Von Struckel had found. He got up finally and sat on the cot once again.

54   "What have you done to her?" he asked. There was no longer any point in pretending.

55   "Nothing—yet," said the colonel menacingly. "No one else even knows of this—yet. The connection between you and the apparently nonpolitical Anne Monsant has been well covered up. I was able to make the connection only by piecing together a whole series of harmless-looking documents and reports. If you give me the information I seek, no one need ever know." Arpady looked up at the officer, seeing the gloat of triumph in his face, and he could believe that no one else knew—yet Von Struckel was the kind of a man who liked to keep an ace in the hole and liked to keep it to himself. But he wondered how long and how far he could trust this man to keep the ace hidden.

56   "How can I be sure?" he asked.

57   "You have the word of a German officer," Von Struckel said indignantly.

58   Arpady sneered. "It will have to do."

388

59   "Now then." The colonel sat down. "I want the names of the agents you dealt with."

60   "I never knew their names," the hypnotist said. "I would go to a place in the country, their headquarters, and I would turn over whatever information I had. I never met the same man twice."

61   "Hm'm. Excellent," Von Struckel muttered. "Take us to this place."

62   Arpady nodded weakly. He had no choice now. "How long have I been here, colonel?"

62   "Three weeks."

64   "It seems like three years."

65   The colonel smiled. "You held out longer than most," he said, not without a note of grudging admiration in his voice.

66   "But not long enough," retorted Arpady sadly. "Is it day or night?"

67   "Night," Von Struckel informed him. "Nearly ten P.M."

68   "Good," Arpady said. "We can go tonight. We might as well get it over."

69   The German rattled the cell door several times, and the three SS men reappeared. They half-escorted and half-dragged the hypnotist up the stairs, pushed him into a bathroom, and threw him a set of fresh clothes.

70   It was while washing his face and hands for the first time in three weeks that Arpady got a glimpse of himself in the mirror. He could hardly recognize what he saw. His scraggly beard had come in white, and his skin was a pale yellow. The chubby face that had always appeared so boyish was gaunt and drawn now, and the deep-set eyes that had fascinated audiences for more than two decades were puffed up.

71   He looked at his hands, rendered useless by the thumb-screws. His legs, shaking miserably in the damp bathroom, were hardly able to support his emaciated body. He thought of Von Struckel, fat and rested. He thought of the SS men, big, hulking brutes in their pressed uniforms.

72   No man could hold out forever in the face of this scientific hacking away of the body to get at the will, he thought. There was no shame in breaking.

73   "Hurry up," bellowed the guard standing in the doorway. Arpady finished dressing and walked out.

389

74   The air pouring in through the open staff car was crisp and fresh. The air had never smelled so good to Arpady before, and he savored it.

75   "Are we on the right road? Are we on the right road?" screamed the colonel, grabbing Arpady's handcuffed hands beside him.

76   "We are on the right road," the hypnotist said softly, putting his hands back in his lap. "Really, colonel, you must learn to relax. I'd hate to have your blood pressure."

77   "We'd better be on the right road, or you won't have any blood pressure at all."

78   The SS man sitting at Arpady's left and the two up front laughed courteously at Von Struckel's bon mot.

79   "Now if I were you," Arpady continued, "I'd probably worry about that. But I am not you, and I choose not to worry. Instead, I choose to concentrate on beauty, which is always calm and relaxing."

80   Arpady threw his head back. "Look at the moon, colonel. You, too," he dug his elbow into the ribs of the man sitting at his left and brought his handcuffed hands down on the shoulder of the SS man sitting beside the driver. "You see," he smiled, "I am not afraid of you. I have nothing left to be afraid of. The moon is very beautiful," said Arpady softly. "You never realize how beautiful until it's taken away from you. How bright the moon is. It is worth noticing while there is time."

81   "Have you ever noticed, colonel," he went on, "how the moon is always racing with the clouds, but the clouds never touch it? Even when a cloud passes in front of the moon, you can always see the moon's luster through the cloud. A very relaxing thought, colonel. It shows that light can never be blocked, only dimmed, and even that only temporarily. See how the clouds pass and the moon shines?"

82   Except for the driver, they were all looking at the moon now, but if the Germans drew any lesson from its light they were quiet about it.

83   "Now this young man," said Arpady, tapping the shoulders of the driver. "This young man knows how to relax. See how he keeps his eyes glued to the road, turning his head neither to the left nor to the right, watching nothing but the rays of the

headlights as they play on the concrete. This young man knows how to relax. He'll go far, I assure you.

84   "Turn right here," Arpady said in the same breath. The staff car veered to the right at the crossroads and continued its journey into the night, three armored cars moving along behind it.

85   "From here on in you go straight," Arpady told the driver. "Keep your eyes on the road, but you'll find you won't even have to move the steering wheel from now on. You might put on a little speed," he added.

86   "If you don't mind," smiled the colonel, "I'm still in command."

87   "Ah, yes, colonel, always in command," Arpady said. "How wonderful it must be to be a superman."

88   "Your sarcasm is not amusing," snapped Von Struckel. "Slow down," he told the driver. The man at the wheel continued at the same speed. "Slow down," barked the colonel grabbing the man's shoulders. The driver's eyes remained on the road, his foot resting on the accelerator.

89   "Command him, superman," said Arpady, smiling. "Use your will. Surely it is stronger than mine."

90   The officer glanced quickly at the SS man beside Arpady. He was staring straight ahead, just like the driver. Von Struckel hit the head of the man sitting in front of him, knocking off his hat. "Make him slow down," he shouted. The man didn't move.

91   The colonel turned to Arpady, a wild look in his eyes. "Tell him to stop."

92   "No," said Arpady calmly.

93   "Tell him to stop," shouted Von Struckel, pulling his gun from its holster. "Tell him to stop or I'll kill you."

94   "Kill me, colonel?" the hypnotist smiled. "But you have killed me. You killed me in that cell at "60" Andrassy Ut, just as you have killed all love and all art and all beauty in your domain. You left me nothing but a little torn bit of loving, hating, thinking free mind. And that is more than enough to kill you with, superman."

95   Von Struckel looked at him desperately. "You will not kill yourself," he said. "No, you must be bluffing."

96   "How logical your mind is, colonel. How precise and in-

human. Well, here's a precise fact for you. In less than two kilometers there's a sharp curve in this road, and there we will see who is right—you with your overwhelming logic or me with the little scrap of dignity that tells me to die."

97   "Stop this car," Von Struckel screamed at the armored vehicle a few hundred feet behind them.

98   "They can't hear you, colonel," Arpady said softly. "It is only about a kilometer now."

99   "Shoot at the tires," bellowed the officer into the wind.

100   "Half a kilometer."

101   Von Struckel turned to the Hungarian beside him, a look of animal fear in his eyes. "Tell him to stop."

102   Arpady smiled. "I find I lack the will," he said as the car crashed through the guardrail and tumbled into the Danube below.

COMMENTARY ON "I WILL NOT TALK"

This suspense story was selected because the author employs the deviation of reversal of struggle discussed in Chapter Three. In the story, the antagonist, Colonel von Struckel, tries to take the honor of Arpady, the protagonist, away from him through torturing him and making him inform.

BASIC PLOT

The basic plot is conflict to eliminate an opponent so that the protagonist may solve his complication and reach a worthwhile goal. The opponent Arpady must eliminate is Colonel von Struckel, and all he symbolically stands for, in order to reach the worthwhile goal of maintaining the honor both of Arpady himself and all he symbolically stands for.

THEME

The story turns upon the nature of man's will. The author has seen that the will of a man can be so strong that it can lead him to endure inhuman punishment, the loss of loved ones, even the acceptance of death—if it is based upon respect and love for humanity and intangible values, such as beauty and freedom. Opposed to this use of the will in Arpady, there is the sort of will shown by Colonel von Struckel, which we can label a false use of will. The colonel's will depends upon a falsification of human freedom and human values and must express itself selfishly in the use of force. His carrying a riding whip symbolizes his necessity to force people to do his bidding. There are some curious ironies in the story: to have so strong a will as Arpady's, it is necessary to will that one would rather cease to exist than betray humanity. Arpady is actually using his own will to carry out the design the colonel has in store for him, but Arpady's will can never be enslaved, as is the colonel's. Though the theme is stated in paragraph 94, it tends, of course, to be much more inclusive since both Arpady and the colonel function as symbols of one of the world's deepest current problems, the will to live through love or to die through hatred. And it is significant that only Arpady can will both of these things. The colonel can will only to die through hatred. He is too self-involved to see that that is what he actually does, and the story's ending proves it.

COMPLICATION

The complication is certainly something unpleasant that happens to Arpady. Had he freedom of choice, he would not have chosen to be arrested by the Gestapo.

The complication is made more interesting than it would seem in real life through certain exaggerations. In real life, such physical tortures as Arpady underwent would not be necessary. The Gestapo employed much more scientific methods to obtain information from prisoners, such as truth drugs like sodium pentathol and brain-washing techniques (the playing of records over and over again while a prisoner slept), etc.

Arpady's minor complication is his arrest by the Gestapo. The author uses the principle of discovery and change to make the complication deeper. When Arpady, who believed the Gestapo had no evidence against him, discovers that Colonel von Struckel has evidence against him, which the German officer obtained from Madame Letitzer, he is forced to change his mind about his status. The complication is made more serious as Arpady undergoes torture to such a point that he begins to wonder if his will is strong enough to resist until he is killed. The important thing at stake, if he cannot resist torture, is his honor.

The author, again, uses discovery and change to make the complication so serious that there seems no hope of a satisfactory solution. Arpady discovers that Colonel von Struckel knows of the existence and whereabouts of his daughter, who is living in German-occupied Paris.

The agonizing decision Arpady is forced to make (the ante-climax) points to the solution. As a result of his decision, Arpady is to be driven in a staff car to the place he used to rendezvous with spies for the Allies. With the bright moonlight and the headlights of the car, Arpady is able to hypnotize the driver and two guards.

The complication is made believable to the reader through Colonel von Struckel's characterization as a cruel, sadistic Gestapo officer completely dedicated to the principles of the Nazis. It is believable that he would inflict such inhuman punishment upon an enemy of Hitler's Germany. Arpady's characterization as a hypnotist with an indomitable will makes it believable he could undergo such torture without breaking, and also makes it believable that he would be able to hypnotize the two guards and the driver of the staff car.

The reader participates vicariously in all the emotions the protagonist undergoes. Conflict is produced as Arpady attempts to resist torture and die with honor, and Von Struckel attempts to extract the information.

PLOT STRUCTURE

The story follows the plot structure of the formula story with the exception of the deviation of reversal of struggle.

BEGINNING (Paragraphs 1 through 32)

1. The beginning is placed in time as close to the ending as possible, with Arpady's arrest upon charges of collaborating with the enemy.
2. There are two scenes set in this story: a brief introductory scene with Arpady performing as a hypnotist and Colonel von Struckel watching; and the scene in Gestapo Headquarters in Berlin. The introductory scene is necessary to dramatize Arpady's powers as a hypnotist and hence to make believable his use of such abilities.
3. The principal characters are introduced with an indication of their approximate ages. Dual points of view are established. Although this is primarily Arpady's story the author shifts the point of view at times to Colonel von Struckel. The story lends itself to a study of a shift in viewpoint; for example, the shift of viewpoint in paragraph 5 that imparts information to the reader about Colonel von Struckel. Arpady would have had no way of knowing Von Struckel applauded "not so much out of appreciation as from a sense of duty"; he would have

had no way of knowing Von Struckel had "seen better hypnotists in Berlin, of course, and he was not much of a theater-goer"; he would have had no way of knowing Colonel von Struckel was there "on business." Again the viewpoint shifts to the German officer in paragraph 26, with the author characterizing the physical appearance of Arpady through Von Struckel. Nevertheless, the inexperienced writer is cautioned, once again, to stick to the single point of view until such time as he has gained the experience and ability to be able to shift the point of view consistently, as this well-known author has done.

4. The complication is presented with Arpady's arrest for collaborating with the enemy.
5. The reader knows from the nature of the prose he is reading a dramatic, suspenseful slick story.
6. The beginning implies what ending is desired. The reader knows that all slick stories are optimistic and that Arpady will somehow solve the complication to the reader's satisfaction.
7. The reader is trapped into reading the rest of the story by the narrative hook in paragraphs 28 through 32, in which Arpady undergoes torture. He reads on to find out if the hypnotist has the will to resist torture and die with honor.

MIDDLE (Paragraphs 33 through 73)

1. The background of circumstances that produced the complication is presented in paragraphs 33 and 34, as the reader learns why Arpady began collaborating with the Allies. This is an excellent example of how to tell the dullest part of the formula story in the quickest way. The reader is transported into the past in the memory of Arpady with the sentence, "History made strange heroes, he mused"; and in one short paragraph the circumstances that produced the complication are given.
2. Deviation: Paragraphs 35 through 42 present a series of attempts by the antagonist, Colonel von Struckel, to take away Arpady's honor by trying to get the hypnotist to inform through torture; these attempts meet with failure.
3. Deviation: A reversal of struggle in the situation of ante-climax is, therefore, presented in which it appears that the antagonist, Colonel von Struckel, is certain to get the information he wants. He has learned of Arpady's daughter and threatens her life. Thus, the reader is convinced that there is no way for Arpady to prevent his loss of honor without sacrificing his daughter's life. During his moment of truth, Arpady discovers that his love for his daughter is greater than his love of honor, and he must sacrifice his honor to save his daughter. In paragraph 53, the moment of truth is not stated, only implied.

395

4. Thus, Arpady makes the agonizing decision to inform in order to save his daughter's life, which points to the solution.

END (Paragraphs 74 through 102)

1. As a result of his agonizing decision, Arpady is to be driven to the place where he used to rendezvous with spies for the Allies. During the drive, he gets the idea of using the moon and the headlights of the car to hypnotize the driver and two guards. The solution is satisfactory to the reader because Arpady dies with honor and in so doing kills the cruel and sadistic SS men and Colonel von Struckel. The solution is made believable to the reader through Arpady's characterization as a hypnotist with an indomitable will and the fact that his will must be innately stronger than the wills of the colonel and his helpers.

The Casanova of
Kearny Street

by C. Y. LEE

1   Santos Beneto lived in a three room apartment across the hallway from mine, with a roommate known as Nightbird Tony, a bellboy in one of the swanky hotels on Nob Hill. Santos claimed he had been a colonel in the Filipino army during World War II, but hard luck had reduced him to the status of a cook in San Francisco. However, he enjoyed considerable fame as the Casanova of Kearny Street, although he was barely five four and by no means handsome. His great feat was his ability to date the most beautiful girls on Kearny without having to buy too many champagnes.

2   It was a great myth on Kearny why Santos, a man approaching forty, dark and short, and by no means a smooth talker, was so popular. Yes, he had a large diamond ring, a shiny gold watch, many suits of smart clothes, and a 1952 Cadillac convertible; but it was no secret that he shared the above items with Nightbird Tony, that they fully utilized this community property on their respective days-off, and that nobody was willing to bet a nickel on the authenticity of their diamonds.

3   Santos and I used to eat sotanghon manok, the hot spicy Filipino food, on Kearny. Our favorite restaurant was Palm Grove, consisting of a beer bar and a long, narrow dining room in the back, brightly-lighted, smoky and noisy, with sailors hitting and kicking the pinball machines in order to score more points. We went there mainly for the excellent, genuine Filipino

397

food. As for girls, Santos' favorite hunting ground was Hot Spot across the street, where only those with a measurement of 45-30-45 were allowed to work or "patronize"; those 50-40-50 ones were banished to the second-class places; as for those under 35-25-35, they had no place on Kearny at all, for the boys on Kearny hated nothing more than bone-bags and spare-ribs.

4   Santos' greatest rival on Kearny was a gambler and ex-lightweight boxer called Three-Eye Jack, who liked to toss insults around, especially when Santos was present. But Santos, the philosopher, quietly enjoyed the fact that Three-Eye Jack could seldom take any Hot Spot girl out without first spending a fortune on those pink drinks, at a dollar-a-shot, whereas he, a man of much smaller means, could do much better with half the money.

5   It was Santos' day-off. We had a pre-dinner beer at Palm Grove. Santos talked about a new Hot Spot girl by the name of Maria and declared his intention to conquer her in about three weeks' time. This was odd, because it never took him more than a week to conquer a girl. Then I learned that this Maria was indeed a hot plate; according to the boys, she had the most sexy voice, which, by God, sounded exactly like the chirping of a canary. There was a lot of betting in Palm Grove on who could take her out first. Santos said Three-Eye Jack had offered to bet him that he could not get a date from her even after buying her twenty champagne cocktails. He had considered the bet and had turned it down. "Have to work on her for a while," he told me excitedly over the beer. "You know why the skunk want to bet? He try to date her the other night. He buy her two dozen champagnes, and all he get is a lousy kiss on the forehead. No wonder he want to bet me a twenty, the skunk."

6   We ordered our dinner as we talked about Maria. Presently Three-Eye Jack arrived, followed by his secretary, a skinny man by the name of Regular. They took a booth not too far away from ours. "Damn," Santos mumbled, "now my meal is spoiled."

7   Three-Eye Jack was a dark, brawny fellow with a flat nose and a scar between his eyes, somewhat resembling a third eye. Some boys on Kearny seriously believed it was a third eye, an

X-ray eye at that, especially when he played poker. "Hey, Casanova," he said to Santos, "have a drink on me."

8   Santos had no objection to being called Casanova, but when Three-Eye Jack called him, there was always a tinge of sneering in his raucous voice. Santos pretended that he did not hear him, and Three-Eye Jack, never giving up, said much louder, "How about the bet, Casanova? Have you changed your mind yet?"

9   Santos filled his glass with beer and drank it. "What's the matter, Colonel?" Regular said. "Have you lost your nerve? Or have you lost the touch with dames?"

10   Again Santos ignored him. "I'll be fair with you, Casanova," Three-Eye Jack said. "I'll bet you two to one you can't even get Maria to see *80 Days Around the World*. How's that?"

11   "Forget it," Santos said, raising a hand casually.

12   "What's the matter, Colonel?" Regular said loudly. "You going to retire? If so, I'll campaign for the title."

13   There was some laughter, which indicated that Santos had already lost a great deal of prestige by refusing the bet. Presently I heard someone greet Tony, Santos' roommate. Santos began to look tense. I realized that he couldn't let his prestige be damaged in front of Tony, who admired him the way a boy admires Superman.

14   "Hey, Tony," someone in the dining hall yelled. "What's the matter with your hero tonight? He no more hot pants. He scared?"

15   Tony came to our table hurriedly. "What's wrong, Santos?"

16   "Ah, nothing. They want a bet."

17   "You want money?" Tony asked, reaching for his wallet. "I still have my paycheck, and plenty of cash."

18   "No," Santos said firmly.

19   Three-Eye Jack came to our table and tossed his wallet on the table. "Look here, Casanova, I've got more than two hundred in this wallet. Two to one you can't even get Maria into your damned convertible tonight. How's that?"

20   There was applause and laughter. Santos picked up his beer; for a moment I thought he was going to dash it into the gambler's face, but to my relief he lifted it to his mouth and took a long drink from it, then wiped his lips with a thumb and forefinger. "OK," he said calmly. "Dish out your cash, Tony; all of it."

21   Tony cleaned his wallet of bills. I also loaned him a ten, so Santos was able to bet fifty. Three-Eye Jack collected the money, counted out a hundred from his own wallet and handed the money to the bartender for safe-keeping. Santos ordered another round of beer and finished his dinner leisurely. When he left to make the date, some boys applauded him, and he acknowledged the applause by raising a hand casually at the door.

22   He returned from Hot Spot half an hour later, puffing on his big cigar and acknowledging people's greetings by waving a hand like Winston Churchill. "How you make out, Santos?" a friendly voice asked at the bar.

23   "Just wait and see," he said, coming to the booth.

24   "When are you going to meet her?" I asked anxiously.

25   He sat down and tapped his cigar on the lead ash tray. "She's meeting me in my car at eleven—in front of this joint." He took a puff on his cigar and added, "Tough, all right. In five minutes she down two champagnes. After six champagnes I get nervous. I have only a twenty left, so I use a bit of strategy. Can you loan me another ten?"

26   I gave him a ten and he quickly stuffed it into his pocket. Tony, who had drifted away to play the pinball machine, hurried back to the booth. "Did you make a date, Santos?"

27   "Yeah," Santos said.

28   "How much drink did you buy?"

29   "Three."

30   "Only three? Gee! How did you do it?"

31   Santos pointed at his head and said, "Use a little bit of this, that's all."

32   "Gee!" Tony said admiringly.

33   Three-Eye Jack came to the booth, closely followed by his secretary. "I hear you made a date, Casanova," he said with a sly smile. "Congratulations." Santos acknowledged it by raising a hand slightly.

34   "Here's to you, Colonel," Regular said, raising his glass, and taking a drink. "However, the boys and I will bet you a fifty she won't show up. Two to one, as before."

35   "Forget it," Santos said.

36   "Why don't you bet, Santos?" Tony said.

37   "I'm no damned gambler, that's why."

400

38   "Boys," Three-Eye Jack said to a few men at his table, "you are out of luck. You should have bet earlier, when his pants were hotter." The men laughed.

39   "Santos," Tony said, "why don't you bet with these skunks? I'll loan you my paycheck. You can make them eat their next meal at St. Antony's."

40   Santos shined his diamond ring with a thumb. "All right, Tony," he finally said, "dish it out."

41   Tony fished out his check and slammed it on the table. "OK, you jerks. Here's one hundred and twelve dollars. Two to one, don't you forget!"

42   "How much do you want to bet?" Three-Eye Jack said to his friends. "C'mon, the rest is mine."

43   Regular and three other men bet fifty. Three-Eye Jack wrote a check for the rest of the amount. "Hope the check can be honored," Tony said, collecting the money. Three-Eye Jack said something in the Filipino language and the men guffawed. At this moment a man named Music came in, jingling his keys and coins in a trouser pocket. He was thin and pale, looking very young despite his Spanish mustache. He came to Three-Eye Jack's table and winked. Three-Eye Jack nodded. "Guess what?" Music said, jingling a tune with his coins.

44   "Three Coins in the Fountain," Regular said.

45   "No. Doggie in the Window."

46   The boys laughed. "I have news for you, Three-Eye Jack," Tony was saying, still angry at the Filipino joke Three-Eye Jack had just told. "You're a washout and I won't tell you why. Tell me, when did you have your last date? 1930?"

47   "Just about, kiddo," Three-Eye Jack said. "That's when you came to this big wide world, and I'm not too proud of it." The boys laughed and Music jingled his coins, and did a fancy dance step. "Hey, Music," Three-Eye Jack said, "tell the gentlemen how you make out at Hot Spot."

48   "I make out fine, Jack," Music said. "I make a date with Maria. Some skunk offered her a twenty to meet him in his car at eleven. I offered her thirty. She is meeting me. She says no Casanova is worth ten bucks."

49   Santos pointed at Music and said to Three-Eye Jack. "How much you pay this queer for the job?" Music stopped jingling his coins and stepped up menacingly. "Say that again!"

50   "Calm down," Three-Eye Jack said quickly, putting a hand between them. "OK, I hired you, what's wrong with that? You proved a point—no Casanova is worth ten bucks. Now go get yourself a beer."

51   Music dusted his clothes as though he had just knocked somebody down. He went to get his beer, mumbling. Presently news got around and more people came into the dining room to wait for one of the greatest events on Kearny, arguing and betting. At ten to eleven, Tony went out to watch the door of the Hot Spot. He returned briefly to report that Music had parked his blue Oldsmobile half a block away from Hot Spot, across the street from Palm Grove.

52   At 11:10 Maria did not emerge. Getting impatient, some bettors drifted to the bar to personally watch the door of Hot Spot. Santos puffed on his cigar, his hand shaking slightly, and stole constant glances at his watch. It was not until 11:20 that the news broke out. Tony burst in and shouted, "Santos, she is crossing the street! She didn't even hesitate!"

53   Santos blew out some smoke like a long sigh. "Tony, go collect the money. And have a coupla drinks on me."

54   "Sure, Santos," Tony said, hurrying to the bar.

55   Puffing on his cigar, Santos started for the door. "C'mon," he said to me. I don't know why I followed him. At the door I thought, "Damned if I don't look like his secretary." I was sure that was exactly why he always wanted me to follow him around. When I got into the back seat of his Cadillac, I saw a sexpot with long black hair and a tight black dress coming toward the car. Santos blew the horn three times. She climbed in and promptly filled the car with lily-of-the-valley perfume. Under the strong street light I could see she was quite a dish, except for her slightly rotten teeth and her voice, which, by God, really chirped like a canary. She sat close to Santos and chirped, "Gimme the other half, honey."

56   Santos tried to hush her but she wouldn't listen; she demanded the other half. Santos started the car and fished out something that looked like a half twenty dollar bill, which Maria snatched and quickly stuffed into her brassiere. I was puzzled for a moment, then I realized that Santos must have cut a twenty dollar bill in two at the Hot Spot, given half of it to Maria and told her she could get the other half in his car.

57   "You know," Maria was chirping, "some other guy offered me thirty, but I come to you, honey."

58   "Sure," Santos said.

59   "You know," Maria said again, "a bird in the hand is better than ten in the tree."

60   Santos turned and asked me where I wanted to go. I said around the corner. He dropped me off around the corner. As I watched his car disappear into the night, I enviously wondered where he was taking her. Probably Samuel's Drive-in. That was the most logical place in San Francisco for a man to show off his Sophia Loren. And I thought, "No wonder the guy is so popular. He's got plenty of guts."

61   And he did, too.

COMMENTARY ON "THE CASANOVA OF KEARNY STREET"

This short story by the author of *The Flower Drum Song* is an excellent example of an off-beat, slick short story. The story not only violates the plot structure but it also violates the popular notions of romance found in the chronological and formula story.

Instead of presenting characters to us who clearly belong to a world which the majority of readers would like to emulate—advertising executives, lawyers, actors and actresses, private detectives, adventurers, etc.—the story presents characters who are just a shade above the underworld, who clearly lack the physical qualities of the usual romantic lead, and who engage in practices which, somewhat reprehensible, do not belong to the world of conventional romanticism. They are drinkers, gamesters, and women chasers. The story thus gives an off-beat portrait of romance, and its title suggests the ironic qualities of the story. For Santos clearly cannot capitalize upon his physical charms or his position in life to win the favors and attention of women: the women whom he chases serve more as a testimonial to his shrewdness and egotism than as romantically alluring figures; they have measurements and the same low scale of values that the men appear to have; and the romantic conquest is, in actuality, not a romantic conquest at all, but a solution of the complication facing Santos, purely in terms of his group's values.

Despite the fact, however, that the story explodes the popular notions of romance by giving us a middle-aged and not too dashing lover making his conquest through a bit of money, neither Santos nor his cronies are, in actuality, unsympathetic. The story seems to say: "Well, this is the way romance is here on Kearny Street—not up in the sky, not shrouded in mists of passionate feeling, pretty plain and perhaps a trifle mercenary—but at least it is the way we experience it." And the speculation of the narrator as to where Santos will go to "show off his Sophia Loren" somewhat testifies to the wistful egotism of both the narrator and Santos about the nature of their conquests, with a hint of true romance still lurking in their hearts.

The reader who wants to write off-beat stories can learn many techniques for doing so by carefully studying this story. The violation of the popular notions about romance should inspire anyone wanting to write off-beat fiction to try his hand at writing an off-beat story that violates some other popularly held notions, such as about mother love, virginity, honesty, good taste, ethics in business, etc.

The reader who wants to write off-beat stories will discover that a good many of them are told, as is this story, from the point of view of a minor character. To have told the story from Santos' viewpoint would have made both Santos and the story unbelievable. Instead, the author tells the story from the viewpoint of a hero-worshiper of Santos content to bask in the Casanova of Kearny Street's limelight. The author makes Santos and the story even more realistic by telling it in the first person. For practice, the reader should rewrite this story from the point of view of Santos. He will then discover how completely unrealistic both Santos and the story become. The right selection of point of view in the off-beat story is very important.

Violation of the plot structure of the chronological or formula story is a part of the technique of writing an off-beat story. This story, like all short stories, is based upon a complication. Santos' complication is that he will lose his title of being the Casanova of Kearny Street if he fails to get a date with Maria. In this particular story, Santos solves his complication. But note the following violations of the plot structures of the chronological and formula story:

There is no series of attempts by Santos to solve his complication, only for him to meet with failure.

There is no one final attempt by Santos to solve his complication only for him to meet with such disastrous failure that the reader is convinced that there is no hope for a satisfactory solution.

There is, therefore, no situation of ante-climax and no agonizing decision that will point to the solution. Without letting the reader or narrator know it, Santos gets Maria to keep a date with him by cutting a twenty dollar bill in two, giving her half of it, and promising her the other half if she will meet him. Here we have a violation of exposition because the author withholds information from the reader, in order to achieve his surprise ending.

The story is a good model to study for off-beat characterization. Santos, a man approaching forty, only five feet four inches tall, is not handsome and by no means a smooth talker, and yet he is cast as the romantic lead. Three-Eye Jack, Regular, Music are all off-beat characters.

In discussing the off-beat story, we stated that every writer would occasionally get an idea for a short story that cannot be plotted satisfactorily as a chronological or formula story. When this occurs the writer is on the verge of writing either an off-beat (or perhaps a quality story) and he should not harness his creativity by thinking of plotting in conventional terms. His major concern should be from which character's point of view the story will be most interesting and believable.

The Fly

by KATHERINE MANSFIELD

1   "Y'are very snug in here," piped old Mr. Woodifield, and he peered out of the great, green leather armchair by his friend the boss's desk as a baby peers out of its pram. His talk was over; it was time for him to be off. But he did not want to go. Since he had retired, since his . . . stroke, the wife and the girls kept him boxed up in the house every day of the week except Tuesday. On Tuesday he was dressed up and brushed and allowed to cut back to the City for the day. Though what he did there the wife and girls couldn't imagine. Made a nuisance of himself to his friends, they supposed. . . . Well, perhaps so. All the same, we cling to our last pleasures as the tree clings to its last leaves. So there sat old Woodifield, smoking a cigar and staring almost greedily at the boss, who rolled in his office chair, stout, rosy, five years older than he, and still going strong, still at the helm. It did one good to see him.

2   Wistfully, admiringly, the old voice added, "It's snug in here, upon my word!"

3   "Yes, it's comfortable enough," agreed the boss, and he flipped *The Financial Times* with a paper-knife. As a matter of fact he was proud of his room; he liked to have it admired, especially by old Woodifield. It gave him a feeling of deep, solid satisfaction to be planted there in the midst of it in full view of that frail old figure in the muffler.

4   "I've had it done up lately," he explained, as he had explained for the past—how many?—weeks. "New carpet," and he pointed to the bright red carpet with a pattern of large white rings. "New furniture," and he nodded towards the massive bookcase and the table with legs like twisted treacle. "Elec-

tric heating!" He waved almost exultantly towards the five transparent, pearly sausages glowing so softly in the tilted copper pan.

5   But he did not draw old Woodifield's attention to the photograph over the table of a grave-looking boy in uniform standing in one of those spectral photographers' parks with photographers' storm-clouds behind him. It was not new. It had been there for over six years.

6   "There was something I wanted to tell you," said old Woodifield, and his eyes grew dim remembering. "Now what was it? I had it in my mind when I started out this morning." His hands began to tremble, and patches of red showed above his beard.

7   Poor old chap, he's on his last pins, thought the boss. And, feeling kindly, he winked at the old man, and said jokingly, "I tell you what. I've got a little drop of something here that'll do you good before you go out into the cold again. It's beautiful stuff. It wouldn't hurt a child." He took a key off his watch-chain, unlocked a cupboard below his desk, and drew forth a dark, squat bottle. "That's the medicine," said he. "And the man from whom I got it told me on the strict Q.T. it came from the cellars at Windsor Castle."

8   Old Woodifield's mouth fell open at the sight. He couldn't have looked more surprised if the boss had produced a rabbit.

9   "It's whisky, ain't it?" he piped, feebly.

10   The boss turned the bottle and lovingly showed him the label. Whisky it was.

11   "D'you know," said he, peering up at the boss wonderingly, "they won't let me touch it at home." And he looked as though he was going to cry.

12   "Ah, that's where we know a bit more than the ladies," cried the boss, swooping across for two tumblers that stood on the table with the water-bottle, and pouring a generous finger into each. "Drink it down. It'll do you good. And don't put any water with it. It's sacrilege to tamper with stuff like this. Ah!" He tossed off his, pulled out his handkerchief, hastily wiped his moustaches, and cocked an eye at old Woodifield, who was rolling his in his chaps.

13   The old man swallowed, was silent a moment, and then said faintly, "It's nutty!"

14   But it warmed him; it crept into his chill old brain—he remembered.

15   "That was it," he said, heaving himself out of his chair. "I thought you'd like to know. The girls were in Belgium last week having a look at poor Reggie's grave, and they happened to come across your boy's. They're quite near each other, it seems."

16   Old Woodifield paused, but the boss made no reply. Only a quiver in his eyelids showed that he heard.

17   "The girls were delighted with the way the place is kept," piped the old voice. "Beautifully looked after. Couldn't be better if they were at home. You've not been across, have yer?"

18   "No, no!" For various reasons the boss had not been across.

19   "There's miles of it," quavered old Woodifield, "and it's all as neat as a garden. Flowers growing on all the graves. Nice broad paths." It was plain from his voice how much he liked a nice broad path.

20   The pause came again. Then the old man brightened wonderfully.

21   "D'you know what the hotel made the girls pay for a pot of jam?" he piped. "Ten francs! Robbery, I call it. It was a little pot, so Gertrude says, no bigger than a half-crown. And she hadn't taken more than a spoonful when they charged her ten francs. Gertrude brought the pot away with her to teach 'em a lesson. Quite right, too; it's trading on our feelings. They think because we're over there having a look around we're ready to pay anything. That's what it is." And he turned towards the door.

22   "Quite right, quite right!" cried the boss, though what was quite right he hadn't the least idea. He came round by his desk, followed the shuffling footsteps to the door, and saw the old fellow out. Woodifield was gone.

23   For a long moment the boss stayed, staring at nothing, while the grey-haired office messenger, watching him, dodged in and out of his cubbyhole like a dog that expects to be taken for a run. Then: "I'll see nobody for half an hour, Macey," said the boss. "Understand? Nobody at all."

24   "Very good, sir."

25   The door shut, the firm heavy steps recrossed the bright carpet, the fat body plumped down in the spring chair, and

leaning forward, the boss covered his face with his hands. He wanted, he intended, he had arranged to weep. . . .

26   It had been a terrible shock to him when old Woodifield sprang that remark upon him about the boy's grave. It was exactly as though the earth had opened and he had seen the boy lying there with Woodifield's girls staring down at him. For it was strange. Although over six years had passed away, the boss never thought of the boy except as lying unchanged, unblemished in his uniform, asleep for ever. "My son!" groaned the boss. But no tears came yet. In the past, in the first months and even years after the boy's death, he had only to say those words to be overcome by such grief that nothing short of a violent fit of weeping could relieve him. Time, he had declared then, he had told everybody, could make no difference. Other men perhaps might recover, might live their loss down, but not he. How was it possible? His boy was an only son. Ever since his birth the boss had worked at building up his business for him; it had no other meaning if it was not for the boy. Life itself had come to have no other meaning. How on earth could he have slaved, denied himself, kept going all those years without the promise for ever before him of the boy's stepping into his shoes and carrying on where he left off?

27   And that promise had been so near being fulfilled. The boy had been in the office learning the ropes for a year before the war. Every morning they had started off together; they had come back by the same train. And what congratulations he had received as the boy's father! No wonder; he had taken to it marvellously. As to his popularity with the staff, every man jack of them down to old Macey couldn't make enough of the boy. And he wasn't in the least spoilt. No, he was just his bright, natural self, with the right word for everybody, with that boyish look and his habit of saying, "Simply splendid!"

28   But all that was over and done with as though it never had been. The day had come when Macey had handed him the telegram that brought the whole place crashing about his head. "Deeply regret to inform you . . . ." And he had left the office a broken man, with his life in ruins.

29   Six years ago, six years . . . How quickly time passed! It might have happened yesterday. The boss took his hands from his face; he was puzzled. Something seemed to be wrong with

him. He wasn't feeling as he wanted to feel. He decided to get up and have a look at the boy's photograph. But it wasn't a favorite photograph of his; the expression was unnatural. It was cold, even stern-looking. The boy had never looked like that.

30   At that moment the boss noticed that a fly had fallen into his broad inkpot, and was trying feebly but desperately to clamber out again. Help! Help! said those struggling legs. But the sides of the inkpot were wet and slippery; it fell back again and began to swim. The boss took up a pen, picked the fly out of the ink, and shook it on to a piece of blotting-paper. For a fraction of a second it lay still on the dark patch that oozed round it. Then the front legs waved, took hold, and, pulling its small sodden body up it began the immense task of cleaning the ink from its wings. Over and under, over and under, went a leg along a wing, as the stone goes over and under the scythe. Then there was a pause, while the fly, seeming to stand on the tips of its toes, tried to expand first one wing and then the other. It succeeded at last, and, sitting down, it began, like a minute cat, to clean its face. Now one could imagine that the little front legs rubbed against each other lightly, joyfully. The horrible danger was over; it had escaped; it was ready for life again.

31   But just then the boss had an idea. He plunged his pen back into the ink, leaned his thick wrist on the blotting paper, and as the fly tried its wings down came a great heavy blot. What would it make of that? What indeed! The little beggar seemed absolutely cowed, stunned, and afraid to move because of what would happen next. But then, as if painfully, it dragged itself forward. The front legs waved, caught hold, and, more slowly this time, the task began from the beginning.

32   He's a plucky little devil, thought the boss, and he felt a real admiration for the fly's courage. That was the way to tackle things; that was the right spirit. Never say die; it was only a question of . . . But the fly had again finished its laborious task, and the boss had just time to refill his pen, to shake fair and square on the new-cleaned body yet another dark drop. What about it this time? A painful moment of suspense followed. But behold, the front legs were again waving; the boss felt a rush of relief. He leaned over the fly and said to it ten-

derly, "You artful little b . . ." And he actually had the brilliant notion of breathing on it to help the drying process. All the same, there was something timid and weak about its efforts now, and the boss decided that this time should be the last, as he dipped the pen into the inkpot.

33   It was. The last blot on the soaked blotting-paper, and the draggled fly lay in it and did not stir. The back legs were stuck to the body; the front legs were not to be seen.

34   "Come on," said the boss. "Look sharp!" And he stirred it with his pen—in vain. Nothing happened or was likely to happen. The fly was dead.

35   The boss lifted the corpse on the end of the paper-knife and flung it into the waste-paper basket. But such a grinding feeling of wretchedness seized him that he felt positively frightened. He started forward and pressed the bell for Macey.

36   "Bring me some fresh blotting-paper," he said, sternly, "and look sharp about it." And while the old dog padded away he fell to wondering what it was he had been thinking about before. What was it? It was . . . He took out his handkerchief and passed it inside his collar. For the life of him he could not remember.

COMMENTARY ON "THE FLY"

How far possible is it to escape from the traits of one's group? This famous short story by Katherine Mansfield raises and answers the question. For the story concerns old men, one of whom, Woodifield, reveals perfectly the group traits of old men—and the other of whom, the boss, has so far escaped from these traits that he can look condescendingly at Woodifield, seated before him, even though he is five years Woodifield's senior.

The story begins:

"Y'are very snug in here," piped old Mr. Woodifield, and he peered out of the great, green leather armchair by his friend the boss's desk as a baby peers out of its pram.

From the very beginning, Woodifield is seen with the general characteristics of the aged. His voice "pipes." He "peers" out of the armchair "as a baby peers out of its pram." He is ordered about by his wife and the girls who allow him to go to the City once a week, and then he "was dressed up and brushed and allowed to cut back to the City for the day." They suppose him a "nuisance" to other people. He is envious of the boss, who, though five years the elder, is "still going strong." Woodifield has something to say to the boss, but he cannot remember, and in the effort, his hands "began to tremble, and patches of red showed above his beard." The boss gives him a drop of whisky—poor old Woodifield's wife will not tolerate it at home— and then he remembers what it was he had wanted to say. He makes the remark about the grave of the boss's only son, wanders away from the sensitive subject to discuss quaveringly how beautifully the cemetery is kept up, and then deserts the question altogether with perceptible brightening, to discuss how "the girls" had been overcharged for a pot of jam on their trip. The mind of the aged veers off the subject of death—is it a natural refuge that the old mind takes to forget what must be so close, the body's end? Is there a kind of numbness, a chilling? Evidently, for the whisky "warmed him." And after the few plaintive remarks about the jam pot, old Woodifield "shuffles" from the office and is gone.

The writer of the quality story, as we have seen, very frequently presents the complication with which the story deals, by means of descriptive imagery, or by means of an example. The example once dealt with, it may have no further dramatic function, though a symbolic function may remain, and this is the case with Woodifield, who has served to give an entirely vivid picture of the generic old man, who has made some kind of compromise with the circumstances of life and death, albeit unwillingly, and who is now hanging onto the fringe of existence, savoring feebly and nostalgically its qualities and sinking slowly into oblivion.

The portrayal of Woodifield serves to intensify by contrast the manner in which the boss has, so far, escaped from the general characteristics of old age. He is "stout, rosy," and he is "still at the helm"; and the contrast with Woodifield serves to introduce the complication that the boss faces. Without the picture of Woodifield to heighten and suggest the norm, we would perhaps find it more difficult to understand the boss's escape from his particular age group. And we would certainly fail to see the one essential way in which the boss does retain a vigor and a vitality resembling the characteristics of a much younger man. What is the boss's complication? Put simply, it lies in his will, his energetic desire to escape the characteristics of his group. The crux is here: in his vanity, his self-assertiveness, his ambitious drive, rather than in any love he bears for his dead son. He is a vain man; he asserts himself against the nature of the world, which crushes and thwarts man's planning. He is, in essence, trying to play the role of God, who directs all human events.

Notice the ironic juxtapositions within the story between the boss's vanity and his latent recognition, frequently even unconscious admission, that he has suffered a crushing blow to his ambitions. He is proud of his office—he points out the new carpet, the new furniture, the electric heating—but he does not point to the picture of his son, for as we learn, "Ever since his birth the boss had worked at building up his business for him; it had no other meaning if it was not for the boy." The boss is proud of his own resiliency, his own comparative youth before the "frail old figure in the muffler." Yet at the same time, many years before, after having received the news of his son's death, he had "left the office a broken man, with his life in ruins." Yet he treats the old office messenger with asperity, and the "grey-haired office messenger, watching him, dodged in and out of his cubbyhole like a dog that expects to be taken for a run."

It is noteworthy, in this series of ironies, that the greatest irony of all lies in the way the boss has valued the memory of his son and the way in which he has wept for him. He has thought of the boy as "lying unchanged, unblemished in his uniform"—death has had no essential victory over the timeful human being—and this is deftly counterpoised against the violent fits of weeping that the boss has done for six years at every fresh remembrance of the boy. In effect, the tears are not for the son, but for the fact of change itself. They mask the driving egocentrism of the boss, a kind of Messianic complex which insists that "Time . . . could make no difference." And yet he thinks, "Other men perhaps might recover, might live their loss down, but not he."

In this presentation of ambivalence, Katherine Mansfield prepares us for the symbolic action that then takes place in the story. The boss rescues a fly from the inkpot, which he then proceeds to drown once more by successive drops of ink. The boss is the deity dispensing the inevitable blows of fate or of change. Yet at the same time, the boss sympathetically identifies himself with the fly: "He's a plucky little devil, thought the boss. . . ." As deity, he is aware of and fascinated by his own powers, the power of killing the fly. As fly, he is aware of and morbidly fascinated by the weakening efforts that he makes with each fresh deluge of ink—or with each fresh deluge of

413

tears until he finds, surprisingly enough, that he can no longer weep for his dead son. The fly's eventual death is the point of catharsis: as flies, not to wanton boys, but to the gods, who kill us for their sport. With this realization, the boss joins his contemporaries: he becomes old. He has faced the final mystery of existence, the puniness of his own powers, the inevitability of death. Vanity yields. There is a "grinding feeling of wretchedness . . ."—perhaps a slight stroke?—and then, after he sends for Macey, a momentary reflex assertion of authority, he falls to wondering what he had been thinking. Of all the traits that characterize old age, loss of memory is probably the most significant. And with the final statement, "For the life of him he could not remember," the boss is within the confines of the group that he has attempted to escape.

An interpretative commentary upon a story has its function, but we are not, here, concerned so much with the meaning of the story as we are with the devices the author has used in setting forth that meaning. The first method, which we have already mentioned, is characterization in terms of a group's general attributes. "The Fly" is a superb example of the way in which an author deals with an idea in terms of the general traits a given group possesses. But there is obviously more to the story than this. The question of structure and the use of the symbolic drowning of the fly need a word or two of comment.

To illustrate the various characteristics of the story's structure, let us first tell it in terms of chronology:

1. A businessman, very vital, self-assured, and energetic, has dedicated himself to his business ventures with great enthusiasm in order to hand a growing business on to his son.
2. His son is very popular with the employees, and this gives the man a strong sense of vanity.
3. He does not realize that his son's popularity may, in fact, be largely due to the fear his employees have of him.
4. The son goes to war, is killed, and the news crushes the father. It saps his zeal. What is the good of life if everything he has worked for has come to nothing?

Now it is worth pausing at this point of the story, for there is here a possibility—at least, considering the story as yet untold and merely being plotted—that the structure will move away from the pulp and slick handling into the approach of the quality story. It is a possibility at this point, one may remark, rather than an inevitability. Pulp and slick stories do handle the question of death as well as other serious subjects, degradation of character, violence, rape, abortion, childlessness, prostitution, dope addiction, and so on. What is primarily characteristic of the pulp and slick approach, however, is that the difficulty encountered is concrete and may be mastered, if the protagonist struggles. For the sake of illustration, let us plot the sequence of events that could possibly occur in the story in terms of a pulp or slick version—and if this sequence of events seems less valuable to a critic in terms of depth, reality, truthfulness, and so on, let him reflect that there is as much depth, reality, and truthfulness implicit in the comic approach to life as there is in the tragic. The only real argument for a critic lies in the esthetic values by which the story is realized, but these values are not a consideration in terms of working out the plot. Pulp and slick versions might develop the story, then, in terms of the following steps:

5. The boss is stunned by the loss of his only son. The loss is a direct blow to his conception of life.
6. He attempts, unsuccessfully, to rid himself of his sense of bewilderment, his sense of anguish, by trying to throw himself into work as a means of forgetting his hopes.
7. In driving himself to forget, he also drives his employees unmercifully, and he finally realizes that in requiring such devotion to himself, a harsh taskmaster, he is only exercising his power and vanity.
8. This moment of discovery leads to yet another discovery—how much of his drive for success has been based on the love of his son? How much on his own vanity?
9. As a result of these discoveries, he ceases to drive himself and others; the realization of his own vanity makes him more human.

Now, of course, the story outlined above is not Katherine Mansfield's story, and it is interesting to reflect upon the reasons. Perhaps the most important reason lies in the basic supposition that a man may see what he does and modify his behavior in terms of his vision— and this supposition follows the pulp-slick writer's viewing the complication as containing an obstacle that the protagonist may overcome. The pulp and slick writer will view the character as primarily conscious and aware, and as a consequence will not use a character who is so unaware that he will try to deny change and death. The quality writer, as we have noted, has adopted, as one of the essential ingredients of his artifice, the idea of the protagonist's blindness, his lack of awareness, his lack of consciousness. Thus, Katherine Mansfield views the complication as one that the protagonist is forced to accept as a part of his life. Hence, we move from the objectively sensible position shown by writers of pulp and slick stories that no one can prevent change or death to the relatively interesting proposition that, given sufficient unawareness, a man may try to prevent their inevitable course. Now let us return to the steps in the quality story and finish them as they actually appear in Katherine Mansfield's story:

5. Although the boss feels a loss of purpose in life through his son's death, the feeling is too superficial to overbalance his vanity. The death of the boss's son only momentarily crushes his ambition.
6. Years later, the vain drive is still there, and we can see the curiously elaborate fashion in which the boss prepares to weep afresh at a reminder of his son's death as one more illustration of his vanity. For his vanity hides the fact of change—"the boss never thought of the boy except as lying unchanged, unblemished in his uniform, asleep for ever"—his vanity obscures death, hides it, and, of course, nourishes his sense of superiority over old Woodifield. All things change except the boss for whom the laws of Nature have been suspended.
7. Hence in the inkpot and fly episode in the story—the boss as a God dispensing change and death, and the Boss as fly with a cherished sense of mortality—these ambivalences come into collision, and the boss becomes startlingly human by changing in front of our eyes.

Even though we have now reached the conclusion of Katherine Mansfield's story, we have not yet arrived at the structure of it. How has the author managed to tell the story so economically, so sparsely, and yet so vividly? It is noteworthy that in the steps of the story, so far as a chronological telling is concerned, old Woodifield is an entirely peripheral character. Indeed, in the chronological structure, he need not enter at all. Let us suppose that he entered when Katherine Mansfield realized that she must show how her main character differed from his associates. How best reveal that a protagonist does not conform to his group's pattern? One of the best ways is to make use of a dramatic foil, and hence in structure, "The Fly" follows that procedure of the writer who delays his complication—though eventually it is stated and resolved—in favor of descriptive detail, characterization, thematic statement, or incidents that imply the complication. (See Chapter Four.)

Woodifield functions to present the complication, but he also aids in several other ways in the story's structure, and perhaps we can discover these by analyzing the story in terms of the various structural steps that the author has utilized. There will be quite noteworthy variations in these steps from those of the formula story:

BEGINNING (Paragraphs 1 through 22)

1. The story's beginning is placed in time as close to the ending as possible, since with the entrance of old Woodifield we see that the boss has attempted, apparently successfully, to escape from his group's general character. Yet only moments after Woodifield has gone, the boss undergoes the change that makes him the same as his contemporaries.

2. The complication is strongly hinted at—that the boss is purposefully defying the laws of change and death through his vanity—but the author is more concerned to indicate the minor problem leading to the complication. The minor problem is the mention of the boss's dead son, a fact that he refuses to accept and yet over which he weeps. Here again, Woodifield is important since he presents the minor problem, and he reveals how a typical old man reacts to the subject of death. Thus, there is a delay in the stating of the complication.

3. Now if we consider the story closely, we will see that the author has foreshortened the structure of it by crowding some of the circumstances that would normally belong in the middle of the story—those circumstances that form the background of the complication—right in at the beginning. Though Woodifield would serve little function in a complication outline, in terms of the structure of the story he is extremely valuable: against his figure, we see the boss denying change; through him, we learn that the boss has been ambitious and successful; and Woodifield introduces the past event that has been so meaningful, the death of the boss's son. Now it is apparent that a part of the middle of this story has been condensed within the implicit contrasts between Woodifield and the boss. Let us return to the real complication of the story for a moment: the real complication is the boss's desire to play God in the face of inexorable change. As we have said, this real complication is hinted at in the contrasts between the two old men. What Woodifield does is to present the minor problem leading to the complication, the death of the boy, and by implicit, rather than explicit, means, he presents the complication itself. Since some of the middle of the story is presented at the very beginning, we observe that a further delay occurs in the explicit statement of the complication. For the mention of the dead boy leads to a recapitulation on the boss's part—not of the major dilemma he faces—but of the minor dilemma. Here certainly is the point at which we can put our finger on one of the quality writer's most significant approaches to character—that the protagonist through his blindness will confuse a minor with a major dilemma. The boss in this story is a tragic, rather than a linear, figure; he attempts to deny change; he struggles to deny change; and he fails. Yet at the same time, the attempt and struggle are not couched in

417

concrete terms, for then the boss would be like the pulp or slick protagonist, conscious of what he is doing and therefore aware of his major complication. In reality, the attempt and struggle are phrased in terms of the minor dilemma leading to the complication, and therefore we hold the figure in our minds as blind to his real difficulty. At no point in this story, in fact, does the boss become really conscious of his major complication, and hence the author prepares us for the way in which she hides from conscious awareness the facet of his character, his vanity, which is the real villain of the piece. One of the best ways to hide the complication is to place it within a symbol, and as do the characters in a good many of Katherine Mansfield's stories, the boss in this story enters into a symbolic action. He becomes a deity and he becomes a fly—that the character is capable of such extremes of viewpoint indicates his blindness to the fact that he can only be the fly.

4. The scene is set, and very skillfully, in the boss's office, for in this setting we can see the essential ambiguity of the boss's attitude: on the one hand, the driving ambition to succeed, and on the other the sense of having been crushed and overwhelmed by the news of the son's death, both emotional attitudes coalescing within the environment.

5. The point of view is established. Though this is the boss's story and he is the focus of interest, the story uses the device of concealed narrator B in paragraph 1. The author briefly enters the thoughts of old Woodifield, of Woodifield's family, makes a brief comment in which is stated an aspect of the complication of the story—"All the same, we cling to our last pleasures as the tree clings to its last leaves"—and then, in subsequent paragraphs, using concealed narrator A concentrates on telling the story from the boss's point of view.

MIDDLE (Paragraphs 23 through 34)

1. The middle of the story ordinarily gives the background of circumstances that produced the complication. Since the boss is unaware of the nature of his complication, and since the author has presented the complication only indirectly, the middle of the story must deal with the minor dilemma of which the boss is conscious. Hence paragraphs 23 through 29 give the background of the minor dilemma and make it more explicit than in the beginning. Here we see the boss attempting to weep afresh over the thought of his dead son, and his failure. He has, many times in the past, achieved some kind of catharsis by weeping, and here again, the minor dilemma points to the complication. The source of his vanity is implicit in his weeping. The boss uses his tears as an illustration that "time . . . could make no difference. Other men perhaps might recover, might live their loss down, but not he." In essence, we confront in these paragraphs (23 through 29) the

blindness of the boss to his complication. He is a sentimentalist who usurps unto his own ego the mode and function of the universe. He thinks that by once caring for someone, he necessarily has committed himself to perpetual grief. This is the denial of change leading to the symbolic presentation of the complication.

2. After having made, then, an attempt once more to weep, and after having failed, the boss should, we suppose, be brought to confront the true complication. But this does not happen. Since the boss has been unaware of the real complication that faces him, he can only be perplexed that his feelings have changed. He no longer feels the same way as formerly. Ordinarily, at this point in the story, the protagonist will face an ante-climactic situation, and since the story has a tragic rather than comic curve, he must be made to appear to solve the complication completely only to have something with which he cannot cope trip him up. Interestingly enough, the ante-climactic situation states the main complication and continues, since it is oblique and buried within symbolism, to hide from the boss himself what he has been doing, what the real complication is he faces. The apprentice writer might, therefore, learn from this story that an effective use of symbolic action may occur when a character, blind to his real dilemma, involves himself in the minor dilemma, leading to the complication, changes toward the minor dilemma since it no longer seems to be a dilemma, and still blind to his main complication, acts out a completely unconscious role through the symbolic statement of the complication. Thus, the symbol has a literalness within the story in terms of action, as well as a figurative quality that captures and condenses brilliantly the complication that the boss never realizes.

3. Now since the boss does not truly see what complication he faces, he can make no decision concerning it. The only decision that he can make is in terms of the role he temporarily plays within the symbolic act. His decision to drown the fly with successive drops of ink points to the resolution of the complication, since in playing the role of the deity, he discovers that he has the power to cause death and change, but that he does not have the power to bring the fly back to life. Katherine Mansfield could have used a series of real actions, rather than one symbolic situation, as a means of delineating the inevitable changes that occur in the boss as he grows older. But the lapse of time would have an effect of obscuring the ironic twist of affairs that occur within the symbol: the boss plays the role of deity to the hapless fly and discovers his own terrible mortality. And again, to have detailed the changes occurring in the boss in a much looser chronology would have made it difficult to bring his vanity into confrontation with any event that would put in proper perspective the vanity of mortal man attempting to assume the majesty and power of universal forces.

END (Paragraphs 35 and 36)

1. The story ends with the boss facing his moment of truth. With the death of the fly—with an instance of mortality that resists change and then must yield to it, no matter how plucky the fly is—the boss confronts a complication that no matter how hard he may struggle, he must nevertheless accept as a part of life. How thoroughly conscious his moment of truth is to himself, how clearly he can see his complication, is a matter of debate. It would appear from the way Katherine Mansfield states the conclusion that the boss retains his essential blindness.

Hence to describe briefly the way in which this story reveals itself as literature, we may note the following:

1. The tightening and economy of structure in which a dramatic foil is used to present the minor and major complications that the protagonist faces, and the use of a symbolic action that will serve the place of a chronological unfolding of literal events.
2. The theme, which underlies the story, that asserts that obviously the human will is insufficient to prevent change, and yet that, nevertheless, some human beings, like the boss, who are incapable of preventing vanity from controlling their actions, are quite unable to accept this fact. Thus, the complication moves outside the power of the protagonist to resolve it.
3. The suggestion of unwilled circumstance that acts upon the blind and powerless individual.
4. The movement of the story into a man's mind—even considering that mind as almost literally a physical thing.
6. The avoidance of the unessential: the author has visualized her material almost perfectly; there is hardly an excess word.

Mac's Masterpiece

by FRANK O'CONNOR

1   Two or three times a year Mac, a teacher in the monks' school, took to his bed for four or five days. That was understood. But when he gave up taking food his landlady thought it was getting serious. She told his friends she wanted to have him certified. Not another day would she keep him in the house after the abominable language he had used to her.

2   His friends, Boyd, Devane and Corbett, came. Mac refused to open the bedroom door. He asked to be allowed to die in peace. It was only when Boyd took a hatchet to the lock that he appeared in his nightshirt, haggard and distraught, a big, melancholy mountain of a man, dribbling, his hair in tumult.

3   "Almighty God!" he cried. "Won't I even be allowed that one little comfort?"

4   They wrapped him in blankets and set him by the fire among his discarded toys, his dumb-bells, chest-developers, Indian clubs, sabers, shot-guns, camera, cinema, gramophone and piano, while Corbett, the bright young man from the local newspaper, heated the water for the punch. At this Mac came to himself a little and insulted Boyd. Boyd was his foil; a narrow-chested, consumptive-looking chemist with a loud voice and a yapping laugh like a fox's bark. He wore a bowler-hat at various extraordinary angles and was very disputatious.

5   "Bad luck to you!" growled Boyd. "I don't believe there's anything up with you."

6   "Nothing up with me!" jeered Mac. "Devane, did you hear that? You know, Devane, that hog, unless you had a broken neck or a broken bottom, he'd say there was nothing up with you. He'd say there was nothing up with Othello or Hamlet.

'Nothing up with you!' Did anybody ever hear such a barbarous locution?"

7   "Come on away, Corbett," said Boyd angrily. "We might have known the old cod was only play-acting as usual."

8   "Don't rouse me now," said Mac with quiet scorn.

9   "Like an old actress when she's going off, pretending her jewelry is stolen."

10   "I won't be roused," said Mac earnestly. "What's that Lear says—'No, I'll not weep, this heart shall crack. . . .' You Philistine, you Christian Brothers' brat, you low, porter-drinking sot," he snarled with sudden violence, "I have a soul above disputing with you. . . . Devane," he added mournfully, "you understand me. You have a grand Byronian soul."

11   "I have nervous dyspepsia," groaned Devane, who was organist in the parish church. He felt himself in two or three places. "I get terrible pains here and here."

12   "I see you now as I saw you twenty years ago with the fire of genius in your eyes," Mac went on. "And now, God help you, you go about the streets as though you were making a living by collecting lost hairpins."

13   Devane refused punch. It made his stomach worse, he said.

14   "You're better off," said Mac, falling serious once more. "I say you're better off. You see your misery plain. You're only a little maggot yourself now, a measly little maggot of a man, hoping the Almighty God won't crush you too soon, but you're a consistent maggot, a maggot by night and by day. But in my dreams I'm still a king, and then comes the awakening, the horror, the gray dawn."

15   He shuddered, wrapped in his blanket. Corbett rose and began to fiddle with the gramophone.

16   "Don't break that machine," said Mac irritably. "It cost a lot."

17   "What you want is a wife," said Corbett. "All those gadgets are only substitute wives. Did you ever get an hour's real pleasure out of any of them? I bet you never play that gramophone."

18   "You have a low mind, Corbett," snarled Mac. "You impute the basest motives to everyone."

19   At that very moment Corbett placed the needle on the record. There was a startling series of cracks and then it began to give

off *La Donna e Mobile*. Mac jumped up as though he had been shot.

20   "Oh God, not that, not that! Turn it off! There, you've done it now."

21   "What?" asked Corbett innocently.

22   "Sunlight on the Mediterranean, moonlight on the Swiss lakes, the glowworms in the grass, young love, hope, passion."

23   He began to stride up and down the room, swinging his blanket like a toga.

24   "The last time I heard that"—he stretched out his arm in a wild gesture—" 'twas in Galway on a rainy night. Galway in the rain and the statue of O'Conaire in the Park and the long western faces like—like bullocks. There they were over the roulette-tables, counting out their coppers; they had big cloth purses. Then suddenly, the way-you-may-call-it organ began . . . Magic, by God, magic! It mounted and mounted and you knew by the shudder down your spine that 'twas all on fire; a sort of—a sort of pyramid—that's it!—a pyramid of light over your head. Turning and turning, faster and faster, the pyramid, I mean, and the lights crackling and changing; blue, red, orange. Man, I rushed back to the hotel, fearing something would spoil it on me. The last light was setting over the church tower, woodbine-colored light and a black knot of weeping cloud."

25   "Bravo, Mac!" said Boyd with his coarse laugh. He stuck his thumbs into the armholes of his waistcoat. "The old warrior is himself again. Haw?"

26   "Until the next time," said Corbett with a sneer.

27   "There'll be no next time," said Mac solemnly. "I'm after being down to hell and coming back. I see it all now. The Celtic mist is gone. I see it all clear before me in the Latin light."

28   And sure enough there was a change in Mac's behavior. He almost gave up drink and began to talk of the necessity for solitude. Solitude, he said, was the mind's true home. Solitude filled the cistern; company emptied it. He would stay at home and read or think. He began to talk of a vast novel on the subject of the clash between idealism and materialism in the Irish soul.

29   But the discipline was a hard one. Though he told the maid

423

to say he was out, he hated to hear the voices of Boyd or Corbett as they went off together down the quay. One evening as they were moving away he knocked at the window and raised the blind, looking out at them and nodding. He tried to assume a superior, amused air, but there was wistfulness in his eyes. Finally he raised the window.

30   "Come on out, man!" said Boyd scornfully.

31   "No, no, I couldn't," replied Mac weakly.

32   " 'Tis a lovely night."

33   "What way did ye come?"

34   "Down High Street. All the shawlies were out singing. Look, 'tis a gorgeous night. Stars! Millions of them!"

35   Softly in a wheezy tenor Boyd sang *Night of Stars and Night of Love* with declamatory gestures. Mac's resolution wavered.

36   "Come on in for a minute."

37   They climbed over the low sill, Boyd still singing and gesturing. As usual, he had an interesting item of news for Mac. The latest scandal; piping hot; another piece of jobbery perpetrated by a religious secret society. Mac groaned.

38   "My God, 'tis awful," he agreed. " 'Tis, do you know what it is, 'tis scandalous."

39   "Well, isn't that what we were always looking for?" exclaimed Boyd, shaking his fist truculently. "Government by our own? Now we have it. Government by the gunmen and the priests and the secret societies."

40   " 'Tis our own fault," said Mac gloomily.

41   "How so-a?"

42   " 'Tis our own fault. We're the intellect of the country and what good are we? None. Do we ever protest? No. All we do is live in burrows and growl at all the things we find wrong."

43   "And what else can we do? A handful of us?"

44   "Thousands of us."

45   "A handful! How long would I keep me business if I said or did what I thought was right? I make two hundred a year out of parish priests with indigestion. Man, dear, is there one man, one man in this whole town can call his soul his own?"

46   "You're all wrong," said Mac crossly, his face going into a thousand wrinkles.

47   "Is there one man?" shouted Boyd with lifted finger.

48   "Bogy men!" said Mac, "that's all that frightens ye. Bogy

424

men! If we were in earnest all that tangle of circumstance would melt away."

49 "Oh, melt away, melt away? Would it, indeed?"

50 "Of course it would. The human will can achieve anything. The will is the divine faculty in man."

51 "This is a new theology."

52 " 'Tisn't theology at all; 'tis common sense. Let me alone now; I thought all this out long ago. The only obstacles we ever see are in ourselves."

53 "Ah, what nonsense are you talking? How are they in ourselves?"

54 "When the will is diseased, it creates obstacles where they never existed."

55 "Answer me," bawled Boyd, spitting into the fire. "Answer my question. Answer it now and let Corbett hear you. How are the obstacles in ourselves? Can a blind man paint a picture, can he? Can a cripple run the thousand yards? Haw?"

56 "Boyd," said Mac with a fastidious shudder, "you have a very coarse mind."

57 "I have a very realistic mind."

58 "You have a very coarse mind; you have the mind of a Christian Brothers' boy. But if you persist in that—that unpleasant strain, I'm more ready to believe that a blind man can paint a picture than that a normal, healthy man can be crippled from birth by a tangle of irrelevant circumstances."

59 "Circumstances are never irrelevant."

60 "Between the conception and the achievement all circumstances are irrelevant."

61 "You don't believe in matther? Isn't that what it all comes to?"

62 "That has nothing to do with it."

63 "Do you or do you not believe in matther?" repeated Boyd, throwing his bowler viciously on to the floor.

64 "I believe in the human will," snapped Mac.

65 "That means you don't believe in life."

66 "Not as you see it."

67 "Because I believe in life," said Boyd, his lantern jaw working sideways. "I believe that in all the life about me a divine purpose is working itself out."

68   "Oh, God," groaned Mac. "Animal stagnation! Chewing the cud! The City Council! Wolfe Tone Street! Divine purpose, my sweet God! Don't you see, you maggot, you clodhopper, you corner boy, that life can't be directed from outside? If there is a divine purpose—I don't know whether there is or not—it can only express itself through some human agency; and how the devil can you have a human agency if you haven't the individual soul, the man representing humanity? Do you think institutions, poetry, painting, the Roman Empire, were created by maggots and clodhoppers? Do you? Do you? Do you?"

69   Just then there was a ring at the door and Devane came in, looking more than ever like a collector of lost hairpins.

70   "How are you, Devane?" asked Corbett.

71   "Rotten," said Devane.

72   "I never saw you any other way," growled Mac.

73   "I never am any other way," replied Devane.

74   "You're just in time," said Corbett.

75   "How so-a?"

76   "We're getting the will versus determinism; 'tis gorgeous. Go on, Mac. You were talking about the Roman Empire."

77   Mac suddenly threw himself into a chair, covering his face with his hands.

78   "My God, my God," he groaned softly between his fingers. "I'm at it again. I'm fifty-four years of age and I'm talking about the human will. A man whose life is over talking about the will. Go away and let me write me novel. For God's sake let me do one little thing before I die."

79   After that night Mac worked harder than ever. He talked a great deal about his novel. The secret of the Irish soul, he had discovered, was the conflict between the ideal and the reality.

80   Boyd, with whom he discussed it one night when they met accidentally, disputed this as he disputed everything.

81   "Idealism, my eye!" he said scornfully. "The secret is bloody hypocrisy."

82   "No, Boyd," protested Mac. "You have a mind utterly without refinement. Hypocrisy is a noble and enlightened vice; 'tis far beyond the capacity of the people of this country. The English have been called hypocritical. Now, nobody could ever talk about the hypocritical Gael. The English had their walled cities, their castles, their artillery, as the price of their hypoc-

426

risy; all the unfortunate gulls of Irishmen ever got out of their self-deception was a ragged cloak and a bed in a wood."

83   "And is that what you're going to say in your novel?"

84   "I'm going to say lots of things in my novel."

85   "You'd better mind yourself."

86   "I'm going to tell the truth at last. I'm going to show that what's wrong with all of you people is your inability to reconcile the debauched sentimentalism of your ideals with the disorderly materialism of your lives."

87   "What?" Boyd stopped dead, hands in his pockets, head forward. "Are you calling me a sentimentalist?"

88   "I'm only speaking generally."

89   "Are you calling me a sentimentalist?"

90   "I'm not referring to you at all."

91   "Because I'm no sentimentalist. I'm a realist."

92   "You're a disappointed idealist like all the rest, that's what you are."

93   "A disappointed idealist? How do you make that out?"

94   "Boyd, I see ye all now quite clearly. I see ye as if I was looking at ye from eternity. I see what's wrong with ye. Ye aim too high. Ye hitch yeer wagon to too many bloody stars at the one time. Then comes the first snag and the first compromise. After that ye begin to sink, sink, sink, till ye're tied hand and foot, till ye even deny the human soul."

95   "Are you back to that again? Are you denying the existence of matther again?"

96   "Materialist! Shabby little materialist, with your sentimental dreams. I see ye all there with yeer heads tied to yeer knees, pretending 'tis circumstance and 'tis nothing only the ropes ye spin out of yeer own guts."

97   Boyd was furious. It was bad enough to have Mac dodging him, telling the maid to say he was out, forcing him to spend long, lonely evenings; but then to call him a sentimentalist, a materialist, a disappointed idealist! In fact, all Mac's friends resented the new state of things. They jeered at the tidy way he now dressed himself. They jeered at the young woman with whom he was seen taking tea at the Ambassadors'.

98   Elsie Deignan was a pretty young woman of thirty-two or -three. She was a teacher in the nuns' school in the South Parish and had literary leanings. As a result of her experiences with

the nuns, she was slightly tinged with anticlericalism. For the first time in his life Mac felt he had met a woman whose conversation he might conceivably tolerate over an extended period. He fell badly in love.

99   The resentment of Mac's friends grew when he was seen walking out with her. And there were strange stories in circulation about the things he was saying in his novel. They were all going into it, and in a ridiculous fashion. They were pleased when Corbett told them that Mac's employers, the monks, were getting uneasy, too. Mac knew far too much about the Order. He had often referred scornfully to the disparity between their professions and their practice; was it possible that he was revealing all this? Corbett swore he was; he also said that one chapter described the initiation of a young man into the Knights of Columbanus, skulls, cowls, blindfolding, oaths and all.

100   "I suppose he thinks he'll be able to retire on the proceeds of it," said Boyd in disgust. "The English will lap that up. I hate a man that fouls his own nest."

101   "Well, don't we all?" groaned Devane, who alone of the gang was disposed to be merciful.

102   "That's different," said Boyd. "We can say things like that among ourselves, in the family, so to speak, but we don't want everyone to know about it."

103   "He showed me a couple of chapters," said Devane mournfully. "I didn't see anything at all in it. Sentimental stuff, that's how it looked to me."

104   "Ah, but you didn't see the big scenes," said Corbett. "And for a good reason."

105   "What reason?"

106   "There are several nasty things about you in it."

107   "He couldn't say anything about me," said Devane.

108   "That's all you know."

109   "By God," said Boyd, "he deserves all he gets. If there's anything worse than a man using his friends for copy, I don't know what it is."

110   Devane, perturbed, slipped away. After a good deal of thought he went along the quays to Mac's lodgings, his head down, his umbrella hanging over his joined hands, a picture of misery. Mac was busy and cheerful. Sheets of foolscap littered the table. He had been drinking tea.

111   "So you're still at it," said **Devane.**

112   "Still at it."

113   "You're a brave man."

114   "How so?"

115   "All the dovecots you're after putting a-flutter."

116   "What the hell are you talking about?"

117   "I hear the monks are very uneasy."

118   "About my novel?" asked Mac with a start.

119   "Yes."

120   "How did they get to hear of it?"

121   "How do I know? Corbett says they were talking to the Canon about you."

122   Mac grew pale.

123   "Who's spreading stories about me?"

124   "I don't know, I tell you. What did you say about me?"

125   "I said nothing about you."

126   "You'd better not. You'll cause trouble enough."

127   "Sure, I'm not saying anything about anybody," said Mac, his face beginning to twitch.

128   "Well, they think you are."

129   "My God, there's a hole to work in." Mac suddenly sat back, haggard, his hands spread wide before him. "By God, I have a good mind to roast them all. And I didn't get to the serious part at all yet. That's only a description of his childhood."

130   "I didn't see anything wrong with it—what you showed me," said Devane, rubbing his nose.

131   "By God, I have," repeated Mac passionately, "a thorough good mind to roast them."

132   "You're too old," said Devane, and his metallic voice sounded like the spinning of a rattle. "Why don't you have sense? I used to want to be a musician one time. I don't want anything now only to live till I get me pension. You ought to have sense," he went on in a still crankier tone. "Don't you know they'll all round on you, like they did on me the time I got the organ?"

133   " 'Tis the curse of the tribe," declared Mac despairingly. "They hate to see anyone separating himself from the tribe."

134   "I don't know what it is," said Devane, "and I don't give a damn. I used to be trying to think out explanations, too, one time, but I gave it up. What's the use when you can read Jane Austen? Read Jane Austen, MacCarthy, she's grand and con-

soling, and there isn't a line in her that would remind you of anything at all. I like Jane Austen and Trollope, and I like Rameau and Lully and Scarlatti, and I'd like Bach too if he was satisfied with writing nice little dance-tunes instead of bloody big elephants of Masses that put you in mind of your last end."

135   Devane left Mac very depressed. The news about the novel had spread. People discussed it everywhere; his enemies said they had never expected anything else from him; his friends were uneasy and went about asking if they shouldn't, as old friends of Mac's, advise him. They didn't, and as a result the scandal only spread farther.

136   With Elsie, Mac permitted himself to rage.

137   "By God, I will roast them now," he said. "I'm going to change the whole center part of the book. I see now where I went wrong. My idea was to show the struggle in a man's soul between idealism and materialism; you know, the Celtic streak, soaring dreams, 'the singing masons building roofs of gold', the quest of the absolute; and then show how 'tis dragged down by the mean little everyday nature of the Celt; the mean, vain, money-grubbing, twisty little nature that kept him from ever doing anything in the world only suffer and twist and whine. But now I see a bigger theme emerging; the struggle with the primitive world—colossal!"

138   "You're marvelous," said Elsie. "How do you think of it all?"

139   "Because I'm it," said Mac vehemently. "I am the Celt. I feel it in my blood. The Celts are only emerging into civilization. I and people like me are the forerunners. We feel the whole conflict of the nation in ourselves; the individual soul and at the same time the sense of the tribe; the Latin pride and the primitive desire to merge ourselves in the crowd. I can see how 'twill go. My fellow will have to sink himself time and time again, and then at last the trumpet call! His great moment has come. He must say farewell to the old world and stand up, erect and defiant."

140   Still, Mac found his novel heavy going. It wasn't that ideas didn't come to him; he had too many, but always there was the sense of a hundred malicious faces peering over his shoulder; the Canon and Corbett; Devane, Cronin, Boyd; the headmaster.

141   Then one evening the maid came to his room.

142   "Oh, by the way, Mr. MacCarthy, the Canon called looking for you."

143   "Oh, did he?" said Mac, but his heart missed a beat.

144   "He said he'd call back another time."

145   "Did he say what he wanted?"

146   "No, Mr. MacCarthy, but he seemed a bit worried."

147   The pages he had written formed a blur before Mac's eyes. He could not write. Instead he put on his hat and went up to Elsie's.

148   " 'Tis all up," he said.

149   "What?" she asked.

150   "Everything. Turned out on the roadside at my age to earn my living what way I can."

151   "Do you mean you're sacked?"

152   "No, but I will be. 'Tis only a matter of days. The Canon called to see me. He never called to see me before. But I don't care. Let them throw me out. I'll starve, but I'll show them up."

153   "You're exaggerating, Dan. Sure, you didn't do anything at all yet."

154   "No, but they know what I can do. They're afraid of me. They see the end of their world is coming."

155   "But did anything else happen? Are you guessing all this or did somebody tell you?"

156   "I only wish to God I did it thirty years ago," said Mac, striding moodily about the room. "That was the time when I was young and strong and passionate. But I'm not afraid of them. I may be a fallen giant, but I'm still a giant. They can destroy me, but I'll pull their damn' temple about their ears, the way Samson did. It's you I'm sorry for, girl. I didn't know I was bringing you into this."

157   "I'm not afraid," she said.

158   "Ah, I'm a broken man, a broken man. Ten years ago I could have given you something to be proud of. I had genius then."

159   After leaving her he called at Dolan's for a drink. Corbett and some of the others were there and Mac felt the necessity for further information. He resolved to get it by bluff. He'd show them just what he thought of all the pother.

160   "I hear the Church is going to strike," he said with a cynical laugh.

161   "Did you hear that, too?" exclaimed Corbett.

162   "So you know?"

163   "Only that old Brother Reilly was supposed to be up complaining of you to the Canon."

164   "Aha! So that's it, is it?"

165   "I hope to goodness it won't be anything serious," said Corbett despondently.

166   "Oh, I don't care. I won't starve."

167   "You're a bloody fool," said Cronin, the fat painter who had done the Stations of the Cross for the new parish church. "Don't you know damn' well you won't get another job?"

168   "I won't. I know quite well I won't."

169   "And what are you going to do? I declare to God I thought you had more sense. At your age, too! You have a fine cushy job and you won't mind it."

170   "Not at that price."

171   "What price? What are you talking about? Haven't we all to stand it and put the best face we can on it?"

172   "And damn' well you paid for it, Cronin!"

173   "How so?"

174   "You're—how long are you painting?—twenty-five years? And worse and worse you're getting till now you're doing Stations of the Cross in the best Bavarian style. Twenty-five years ago you looked as though you might have had the makings of a painter in you, but now what are you? A maggot like the rest of us, a measly little maggot! Oh, you can puff out your chest and eat your mustache as much as you like, but that's what you are. A maggot, a five-bob-an-hour drawing master."

175   "MacCarthy," said Boyd, "you want your backside kicked, and you're damn' well going to get it kicked."

176   "And who's going to do it, pray?" asked Mac coolly.

177   "You wait till you get the Canon down on you; he won't be long about it."

178   "Aha," said Mac. "So the Canon is our new hero! The Deliverer! This, as I always guessed, is what all the old talk was worth. Ye gas and gas about liberty of conscience, but at the first whiff of powder ye run and hide under the Canon's soutane. Well, here's to the Canon! Anyway, he's a man."

179   "Are you accusing me of turning me coat?" bawled Boyd.

180   "Quiet now, Boyd, quiet!"

181   "Are you?"

182   "Boyd, I won't even take the trouble to quarrel with you," said Mac gravely. "You've lost even the memory of a man. I suppose when you were twenty-five or so you did hear the clock, but you don't hear it any longer." He sipped his pint and suddenly grew passionate. "Or do you? Do you? Do you hear the inexorable hour when all your wasted years spring out like little toy soldiers from the clock and present arms? And does it never occur to you that one of these days they'll step out and present arms and say: 'Be off now, you bloody old cod! We're going back to barracks!' "

183   It was late when he left the pub. He was very pleased with himself. He had squelched Cronin, made Boyd ridiculous, reinstated himself with the gang, proved he was still the master of them all. As he came through the side streets he began to feel lonely. When he came to the bridge he leaned over it and watched the river flowing by beneath.

184   "Christ, what a fool I am! What a fool!" he groaned.

185   For a long time he stood on the quay outside his own lodgings, afraid to go in. The shapes of human beings began to crowd round him, malevolent and fierce, the Canon, the head, Cronin, Boyd, Devane. They all hated him, all wished him ill, would stop at nothing to destroy him.

186   In the early morning he went downstairs, made a bonfire of his novel, and sobbed himself to sleep.

COMMENTARY ON "MAC'S MASTERPIECE"

After first reading this story, many people will ordinarily be puzzled, for the story makes several unusual demands. The chief demand is an understanding of the Irish temperament as it is defined in the characters of Mac and his cronies, rather than in plotted action. The other demands are an alertness to the incongruous, particularly in Mac's speech and behavior, and the ability to conceive in all the characters—and again, particularly in Mac—that the disparity between their idealism and their materialism shapes their whole being. Of course, in this latter point, it is Mac who most clearly exemplifies the temperament of a Don Quixote, tilting at windmills; but he is a Don Quixote aware of the forces that unseat him in all his jousts. Mac is defeated from the very start.

It is this latter point that makes calling Mac a linear character an accurate term. True enough, the story presents him in an attempt to work his way out of the emotional and moral morass that he believes has swallowed up the Irish spirit. He will write a novel exposing the sores that disease the will and prevent the Celt from achieving a civilization of grandeur. He makes the struggle, and he fails. But the action is only one more exemplification of what he apparently has done consistently throughout his life. "Two or three times a year," we learn right at the very start of the story, "Mac . . . took to his bed for four or five days." And Boyd's scornful comment that "the old cod was only play-acting as usual" puts Mac's behavior in its proper perspective. At times he has the enthusiasm and zeal of the outraged idealist. At other times, the zeal flags, and he goes off into neurotic and defeated self-pity. The attempt by Mac to write a novel—which appears to form the action of the story—is one other way of illustrating what we already have learned of Mac in the opening paragraphs, 1 through 27. From his death bed, he arises a ruined figure to sit among his chest-developers, and then stirred by his foils (as well as by the punch), he "strides" about the room once more fired by his visions of what is wrong with all of them.

One may well ask, also, how certain Mac is of his success in writing the novel. Is he not aware of "play-acting" once more? "He almost gave up drink and began to talk of the necessity for solitude." But solitude is wormwood. He stares wistfully after his friends, and then in the midst of his solitary discipline, invites them in (paragraph 36), only to get fired up all over again by his conversation. He talks his way into enthusiasm through his astute criticism of his companions— "Ye aim too high. Ye hitch yeer wagon to too many bloody stars at the one time. Then comes the first snag and the first compromise. After that ye begin to sink, sink, sink, till ye're tied hand and foot"— and he thus reveals perfectly the dilemma that traps him in writing his novel. For he keeps changing the stated purpose of his novel, and as he works, "It wasn't that ideas didn't come to him; he had too many, but always there was the sense of a hundred malicious faces peering over his shoulder. . . ." The mere threat of his losing his job leads him to profess the outraged desire to "roast them all," but his face twitches, his heart misses a beat now and then, and finally he gives up his dream altogether when he seeks out the truth by bluffing as to whether or not the Church actually is going to get rid of him. Frightened, he insults his friends, drinks, and for a time deceives himself into thinking that his defeat is victory, only to admit when he is once more alone that he is a fool.

In Mac, we have a superb illustration of the linear character caught in a dilemma. Like certain linear characters, he is totally aware of himself and his environment—he knows what the curtailments are that inhibit him—and yet he cannot free himself. He is enmeshed, takes refuge in his understanding, which only exacerbates the dilemma, spinning him around, so that he cannot commit himself to the real discipline that his struggle has to involve. Unlike some linear stories, however, this story exhibits a tragic curve, it may be thought, and hence is a departure from the type. But is this really so? Rather than a tragic curve—again let us remember the artifice involved in dealing with a story's complication that we assume the complication to be faced and resolved once and for all within the story— it would be more accurate to speak of it as a comic line with pathetic overtones, for we cannot take Mac's struggle seriously. We know that once more, he is only "play-acting"—and the dramatization of his play-acting is a handy way for the author to show Mac's habitual behavior. Mac is an individual whose insights into the nature of his countrymen must always confront the very forces in himself that make his friends what they are: the cheapening of his own ideals through fear and materialism; the sudden shifts from heightened poetry into "barbarous locution"; the magic vision that descends into coarseness; the indomitable human will trapped in "irrelevant circumstances"; the divine purpose as seen in the "consistent maggot"; the enthusiasm that gets wrapped in neurotic fears of age and decay; the striving of the individual that becomes lost in "the sense of the tribe"; the "Latin light" of the intellect, clear, cold, and precise, foundering in the "Celtic mist," which though soaring and visionary is too much imbued with the sentimental and worldly.

Like the linear character, too, Mac exhibits the dominant moods of wryness and pathos. He is a comic figure, for he is a figure of incongruity, and the incongruous always forms the basis of laughter. It is in the nature of comic laughter to shift its tonal values in terms of the serious things hinted at behind the laugh. The more serious the disparity, the more wry, perhaps even the more bitter, the laugh. We certainly find our amusement—to adopt an example Henry Fielding once used—to be relatively light when we see a ragged ne'er-do-well step from a resplendent coach and six. But the disparity between Mac's insight into the nature of his country—"Between the conception and the achievement all circumstances are irrelevant"—and his foundering in those very circumstances raise some serious questions indeed, and our laughter turns into wryness. Mac is a good deal more than a buffoon, and yet he is a gross and palpable fool whose emotional reactions toward life—half completely correct and justifiable—can never serve to give him that inner certitude and conviction necessary for the completion of the task his insight imposes.

At the same time that Mac is comic, he is also tragic—or as tragic as a failure to struggle against the odds will allow him to be. Such a neutralization of tragedy ends in pathos—and the pathos that Mac feels for himself at the end is partially shared, even as he laughs, by the reader. The story reveals the curious combination of attitudes so characteristic of the linear tale—no one mood clearly cut, sculptured as it were, by artifice into a dominant (and therefore, more exaggerated) emotion. What makes the story technically interesting is the possibility of seeing Mac as truly a tragic figure, but this would be to go against the true-to-life quality that the author has attempted to capture. It is interesting to speculate on the changes that would have to occur in the story so that the comic elements of Mac would not detract from his tragedy. For one thing, the attempt he makes would have to be the only attempt he has made in life to "set the record straight." He would have to struggle against the fate that imbued his character with the damaging traits that have weakened and stultified those around him. And his struggle would have to be serious. But then, there remains the impossibility of making such an attempt serious; for the Nemesis against which Mac struggles is too clearly of the comic variety: it is the Nemesis of Mac's own Irish nature. Tragedy is not so clearly possible when it must confront, in its rationale, fate working within the character as an incongruous split between desire and achievement. Perhaps, indeed, the source of whatever pathos one feels for Mac stems from the recognition of his being a comic figure trapped in a serious situation.

There are many other things in this story that should interest a writer: the vital dialogue, the methods by which the author motivates his characters, and swift and graphic characterizations, the smooth transitions, the use of dialogue for expository purposes, and so on. But rather than point out these things, we feel it better for the story to be read and reread in the light of our comments on technique and craftsmanship, so that the reader discovers for himself the way in which a great contemporary author has constructed an excellent tale.

The Corn Dies

by JEAN GIONO

1   A splendid harvest. Tight in the ear, short-strawed, pale-bearded, yet sparse enough to show the stony soil beneath. And still the mass seemed solid, and swung its thick pile from side to side in the breeze, like a huge brass platter. There it stretched, grave and serious bordered by pale oats beginning to ripen too. At moments some wild impulse, some girlish restlessness, would take them. Then they raced to the skyline with ragged streaming locks. From that vantage point they gazed down on the opposite slope, its Val Noir, its Vaudrey Valley, its Val d'Enchat or its Combe de Pierre Mousse. There was never anything else. They would always have to stay where they were, with only the fir plantations, the sombre trees and the dense foliage to look at, as though every black ram in the world had been flayed, and the pelts spread out to dry over every inch of ground, and cover every tree. And then the little oats would seem to shudder and begin to rush downhill again, passing like a pale wind over the lovely cornflowers that lit up bright as stars.

2   The fields of corn were dancing. Weighed down and solemn. Beating with huge freckled hands on a limp drumskin. It thudded as the heart thuds, the very earth seemed reverberating with its muffled kroom-kroom. The fields of corn were dancing, shooting a frantic lark into the air from time to time, which trilled over and over:

"Brrrning, Brrrning . . ."

till the sky's blue waves swept it under.

3   The Hebron no longer existed. Now all its vast body swarmed with wild mint, goats and grass snakes. The huge rocks, like

caps to its watery knees, stood out grimly in the litter of bleached bones and pebbles: the lovely watery leg no longer curved closely about the rock. It was all dead and motionless. The great arms of the mountain stream that, all withered, still stretched as occasional sumps among the alders, were covered with swarms of flies sucking the putrid water. In the forest vale nothing stirred. The woodcutters had departed for the remote high glades. From time to time a woodman or so would come out of the trees. There they stood a moment in the clearing, blinking at the hot sun, before beginning to cross the dry river. The stout boots echoed among the stones. Climbing they would reach La Columette's, and there get their wine-gourds filled. Pale as turnips they were, smelling of fungi and the dark. Yet half an hour at the iron tables of the café, and all the coolness had been drained out of them. They would begin to sweat, and scratch themselves, and smell like ancient leather. Then they would cross over the Hebron again, making for the remote depths of the forest.

4   It was no good gazing at the poplars. Frail as smoke though they were, they stood as motionless as cast iron.

5   The village wash-house. Now and then the pipe would purl a drop, and the pool would tremble slightly. But the second after it was flat and dead as ice, revealing through the depths the accumulated soap and dirt of innumerable washing-days. So densely did it cling together, there in the depths, it seemed a forest underwater.

6   Only the wheat went on dancing, kroom, kroom, kroom, thudding always deeper and more strongly as the heat increased, while everything in which the life was frail slowly perished, and everything in which the life was firmly, cautiously, rooted, the dense woods, the watery grottoes, and the mountain tarns, huddled closer in upon themselves, striving to retain their moisture. Meanwhile the corn danced, rubbing its freckled hands over the limp drumskin, kroom, kroom, endlessly, uninterruptedly, both day and night, dancing thuddingly like a heart.

7   Samsombre met Simon in the village square.

8   It was full noon, and the air was oppressive: oppressive and glittering like a marble haystack.

438

9   "Well?" said Simon.

10   "To-morrow!" said Samsombre.

11   The coolness had all gone from the shadows under the elm, and the sick fountain moaned and hiccoughed and gave forth a mossy smell.

12   For a moment they stayed there, hardly daring to venture into the sun again.

13   Boromé came round the corner. He saw them and stopped.

14   "To-morrow!" shouted Samsombre.

15   "Your place?" asked Boromé.

16   "Yes."

17   Sailor came out of Columette's.

18   "To-morrow!" shouted Samsombre.

19   "Good," said Sailor.

20   "I'll tell Clodomir," said Simon, "and Jofroi. Barbe-Baille and Doron. You see Martin, Picollet, Pélissier, Belfruit and Cateland."

21   "We'll begin with the big field," said Samsombre, "the one near Durban's land. How will he manage this time, I wonder. His corn should be ready for cutting too."

22   "That's true," said Simon. "But he's generally back round this time."

23   After a moment Samsombre said:

24   "My word, it's hot. Well, so long."

25   "So long," said Simon, ". . . till to-morrow."

26   The vast silence of high summer encompassed them.

27   That evening Samsombre called on the priest.

28   "Well, will you be coming to-morrow?" he said to him.

29   "Of course," M. Lignières made answer. "What makes you ask?"

30   "Oh, nothing . . ." said Samsombre, ". . . but the years pass—you never know . . . one goes on getting older."

31   M. Lignières rested a bony hand on Samsombre's arm, and first he said:

32   "You're sweating."

33   "It's hot," said Samsombre.

34   "For that sort of thing," said M. Lignières, "one's never too old. Of course I'll go. At least I can be of some help. Which are we doing first?"

35   "The big field."

36 "You've seen the others?"

37 "Yes."

38 "When do we start?"

39 "At three."

40 "Would you like me to ring the church bell?"

41 "Ah! that's an idea," said Samsombre.

42 "Good. What could have made you think," said M. Lignières, "that I shouldn't go harvesting with you this year. We haven't stopped needing each other's help, have we? Well, till to-morrow, then."

43 "Good-bye, Lignières," said Samsombre.

44 "Funny," he thought, "why, I left the 'Sir' out."

45 At three in the morning the church bell rang. People were already afoot. But first to leave was Samsombre, with the mare carrying the sack of bread, the two hams and the wine-barrel.

46 Simon carefully picked out a scythe and then a stone. There were three of them. He weighed them one against the other.

47 "I'm going," said Marie.

48 "It's a long way."

49 "I should be afraid alone here," said Marie. "There won't be a soul left in the village."

50 "Is it heavy?" asked father.

51 "No," said little Jean.

52 He was carrying the billhook and the water-bottle. As they passed by Boromé's house, he threw a glance into the stable. It was empty, except for a big half-finished basket standing there. As they came to the threshing-floor by the crossroads, he gazed down on the meadows. The willows were scarcely distinguishable. It was light enough, but a heavy mist obscured everything. Overhead there was the sound of Samsombre's mare picking its way over the stones. Barbe-Baille blew the lamp out, opened the door, peered at the dawn and put down his scythe: then shut the door, picked up the scythe and started.

53 The women, Adeline, Mélanie, Héloise, Maxima, Zélie and Mariette, came down the street. They had their heavy boots on. Colombe Boromé was taking the short cut.

54 "Oh! Colombe!"

55 M. Lignières came out of the church, locked the door, raised

an arm and slid the key under one of the beams of the porch. He was wearing his corduroy trousers, and a gleaming white, newly washed shirt. His face was shaved and shining, and his hair was newly cut. A happy smile played over his lips.

56 In front of Picollet's house he shouted.

57 "Irma."

58 "What," she said from the window, buttoning her cotton blouse.

59 "Is my scythe ready?"

60 "It's just inside, M. le curé. Behind the door. I won't come down, I'm still dressing. Picollet's gone off already. Oh, that man. Behind the door . . . have you got it?"

61 "Don't bother. I've got it. Hurry," said M. Lignières, "or you'll be last."

62 Bearing the scythe on his shoulder, he set off.

63 Adeline and Mélanie seemed to have muscles of iron. Already they were up by the maples. Little Jean walked behind father. The billhook now rested on his shoulder. Father takes a step, I take a step. What big steps I'm taking. . . . He was wearing lovely corduroy trousers, whose rustling made sweet music in his ears, and boots as hard as horn. Héloise, Zélie, and Mariette were taking the short cut. Maxima had stopped where the roads branched, and was wondering:

64 "Which road shall I take?"

65 Barbe-Baille was coming up the hill behind her with his long legs. Then Sailor, Boromé and Philomène Samsombre, leading her two children by the hand, while a little behind came Simon, bringing up the rear.

66 They took the road, and Maxima fell in with them. The three others went up by the fields.

67 On the bluff high over them, Samsombre's field came in sight, one mass of corn.

68 As they went pebbles were constantly rattling downwards beneath their feet. Heads began to appear higher than the boxtrees.

69 Slowly the light grew stronger, but the heat was still bearable. Yet so still and heavy was the air that only by taking great gulps was it possible to breathe.

70 Marie shut her door and began to climb the road. Her crutch

made progress difficult. The village was as silent as a stone. It took her a long time to pass the first slopes. At last she was on the other side.

71   "How shall we begin?"

72   "Following the rise," says Samsombre.

73   The cornfield is as steep as a wall.

74   Simon puts an edge on his scythe. Lignières puts an edge on his scythe. Barbe-Baille shoots out his arm in a great sweep. Boromé keeps step with him. Samsombre attacks the corner. Sailor takes off his shirt. Three are already deep in the corn. Four are in line, six over by the alders, four over by the oaks. The women are waiting for the first swathes. Adeline is already gathering them up. Zélie leans forward. Mariette advances. Héloise moves her arms in readiness. Maxima tucks up her sleeves.

75   The ten by the alders mow upright. The four by the oaks move obliquely; the fifteen in front sway together. Simon is next to Lignières, Lignières is short in the arm. He does his best, but leaves a wisp standing after every fourth sweep of the scythe. Simon makes a fifth sweep to the right and mows the wisp through. Lignières takes a short step to the left after each cut. There are no wisps now. Simon straightens up. At intervals his scythe sweeps inquisitively out towards Lignières. Boromé makes his sweep, then raises the left foot.

76   Mariette catches the sheaves up. She twists a string of straw, she ties the sheaf, she casts it back. Héloise goes so fast, she is almost under the reapers' feet.

77   "Mind your head."

78   Mélanie, Maxima, Zélie pile it into shocks.

79   Little Jean cuts binders with his hook. Leonard twists them. Mille carries them to the women. Little Jean stops. Now Leonard takes the hook. Mille twists binders, Little Jean takes them off.

80   Mariette sends out a hand behind, takes hold of the twist, embraces a sheaf, ties it up and throws it behind. Mélanie takes it and Zélie places it. Héloise throws down her sheaf, Maxima takes it, Zélie places it.

81   "Oh! my back."

82   Simon raises his scythe. Lignières advances. Boromé finishes

the cut and raises a foot. The corn topples over between all three, like water flowing.

83   The center of the field still sings its "kroom, kroom, kroom." Not a breath of wind. It is hot. They are thirsty. Little Jean carries the waterbottle to his father. Old Jofroi never touches wine at work. Mariette sends out a hand behind. There is no binder waiting. Her head turns: ". . . Well, children!"

84   "Here," says Leonard.

85   She clasps the sheaf, ties it, flings it away. Zélie places it. Simon sweeps his scythe into a dense mass of corn with a mighty swing of the shoulders. Lignières raises his scythe. Boromé slips on a rock. The corn goes on flowing. Simon takes a stone and puts an edge on his blade. He goes back to his mowing. Lignières sharpens his blade. Samsombre does likewise. Boromé wipes the sweat off his brow, and hitches his belt up. Old Jofroi is over by the alders. He raises the pitcher, and spurts the water into his mouth. His face is scarlet. He draws in his loins. The pains in his back were bad before setting out. He makes a grimace, straightens himself up and begins to mow again, limping as he starts. Those over by the alders go on relentlessly devouring the corn. The women can no longer keep pace tying up the sheaves. Those over by the oaks have broken their line: the prim straight line now looks crooked as a goat's leg. Sailor lags behind. He had stopped to fasten his woolen body-belt. It came undone, and now has to be wound round himself again.

86   The sun can be felt rising on the other side of Ferrand, about to burst forth. The mountainside facing the sun is intensely blue, darting with rays, a floating powdery blue.

87   Simon reaps with a slow wide sweep that mows beautifully. He is tall. As he cuts he throws his body forward. His reach is long; he leaves a wide clear space all round him. Lignières can still do pretty well for his age. But he stands too stiff. His loins don't do their part, it's suppleness he lacks. He thinks he can do it all with his shoulders, and his scythe turns up as he cuts. His mowing is not even. Boromé is best of all. He is far in front. He eats up the corn like a rat. There is always a pocket round him.

88   Mariette counts as she follows in Simon's wake.

89   "One, two, three."

90   Behind Lignières, three: behind Samsombre, four: behind Boromé, five. Five sheaves and they must step three paces forward to catch up, he is so far in front.

91   Suddenly the sun bounds over Ferrand peak, beginning to bear down on everything with its vast trenchant might. The air is full of the sound of corn, the stertorous breathing of the men, the singing flight of scythes, and the women's sighs. Lignières stops. He rests his scythe against his body, takes off his shirt. Immediately a horn of wheat appears in front of him. A salient of standing wheat advancing on him. Simon is pressing forward on his left. Samsombre on his right. Lignières, his torso bare, sets to again. Mariette picks up his shirt and puts it near the shock. Simon stops, leans the scythe against his hips, takes off his shirt. Lignières catches up to Simon. Mariette picks up the shirt and puts it near the shock. Samsombre takes off his shirt, Mariette gathers the sheaf, ties it up, gives it to Zélie and gives her Samsombre's shirt. Boromé takes off his shirt and tightens his belt. The four backs are scarlet. Lignière's shoulders are hairy. Old Jofroi cries:

92   "Jeannot."

93   Little Jean runs through the stubble.

94   Father takes off his shirt. He has huge tufts of grey hair on his chest like a ram, and bundles of knotted muscles in his shoulders. They quiver on both sides of his head like the beam of a balance, when he picks up his scythe again, and hurls himself on the corn.

95   Sailor seems to be dancing with his arms high over his head. He is kicking an ant heap to pieces. Zélie unbuttons her blouse, tucking the collar in. She opens the neck as much as she can. It shows the skin all scarlet, and she rubs her buttocks with the flat of her hand.

96   Simon raises his scythe; so do Lignières, Boromé, Samsombre. Working in unison they sweep through the corn in a wide arc, and it sinks down suddenly in front of them. For a moment, all are working to the same rhythm, left-right in cadence, in step, with the same thrust of the foot. That helps. They speed forward. Lignières bites his lips. It is hard to keep up. Simon is thirty-five. Boromé's muscles are hard as iron, and Samsombre is cutting his own corn. Zélie has taken off her bodice, now she wears only her chemise, open at the neck, and a petticoat.

Mariette does the same. Leonard takes his shirt off. Little Jean cuts more binders. Leonard twists them, Mille takes them to the women. A score of swathes are waiting to be gathered. Mariette sends out a hand, takes hold of a twist, gathers the sheaf together, ties it, stands erect again, draws in her loins and throws the sheaf back. Mélanie takes it, stands erect and carries it to the shock. Simon raises his scythe. Lignières sweeps outwards. Boromé swings back. Samsombre is in his element. The corn falls in front of them like the waters of the Hebron when it leaps over the rocks, and full of mud, cascades through the valley, with great webbed feet, and spumy flying manes like a troop of horses.

97 The sun spins in the sky like a chalk crusher. All the dust of the earth seems to be filling the sky. There it remains, dense, unyielding, motionless. The trees, the very grass are white with it. The toppling wheat smokes as if on fire, and sends up clouds of dust that quiver and gleam in the drab air. Not a vestige of colour remains on the mountainside. The earth is grey, the corn is grey, the sky is grey. The heat sinks down on the world like a mountain of cinders.

98 Simon, Lignières, Boromé, Samsombre, naked to the waist, go on battling with the grain. When they straighten up, all that is visible is the colour of the eye, shadowed by a hat. The rest is a compost of dust and sweat and blood. The blood held off only by the frail skin.

99 Over everything the same greyness. Everything burns and the wheat smokes. Those over by the alders are naked. Those over by the oaks are naked. Sailor has taken off his belt: he ties his trousers with a wisp of straw. The fourteen scythes pierce into the corn, the legs move forward, the feet trample the stubble, hands twist binders, hands stretch out for twists, tie sheaves, add sheaves to shocks. Fists clench handles of scythes, press down on scythes, draw back, clutch tighter, balance and swing out again. Feet move forward, backs bend, loins ache, heads buzz, eyes throb. Teeth bite, and noses pump up air. Mouths gasp, throats are afire. Pangs of anguish shoot long flames through spines. The earth is grey, the sky is grey. The sun crushes all things under it. Fists clench. Feet move forward. Hands gather up corn. Arms shuffle sheaves. Hands take twists. Fingers tie knots, shoulders cast sheaves, hands catch sheaves

by ties, arms pull, shoulders lift, hands set them to the shock. The earth is grey, the corn is grey. The sun crushes its chalk faster than ever. Breasts ache, loins ache, thighs ache, heads weigh tons, and the hair is an intolerable weight. Eyeballs quiver, teeth bite, petticoats burn the thighs like fire.

100   Little Jean, flat on his stomach in the grey shadow, lies still and motionless. His face is turned to the earth. Leonard no longer moves. Mille no longer moves. Over by the alders, over by the oaks, over by the straight cut there are no more men now, no more women. Nothing but hands, arms, fists, legs, feet, calves, shoulders, fingers, teeth, mouths, loins, buttocks, breasts, thighs still pulsating with the struggle against the heat, against the corn, against the sun. The vast solitary sun crushes its chalk of summer down on the whole universe.

101   Lignières puts down his scythe.

102   "Oh," he says, drawing in his loins and straightening his back.

103   Simon stops, Samsombre stops, Boromé and Sailor, in the distance Héloise, Zélie, Mélanie, Maxima, Adeline, those by the alders, those over by the oaks, each and all come to a stop. It is too hot. The four in the distance away there, by the alders, can be seen stopping, looking at each other. They raise their hands in the air, towards those taking the straight cut, for Samsombre is among them, the master for the day. Samsombre puts his fingers to his mouth and whistles. Those by the alders put their scythes on their shoulders and move towards the shadow of the oaks. The others have put their scythes on their shoulders and are walking towards the maples.

104   "A good morning's work," says Lignières.

105   "A long morning," says Simon.

106   Samsombre goes off to the mare where the bread, the ham and the wine are. He drags his leg as he walks.

107   Marie is waiting under the maples. She has got ready beds of dried leaves for all of them, but Simon's heap is thickest. Not that it is noticeable though, she has only bedded them more tightly down. He will notice the difference when he throws himself upon it.

108   Lignières lies down. So does Boromé. Simon too. And he pulls his hat down over his eyes.

109   Samsombre returns carrying a bag of bread and a ham.

110	"I'm going for the wine."
111	He goes off dragging his leg, and returns with a small barrel.
112	"Oh! Lignières!"
113	"Oh!"
114	Lignières pushes his hat up off his face.
115	"Here!"
116	Samsombre holds out the bread and ham.
117	"Cut it," says Lignières.
118	"This much?"
119	"Yes, thanks."
120	"Oh, Simon!"
121	"Cut it."
122	"Is this all right?"
123	"Yes, that's right."
124	"Oh! Boromé!"
125	Boromé sits up on the leaves and gets out his knife.
126	"Marie, help yourself."
127	"Lie down, Samsombre," she says, "I'll take the food over to those by the alders, and then over to those by the oaks. Let me be of some use!"
128	"Good," says Samsombre.
129	He takes some ham and lies down. Simon eats lying down. He bends his right arm, and bites the bread. He bends his left arm, and bites the ham. Then both arms fall at his side and he goes on chewing for a long time.
130	Lignières is lying on his side. Boromé is sitting up.
131	Marie takes the bag, she tucks the crutch under her arm, and goes off toward the alders.
132	The cornfield no longer sings. Softly, with what is left of the standing wheat, it sighs a little iron sigh. The sun beats down so heavily, you can hear the trees crack.
133	Marie, the only moving figure, crosses the empty field.
134	Samsombre sits up. Boromé, his face buried in the leaves, snores. Lignières sleeps. He clenches his lips, but he does not move. Simon sleeps. Marie, sitting, gazes beyond the leaves at the vast face of the sun. Not a movement. The earth is glittering and dead like marble. Samsombre whistles.
135	Lignières is first to rise. The first two, three, steps, he seems to be walking on knife blades.

447

136   Away off, they come out of the shade of the alders. They tramp towards the wheat like huge staggering beetles with the scythe blades trembling over their heads.

137   Little Jean wakes in bewilderment, hardly able to breathe, his nose and his mouth blocked. A violent fit of sneezing buffets him like a diver who has hit his head on the bottom.

138   "Forward march!"

139   At five, Samsombre's field is finished. A hundred shocks, each a score of sheaves. At the top of the field, the ears were small, the straw short and the sheaves like children born before their time. Then they all ate, standing, silent in the midst of the flat field.

140   The first arrivals were waiting in front of the church. They sat down on the steps.

141   "Well, what about to-morrow?" said Samsombre.

142   They looked at each other.

143   "To-morrow, we could go over to my place," said Boromé, "if you'd care."

144   "Yes," said Sailor, "only next, we ought to be thinking of mine, it mustn't be left too long in the valley. It's out of the sun too much."

145   "Mine, that can wait," said Boromé.

146   "Mine too," said Sailor.

147   "Best begin with Sailor's field."

148   "Well, then we'll meet at the same time."

149   "The only thing is," said Lignières, "you'd better not put too much reliance on the church bell. To-morrow's Sunday: I'll be saying Mass before we leave."

150   He took the key from under the beam in the porch, and opened the church door.

151   The bell rang towards three the next morning. Four or five soft strokes rose like bubbles into the green of the dawn, and burst softly, high in the air on Ferrand brow.

152   Simon rose.

153   There were lights in the church.

154   Adeline and Mélanie were walking down the street.

155   Barbe-Baille opened his door, put down his scythe, shut the door, took up the scythe and departed.

156   "Babeau, my back aches," said Jofroi. "I'm getting old."

157   He got up . . . his knees creaking.

158   "Devil take it," he swore, his hands on his buttocks.

159   Little Jean was still asleep.

160   "Oh!" said Jofroi touching his chin.

161   Little Jean awoke. The first thing he saw was his father standing by his bed. He was so full of the grey wheat he could almost vomit. The dawn was ripening gradually.

162   "Not tired?" asked Boromé, that evening, when they stood in front of the church.

163   "Forty-three shocks," thought Sailor, "if the yield's all right, I shan't do badly."

164   "Well, same time to-morrow."

165   Lignières took the key from under the beam in the porch and opened the church.

166   The bell rang at three again.

167   Simon got up.

168   Adeline went down into the street. She knocked at Mélanie's door.

169   "Mélanie!"

170   After a moment the window opened.

171   "I'm dressing."

172   Barbe-Baille shut his door, took his scythe and departed.

173   "Let the child stay at home to-day," said Babeau.

174   Jofroi had gone closer to the window. His naked foot was resting on a chair. He was cutting his corns with a knife.

175   Sailor passed by his barn. He gazed at the bare earth. He counted his steps. "One, two, three, four."

176   He was picturing his corn.

177   "I'll borrow a plank from Taillas," he said.

178   Footsteps sounded upon the road.

179   Mélanie went by, loins limp and with trailing feet. Boromé's horse followed slowly after, bearing the three bags of bread and ham. Barbe-Baille walked with his scythe on his shoulder, bending beneath it as though it were socketed into a pine. . . .

180   "You're resting to-morrow?" asked Babeau.

181   "No, to-morrow's our turn."

182   "You might have said so sooner."

183   "If that's all you think one has to think about?"

184   "But all the things I've got to get ready. The ham, the bread, everything. Heavens! And how do you feel in yourself . . . your back?"

185   "It'll do," said Jofroi.

186   He sat down in his wooden armchair, put his hands on his knees and slowly let the small of his back sink against the back.

187   "There," he said sighing.

188   With all his weight he leant against it.

189   Marie was melting some salt in a basin of water. Simon was lying face down on his bed. Marie soaked a towel in the water. Then she went to him.

190   "Where is it?" she said.

191   Simon sighed.

192   "There," he said.

193   He pointed to the crease in his loins, just over the buttocks.

194   "Take your hand away."

195   She laid the cold biting towel on the skin that the heat and sweat had split open.

196   "God damn it for a life," moaned Simon.

197   Lignières was stretched out on his bed. Without moving his body, he put out an arm and picked his stick from the floor. Then holding it carefully, he knocked a piece of bread off the table onto the floor. With his stick he went on drawing it closer, till he could take it with his hand. Then he began to eat, the crumbs crunching in his mouth like maize.

198   "What time are they starting?" said Babeau.

199   Jofroi opened an eye.

200   "At three."

201   "That bitch of a bell," said Simon, then awoke.

202   The bell was ringing. There was the dawn all clad in green. Nothing moved in the whole universe. The earth was more motionless than ever, now that so much corn was cut.

203   Marie slept.

204   Simon rose. He bent down for his boots . . . stumbled. . . .

205   "God damn it for a life!" he muttered in his teeth.

206   There were balls of fire under his knees. They burst between his thighs and legs whenever he bent his knees, and sparks of fire shot into the flesh like red-hot iron. A belt of

thorns tore at his thighs. The collar of his shirt weighed heavier than a horse-collar.

207   "Marie!"

208   He touched her cheek.

209   "I'm off."

210   She tried to rise. But only her scrawny chicken's neck lifted itself up.

211   "I'm done," she said.

212   "Stay here then."

213   She watched him go. His feet dragged. He was as full of mutterings as water about to boil.

214   "Jofroi, Jofroi," called Babeau.

215   He lay there like a stone, then buried deep in sleep, asked:

216   "What?"

217   "Three o'clock."

218   "Good," he said.

219   She shook him.

220   "It's our turn to-day."

221   He woke.

222   "What?"

223   "They're coming to us. It's our corn to-day."

224   He looked at the green dawn.

225   "It's a dog's life," he groaned.

226   Barbe-Baille opened his door, put down his scythe, shut the door, put out his hand to the scythe, and moved his loins forward and back two or three times to prove the extremity of their pain. He took his scythe and departed.

227   That night, Boromé went through the motions of sitting down a few times, to test how far those legs of his would still serve him.

228   "Aie!" he said at last.

229   Colombe sighed.

230   "Oh, that corn, that corn! And they won't be finished till Sunday."

231   She could hear her man yawning in the room above; it sounded like the bellowing of a bull.

232   A hundred shocks at Samsombre's, forty-three at Sailor's, fifty-eight at Boromé's, sixty-four at Jofroi's, forty at Simon's, twenty, sixteen, thirty-four, Saturday, Sunday, Monday, Tuesday. The earth is dead, the sun beats more and more fiercely down, bearing down so heavily on the earth that nothing moves

now, nothing at all; it crushes so much powdered chalk and stifling air that the whole universe is white, at the last gasp. And yet the corn of Mariette, Adeline, Héloise, Durban, Taillas, Zélie, and Barbe-Baille is still standing.

233   Three o'clock.

234   The bell rings.

235   "Oh, curse and blast it," groans Simon from his bed.

236   "Jofroi!"

237   Not a movement.

238   "Jofroi," Babeau says to him, "don't go, you'll kill yourself at your age."

239   "They've done for me," says Jofroi.

240   And gets up.

241   "God in heaven!" he cries.

242   "Damn it for a life!" mutters Boromé between his teeth.

243   Barbe-Baille throws open his door, puts down his scythe.

244   "The bitch's bastard!"

245   Lignières comes out of church. He leaves the door open. He has grown as thin as a whistle. He stretches himself, and as he does so groans.

246   "Oh! Suffering Christ, our Saviour!"

247   Towards five in the morning, the bell began to ring softly. Simon heard it.

248   "Curse!" he thought. "The corn!"

249   Heavy waves of grey corn swirled through the still air on the vibrations of the bell. A ball of dust exploded inside his head. His ears were full of the sound of corn; the spatter of raining chalk dust and the throbbing of the sun. He turned over to shut its rays out of his eyes.

250   "Curse!"

251   Huge nails of pain pierced him through and through.

252   "But we finished, we finished yesterday! Why are they ringing?"

253   The ringing came to an end.

254   "Ah!" he sighed.

255   A frightful weariness seemed to crush all his muscles.

256   When M. Lignières had finished ringing, he came down. He was still in his corduroy trousers and heavy boots, just as he

had thrown himself down to sleep. He ran his hand over his week-old beard. It pricked like stubble where it covered the jaw, stretched up to his eyes, and along his nose, and filled the hollows in his cheeks.

257   The church door opened, screeched and fell shut again.

258   He looked. Héloise Catelan had just entered.

259   "It's time to begin," M. Lignières told himself.

260   He had to sit down on his bed to pull off the corduroy trousers, and get into his light buckled shoes. . . . His nose was full of earthy dust. . . . The air he breathed still tasted of flaming summer. . . . He licked the corner of his lips. . . . It was salty with all his dried-up sweat, and rough as a hog's back.

261   Then stretching out his two tired arms.

262   "It's only because I can't. . . ." he told himself.

263   He slipped his surplice over the dirty shirt. There was blood on both his hands.

264   He looked into the church. Four were waiting. Then he called.

265   "Clarisse!"

266   "Monsieur l'abbé?"

267   She came up to him.

268   "You serve me at Mass," he said.

269   "An old woman like me?"

270   "Yes, take the sacring bell, go before."

271   "You will tell me what to do, monsieur l'abbé?"

272   "Yes, I'll tell you!"

273   They went into the church together. It was broad daylight.

274   "Will you get me a chair?" said M. Lignéres. "I know it isn't seemly, but I'm tired."

275   He watched her as she fetched the chair.

276   Héloise, Lydia, Augusta gazed at M. Lignières and his week-old growth.

277   "I'm tired," he said aloud. "There's been ten days of it."

278   "At your age," they replied, "you shouldn't be."

279   A pigeon flew in through the open window, and Augusta, fluttering her apron, tried to frighten it away.

280   "Let it be," said M. Lignières, "it's not doing any harm."

281   He moved his chair closer to his book.

282   "I'll read to you sitting, if you don't mind?"

283   "Oh, please! monsieur l'abbé," they said, all together.

284   "In a moment I'll stand up," he said, with a soft apologetic laugh. The pigeon pecked at the stoup. Then it began to spill the water over itself, and beat its wings. It was all white, all clean, all steaming in the scattering water.

285   "Pigeon," said M. Lignières, "if you want to stay, stay, but keep quiet and listen."

COMMENTARY ON "THE CORN DIES"[1]

One of the three basic plots of the pulp and slick story we described was conflict to avert disaster. Of course, disasters may be man-made. But usually, a disaster is one that nature imposes upon man. Many a successful pulp and slick story has utilized the theme of man against nature, for it is one of the primitive conflicts that man has faced, and despite a civilization which evermore encroaches upon the prerogatives of nature by means of superhighways, stream and flood control, the moving of mountains, and the study of ways in which to seed clouds over deserts, nature still claims a power that transcends man's abilities to overcome its ravages, to subdue its whirlwind blasts, or to do other than fly from its tornadoes. The story which we are now examining takes this oldest theme of literature and puts it into sophisticated terms. Let us study it, not only in terms of its own inherent techniques, but also in terms of its difference from what the commercial writer would do with such a conflict.

One of the most obvious and most immediate distinctions between this story and the pulp or slick versions of it is that the story embraces as protagonists not one man alone, but a whole village. The characteristic attribute, as we have seen, of the quality story, is that it tends to enlarge and extend the significance of the conflicts of pulp or slick fiction. "The Corn Dies" is one more example that illustrates the tendency. And because the story seems to sweep over a whole range of people, not simply over one protagonist, it develops other distinctions, in terms of point of view, of theme, of description, of characterization, of ultimate meaning.

The reader will recall that of the three plots of quality stories, only

[1] The reader unfamiliar with European civilization will immediately assume that *corn* in the title means what Americans mean by the word—excepting, of course, the slang sense. The word as used here means grain or, more specifically, wheat.

one of them met at certain points with the three plots of pulp and slick stories. "The Corn Dies" illustrates that form of essentially comic plot in which the protagonist solves the complication through his own efforts, or has it solved for him by accident, providence, chance, coincidence, or by another character. Obviously since the protagonists solve their difficulty through their own efforts in the story, its plot is identical with the pulp and slick statement of the plot based on conflict to avert disaster.

We have chosen this story because it represents the comic curve of the quality story, as well as the enlargements we have just mentioned. The villagers face a natural disaster. In communal effort they band together and seek to avert it. One can imagine that, in a primitive agricultural setting, not to get the ripened grain in would wreak havoc on the whole community. As a consequence the villagers, understanding without overt statement that their individual selves are threatened by what exceeds their own individual lives, band together, sacrificing their own ease in order to produce their own salvation.

The word *salvation* has, here, multiple meanings. For what is at stake if the villagers do not succeed, is, of course, their economic well-being, if not their own physical lives. But also, so directly representative of the questions of sacrifice, submergence of self, and eventual resurrection in the common good does this story state itself, that other meanings emerge. Here, then, is another way in which the theme of this story enlarges itself. For the comedy is not based alone on the physical life of the individual, but on his spiritual life as well—and to speak of the individual is, to an extent, a falsity, for the whole community undergoes the threat of physical disaster, faces it, and saves itself. For the word *salvation* to have meaning, then, the village priest must occupy some position of special trust. He must identify himself with the common good so much as not to be above the flock that he tends, yet at the same time he must retain that vestige of respect and significance that is entailed in his position.

The comic quality of the story is to be seen in terms of nature's being a worthy antagonist of man. For true comedy implies, it seems to us, that deep values in man are required for his success against any antagonist. His success over odds of a profound sort testifies to his having the spiritual qualities necessary for that success. For if there is man's conflict against nature, there is also nature's conflict against man. That is, the threat of financial and physical disaster that the villagers undergo is attended by still other threats as well, against their culture, values, and traditions. The author never loses sight of the fact that nature is neither malevolent nor beneficent. Man's surroundings are his source of travail as well as his source of spiritual release. Yet at the same time as the author maintains such a strict objectivity, nature in the story tends to subvert all the values that the villagers hold. It begins by testing their physical stamina; it ends by testing their spiritual stamina. While nature provides the villagers with groaning plenty, it makes them groan quite literally to obtain that plenty: nature in old joints and withered sinews, nature in terms of mere physical temperature and comfort, nature in terms of sufficient rest to maintain the strength to capture the goods that it seems to shower upon the villagers, for it is after all an excellent harvest—"A splendid harvest. . . ." the story begins. Man is, therefore, under the penalty as well as the blessing that nature provides. Yet we have a feeling consistently throughout the story that man is always more than his mere environment. He exists as a willful, purposeful agent seeking to obtain what he needs, striving to redeem himself even though his redemption is against the very nature of his bones, cursing his plight, yet willing even in the midst of his own deep, natural slumber, to continue to wage the battle.

So much for the general theme and conflict of the story. Let us look at it in more specific ways. Perhaps the best way is to examine a little the history of the story's author, for the history reveals what any sensitive reader of this story can immediately determine, a talent for accurate visual impression. It is no surprise then to find that Jean Giono is a famous scenarist, most famous in this country for his movie *The Baker's Wife,* but for a relatively sophisticated audience, several novels as well, *Harvest* (1930) and *Song of the World* (1934). That he works best in terms of the physical side of things shows up in "The Corn Dies," for it betrays what seems to be one of the most significant elements in his view of existence, the simple, the unsophisticated, the primitive.

What will puzzle the reader, at first then, will be the pictorial aspect, a matter not at all puzzling were he to view the story in terms of the motion picture, the medium where pictorial quality is one of the supreme achievements. The adaptation of cinematic techniques to the story helps in establishing the point of view. The narrator of the story is as omniscient as the camera lens, but also like the camera lens, incapable, so it would appear, of contributing more to what he views, or what it views, than is actually there. As a consequence, this story uses the point of view of the concealed narrator B. The lens sweeps across the wheat field, the valley, the forests nearby, the wood-cutters, the village wash-house, the meeting of people, the shifts from one person to another, from one consciousness to another. And then there are the relatively abrupt transitions, a clear violation, as we have indicated within the text, of the story writer's usual direct intentions to make his story flow as smoothly in terms of time as possible, so that a developing action will seem to develop with inevitability. But here, the abrupt transitions are as abrupt as the sweep of the lens shifting over what is viewed. A different kind of flowing rhythm is contained here, cyclical in terms of the development of day, the growth toward high noon, toward the heat of the afternoon, then the slackening toward evening and slumber. The author is attempting to recreate the primitive conditions of man, not only in terms of his complication—the getting in of the harvest—but also in terms of his daily rhythmic and cyclical actions as they would appear were we involved in them: the consciousness of time as the consciousness of the moments when a duty comes announced and unwished, the having to get up at the ringing of a bell; or the consciousness of the day as it grows hot when one sweats and swelters and dreams of coolness and evening; or the consciousness of food and wine as momentarily a man lies down and slumbers at the same time as he is eating. The abruptness of the transitions testifies organically then to the numbness that seems to creep over the mind in the facing of the major complication.

The story has an immediate, visual impact, and it is noteworthy that the pictorial and perfectly literal views it presents are full of symbolic overtones. The fields of grain, so full of "girlish restlessness," are nevertheless "solid . . . like a huge brass platter." The poplars, though "frail as smoke . . . stood as motionless as cast iron"; or "the first two, three, steps, he seems to be walking on knife blades. . . ." Those who had started out freshly dressed, and cleanly shaven, "they would begin to sweat, and scratch themselves, and smell like ancient leather"; they undress themselves by degrees and reveal the animal —"Father . . . has huge tufts of grey hair on his chest like a ram . . ."; they become things, almost completely dismembered, animalistic things—"nothing but hands, arms, fists, legs, feet, calves, shoulders, fingers, teeth, mouths, loins, buttocks, breasts, thighs still pulsating with the struggle . . ."; they curse, it "is a dog's life"; it is the life of an animal—"the collar of his shirt weighed heavier than a horse-collar." And at the very end, they have not been defeated, for M. Lignières conducts a mass, his lips "salty with all his dried-up sweat, and rough as a hog's back," his surplice hiding his dirty shirt, his hands bleeding. And what is left of nature in the story? It is the pigeon that flies in through the open window and cleanses itself in the water: "It was all white, all clean, all steaming in the scattering water." The fatigued tolerance of M. Lignières at the end is for nature that has not crushed them, but from which they are distinct in their own urge to worship. And looked at visually, the pigeon would seem to state that their worship is a natural thing, too, for it connotes the dove of Christian symbolism.

There are many things in the story that repay study: the concreteness of the descriptions; the abrupt shift from past to present tense (paragraphs 71 through 139); the methods by which the author gives the sensations of the actions of a number of people; the use of short sentences; the submergence of individual characterization for the sake of a group image. But of chief note is the comedy of this story that illustrates that the most timeworn themes, looked at with an original eye, can become the substance of fine creative writing.

Index

Index